# THE EUROPEAN WORLD 1500–1800

## An Introduction to Early Modern History

### Third Edition

**Edited by
Beat Kümin**

Routledge
Taylor & Francis Group

LONDON AND NEW YORK

Assistant editor and website editor: William H. Rupp

Third edition published 2018
by Routledge
2 Park Square, Milton Park, Abingdon, Oxon, OX14 4RN

and by Routledge
711 Third Avenue, New York, NY 10017

*Routledge is an imprint of the Taylor & Francis Group, an informa business*

First edition published by Routledge 2009
Second edition published by Routledge 2014

*British Library Cataloguing in Publication Data*
A catalogue record for this book is available from the British Library

*Library of Congress Cataloging in Publication Data*
A catalogue record for this book has been requested

ISBN: 978-1-138-11914-7 (hbk)
ISBN: 978-1-138-11915-4 (pbk)
ISBN: 978-1-315-14161-9 (ebk)

Typeset in Goudy Old Style
by Florence Production Ltd, Stoodleigh, Devon, UK

**Visit the companion website: www.routledge.com/cw/kumin**

Printed and bound in Great Britain by
TJ International Ltd, Padstow, Cornwall

# Contents

Contents vii

# Figures and acknowledgements

The authors and Routledge would like to thank the copyright holders of illustrations featured in this book. Every effort has been made to contact copyright holders and to obtain necessary permissions. Please advise the publisher of any errors or omissions, and these will be corrected in subsequent editions.

## PART VII

# Tables and diagrams

# Notes on contributors

All authors have a current or past association with the University of Warwick and the early modern core module 'The European World'. Institutional affiliations appear only for those now based elsewhere.

**James E. Baldwin** is Lecturer in Empires of the Early Modern Muslim World at Royal Holloway, University of London. Previously he taught at the University of Warwick and was a Leverhulme Trust Early Career Fellow at the University of Warwick and Queen Mary, University of London. He has also been a Senior Fellow at Koç University, Istanbul, and a Visiting Research Fellow at Harvard University.

**Humfrey Butters**, Emeritus Reader in History, was twice a Fellow at the Harvard University Center for Italian Renaissance Studies, Villa I Tatti, Florence. His main works include *Governors and Government in Early Sixteenth-century Florence (1502–1519)* (1985) and the edition with historical commentary of volumes VIII and IX of the complete correspondence of Lorenzo de' Medici (Il Magnifico) (2001 and 2002). He is also a foreign member of the Deputazione di Storia Patria per la Toscana.

**Bernard Capp**, Emeritus Professor of History, is a Fellow of the British Academy and a specialist in early modern English history. He is the author of *The Fifth Monarchy Men* (1972), *Astrology and the Popular Press* (1979), *Cromwell's Navy* (1989), *The World of John Taylor the Water-Poet* (1994), *When Gossips Meet: Women, Family and Neighbourhood in Early Modern England* (2003), and *England's Culture Wars* (2012). He is currently completing a book on sibling relationships in the early modern family.

**Henry J. Cohn**, Emeritus Reader in History, also formerly lectured at Glasgow and Leicester universities. He specializes in German history of the fifteenth and sixteenth centuries: government, representative institutions and the social and economic consequences of the Reformation. He is author of *The Government of the Rhine Palatinate in the Fifteenth Century* (1965 and 1991; German edition 2013), and edited *Government in Reformation Europe* (1971) and *Parliaments, Estates and Representation*, vols 22–27 (2002–7).

**Stéphane van Damme** is a Professor in History of Science at the European University Institute (Florence). His research interests focus on early modern scientific cultures including scientific capital cities, antiquarianism and natural history of metropolis. His last publications include *Sciences en société de la Renaissance à nos jours* (2017) and the edited collection *Histoire des sciences et des savoirs. vol. 1, de la Renaissance aux Lumières* (2015).

**Jonathan Davies,** who gained his PhD at the University of Liverpool, is an expert on Renaissance Italy. He is the joint coordinator of the Warwick History of Violence Network and the editor of the essay collection *Aspects of Violence in Renaissance Europe* (2013). His monographs include *Florence and its University during the Early Renaissance* (1998) and *Culture and Power: Tuscany and its Universities 1537–1609* (2009).

**Janet Dickinson** specializes in the history of early modern England and Europe, with particular interests in cultural and political history. Her first book, *Court Politics and the Earl of Essex* was published in 2011. Current projects include work on the nobility and the experience of royalist exile in the mid-seventeenth century. She teaches for New York University in London and is Senior Associate Tutor at the Department for Continuing Education at the University of Oxford.

**Anne Gerritsen** is Professor of Chinese History, having gained her PhD in East Asian Languages and Civilizations from Harvard University. She has published on the role of temples in the formation of literati communities in Jiangxi province and on the local manufactures and global trade in Chinese porcelain, and has edited several volumes on material culture, global connections and the exchange of gifts in the early modern world.

**Kevin Gould** is a Principal Lecturer in late medieval and early modern European history at Nottingham Trent University. His research explores confessional militancy within the urban centres of France during the Reformation. Publications include a monograph entitled *Catholic Activism in South-west France, 1540–1670* (2006).

**Steve Hindle** is the W. M. Keck Foundation Director of Research at the Huntington Library, California. Previously, he taught historiography and early modern history at Warwick. He has worked extensively on the history of rural communities in early modern England. He is the author of *The State and Social Change in Early Modern England* (2000) and *On the Parish? The Micro-Politics of Poor Relief in Rural England, c. 1550–1750* (2004). His next monograph, a study of the Warwickshire parish of Chilvers Coton, is provisionally entitled 'The Social Topography of a Rural Community in Seventeenth-century England'.

**Colin Jones** CBE, currently Professor of History at Queen Mary University of London, was a member of Warwick University's History Department from 1996 to 2006. He is a specialist on the history of France, especially from the seventeenth to the nineteenth centuries (including the French Revolution), and the history of medicine. Recent books include *The Smile Revolution in Eighteenth-century France* (2015), *The*

*Great Nation: France from Louis XIV to Napoleon* (2002), *Paris: Biography of a City* (2004: winner of the Enid MacLeod Prize for Franco-British studies) and *Charles Dickens, A Tale of Two Cities and the French Revolution* (co-editor: 2009). He is a Fellow of the British Academy.

**Mark Knights** works on early modern British history and has a particular interest in political culture and discourse. Recent publications include *The Devil in Disguise: Delusion, Deception and Fanaticism in the Early English Enlightenment* (2011) and *Representation and Misrepresentation in Later Stuart Britain: Partisanship and Political Culture* (2005). He is currently writing a book for OUP about corruption in Britain and its empire, from the reformation to nineteenth century reform, a taster of which is available at http://www.transparency.org.uk/publications/old-corruption-what-british-history-can-tell-us-about-corruption-today/

**Beat Kümin**, Professor of Early Modern European History, works on local communities in England and the Holy Roman Empire c. 1400–1800. His current research focuses on the political culture of imperial villages in the German lands. Publications include *Drinking Matters: Public Houses and Social Exchange in Early Modern Central Europe* (2007); *The Communal Age in Western Europe c. 1100–1800* (2013); the anthology *A Cultural History of Food in the Early Modern Age* (2012); and the co-edited collections *The World of the Tavern: Public Houses in Early Modern Europe* (2002) and *Pfarreien in der Vormoderne* (2017).

**Anthony McFarlane**, Emeritus Professor, has a BSc (Econ.) from the London School of Economics and a PhD in History from the University of London. He works on European colonialism in the Americas, especially Spanish America in the late colonial and early independence periods. Publications include *Colombia before Independence: Economy, Society and Politics under Bourbon Rule* (1993), *The British in the Americas, 1480–1815* (1994), and *War and Independence in Spanish America* (2014). He is also the co-editor of *Reform and Insurrection in Bourbon New Granada and Peru* (1990) and *Independence and Revolution: Perspectives and Problems* (1999).

**Angela McShane** is currently Senior Tutor for Research Supervision in the V&A's Research Department, and Research and External Engagement Fellow for the University of Sheffield's Arts and Humanities Faculty. She was formerly Head of Early Modern Studies for the V&A/RCA postgraduate programme in History of Design. She has published widely on the subject of seventeenth century political broadside ballads and the material culture of intoxication.

**Peter Marshall** is Professor of History and works on the religion and culture of the British Isles in the early modern period. His books include *Mother Leakey and the Bishop: A Ghost Story* (2007), *The Reformation: A Very Short Introduction* (2009) and *Heretics and Believers: A History of the English Reformation* (2017).

**Luca Molà**, currently seconded to the European University Institute, obtained his PhD from Johns Hopkins University, Baltimore, and was a Fellow of the Harvard Center for Renaissance Studies at Villa I Tatti, Florence, in 1998–99. He specializes in the Italian Renaissance, the early modern economy – especially trading communities, artisans and industrial production – and the culture of technological change. Publications include *The Silk Industry of Renaissance Venice* (2000) and the co-edited collections *La seta in Italia dal Medioevo al Seicento* (2000) and *Il Rinascimento Italiano e l'Europa, vol 3: Produzione e techniche* (2007). He is co-editor of a 12-volume series on the Italian Renaissance and Europe (2005–14).

**Giorgio Riello** is Professor of Global History and Culture. He is the author of *A Foot in the Past* (2006), *Cotton: The Fabric that Made the Modern World* (2013) and *Luxury: A Rich History* (2016; with P. McNeil). He was awarded the Philip Leverhulme Prize in 2011. He has also been a visiting fellow at Stanford University, and The National University of Australia, and a visiting professor at The European University Institute and the Max Planck Institute for the History of Science in Berlin.

**Penny Roberts** is Professor of Early Modern History. Her research specialism is the social, religious, cultural and political history of sixteenth-century France. Her publications are principally focused on the period of its religious wars (*c.* 1560–1600), including *Peace and Authority during the French Religious Wars, c. 1560–1600* (2013) and *Ritual and Violence: Natalie Zemon Davis and Early Modern France* (co-ed., 2012). However, her teaching interests range much more widely, encompassing pre-modern European history from *c.* 1200 to 1700.

**William Rupp** obtained his PhD from the University of Warwick. He has taught in the Department of History and works currently as an academic developer. In addition to being assistant editor and website editor for *The European World* (2009, 2014) he also co-edited *Globalization in Practice* (2014). His research focuses on travel and national identity creation in early modern Britain.

**Claudia Stein** is an associate professor whose research interests include the history of medicine and science from 1500 to today. She works on the history of disease and the body, the history of human nature, visual and material culture, and, more recently on the history of capitalism. She is the author of *Negotiating the French Pox in Early Modern Germany* (2009) and is currently in the last stages of preparing the monograph, *The Spectacle of Hygiene: Capitalism, Visual Culture and Medicine in Britain and Germany, 1880s–1930s*.

# Preface to the first edition

*The European World 1500–1800* offers a concise introduction to early modern history. Unlike other textbooks, it derives from an actual university module taught at the University of Warwick. Examining a variety of topics from different perspectives, the tutors/authors convey something of the complexity of early modern experience while adhering to a set of common objectives. We hope that the result can serve in a variety of contexts: as a resource for comparable surveys, as background reading for more specialized courses or simply as a quarry for general information on the period. I would like to thank four groups of people for their support of this project. First and foremost, my colleagues – past and present – who agreed to participate in such a venture at a time when most academics prioritize research publications. I am particularly indebted to Humfrey Butters for not only accepting a disproportionate share of commissions, but also – like Anne Gerritsen and Penny Roberts – commenting on other chapters. Second, William Rupp – who supported all editorial tasks in a highly effective manner – and the Routledge team, especially Anna Callander, Elizabeth Clifford, Emily Kindleysides, Victoria Peters and our principal contact, Moira Taylor, who steered *The European World* through the production process. Third, the group of external readers including Stephen Bowd, Marc Forster, Adam Fox, Thomas Leng, Marc Saperstein, Paul Warde and Retha Warnicke, whose suggestions on various sections greatly benefitted individual chapters as well as the volume as a whole. Last but not least, thanks must go to generations of Warwick second-years for their constructive feedback on successive variations of 'The European World'. This book is dedicated to them.

B. K.
Warwick, Summer 2008

# Preface to the second edition

*The European World 1500–1800* seems to have been well-received by students and tutors alike. Direct feedback – as well as reviews and extensive surveys conducted by the publisher – suggest that the consistently thematic approach and the multiplicity of voices are welcomed by readers. The second edition thus tries to develop the format rather than to make substantial changes. Three principal features distinguish this book from the first version published in 2009: the inclusion of three new chapters (on the theory and practice of politics, the impact of war and a comparative examination of the English/French revolutions), a re-launch of the companion website (offering enhanced access to primary evidence, colour illustrations and supplementary materials) and the use of an optic marker 🔵 to highlight the availability of digital resources throughout the text.

Throughout the preparatory stages, I have accumulated many debts: again, first and foremost, to my colleagues for agreeing to revise/update existing contributions and – in the case of Humfrey Butters, Bernard Capp, Jonathan Davis, Colin Jones and Luca Molà – accepting to write new chapters. Second, to assistant editor William Rupp, who shouldered an even more extensive range of duties this time round (particularly relating to the website); and, third, to the Routledge team, especially Alexandra McGregor, Laura Mothersole, Victoria Peters, Eve Setch and Michael Strang who supported us at various stages of the revision process.

The book remains dedicated to all students who embark on the discovery of the early modern period: at Warwick, in the Anglophone world and – as History continues to go global and digital – hopefully beyond.

B. K.
Warwick, Spring 2013

# Preface to the third edition

This revision of *The European World 1500–1800* coincided with turbulent times, when issues relating to Brexit, borders and migration have come to dominate the news agenda. Questions of what 'Europe' is and stands for are asked with ever greater urgency. A better understanding of socio-economic, religious, cultural and political developments during its formative centuries – what this textbook hopes to facilitate – may help to advance discussions and place arguments in wider historical contexts. Within the field of early modern studies, meanwhile, the quincentenary of Luther's Ninety-Five Theses has stimulated a wealth of activities, some of which are reflected below.

The third edition places yet greater emphasis on comparative perspectives. Part IV 'The wider world', inserted at the centre of the volume rather than its margins, unites all dedicated contributions and offers three new chapters on the Ottoman Empire, European settlement overseas and the global exchange of goods. A fourth additional survey, on sickness and health, complements our coverage of socio-economic topics. Readers will also find integrated timelines at the beginning of each thematic part and an entirely reconfigured companion website, providing easier access to primary sources, visual materials and timeline information.

I remain indebted to the support of all authors and particularly to James Baldwin, Anne Gerritsen, Anthony McFarlane, Giorgio Riello and Claudia Stein for writing/collaborating on the new chapters; to assistant / website editor William Rupp for taking charge of our digital presence as well as many other tasks; and to the members of the Routledge/Taylor & Francis team – especially Catherine Aitken, Morwenna Scott, Laura Pilsworth and Sarah Adams – who guided *The European World* through the planning and production process.

B. K.
Warwick, Autumn 2017

# Abbreviations and symbols

| | |
|---|---|
| BCE | Before the Common Era (used for dates before the year '0') |
| SMALL CAPS | denotes a term explained in the Glossary |
| * | precedes recommended survey texts in chapter bibliographies |

## Journals

| | |
|---|---|
| EHR | *The English Historical Review* |
| P&P | *Past and Present* |
| SCJ | *Sixteenth Century Journal* |

## General online resources

| | |
|---|---|
| ECCO | 'Eighteenth Century Collections Online': <http://www.gale.com/primary-sources/eighteenth-century-collections-online/> |
| ED | 'EuroDocs: Online Sources for European History': <http://eudocs.lib.byu.edu/> |
| EEBO | 'Early English Books Online': <http://eebo.chadwyck.com/home> |
| EW | 'European World Textbook Website': <http://www.routledge.com/cw/kumin> |
| Historical Abstracts | <http://www.ebscohost.com/academic/historical-abstracts> |
| HHTP | 'Hanover Historical Texts Project': <http://history.hanover.edu/project.php> |
| IHSP | Paul Halsall (ed.), 'Internet History Sourcebooks Project' <http://www.fordham.edu/halsall/> |
| WGA | 'Web Gallery of Art': <http://www.wga.hu/> |

All online addresses cited in this book were operational at the time of going to press.

# PART I

# STARTING POINTS

# Introduction

*Beat Kümin*

## Approaching the early modern period

Upon awakening on 1 January 1500, Flemish merchants, French ladies-in-waiting, Neapolitan fishermen, Muscovite PEASANTS and Castilian nuns would have had little grounds to suspect the dawning of a new era. It was not necessarily the beginning of a new year either, given that 25 March served as the starting date in many regions. On that day, as from time immemorial, nobles prided themselves on their lineage and lordship, while commoners cherished bonds of kinship and neighbourhood. Women found themselves subordinate to men, poor people depended on acts of charity, and marginal groups struggled for acceptance. The Church occupied a towering position in everybody's lives, even though reformers and heretics had started to shake its foundations. Few Europeans could read or write and only a select number had ever ventured beyond the boundaries of their principality or diocese.

From a historical perspective, however, these people lived in exciting times. Mediterranean sailors explored waters well beyond familiar coastlines, while scholars rediscovered works from ANTIQUITY which challenged the medieval worldview in fundamental respects. Benefiting from population losses caused by plague, most dramatically the BLACK DEATH in the late 1340s, labourers and smallholders found opportunities to earn better wages and to cultivate larger holdings. The recent invention of the printing press, furthermore, offered Europe its first instrument of mass communication.

A complex blend of continuity and change, of course, characterizes any point of the historical process, and periodization – a useful tool to structure information from the past – is a notoriously difficult task (Eisenstadt and Schluchter 1998; Starn 2002). Common criteria are changes in ruling dynasties, technological breakthroughs, demographic crises and the emergence of new cultural movements. These, however, rarely coincide and the identification of actual transition dates depends very much on regional context, socio-economic variables and the observer's perspective. The Italian scholar Petrarch distinguished between the 'old' age of Antiquity, the 'dark' Middle Ages and his own 'new' age already in the fourteenth century, but the notion of a distinct *early modern* period is relatively recent. It gained wider currency (and institutionalization in specialized journals, organizations and curricula) only from the mid-twentieth century, albeit with significant chronological variations: the accession of the Tudors in 1485 and the late seventeenth century serve as period boundaries in English historiography, the Reformation from the early 1500s and the end of the Holy Roman Empire in 1806 in the German-speaking world. Other interpretations locate its beginnings in the RENAISSANCE (starting in late medieval Italian CITY-STATES) or Columbus's first transatlantic voyage in 1492. In recognition of the multiplicity of transformations and the gradual nature of many processes, most historians now perceive a broad transitional phase between the medieval and early modern periods, spanning the century from c. 1450 to c. 1550. This book operates with a similarly flexible starting date.

The following two hundred years offer a number of further notable landmarks, especially the Scientific Revolution from around 1600, the new system of international relations created by the Treaty of Westphalia in 1648 or the beginning of the Enlightenment c. 1700, but the next major cluster of transformations appears in the decades around 1800, the approximate date chosen as the end point for this survey: economists highlight the agricultural and early INDUSTRIAL REVOLUTIONS in pioneering regions like England, political scientists the proclamation of principles of 'liberty, equality and fraternity' in the French Revolution of 1789 and communication historians the advent of the railway in the nineteenth century. What had been an 'early' form of modernity – i.e. a period with 'advanced' features such as rival confessions, print media, growing mobility (Box 1) and expanding state power, but persisting elements of medieval culture like political inequality, religious intolerance and the predominance of agricultural production – gave way, very gradually and incompletely it has to be said, to an era shaped by individual rights, mechanization and the expansion of mass communication.

## Box 1

'[My heart] delights in pure joy, because . . . our coachman is such a gallant fellow, who speeds up as soon as the road affords the slightest opportunity.'
(Wolfgang Amadeus Mozart 1769)

'The speed of the postilions stunned everyone, and as reluctant as I was to pass through these splendid areas in such terrible haste and during the hours of darkness as if in flight, I still rejoiced at having such a favourable wind to accelerate my journey to where I desired to be.'
(Johann Wolfgang von Goethe 1786)

Pre-modern life did not need to be slow and static. Apart from introducing us to two cultural icons of the period, these two brief extracts from a letter and travel report highlight the dynamic and increasingly mobile character of European society in the late eighteenth century. Stagecoaches were typically early modern in the sense that they formed part of a 'communication revolution' based on the availability of regular and reliable transport through space, while relying on purely natural (horse) power and the legal protection of territorial princes (Behringer 2003, 546, 644).

Over the last century, scholars have offered a variety of conceptual frameworks to explain the major developments between c. 1500 and c. 1800. These usually take the form of modernization theories, i.e. attempts to trace the origins and developments of fundamental characteristics of present-day European society. Examples include perceived early modern tendencies towards centralization (of political power), bureaucratization (of rule), codification (of laws), CONFESSIONALIZATION (of religious beliefs) and disciplining (of human behaviour). German sociologist Max Weber (1864–1920), one of the most influential voices in these debates, related long-term processes of rationalization and disenchantment to the relatively ascetic and 'this-worldly' character of Protestantism, i.e. ultimately religious causes, while MARXIST historians interpreted the early modern period as a transitional stage between FEUDALISM and CAPITALISM, thus placing the main emphasis on material and socio-economic factors (Morrison 1995). However, such linear and uniform models are now viewed with considerable scepticism, partly because of the experience of multiple pathways to modernity pursued in different areas of the globe, but also due to contrasting evidence within Europe itself. Mediterranean societies in the age of BAROQUE, to cite one stimulating recent thesis, valued leisure pursuits and ostentation over and above social discipline and the accumulation of capital, providing an example of 'intended backwardness' and the existence of an element of choice in the period (Hersche 2006). One early insight, therefore, is the danger of hasty generalizations.

## The spatial setting

The continent under examination here is extremely diverse. Encompassing coastal regions, fertile plains as well as high mountains, its natural conditions have always fostered different kinds of socio-economic regimes. Historians usually reject environmental determinism, but human agency was framed by (and interacted with) natural conditions. One key variable, the prevailing climate, posed particular challenges from the sixteenth century, when wetter summers and colder winters reduced harvest yields and caused widespread hardship (Pfister in Scott 2015). Culturally, given the sheer number of divisions, disagreements and open conflicts throughout the early modern period, we can legitimately ask whether there was such a thing as 'Europe' at all. In contrast to more recent times, we find its peoples and protagonists preoccupied with local concerns and regional power struggles rather than attempts to promote shared values and forge closer integration. And yet, a number of bonds existed: the religious framework of Christianity, the enduring legacy of the Roman Empire (and, with renewed vigour from the 1500s, ROMAN LAW), Latin as the *lingua franca* of learned people throughout the Continent and a much higher number and autonomy of cities than in other parts of the globe (Anthony Pagden in Cameron 1999). Closer contact with other cultures in the wake of voyages of discovery, furthermore, sharpened the awareness of Europe as a meaningful entity, also in a geographical sense, even though the readiness to engage with these societies remained limited and over-shadowed by almost universal notions of European superiority (Figure I.1; Greengrass 2014).

Europe was thus (increasingly) embedded in a wider intercontinental framework and it accommodated representatives of 'the other' within its own boundaries: Jews had lived in many towns from the High Middle Ages, carving out livelihoods in a generally hostile climate, with periodic bouts of prosecution and (sometimes repeated) expulsions, most famously from Spain in 1492. In the south-east of the Continent, the Ottoman Empire expanded ever further and its armies besieged the Habsburg capital of Vienna on two occasions, in 1529 and 1683. Trade links and diplomatic contacts notwithstanding, 'fear of the Turk' was another, recurring reason for reflection on European identity (see 'European relations with the Ottoman world' in Part IV).

The title *European World* reflects the book's focus on a specific Continent (indeed predominantly its Central and Western areas) and the spatial horizons of its inhabitants rather than an 'isolationist' perspective or an implicit claim of pre-eminence. A dedicated central section of this volume highlights wider geographical,

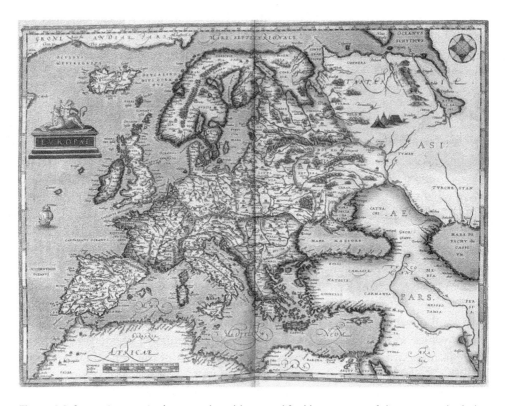

**Figure I.1** Strong interest in the natural world, exemplified by voyages of discovery and schol-arly enquiry, fostered remarkable advances in cartography. This map appeared in Theatrum Orbis Terrarum, the 'first modern atlas' published by an Antwerp engraver and geographer. Ortelius 1570, 'Map of Europe' © Royal Geographical Society, London, UK / Bridgeman Images.

economic and cultural connections throughout the period, including the intensification of exchange with Africa, Asia and the New World as well as different forms of
European settlement there (Part IV). Alongside, of course, there were countless
developments and interactions within or between overseas regions which fall beyond
the scope of this volume.

## Objectives of *The European World*

Some early modern survey works take the form of monographs (Koenigsberger 1987;
Merriman 2004; Wiesner-Hanks 2006), others of essay collections (Cameron 1999),
readers (Collins and Taylor 2006), practical companions (Cook and Broadhead 2006)
or comprehensive handbooks (Scott 2015). As a collaborative introduction based on
a team-taught university course, this textbook adopts a distinctive approach. It
pursues four principal objectives:

- First and foremost, *to portray the early modern period in its own right*. Rather than
  as a precursor to the society of today, it appears as an era with distinctive and
  contrasting features. Contributions thus acknowledge the coexistence of, say,
  subsistence agriculture and market gardening; Enlightenment and 'superstition';
  monarchies and republics; custom and innovation; stagnation and expansion.
- Second, *to examine the entire breadth of the social spectrum* (Part II). Individuals and
  groups experienced, and in turn influenced, early modern processes in specific ways.
  A general account thus needs to look beyond traditional elites, not just in terms
  of economic and cultural contributions, but also fields like religious and political
  thought (Box 2).
- Third, *to convey an impression of the richness and diversity of the sources*. Throughout
  the book, authors will highlight 'voices from the past'. Early modernists find
  themselves in the comparatively fortunate position of having neither a dearth
  nor a deluge of information (as do medievalists and modernists respectively).
  Methodological problems like fragmentary survival, uneven regional coverage and
  bias towards male social elites pose great challenges, of course, but the empirical
  base is substantial and varied. It includes above all written materials – books,
  pamphlets, diaries, travel reports, law codes, court proceedings, tax registers,
  sermons, petitions (many now easily accessible through web resources like EEBO
  and 'Early European Books') – but also visual evidence – paintings, woodcuts, maps
  – and material objects – palaces, muskets and drinking vessels, to name but a few.
  The records allow quantitative as well as qualitative approaches and illuminate a
  vast range of themes (see also IHSP and Sangha and Willis 2016).
- Fourth, *to highlight the plurality of scholarly approaches*. The collaboration of authors
  specializing in different themes, regions and centuries serves to illustrate the
  diversity of research in the field. Over recent decades, early modern history
  has absorbed fruitful impulses from neighbouring disciplines and other periods

**Box 2**

'I . . . the Supreme Authority of England . . . shall be and reside henceforward in a Representative of the People consisting of four hundred persons . . . in the choice of whom (according to natural right) all men of the age of one and twenty years and upwards . . . shall have their voices,'

'X . . . we do not impower or entrust our said representatives . . . to make any Lawes, Oaths, or Covenants, whereby to compel by penalties or otherwise any person to any thing in or about matters of faith, Religion or Gods worship or to restrain any person from the profession of his faith.'

('An Agreement of the Free People of England', 1649;
Haller and Davies 1964, 326–27)

In the late 1640s, when Parliament's defeat of King Charles I prompted fundamental reflection on the English constitution, the LEVELLER movement developed a radical vision of political and religious change: in numerous petitions and pamphlets, artisans and tradesmen called for a government based on elected representatives of the people and for the peaceful coexistence of different beliefs. This precociously 'modern' programme proved unacceptable for England's ruling elite ('Riot and Rebellion' in Part VI).

(Walker 2005; Web resources). Historical anthropology has attuned us to the significance of kinship bonds, mentalities and rituals; postmodernists have warned against a naïve trust in the 'objectivity' of textual sources; and gender studies have readjusted perspectives towards a fuller recognition of the contribution and experience of both sexes. In general, early modern studies have undergone a 'cultural turn', in the sense that the traditional concentration on reigns and events has been complemented by growing interest in communication processes, identities, perceptions and representations (Part V). There are also passionate debates, e.g. about the pros and cons of innovative genres like MICROHISTORY (Ginzburg 1980) or seminal concepts such as the civilizing process and the emergence of the bourgeois public sphere ('Courts and centres' in Part VI; 'Enlightenment: in Part V). As a result, early modern studies constitute a lively and rewarding field of study.

## Thematic structure

Having sketched vast geographical connections, several centuries of change and the need to cover a multitude of aspects, a note of caution needs to be sounded. No one work of synthesis, let alone an introductory survey like *The European World*, can aim for comprehensive coverage. In pragmatic recognition of what can be done (and what most students are likely to need), this book adopts a primarily thematic structure. Readers find the materials arranged in six parts dedicated to 'Starting points'. 'Society

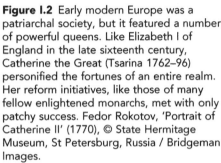

**Figure I.2** Early modern Europe was a patriarchal society, but it featured a number of powerful queens. Like Elizabeth I of England in the late sixteenth century, Catherine the Great (Tsarina 1762–96) personified the fortunes of an entire realm. Her reform initiatives, like those of many fellow enlightened monarchs, met with only patchy success. Fedor Rokotov, 'Portrait of Catherine II' (1770), © State Hermitage Museum, St Petersburg, Russia / Bridgeman Images.

and economy', 'Religion', 'The wider world', 'Culture' and 'Politics', concluding with an 'Epilogue' sketching the state of play at the dawn of the modern era. It goes without saying that this neither implies firm boundaries between spheres (all of which were inextricably intertwined in actual practice) nor a static view of the centuries between 1500 and 1800 (far from it, as each author will be at pains to emphasize). For practical purposes, however, this seems a viable compromise between the complexities of early modern experience and the need to divide the learning process into manageable portions.

While attuned to developments in recent research, the following contributions also engage with 'classic' themes like Renaissance and Reformation, state building and ABSOLUTISM, international relations, the rise of trade and European expansion. 'Great men' (and women; Figure I.2) are not written out of the story, but the emphasis lies on the experience of wider society and the ways in which individuals illuminate more general trends in their respective environments.

Collectively, the authors aim to provide a concise outline of three hundred years of European history. To facilitate understanding of often complex processes and issues, all parts of the book feature a thematic timeline and each chapter suggestions for seminar discussion and guidance to further reading, while appendices contain maps from different periods and a glossary of technical terms (for associated online resources see Box 3). Many aspects can only be touched upon, but if *The European World* manages to whet readers' appetite for closer engagement with some of the topics raised here, then it will have served its purpose.

## Assessment: early modern Europe

If, in conclusion, we attempt to gain a bird's-eye perspective, *The European World* paints a highly differentiated picture of the centuries between 1500 and 1800. Some chapters emphasize feudal ties and religious fervour as legacies from the Middle Ages, others detect peculiar features like the full-blown witch-hunt or the golden age of the Dutch Republic, others yet point to innovative forces like PROTO-INDUSTRIAL forms of production and the clash of rival ideologies.

Faced with such a complex blend of transformations and traditions, what are the structures and processes that, in combination, we can identify as defining this particularly European form of early modernity? Regional, social and gender variables inevitably complicate the analysis, but the following elements seem to characterize the period examined here:

- *socially*, a hierarchical and PATRIARCHAL structure built on households, ESTATES and corporations, in which a growing emphasis on merit enhanced the standing of middling groups in general and the professions in particular;
- *economically*, within a still largely agricultural system, the existence of early forms of industrial production and the increasing importance of global trading networks catering for an emerging consumer society;
- *religiously*, the differentiation of Christianity into 'confessions' and, in the longer term, a reluctant acceptance of pragmatic coexistence;
- *culturally*, a widening of spatial horizons; a move from received knowledge towards experimentation; frictions between social disciplining and popular customs; and a gradual supplementation of face-to-face exchange with various forms of written and long-distance communication;
- *politically*, ever larger-scale warfare, state formation and a power shift towards the centre, albeit in practice through processes of negotiation rather than unilateral commands.

The early modern centuries were highly dynamic, allowing individuals and communities to combine elements from this list into peculiar mixtures which were neither unambiguously 'medieval' nor 'modern'. Europeans had options within strong environmental and cultural constraints. Increasing evidence for informed reasoning, profit orientation and religious toleration did not force the Continent on the road to democracy, industrial capitalism and secularization, just as absolutism and growing armies did not predispose it to totalitarianism and successive world wars. Much rather, as indeed in any period, we see societies engaging with the specific challenges and opportunities of their time.

The (often scarcely documented) interplay of agents, time and space in ever-changing constellations explains why history is not an exact science, but an ongoing evaluation of motives, causes and outcomes. New sources, approaches and periodic reassessments of the field can help us to advance our knowledge of the past – a process which this book hopes to encourage and contribute to.

## Discussion themes

1. Why is historical periodization a difficult task?
2. Where can historians find information on the early modern period?
3. Did contemporaries have an awareness of being 'European'?

## Bibliography

### (A) Sources

Haller, William; Davies, Godfrey eds (1964), *The Leveller Tracts 1647–53*, Gloucester, Mass

Ortelius, Abraham (1570), *Theatrum Orbis Terrarum*, ed. R. A. Skelton, facsimile edn, 1964, Amsterdam

Sangha, Laura; Willis, Jonathan eds (2016), *Understanding Early Modern Primary Sources*, London

### (B) Literature

Behringer, Wolfgang (2003), *Im Zeichen des Merkur: Reichspost und Kommunikations-revolution in der Frühen Neuzeit*, Göttingen

* Cameron, Euan ed. (1999), *Early Modern Europe: An Oxford History*, Oxford

* Collins, James B.; Taylor, Karen L. eds (2006), *Early Modern Europe: Issues and Interpretations*, Oxford

Cook, Chris; Broadhead, Philip (2006), *The Routledge Companion to Early Modern Europe 1453–1763*, London

Eisenstadt, Shamuel N.; Schluchter, Wolfgang eds (1998), 'Early Modernities', special issue of *Daedalus* 127

Ginzburg, Carlo (1980), *The Cheese and the Worms: The Cosmos of a Sixteenth Century Miller*, London

Greengrass, Mark (2014), *Christendom Destroyed: Europe 1517–1648*, London

Hersche, Peter (2006), *Muße und Verschwendung: Europäische Gesellschaft und Kultur im Barockzeitalter*, 2 vols, Freiburg i.B.

\* Koenigsberger, Helmut G. (1987) *Early Modern Europe*, London

Merriman, John (2004), *A History of Modern Europe*, 2nd edn, vol. 1, New York

Morrison, Kenneth L. (1995), *Marx, Durkheim, Weber: Formations of Modern Social Thought*, London

\* Scott, Hamish ed. (2015), *The Oxford Handbook of Early Modern European History, 1350–1750*, 2 vols, Oxford

Starn, Randolph (2002), 'The early modern muddle', *Journal of Early Modern History* 6, 296–307

Walker, Garthine ed. (2005), *Writing Early Modern History*, London

\* Wiesner-Hanks, Merry E. (2006), *Early Modern Europe, 1450–1789*, Cambridge

## (C) Web resources

EEBO: 'Early European Books: Printed Sources to 1700': <http://eeb.chadwyck.co.uk/>

ECCO: <http://gdc.gale.com>

EW <www.routledge.com/cw/kumin>

EBSCO Historical Abstracts / IHSP above: <http://www.ebscohost.com/academic/historical-abstracts>

'The European Library', an aggregated online catalogue: <http://www.theeuropean library.org/tel4/>

# Europe in 1500

*Humfrey Butters*

Anyone seeking to draw a distinction between the Middle Ages and the early modern period can point to the extraordinary changes that occurred in the sixteenth and seventeenth centuries ('Introduction' above); but Europe underwent dramatic transformations in the Middle Ages as well, and many of the principal features of the sixteenth-century landscape, political and social, economic and religious, had arisen or developed before, often long before, 1500.

## Political structures

If a canny political observer, say a Venetian ambassador, had been asked in 1500 to single out the predominant form of government in 'Europe', which term he would probably have taken as referring to the community of Christians, he would have answered monarchy, the rule of one man as king, prince or *signore*, or, far more rarely, of one woman. Monarchical regimes were divided between those, the majority, which observed the principle of hereditary succession, and those, like the Holy Roman Empire or the Papacy, which were elective. Monarchical rule was an even more pronounced characteristic of the European political scene than it had been 250 years earlier. Between 1250 and 1350, for example, in most of the CITY-STATES of northern and central Italy, republican government was replaced by the rule of one man, the *signore* (Jones 1997; 'The Renaissance' in Part V). In France and Germany in the twelfth and thirteenth centuries there were many cities which, though rarely attaining the condition of city-states, had considerable powers of self-government; but by the end of the fifteenth century most of these had been firmly subjected to royal or princely government. The Swiss city republics, still formally part of the Empire in the fifteenth century, constituted a counter-example to this trend, as did the sixty-five imperial free cities.

In an overwhelmingly, though not exclusively, Christian world monarchy was not to be found solely in secular society: the Catholic Church too was subject to one man, the Pope, who claimed not merely to be the heir of St Peter, to whom Christ had entrusted the care of his Church, but also to have the right, albeit a much disputed one, to be able to interfere in the government of kingdoms when he deemed it appropriate, and even to depose rulers for sin or negligence.

Not all monarchical regimes, however, grew more powerful. The Holy Roman Emperor, for example, whose authority in theory extended over most of northern and central Italy, the German lands (increasingly referred to as the 'German nation'), of which he was king, Bohemia and parts of Burgundy, was much less formidable in 1500 than his great predecessor Frederick Barbarossa had been in the twelfth century. An alliance of the Papacy with a powerful group of Italian COMMUNES and, in the second half of the thirteenth century, with the house of Anjou, had destroyed imperial power in Italy; while in Germany the growth in the powers of the imperial electors who chose the emperors was such that by the fifteenth century, in practice, the imperial constitution seemed to have two heads rather than one; but even that is too simple a description, for the wider body of German territorial princes exercised virtually all the key functions of government within their own territories (Box 1).

## Box 1

'Every nobleman, however modest his standing, is king in his own territory; every city exercises royal power within its own walls.'

(Offler 1965, 220)

While overstated, this comment by a Heidelberg professor in 1408 reflects the political fragmentation in the Holy Roman Empire, where territorial princes, prelates and Imperial Free Cities limited monarchical power.

The Papacy was another monarchical institution that suffered a loss of power in the fourteenth and fifteenth centuries, finding itself increasingly forced to make compromises with lay rulers with regard to the government of the clergy within their dominions, in particular in matters of taxation, appointments to BENEFICES and judicial appeals. The Great Schism (1378–1417), during which there were two and, in its later stages, three rival claimants to the papal throne, gave a great opportunity to the conciliar movement, because to end the scandal it was necessary to summon a council of the Church, which met at Constance. Most conciliarists wanted councils to be a regular feature of the government of the Church and to be superior to popes. The popes eventually managed to defeat this movement, but to do so were forced to make large concessions to lay rulers, in order to win their support ('Church and people at the close of the Middle Ages' in Part III).

One monarchical state that had disappeared entirely was the Byzantine Empire, the last surviving part of the Roman Empire that had dominated the later centuries of classical ANTIQUITY. In 1453 its capital, Constantinople, was captured by the Ottoman Turks, who for more than two hundred years afterwards posed a major threat to the Christian powers.

The largest country in Europe was Poland-Lithuania, fruit of a personal union that became a constitutional one (1569). Here, as in the case of Germany, the rulers' dominions were extensive, but their authority was weak, and the monarchy elective (Appendix Map 1). By contrast with many other European states, Poland had a strong DIET, or representative assembly, which was a bastion of noble constitutional privilege.

If our Venetian ambassador had been asked to name the principal secular powers in Western Europe in 1500, he would almost certainly have nominated France and Spain. Thirty-three years after the Treaty of Troyes (1420: Web resources) had made Henry V heir to the French throne, France had emerged victorious from the Hundred Years War, while England's defeat consigned it for a very long time to the second rank of European states. In the second half of the century opportune princely deaths and a Breton marriage had greatly swelled the resources of the French crown (Lewis 1968). Spain had been 'created' by the marriage of Ferdinand of Aragon and Isabella of Castile, who brought stability to the two kingdoms and conquered Moorish Granada in 1492. 'Composite' states like Spain were common features of the political landscape before and after 1500. In 1494 the French king Charles VIII invaded Italy to make good a claim to the kingdom of Naples and thus precipitated the Italian wars which lasted, in discontinuous fashion, until the peace of Cateau-Cambrésis in 1559 put the seal on Spain's victory (Bonney 1991, ch. I.2).

## Society and economy

Despite the existence of significant urban clusters, for example in northern and central Italy, Castile, the Low Countries or the Rhineland, the great majority of a ruler's subjects were likely to be country-dwellers, of whom the most numerous element was the PEASANTRY, but the most important in point of riches, power and social standing was the nobility (Bautier 1971; 'Rural society' in Part II). This group, together with the ruler and the Church, possessed most of the land in most states. The European nobility was a very heterogeneous class: Italian nobles, for example, had residences in the city and in the country and were often involved in commercial activities; in other parts of Europe such as France, nobles tended to live apart from towns and to avoid commerce, considered incompatible with noble status. The English nobility paid direct taxes; the French nobility was largely exempt from them. In France, Spain and Italy feudal or seigneurial jurisdiction was common, although in some Italian provinces it was almost entirely absent; in England it had largely disappeared. Almost everywhere there was a distinction between the titled nobility and the gentry, particularly sharp in England thanks to the existence of the House of Lords (McFarlane 1973).

Nobles were considered to be the natural advisers of kings and princes and played a crucial role both in central and in local government; they were normally overrepresented in the upper ranks of the Church; and they continued to be the military caste *par excellence*. Noble values such as loyalty, honour, courtesy, physical bravery and generosity were reflected in the epics and romances of the age.

The importance of medieval towns and cities should not, however, be underestimated (Epstein 1999). In some respects they played a more significant role than they had in the ancient world. Not merely had urban settlements sprung up in areas where there had never been towns or cities before; new economic instruments and institutions were developed which taken together created an early form of commercial CAPITALISM for the first time in European history. The Italians were at the forefront of these developments. Venice and Genoa dominated east–west trade (Web resources), the so-called 'spice trade', and from the thirteenth century onwards it was Italians, and particularly Florentines, who developed international banking. Two centuries later, however, the Fuggers of Augsburg, merchants who exploited the key commercial links between southern Germany and Venice, founded a great banking house as well (Figure I.3). Merchants came to enjoy a far higher social standing than in classical Antiquity, and, in complete contrast to the ancient world, they began to play a leading role in the government of many cities. No contemporary denounced these developments more eloquently than Dante did in the early fourteenth century in his *Divine Comedy*, subsequently winning for himself the devoted admiration of Karl Marx (Box 2).

## Box 2

In canto 16 of Dante's *Inferno*, the poet and his guide, the classical Roman poet Virgil, encounter the souls of three distinguished Florentines, one of whom asks Dante if 'courtesy and valor' were still to be found in Florence. Dante replies as follows:

'The new people and the sudden gains have engendered pride and excess in you, O Florence, so that already you weep for it!'

(*Dante 1989, xvi. 167*)

In the thirteenth century the term 'borjoisie' appears for the first time, though without its modern meaning, being normally synonymous with 'citizens' or 'burgenses', a privileged category within the wider group of town-dwellers; for Christine de Pisan, the fifteenth-century French political theorist and social observer, the 'bourgois' were the upper class of the towns, the old families (Lewis 1968, 246). Below this social group in every city were to be found the artisans, organized like many of their social betters into GUILDS, of which medieval Paris had at least a hundred. Below them were the industrial workers, such as those employed in the production of textiles, Western Europe's most crucial industry, in cities such as Ghent, Bruges and Florence ('Urban society' in Part II).

The commercial revolution also had a dramatic effect on the countryside. By 1500 the medieval MANORIAL system, based on labour services and the widespread use of SERFDOM, had largely disappeared from Western Europe and had been replaced by customary or commercial rents, SHARE-CROPPING or wage labour, a development that in northern and central Italy had taken place nearly two centuries earlier. In Eastern Europe and Russia by contrast, where towns were much less important and the power of the landed nobility generally greater, serfdom and labour services throve. Famine was a constant threat in this rural world, though its incidence had been greatly

**Figure I.3** Medieval towns boosted economic differentiation and commercial exchange. A portrait by Germany's greatest painter, Albrecht Dürer, of Germany's wealthiest private citizen, Jakob Fugger, the Rich (oil on canvas), Dürer, Albrecht (1471–1528). Bayerische Staatsgemaelde-Sammlung, Augsburg, Germany / Bridgeman Images.

reduced, in the short term at least, by that other great threat to late medieval society, the plague, which had helped to bring a terrifying end to the early fourteenth-century crisis of overpopulation. Peasants were also vulnerable to the ravages of armed conflict: in the Hundred Years War, for instance, the English rarely chose to fight pitched battles, having recourse rather to *chevauchées*, military expeditions whose main purpose was to harry the rural population, depriving them of crops and cattle (Web resources).

## Cultural horizons

In a world of which war, plague and famine were abiding features, most Europeans, regardless of social origin, looked for moral direction, for hope and for consolation to the Church: its liturgy gave meaning to their lives, providing the year with a sacred punctuation; its use of visual aids and potent symbols conveyed dramatically to the illiterate majority, but not only to them, the warnings and assurances of the Christian message; the saints and the Virgin Mary could be turned to at times of tragedy and despair; and the doctrine of PURGATORY gave the living an effective means to help their dear departed, confident that the same would be done for them in their turn (Duffy 1992).

Their Christian beliefs did not deter the literate from studying the classics, any more than they had prevented the great early Fathers of the Church, St Augustine and St Jerome, from doing so. A central element in the medieval educational curriculum was the seven liberal arts, and those studying them were brought into frequent contact with the works of classical authors; the same was true, at a higher level, of anyone reading for a doctorate at a European university. Universities were one of the most enduring creations of the Middle Ages. A classical education based on Latin and, though to a much lesser extent, on Greek, was coming to be regarded as an essential element in the formation of a gentleman. The development of the printing press by Gutenberg powerfully assisted the work of HUMANIST educators ('From pen to print' in Part V).

## Rulers and subjects

The revival of a money economy, discussed above, also had major implications for government and for power relations. If rewards took the form of wages or pensions, and not of lands, they could be cut off at source if the recipient proved disloyal, whereas lands might have to be physically repossessed. In the history of the state in Europe between the fall of Rome and the modern era few developments were more momentous than this. The evolution of medieval warfare provides a particularly clear example of this phenomenon: mercenaries appear on the scene early, and gradually the unpaid military service of fief holders was replaced by money fiefs or by indentures, that is contracts of hire, known in Italy as *condotte*. The final stage was reached in the fifteenth century when, north and south of the Alps, rulers started to deploy standing armies (Contamine 1986).

The pay of soldiers had to come out of taxation, direct and indirect, for the 'ordinary revenues' rulers derived from, for example, crown lands and rights were insufficient for this task; but since persuading taxpayers to pay taxes, especially direct ones, and then collecting those taxes took a long time, rulers increasingly had recourse to extensive borrowing from their subjects or from foreign bankers, a further instance of the impact of the commercial revolution on the practice of government ('The theory and practice of politics and government 1500–1800' in Part VI). Taxes could be indirect, for example customs and sales taxes, or direct, on real estate, mobile wealth or persons (in France the *taille personelle*).

From the thirteenth century onwards the process of winning agreement to taxation often involved consulting a representative assembly such as the Aragonese *corts*, the English Parliament, the Polish *sejm* or the Estates General in France. Periods of war often favoured such assemblies, since they could use the power of the purse to win further rights; but in France after 1439 the king was able to impose taxation to pay for his standing army without seeking the consent of an Estates General, although his representatives had to negotiate with provincial ESTATES in the areas of France that still had them (*pays d'états*). Because of a strong attachment to provincial institutions and nobles' lack of interest in consenting to taxes from which they were exempt, the French put little pressure on their king to convoke an Estates General, and in 1468 the only one convoked in Louis XI's reign begged the king not to summon it again.

Representative assemblies often did more than consent to taxation, and the English Parliament's right to legislate served to distinguish it from the Estates General in France, whose lack of lawmaking powers provided ammunition for those contemporaries who found the French monarchy worryingly unlimited. Nor were they only to be found in strong monarchies: the Swiss Confederation, for example, had its *Tagsatzung*. Nor, moreover, were they exclusively upper- and middle-class affairs: peasant assemblies can be found, for example, in Frisia, Holland and the Swiss rural republics, since the initiative for developing representative institutions might come from rulers who saw them as highly useful devices for rallying support or obtaining rapid approval for taxes; but it could also come from communities that viewed them as useful instruments for the defence of their rights and interests. In the second half of the fifteenth century in Germany and England, however, the BALANCE OF POWER between prince or king and representative assembly was tilting in favour of the former ('Centre and periphery' in Part VI).

Administration became increasingly professional from the twelfth century onwards, thanks largely to the growth of the universities, which produced a continuous supply of law graduates destined for a career in the government of Church or state. Their training in ROMAN LAW, which in many countries was the basis of civil law and powerfully shaped canon law, provided them with words, concepts and arguments that enabled them to discuss and advocate conceptions of the state, sovereignty and corporate representation, even though the word 'state' did not acquire something close to its modern meaning till the sixteenth century (Black 1992).

Rulers were quite aware of the psychological foundations of authority, and by the fifteenth century the view that power was based on reputation was already a cliché. Public ceremonial was employed to impress subjects with the majesty of kings and kingship, at coronations for example, or when kings made formal entries into cities or were buried. Where possible the sacral nature of kingship was stressed: the kings of France and England claimed special healing powers and were anointed at their coronations, as bishops were at their consecrations.

But rulers, in order to secure or maintain their subjects' respect, or at least obedience, did not rely solely on force, on the efficiency or justice of their administrations, on the arguments of their lawyers or on the ideas expressed in rituals: they were well aware that they had to use the resources of PATRONAGE at their disposal – lands, offices, pensions or judicial pardons. This is one reason why the courts of rulers played such a crucial role in government, for it was there above all that their subjects, in person or through kinsmen, friends or patrons, could present them or members of their immediate entourage with requests for favour or redress. This was governance at its most reactive, well suited for a world lacking the modern ideal of an apolitical civil service. In some states, such as France, one could acquire office by purchasing it from its holder ('Courts and centres' in Part VI).

The civil wars and rebellions that occurred, for example, in England, France, some of the Italian states, Aragon and Castile in the fifteenth century might be taken to indicate that the resources of governments were not invariably enough to secure obedience; but these upheavals were protests against the misuse of those resources, not against their inadequacy. Even popular uprisings, though sometimes accompanied by expressions of socially radical views, were often reactions to innovations or, as in the case of the Jacquerie (1358), to the failure of the authorities to discharge their responsibilities by protecting the peasants from the military incursions of foreigners. In the main the peasants' world was one of deference and custom; but deference could be the result of calculation rather than of genuine respect ('Riot and rebellion' in Part VI).

Nor did the literary culture of the age inspire their social betters to dream dreams of profound social change or thoughts of progress. The courtly love tradition and the RENAISSANCE movement were hardly seen as politically or socially dangerous; and the influence of both can be seen in Castiglione's *The Book of the Courtier* (Web resources), perhaps the most influential treatment of its subject ever written. In Aristotle's and Cicero's works could be found defences of republicanism, but not of anything more radical; and the Roman historian Tacitus, who was becoming fashionable around 1500, was certainly no democrat (Box 3).

---

### Box 3

Tacitus judged the Roman populace to be 'eager for political changes and, at the same time, fearful of them' (Tacitus XV, 46) – a similar tension characterized Europe around 1500 as well.

---

## Perspectives

Classical culture, commercial capitalism and Christianity were all products of the Mediterranean area; before 1500 two events occurred, however, one long-term consequence of which was a reduction in the significance of that region and a shift of economic power to Northern Europe: Columbus reached the New World in 1492, and in 1498 Vasco da Gama established the direct route to India via the Cape of Good Hope (Figure I.4). Another long-term consequence of these voyages was the slow but momentous process of globalization that has played such a notable part in shaping the modern world ('Expanding horizons' in Part IV).

## Discussion themes

1. Was Europe in 1500 a primarily rural world?
2. Assess the social standing of merchants around 1500.
3. How important was the role played by religion in Europe before the Reformation?

## Bibliography

### (A) Sources

Dante Alighieri (1989), *The Divine Comedy: Inferno*, trans. S. Singleton, vol. 1, Princeton, NJ

**Figure I.4** European exploration of the 'New World' from around 1500 built on medieval contacts with Mediterranean and Asian societies. 'Marco Polo's Travels' recount his journey to the court of the Mongol ruler, the Great Khan, towards the end of the thirteenth century. Miniature of Venice from 'Marco Polo's Travels' (*c.* 1400). © Oxford, Bodleian Library, MS Bodley 264, f. 218.

Tacitus, Cornelius (1986), *Annales XI–XVI*, S. Borzák and K. Wellesley (eds), Leipzig


**(B) Literature**

Bautier, Robert-Henri (1971), *The Economic Development of Medieval Europe*, London

Black, Anthony (1992), *Political Thought in Europe 1250–1450*, Cambridge

Bonney, Richard (1991), *The European Dynastic States 1494–1660*, Oxford

Contamine, Philippe (1986), *War in the Middle Ages*, trans. M. Jones, Oxford

Duffy, Eamon (1992), *The Stripping of the Altars: Traditional Religion in England c. 1400–1580*, New Haven, Conn.

Epstein, Steven (1999), 'Urban Society', in: *The New Cambridge Medieval History*, vol. V: *c. 1198–c. 1300*, ed. D. Abulafia, Cambridge, 26–37

Jones, Philip (1997), *The Italian City-State 500–1300*, Oxford

Lewis, Peter (1968), *Later Medieval France: The Polity*, London
* Linehan, Peter and Nelson, Janet eds (2003), *The Medieval World*, London
McFarlane, Kenneth (1973), *The Nobility of Later Medieval England*, Oxford
Najemy, John ed. (2004), *Italy in the Age of the Renaissance*, Oxford
Offler, H. S. (1965), 'Aspects of Government in the Late Medieval Empire', in: *Europe in the Late Middle Ages*, ed. J. R. Hale, J. R. L. Highfield and B. Smalley, London, 217–47

### (C) Web resources

Castiglione, Baldesar (1528), *The Book of the Courtier*, trans. Sir Thomas Hoby (1561): 'Renascence Editions' http://www.luminarium.org/renascence-editions/courtier/courtier.html
'Hundred Years War: Treaty of Troyes (1420) and Conditions in France in 1422', IHSP: <http://www.fordham.edu/halsall/source/1420troyes.html>
'Partnership Agreements: Purchase of Shares in a Ship (1248)', IHSP: <http://www.fordham.edu/halsall/source/1248pship3.html>

# PART II
## SOCIETY AND ECONOMY

# Gender and family

*Bernard Capp*

## Introduction

A popular story in early modern England told the adventures of Long Meg of Westminster, a doughty young woman who dressed as a man, fought and overcame male adversaries and performed heroic feats in Henry VIII's wars against France. Contemporaries were always intrigued by the idea of turning gender roles and assumptions upside down. But these flights of fancy usually ended with the restoration of conventional values and Meg's story, too, ends with her marrying and vowing to be a respectful and obedient wife (Mish 1963). Gender constituted one of the key foundations of the European order, shaping almost every sphere – social, economic, religious and political. Though there were significant changes over the early modern period, as we will see, the fundamental assumptions underpinning educated and popular thinking, very different from those of today, survived intact. Reaching back to classical and biblical times, they were rarely challenged, and inevitably they influenced relationships within the family too. The ideal family was seen as a loving partnership, but one in which the husband's supremacy was sacrosanct. Then as now the family was perceived as the social unit best equipped to raise children and transmit society's values to the next generation. In many other respects, however, the family differed sharply from its modern equivalent, in character, function and composition. It possessed a political and economic as well as a social dimension; its composition was unstable (through death, rather than divorce); and it frequently contained members biologically unrelated to either parent.

## Gender

It was an axiom throughout Europe that the two sexes possessed very different characteristics, and that the male was superior. Such beliefs, standard for centuries, rested on several interlocking ideas. The Christian religion was essentially male-orientated, like the Judaic tradition from which it had sprung. God had created Adam first, with Eve as his companion and 'helpmeet'. Eve's weakness in the face of temptation had triggered man's fall and expulsion from the Garden of Eden. The New Testament reinforced the message, with Jesus choosing male disciples and St Paul preaching the duty of obedience by women. The Protestant Reformation further strengthened religion's male character by rejecting the cult of saints and of the Virgin

Mary. This religious teaching was supported by medical science stretching back to the Greeks. Aristotle had taught that women were imperfect men. For centuries physicians explained that the human body was composed of four 'humours', and that the balance found in women (primarily cold and moist) made them intellectually, morally and physically weaker. Some physicians believed there was only a single sex, with the humoral balance alone responsible for creating male and female sexual identities, so that a man might turn into a woman, or vice versa, should the balance be reversed (Laqueur 1990). Such fears may have contributed to nervousness about gender roles and alarm whenever women imitated male dress or men behaved effeminately. Other factors also underpinned traditional gender roles. Physical strength remained an essential requirement in many occupations, including agriculture, which gave men an obvious advantage. Though manual work made many women physically strong, this was offset by repeated pregnancies and the care of small children. Equally important was the power of custom. Gender-based assumptions had led in many areas to the exclusion of women from education, from many trades and from the professions. Without education or training, women inevitably appeared incapable of taking on male roles. Moreover, most people naturally absorbed the ideas and values of the society in which they had grown up, and even strong-minded individuals tempted to challenge them could not point to any place or time when things had been different (Box 1).

---

### Box 1

'That the Custom of the World has put Women, generally speaking, into a State of Subjection, is not deny'd; but the Right can no more be prov'd from the Fact, than the Predominancy of Vice can justifie it . . .

I do not propose this to prevent a Rebellion, for Women are not so well united as to form an Insurrection. They are for the most part Wise enough to Love their Chains, and to discern how very becomingly they set.'

(Astell 1706, 72, 82)

A proto-feminist, Mary Astell made biting observations about marriage and male authority, but saw no prospect of change and regarded women as complicit in their subordination.

---

Throughout Europe, early modern society can be described as PATRIARCHAL, with male authority underpinned within the family and in society at large by a web of laws, regulations and custom. We should also note, however, the importance of regional variations. ROMAN LAW, religion and custom combined to limit women's freedom and rights far more severely in southern Europe than in the north. Foreign visitors sometimes described England (with considerable exaggeration) as a paradise for women; no one spoke in such terms of Spain or Italy, where middle- and upper-class women were largely confined to the home.

# Gender and education

Knowing that gender would be a major factor shaping their children's future, parents raised them accordingly. Informal 'dame' or charity schools taught reading, writing (usually only for boys) and basic religious principles. Beyond that, girls were steered towards practical skills such as sewing and embroidery, with formal schooling kept primarily for boys. In Electoral Saxony, 50 per cent of parishes had licensed schools for boys by 1580, while only 10 per cent had schools for girls, who moreover attended only for short periods and received a narrow, mainly practical education. In Italy, a survey of schools in Venice in 1587–88 found 4,600 male pupils and only 30 girls (Wiesner 1993, 122–23). In England too, grammar schools were for boys. A teacher appointed to a school at Crosby, near Liverpool, in 1651 was horrified to discover that some parents wanted their daughters also to attend, and quickly resigned in the face of such 'barbarity' (Guildhall Library, London, MS 34010/7, f. 388v–9). Girls' boarding schools began to spread from the mid-seventeenth century, especially near London, though their syllabus was geared more to music and dancing than to academic study. Literacy rates remained everywhere much lower for women than for men: in England, only about 10 per cent of women could write their names in the early seventeenth century. Even Shakespeare's daughter learned only to read, not to write. In Amsterdam, where educational provision was relatively good, a quarter of the men and half the women marrying in 1730 could not sign their names (Hufton 1995, 424). Among the landed elite, girls were educated at home by private tutors. Some became highly accomplished, especially in the RENAISSANCE period, but no one envisaged young women going to university.

Education was about absorbing values as well as skills, and concepts of honour and reputation remained firmly gender-based. For women, chastity and fidelity were everywhere the prerequisites for a good name. While qualities such as thrift and good neighbourliness might win praise, they could not restore a reputation ruined by sexual promiscuity. In the case of men, honour and reputation were much less uniform, and more closely linked to an individual's age and his social, economic and marital status. To be respected, a man generally needed to be married, economically independent, and able to maintain and govern his own household. He also needed to display 'honesty', keeping his word and paying his debts. Many men, such as labourers, apprentices and servants, could not hope to meet these criteria. Some of the young and single, with few resources and no family responsibilities, responded by developing their own rival codes of honour and worth. Within their own circles they might aspire to a radically different kind of 'good name', based on their prowess in sport, fighting, heavy drinking or sexual promiscuity (Shepard 2003). Among some sections of the aristocratic elite we find a similar scorn for respectable values, and a similar culture of drinking, gambling, fighting and promiscuity.

## Work

Throughout Europe most boys were destined for a life working the land, either on a family holding or by becoming a live-in farm servant in their teens. They learned skills on the job. Many young women also helped on the family farm or were hired as dairy-maids. And it was expected, indeed required, that a farmer's wife would play an active role, taking responsibility for the poultry, pigs and vegetable garden, running the dairy, and helping with hay-making and harvest (Figure II.1). In the towns, a minority of young men, mostly from more prosperous backgrounds, entered a craft or trade, working as an apprentice and later JOURNEYMAN for an established MASTER. In a family business, we often find women working alongside their husbands, usually taking charge of selling produce at market. Often, too, a widow enjoyed the right to continue the business after the husband's death. Increasingly, however, guild regulations were tightening to exclude women from membership. Many powerful German GUILDS barred female servants from working in the shop, and often a master's wife, widow and daughters too. Women were seen as unwelcome competition, and their mere presence (and that of lower-class or illegitimate men) was perceived as compromising the 'honour' of the guild (Wiesner 1998, 163–96; similarly for Spain: Perry 1990, 17–18). Almost everywhere, women were pushed into lowly and marginal occupations that had never been organized into guilds. In a few trades which men had never colonized, such as lace-making and MILLINERY, they could sometimes earn reasonably good incomes. Far more often they entered domestic service or worked in poorly paid activities such as spinning, knitting, laundering, sewing or nursing. Women also worked in large numbers in alehouses, taverns and 'fast-food' urban cook-shops or as street vendors, and they dominated the huge second-hand clothing market. The poor of both sexes would often follow several occupations, switching according to season and circumstance. Thus one London woman explained in 1687

**Figure II.1** Men and women collaborate during the grain harvest in eighteenth-century Germany. Mayer 1770, facing 247. 'Reapers in a Field' from Johann Friedrich Mayer, Fortsetzung der Beytrage und Abhandlungen zur Aufnahme der Land- und Hauswirthschaft (Frankfurt a.M., 1770). © Wüttembergische Landesbibliothek, Stuttgart, Gew.Oct.4072.

that she worked at home winding silk on rainy days, but as a porter at Leadenhall market when it was fine (Capp 2003, 43). Whatever they did, women generally had to juggle paid work with the demands of child-care and running the home ('The early modern Economy' in Part II).

## The public sphere

In most places women were excluded from the political world. At the very highest level, gender and dynastic principles sometimes collided, as in France, where Salic law forbade a woman to inherit the throne. By contrast Isabella of Castile and Elizabeth Tudor ruled successfully, though Henry VIII had feared that only a son would be able to preserve his dynasty (Box 2).

**Box 2**

'To promote a woman to bear rule, superiority, dominion or empire above any realm, nation, or city is repugnant to reason, contumely to God . . . it is the subversion of good order, of all equity and justice.'

*(Knox 1994, 8)*

For the Calvinist John Knox, writing in 1558 and swayed in part by religion, gender outweighed dynastic right.

There were later successes too: Maria Theresa in Austria, Catherine the Great in Russia and several female heads of small German territories. But nowhere did such examples lead to any wider reappraisal. Ministers, officials, diplomats were always male and so were urban magistrates. In practice, however, some aristocratic women, such as members of the Guise family, were able to play very active roles in the bloodthirsty politics of late sixteenth-century France. Moreover, women often occupied a significant position at royal and princely courts, wielding informal power through the personal influence they might have with a king, minister or favourite ('Courts and centres' in Part VI). Similarly, contemporaries recognized that the wife of a landowner, local magistrate or parish officer might be more forceful than her husband, and that winning her support could offer their best chance of securing a favourable decision.

Among the poor, women quite often became involved in popular politics of a very different kind, in riots and demonstrations, where gender could play to their advantage. Women protesting over grain supplies or ENCLOSURES were less likely to face retribution; magistrates recognized that a female rebellion was unthinkable and might therefore feel more able to make concessions without losing face ('Popular culture(s)' in Part V). And at the neighbourhood level, women played an important role in shaping local public opinion, through their 'gossip networks'. Public opinion was a weapon of some significance, for retaining a 'good name' mattered to both men and women. By ostracizing, mocking or rebuking troublesome neighbours or violent, unfaithful husbands, women might shame offenders into mending their ways, and if that failed, their pressure might trigger intervention by parish officers. Equally, they might rally to support a respected woman who had come under threat. Margaret Graeme, a Norfolk villager accused of witchcraft in 1590, was defended by several respectable female neighbours who had known her for over 20 years and testified to her good character. Proceedings against her went no further (Capp 2003, 286, 311–18).

Gender was equally reflected in the judicial system. Judges, lawyers and juries were male, and the law regarded husband and wife as one person, the man. That generally gave him control over the money and goods his wife had brought to the marriage and any money she might earn, though control over land she had brought remained more limited. While all this was to the husband's advantage, he also became liable for any debts his wife might incur, and if they committed a crime together, the court would usually hold him solely responsible. As today, most crime was committed by men. Certain categories, however, such as witchcraft, were primarily associated with women, in most parts of Europe ('Witchcraft and magic' in Part V), and a double standard meant that women found guilty of adultery or premarital sex were usually punished more severely than the men involved. Unmarried mothers suspected of infanticide were assumed to be guilty unless they could prove their innocence and faced almost certain execution until attitudes softened in the eighteenth century.

## The family

The early modern family displays both parallels with and significant differences from the family today. By no means everyone married: in Western Europe roughly 20 per cent of women remained single throughout their lives, and the figures are probably similar for men (Bennett and Froide 1998). For some it was a matter of choice. In Catholic countries a religious vocation might lead men into the priesthood or a monastery, while women might enter a convent, either from choice or because their families were unable to raise a DOWRY to secure a husband. For others, poverty, physical disability or the ravages of illness left them unable to find a partner. Unmarried women might spend a lifetime in domestic service, with others working 'at their own hands' to earn a living. In most of Northern Europe the NUCLEAR family was the norm, as today, comprising a married couple and their children, with an average family size of four to six. In the Mediterranean region, by contrast, it was common to find larger and more complex families. EXTENDED or multiple families contained more than two generations and/or brothers and sisters of the main householder (Flandrin 1979, 50–92). In Italy a teenage bride might often marry a much older man and begin married life living in his parents' home, in a very subordinate position.

Perhaps the most striking difference between the modern and early modern household is the presence of people not biologically related to the householders.

Farmers might have live-in farm servants, while many modest urban households contained at least one maidservant, often one or two apprentices and perhaps an older journeyman. Two factors lie behind this. First, the home was frequently also the work-place, with the household containing employees as well as parents and children. Second, domestic chores such as washing and cleaning were arduous and time-consuming, making help essential, especially if the wife had children to care for and was helping with her husband's farm or trade (or supplementing their income through part-time work). Hiring a young maidservant made good economic sense, for domestic labour was cheap; an English maidservant in 1600 might expect no more than £2 a year, plus board and lodging. In the poorest families, even children as young as five or six were pressed into assisting with simple tasks that helped to boost the family income. By their early teens poor children might be sent out as live-in servants, which guaranteed them food and shelter and created space in a cramped cottage for the younger siblings. Poor households were generally small; only the well-to-do, able to keep their children at home and employ servants, presided over large households.

It was generally accepted that husband and wife should play different but complementary roles within the marriage. The former was to provide for and govern the household, while the latter managed the home. Among the landed elites, dynastic and financial concerns outweighed the interests and wishes of the individual, and marriage formation was usually a family matter, arranged by parents who bargained hard over the dowry (the bride's contribution) and JOINTURE (what she would receive, if left a widow). The young couple, especially the bride, often had little choice over the arrangement. Moving down the social ladder, a merchant would often wait years until his business was securely established and then choose a much younger bride, who would be guided by her parents. There was far greater freedom of choice in the lower levels of society, where there was little property at stake. Moreover, with bride and groom often in their mid- to late twenties, they might well have left the family home over ten years earlier by the time they wed, which inevitably reduced parental control. Even the poor, however, usually looked for parental approval and support. It took years for young folk on low wages to accumulate the modest savings needed to set up a home, and material help from parents or employers (or both) was often essential to give their marriage a secure foundation.

Without effective means of birth-control, fertile women often became pregnant every two or three years. A high birth-rate did not lead on to large families, however; many children died in infancy (over a quarter before the age of ten). Only rarely did both husband and wife survive into old age. Repeated pregnancies inevitably threatened a woman's life and health, while (perhaps surprisingly) male mortality was generally even higher. Dangerous occupations, such as mining and seafaring, almost guaranteed an early death, while strenuous farm labour took a heavy toll, and plague and other diseases swept away thousands while still young. Widowers (and to a much lesser extent widows) often remarried quickly, for practical reasons: it usually took two adults to earn an adequate income, run a home and look after children. For those men and women who did reach middle age, failing strength resulted in lower wages, and old age generally spelled poverty, especially for widows living alone. There was no retirement age, and the Norwich Census of the Poor (1570) records many men and women in their seventies and eighties still working to earn a few pence.

An earlier generation of scholars such as Lawrence Stone argued that married couples felt little affection or warmth for each other or their children. Philippe Ariès even denied that childhood was recognized as such. These views no longer command support. Apart from royal and aristocratic marriages, arranged for political and dynastic reasons, most couples cherished the ideal of a relationship based on affection, trust and partnership (Houlbrooke 1984, 96–126). It was an ideal reflected in popular songs and ballads. As today, the reality often fell short, and many couples lived unhappily with poverty and drink breeding bitterness and domestic violence. In other cases one partner, usually the man, simply deserted, and some married again, bigamously. But we can also find many letters and diaries that record deep love and affection between couples, pride in their children's progress, and devastating grief when a child died. They remind us how much we share with our ancestors, however different their world (Box 3).

---

### Box 3

'Honest, kind, dearest, closest bridegroom:

With longing and heartfelt joy I received your letter ... Kind and dearest treasure, with this letter I am sending a little string which you may bind [about your wrist] on my behalf and thereby think of me ...

Magdalena, y.l.b.' [your loving bride]

(Ozment 1989, 39–43)

Magdalena Paumgartner writing to her fiancé Balthasar, a Nuremberg merchant, in 1582. The couple's letters show a happy marriage based on affection and a close working partnership.

---

## Assessment: continuity and change

The early modern period witnessed several significant changes affecting both gender and the family. The Protestant Reformation was at best a mixed blessing for women ('The long Reformation' in Part III; Roper 1989). In theory, justification by faith alone made men and women spiritual equals and removed (male) priests as indispensable intermediaries. It elevated the status of marriage, rejecting celibacy as a superior state, and through sermons and domestic conduct-books promoted the values of married love, mutual responsibilities and mutual rights. New marriage laws in towns such as Zurich enabled both husbands and wives to sue for divorce and to remarry, if their partners had committed serious faults such as adultery and reconciliation proved impossible (Ozment 1983, 80–99). But Protestants always stressed the father's authority, and – just like Catholic reformers – they were anxious to regulate marriage more tightly by discouraging informal weddings based on the simple exchange of vows, demanding parental approval and prosecuting couples for premarital sex. Divorce remained everywhere difficult to obtain (and impossible in Catholic countries, as well as in England). In the religious sphere itself, Protestantism removed women's option of a religious vocation and the possibility of achieving any position of authority. In the event, some women carved out new forms of vocation for themselves, and in Germany, France and elsewhere we can find devout women using their personal interpretation of scripture to challenge the authority of the Catholic Church or a non-believing husband. Others felt a call to spread the gospel by preaching or writing, and women played a leading role in the evangelical missions of the early Quakers and early METHODISTS. Over time, however, Protestant movements generally became more conservative and restrictive. The Catholic Reformation, for its part, triggered a burst of female religious activity, finding expression in lay orders devoted to working with the poor and sick, such as Angela Merici's Ursulines in sixteenth-century Italy.

There were other significant changes. Guild controls gradually weakened over the period, and women played a prominent part in the PROTO-INDUSTRIAL cloth and silk industries, if mainly in ill-paid work at home as spinners and silk weavers. Opportunities for women also opened up in the burgeoning retail sector and there were broader changes in the prevailing views of gender. By the eighteenth century the humoral understanding of the body was losing ground, and women were increasingly seen as frail rather than threatening, needing protection, not control. Both views, of course, reinforced men's perception of patriarchal authority as natural and essential. Public debate over relations between the sexes continued throughout the period, increasingly aired in print. Many writers, drawing on scripture and history, pointed to striking examples of pious, brave and intelligent women. One sixteenth-century French poetess argued daringly that Christ had been incarnated as a man only because a female saviour would have been unacceptable in the Jewish society of his time (Davis 1975, 188). Shakespeare created numerous heroines for the stage who were intelligent, witty and forceful. And if the combative Katharina was eventually subdued in *The Taming of the Shrew*, the tables were turned in John Fletcher's sequel, *The Tamer Tamed*. Proto-feminists argued that women were by nature the equals of men and held back only by lack of educational opportunity. But in practice assertions of the intrinsic 'worth' of women posed little real threat to male control. Any woman who posed a more direct challenge was quickly silenced. One who had mastered enough legal expertise to practise as a solicitor in London was arrested in 1654 and dispatched to the Bridewell, among vagrants, pickpockets and prostitutes (*Calendar 1654*, 67). At the very end of our period, in 1793, the French actress Olympe de Gouges was guillotined by the JACOBINS, after daring to demand political rights for women as well as men. Even in the French Revolution, gender equality remained a shocking idea. If history is mainly about change, in gender relations the continuities are more striking.

## Discussion themes

1. How far did practical considerations modify the conventional view of appropriate gender relations, within the family and beyond?
2. Do you agree that continuity is more evident than change in this period?
3. 'There was less agreement on appropriate patterns of behaviour for men than for women.' Do you agree?

## Bibliography

### (A) Sources

Astell, Mary (1706), *Reflections upon Marriage*, 3rd edn, London

*Calendar of State Papers. Domestic Series: 1654* (1880), ed. Mary A. E. Green, London

Knox, John (1994), 'The first Blast of the Trumpet against the Monstrous Regiment of Women' [1558], in: *John Knox on Rebellion*, ed. Roger Morgan, Cambridge, 3–47

Mayer, Johann Friedrich (1770), *Fortsetzung der Beyträge und Abhandlungen zur Aufnahme der Land- und Hauswirthschaft*, Frankfurt a.M.

Mish, Charles C. ed. (1963), 'The Life of Long Meg of Westminster' [1620], in: *Short Fiction in the Seventeenth Century*, New York, 79–113

Ozment, Steven ed. (1989), *Magdalena & Balthasar: An Intimate Portrait of Life in Sixteenth-Century Europe*, New Haven, Conn.

### (B) Literature

Bennett, Judith M. and Froide, Amy M. (1998), *Singlewomen in the European Past 1250–1800*, Philadelphia, Pa.

Capp, Bernard (2003), *When Gossips Meet: Woman, Family and Neighbourhood in Early Modern England*, Oxford

Davis, Natalie M. (1975), *Society and Culture in Early Modern France*, Stanford, Ca.

Flandrin, Jean Louis (1979), *Families in Former Times; Kinship, Household and Sexuality*, trans. Richard Southern, Cambridge

Houlbrooke, Ralph (1984), *The English Family, 1450–1700*, London

*Hufton, Olwen (1995), *The Prospect Before Her: A History of Women in Western Europe 1500–1800*, London

Laqueur, Thomas (1990), *Making Sex: Body and Gender from the Greeks to Freud*, Cambridge, Mass.

Ozment, Steven (1983), *When Fathers Ruled*, Cambridge, Mass.

Perry, Mary E. (1990), *Gender and Disorder in Early Modern Seville*, Princeton, NJ
Roper, Lyndal (1989), *The Holy Household: Women and Morals in Reformation Augsburg*, Oxford
Shepard, Alexandra (2003), *Meanings of Manhood in Early Modern England*, Oxford
*Wiesner, Merry E. (1993), *Women and Gender in Early Modern Europe*, Cambridge
—— (1998), *Gender, Church and Society in Early Modern Germany*, London

## (C) Web resources

'Early Modern Resources', with links to 'Bodleian Broadside Ballads', 'Parents and children', 'Women's writing' etc: <http://earlymodernweb.org/resources/>
'Defining Gender 1450–1910': <http://www.amdigital.co.uk>
Halsall, Paul ed., 'Internet Women's History Sourcebook' (1998–), IHSP: <http://www.fordham.edu/halsall/women/womensbook.asp>

# Rural society

*Steve Hindle*

## Landscapes and victuals

At the end of the Middle Ages, most Europeans lived in rural surroundings in settlements of less than 5,000 inhabitants, and despite the growth of the urban sector, this still remained true in the middle of the eighteenth century. Environmental conditions, emphasized as crucial factors of early modern experience in a seminal study of the Mediterranean world (Braudel 1972), were highly varied – ranging from Atlantic and Alpine to harsh Continental climates; from coastal regions and fertile plains to mountainous areas; and from soils suitable for cereal farming and viticulture to those more appropriate for grazing and market gardening. Prominent European products included barley and wheat in the north, olives and grapes in the south, but also imports from the New World: maize in some areas (like northern Italy) from the late sixteenth century, potatoes towards the end of our period. For the vast majority of the population, however, typical diets were cereal-based, and the average European ate less meat in the seventeenth century than his ancestors had done in the late Middle Ages. Men, and to a lesser extent women, drank wine (in the south and west) and beer (in the north and east of the Continent) on a regular basis, while variables like region, prosperity and seasons affected the consumption of other key victuals like vegetables, fruit, fish, spices and dairy products. The rhythms of plenty and want – both across the agricultural year and over the *longue durée* from 1500 to 1800 – remained basic characteristics of early modern rural life (Albala 2003).

## The importance of the harvest

Throughout the early modern period, agriculture remained central to the everyday concerns of most European families. In rural society, virtually all men, women and children were involved at various levels in the agrarian economy – as producers of foodstuffs either for the provision of their own households or for sale at market, as processors of agricultural goods (especially wool for textiles and hides for leather) in the manufacturing industries (which were commonly located in the countryside) and as purchasers both of food and drink and of consumer goods ('Gender and family' in Part II). To this extent, the harvest was the heartbeat of the whole economy.

The strength of that heartbeat depended fundamentally on the weather. In most parts of Europe, a typically sized 20-acre (8-hectare) holding might just be expected to feed a family of five. In a 'normal' harvest year, when YIELD–SEED RATIOs of 4:1 prevailed, 20 acres might produce as much as a pound in weight of bread per person per day for three people, assuming that a quarter of the harvested grain was kept back for seed corn for the following year. More productive soil and better weather might result in the yield–seed ratio of 8:1 which characterized a super-abundant harvest, feeding as many as an additional ten individuals. The falling ratios characteristic of poor terrain or disappointing weather might, correspondingly, have a devastating impact. Throughout the sixteenth and seventeenth centuries, however, it has been estimated that yield–seed ratios of about 6:1 were the most that the more productive regions of Europe could be expected to produce (Overton 1996). To this extent the agricultural economy provided little more than a precarious living for most self-provisioning households, with budgets teetering on the margins of balance, and posing very serious questions about many families' capacity to pay rent, especially if a landlord demanded payment in cash. Many farmers were thus dependent on selling goods and labour services to their landlords in order to keep a roof over their heads. The position of those landless labourers who could not self-provision from arable plots was even more precarious, for the quality of their diet rested on their ability to pay a market price which was by definition dependent both on medium-term levels of supply and demand and on the short-term vicissitudes of scarcity and plenty.

Economic fortunes were, therefore, bound up in the quality of the harvest, which, given the need to keep a proportion of the crop for next year, had implications not only for immediate consumption but for the following year's production. Years of scarcity (or 'dearth', a period of high prices caused either by harvest failure or by market inefficiency) were in fact very common throughout early modern society. In the period between 1480 and 1620, one in four harvests could be classified as poor, and some years, especially in the adverse weather conditions of the mid-1540s, late 1590s and early 1620s, were disastrous with runs of two, three and even four consecutive harvest failures causing not only dearth but actual famine, a crisis of subsistence characterized not only by increased mortality but by falling fertility. Throughout the whole period from 1500 to 1800, most generations would have experienced dearth at least once during their lifetimes with only the more productive agricultural economies of Northern and Western Europe, especially in the lowland zone of the British archipelago, avoiding the shadow of harvest failure before 1700, perhaps even as early as 1650 (Walter and Schofield 1989). Even when there were runs of good harvests, however, contemporaries could never be entirely confident that the MALTHUSIAN TRAP had been sprung, and the diaries and correspondence of the period are full of neurotic concern about the implications of summer rainfall. The fear of creeping malnutrition, if not actual starvation, stalked most of Europe until the agricultural revolution of the late eighteenth and early nineteenth centuries.

Harvest shocks also had profound implications for industrial activity in the countryside, for most manufacturing involved the making of consumer goods from agricultural products, and much trading activity depended on the supply of woollen cloth. All this is to say nothing of the implications for rural industry of falling demand for manufactured goods in those days when harvest failures forced households in town and countryside alike to spend more of their income on the earthly necessities of food and drink. Little wonder that so many early modern men and women watched the skies with apprehensive anxiety (Box 1).

---

### Box 1

'This time God was good and gratious to mee and mine, in our peace and provisions for us, yet all things were wonderfull deare, wheate 9s, malt 4s8d, rye 7s6d, oatmeal 8s per bushel and cheese 4d ob [41/2 pence]. All things deare, yet the season was indifferent warm and drye. Beggars many, givers few, lord of thy bounty provide for the poore, I constrained myself to do more th[a]n ordinary for our poore, it is better to give than to receive, and yet poore people were never more regardless of God then now adayes.'

*(Earls Colne, Essex; Web resources)*

Extract from the diary of Ralph Josselin, clergyman of Earls Colne (1–16 December 1649).

---

## Agrarian economies

The centrality of the harvest to the rhythms of rural life notwithstanding, it is important to emphasize that the agrarian economy and the rural social relations to which they gave rise were not uniform even within (let alone between) most European states, and that there were a great many distinctive *pays*, or 'countries', scattered across the Continent, in which specialized local and regional farming patterns prevailed (Scott 1998; 'The early modern economy' in Part II). The geographical diversity of this vast terrain of interlinked and overlapping rural economies cannot be exaggerated: soil type, topography and climate varied immensely and minutely, and never exercised a purely deterministic influence over patterns of settlement, TENURE or labour. After all, the landscape was in large measure a product of human initiative: the natural environment was made and remade by the decisions of men to drain marshes, clear forest or cultivate marginal land. Indeed, with the growing pressure of population on the resources of the agricultural sector, men were forced from the mid-sixteenth century to make war on forest and fen with zeal unknown for three hundred years (Thirsk 1967). These caveats notwithstanding, it is conventional to make a fundamental geographical and topographical distinction in the agrarian economy between those lowland zones in which mixed farming (the cultivation of arable crops, the fattening of cattle for milk and other dairy products) prevailed and the upland regions where sheep were grazed to produce wool. This crude ideal-typology fails to take account of the much more variegated realities of the rural landscape, where certain types of environment such as coastal marshes might permit the coexistence of arable cultivation, meadow and high-quality pasture.

A more sophisticated classification of rural society into farming regions should distinguish not only lowland fielden zones from upland pastoral zones, but also different types of pastoral activity practised in woodland or BOCAGE, in fenland and marshes and in moorlands. Each of these might be in turn associated with a distinctive agrarian order. Farming could be practised on open fields, usually across three or four common fields where tenants held strips of land in scattered parcels and obeyed common rules of cultivation stipulated by MANORIAL courts in which they themselves had an active voice ('Centre and periphery' in Part VI). But it might increasingly be undertaken in severalty, that is on land enclosed by hedges and ditches over which the landlord exercised absolute rights in property and where tenants had lost traditional customary privileges of grazing livestock or collecting fuel. In this system, even pasture might be held individually. Furthermore, various combinations of topography and farming systems might in turn give rise to differentiated patterns of settlement and architecture, nucleated villages being much more characteristic of those lowland regions where common field agriculture was still practised, scattered settlements being much more likely to spring up at the margins of wood-pasture zones where sheep were reared and their wool knitted for textiles (Figure II.2).

**Figure II.2** In wood-pasture zones settlements developed at the margins of the forests: at Ludgershall (Buckinghamshire, in the foreground), houses originally erected by squatters engaged in woodland clearance were clustered around either side of the high street leading to a large village green. Sixteenth-century map of Ludgershall and Wotton Underwood (ref ST Map 69; CD #MS 167). © Huntington Library, Art Collections and Botanical Gardens, San Marino, California 9112080.

Despite this differentiated map of agrarian activity across Europe, it would be a mistake to think in terms of a random scattering of autonomous farming regions both within and across states. Local agrarian economies were gradually becoming integrated by processes of specialization and interdependence into regional, national and ultimately even international markets for food and consumer goods. These links were provided first by markets for agricultural produce but increasingly too by the demand for new consumer goods. By the late seventeenth century, regional, national and international trade facilitated market penetration into the humblest households, and the exchange of agricultural goods and services was no longer exclusively local. Even in the late sixteenth century a corn-deficient area like the north-east of England was importing grain not only from the granaries of East Anglia but from the ports of the Baltic and the agricultural hinterlands which they served. The citizens of Newcastle owed their bread as much to Danzig as they did to King's Lynn. Nonetheless even by the end of the period there was no single European market for agricultural goods, but a series of regional markets in which very large-scale operations were possible.

## Rural social relations

Involvement in the market-place varied not only geographically, however, but also socially. An understanding of relations within rural society depends upon recognition of the relationships between various groups within the rural economy. The landowning class was not consistent in its characteristics across Europe, with the aristocracy of Eastern Europe long enjoying feudal privileges which their western cousins had begun to lose. Nonetheless, the greater and lesser nobilities throughout the Continent expressed their social power, whether it had been achieved by military glory, bureaucratic service, economic success or inheritance, in their ownership of land. Although nobility and gentility might be achieved, perhaps even earned, as well as inherited, it was instantly recognizable in the lifestyle of landlords, men of leisure who seldom farmed their own ESTATES but derived their income from rent. In their dress, their diet, their education and above all in the houses they built and beautified for their posterity, the landed classes fashioned roles for themselves in the theatre of the great, and in turn had their status recognized by rulers who came to depend on them for the holding of local office and the exercise of royal authority (Dewald 1996).

If the landed classes were relatively easily recognized (especially by one another, for contemporary elites claimed to know a real gentleman when they saw one), their tenants are a far more amorphous group. Many, especially in North-western Europe, could no longer reasonably be described as PEASANTS in the sense of basic subsistence farmers. However, particularly in the east, a more recent definition as family-based agriculturalists with limited market involvement seems appropriate (Scott 1998, 1–2). 'Peasants', it should be added, is a technical term (without condescending or sentimentalizing associations) for inhabitants of a rural world in which the force of custom was central. The country-dwellers of early modern Europe might have idealized the past as a lost world of honest plain dealing, a normative agrarian order in which resources were equitably allocated, but they did so in order to preserve such tradition for future generations. To this extent, tenants were no less concerned than their landlords with perpetuating their lifestyle for posterity.

The circumstances of those who farmed land therefore varied widely across Europe and their fortunes depended on a series of factors, but most fundamentally upon the nature of their tenures, the terms on which they held their land, and the size of the farms that they occupied. In both respects it is fundamental to recognize variations in the proportion of tenants who were owner-occupiers, which is often seen as a characteristic for the peasant class in pre-industrial society: in fact, as few as 25 per cent of English farmers were owner-occupiers, and the rest were tenants of either individual or institutional landlords (Whittle 2000).

In terms of tenure, the most fundamental distinction was between those who held land on customary terms and those who paid commercial rents. Custom was *lex loci*, the law of the locality, and could vary enormously even within a particular region: within customary economies, landlords and tenants might enjoy various privileges but they would more usually be guaranteed in a local manorial court in which tenants enjoyed significant rights and responsibilities. Most customary tenants were the descendants of serfs (freed several centuries earlier in the west than in the east), and they generally fell into two types. The first, most characteristic of the more traditional agrarian regimes east of the Elbe, were merely tenants-at-will, holding land only at the lord's pleasure for a specified period for a specified rent, usually payable as labour service, and enjoyed no legal rights except over the crop they were growing at the time of their eviction (Hagen 2002). The second, more characteristic of the west and especially of England, were those who enjoyed rights guaranteed by local custom negotiated over many centuries and 'whereof the memory of man ran not the contrary'. They nonetheless enjoyed varying degrees of security: they might enjoy a right of inheritance or hold the farm for a specified number of years or lives; they might enjoy fixed or negotiable rents; and they might gain access to their holding by the payment of a fixed or customary fee or fine. These customary tenures were the characteristic product of an economic context in which relatively low prices and high demand for labour encouraged landlords to offer sympathetic terms to their tenants in the hope of retaining a supply of labour and a regular if nominal income.

But the changing economic context of the mid-sixteenth century, bringing with it labour surplus and rising prices, encouraged many landlords to be more demanding of their tenants in order to maximize their incomes. Hence the tendency, most marked in Western Europe, towards the commercialization of the land market (Whittle 2000; Sreenivasan 2004). The result was a system of commercial leasing in which land was held by formal contracts which stipulated economic (rather than nominal) rents and penal conditions. These leases specified finite, often relatively short (perhaps as few as seven years) periods of tenure, and after they had expired they had to be renegotiated in competition with others. Commercial leases of this kind had been by no means unknown before the price revolution of the sixteenth century (though they had often been arranged on longer tenures at lower rents) but they became increasingly common as landlords practised 'fiscal seigneurialism', the tendency to exploit their resources to the full (Manning 1988). By the end of the sixteenth century, most leasehold land was so expensive that only very substantial farmers could afford to purchase it, with the result that most small leaseholders were often bought out by their larger neighbours and were increasingly forced out of the land market altogether. By the early eighteenth century, the English land market, the most commercialized in Europe, was characterized by a very significant proportion of labourers who occupied cottages without gardens, let alone access to more substantial plots, and made a living dependent only on their ability to sell their labour at the annual hiring fair ('Marginals and deviants' in Part II).

In terms of farm size, the actual amount of land cultivated by an individual farmer might vary enormously. Even in the late medieval period, the peasantry had not been a homogeneous group, and the degree of differentiation within the farming classes began to increase significantly: larger farms emerged as the marked shortage of tenants caused by the demographic contraction of the late Middle Ages made more and more tenancies available for those who were producing sufficient surplus to buy them up. Land gradually accumulated into fewer and fewer hands, so that the period saw the emergence of substantial peasants – those who were prepared to take on more land and the perceived opportunities for marketing the surplus which it represented. By the end of the sixteenth century, Western Europe in particular had seen the emergence of a highly differentiated rural population, though of course the extent of this differentiation varied and was probably far greater in lowland arable than in upland pastoral regions.

## Historiographical perspectives

There has been long-standing historiographical preoccupation with FEUDALISM, that pyramid of reciprocal bonds of labour, dues and advice offered to lords by tenants and VASSALS in return for protection. Controversy has raged in particular both over the definition of feudalism and over the chronology of its crisis and decline (Reynolds 1994). Most commentators agree, however, that feudal relations loosely defined remained characteristic of most of Eastern and some of Western Europe until the end of our period. Almost as much ink has been spilled over the relative significance of class struggle (mediated by the state in its role as arbitrator of disputes in the law courts) and demographic and socio-economic developments in causing rural change. Attention has focused in particular on the extent to which agrarian class relations were more conducive to exploitation, individualism and CAPITALIST economic development in England, as argued by Robert Brenner, or in France, as argued by Croot and Parker (Aston and Philpin 1985).

More recently still, there have been further exercises in the comparative history of rural society, calling into question the conventional emphasis on the stark differences between Western and Eastern Europe. The view that the west was liberated early from feudalism has been undermined by growing awareness of the sheer variety of tenurial patterns and of the 'revival of SERFDOM' around 1500 (Scott 2002, 170–76); while the east looks less traditional in light of recent discussion and recognition of strong market involvement and of the limits of seigneurial autocracy in the region's characteristic DEMESNE economies (Hagen 2002; Ogilvie 2005). Long-standing models of decline or even crisis among European aristocracies have been similarly reassessed. As a landowning elite with a strong military identity, the nobility certainly faced challenges in the early modern period: from 'common' soldiers in the ever-growing infantry armies, from upwardly mobile 'bourgeois' gaining their wealth by trade, and from the expansive tendencies of a state keen to eliminate intermediate powers. And yet established elites proved resilient, adapting to the new circumstances by accepting high administrative and military office ('service nobility') and investing in major economic initiatives (Dewald 1996).

The notion that agrarian society in general, and production techniques in particular, underwent an agricultural revolution in the seventeenth and eighteenth centuries remains deeply rooted in the scholarship. Although it was once fashionable to argue for an early chronology of agricultural improvement, emphasizing technical innovation in the seventeenth century, it is now commonly accepted that it was not until the century after 1750 that the decisive breakthroughs took place (Overton 1996).

## Assessment

Rural society was a topographical and social patchwork in which the fortunes of rich and poor alike were bound up with the quality of the harvest, itself dictated by patterns of soil type and the rhythms of climatic change. More fundamentally, access to land, and the terms on which such access was permitted, dictated the ability of each of the groups within the social order to respond to the market opportunities represented by the fundamental economic changes of the early modern period. To this extent the degree to which landlords and tenants could challenge or mobilize the power of custom was a fundamental issue in rural social relations, and it might be suggested that the politics of custom – negotiated between landlords and tenants not only in local courts but increasingly in the central courts of developing sovereign states – constituted one of the most significant social dramas of the age. After all, life chances depended fundamentally on access to land and the food it yielded, and those who could produce sufficient not only to provision their own households but to sell the surplus in the market-place enjoyed a realistic possibility not only of making shift to survive but also of participating in the consumer revolution of the seventeenth and eighteenth centuries.

## Discussion themes

1. Is it possible to speak of class conflict in rural society in this period?
2. What was the significance of custom to landlord and tenants?
3. Who were the beneficiaries and casualties of economic change in the countryside?

## Bibliography

### (A) Sources

Bettey, J. H. ed. (2005), *Wiltshire Farming in the Seventeenth Century*, Trowbridge

### (B) Literature

Albala, Ken (2003), *Food in Early Modern Europe*, Westport, Conn.
Aston, T. H. and Philpin, C. H. E. eds (1995), *The Brenner Debate: Agrarian Class Structure and Economic Development in Pre-industrial Europe*, Cambridge
Braudel, Fernand (1972), *The Mediterranean and the Mediterranean World in the Age of Philip II*, trans. Siân Reynolds, London
* Dewald, Jonathan (1996), *The European Nobility, 1400–1800*, Cambridge
Hagen, William W. (2002), *Ordinary Prussians: Brandenburg Junkers and Villagers, 1500–1840*, Cambridge
Manning, Roger B. (1988), *Village Revolts: Social Protest and Popular Disturbances in England, 1509–1640*, Oxford
Ogilvie, Sheilagh (2005), 'Communities and the "Second Serfdom" in Early Modern Bohemia', *P&P*, 187, 69–119
Overton, Mark (1996), *Agricultural Revolution in England: The Transformation of the Agrarian Economy, 1500–1850*, Cambridge
Reynolds, Susan (1994), *Fiefs and Vassals: The Medieval Evidence Reinterpreted*, Oxford
* Scott, Tom ed. (1998), *The Peasantries of Europe: From the Fourteenth to the Eighteenth Centuries*, Harlow
—— (2002), *Society and Economy in Germany, 1300–1600*, Basingstoke
Sreenivasan, Govind D. (2004), *The Peasants of Ottobeuren, 1487–1726: A Rural Society in Early Modern Europe*, Cambridge
Thirsk, Joan (1967), 'Enclosing and Engrossing', in: *The Agrarian History of England and Wales, Volume IV: 1500–1640*, ed. idem, Cambridge, 200–55
Walter, John and Schofield, Roger eds (1989), *Famine, Disease and the Social Order in Early Modern Society*, Cambridge
Whittle, Jane (2000), *The Development of Agrarian Capitalism: Land and Labour in Norfolk, 1440–1580*, Oxford

## (C) Web resources

'Earls Colne, Essex: Records of an English Village, 1375–1854': <http://linux02.lib. cam.ac.uk/earlscolne/>

'H-Rural' network: <https://networks.h-net.org/h-rural>

# Urban society

*Penny Roberts*

In contrast to today, only some 10 to 20 per cent of the early modern European population lived in towns, many of which were tiny by modern-day standards. The influence and importance of urban society, however, was disproportionately great, because towns were the political, economic, administrative and cultural centres of their localities. The exact number of town-dwellers is open to debate, not just because of the uncertainties of early modern statistics and regional difference, but also on account of problems of definition which have exercised urban historians for decades. One of the issues is the degree to which urban centres overlapped with rural society and its activities. The extent of urbanization differed between states and was dependent on a number of factors. Although the urban population of Europe increased considerably between 1500 and 1800, most of that growth was concentrated in the larger, regionally significant towns. Thus, both expansion and stagnation were characteristic of the period. Urban society also experienced, accommodated and influenced social, economic and cultural change.

## Urban geography

Early modern European towns varied enormously in size and concentration (Figure II.3). In 1500, northern Italy and the southern Netherlands were the most heavily urbanized areas, having been the economic powerhouses of the medieval European economy. The largest towns housed over 50,000 inhabitants. Italy contained most of these – Venice, Milan, Genoa, Florence, Rome, Naples and Palermo – while other countries had only one, such as London, Paris and Lisbon. In Spain only Seville and Granada competed for this status, and Istanbul was the sole contender to the east (alongside the further-flung capitals of Mughal Delhi and Persian Isfahan, which underlines how unusually urbanized Europe was by world standards). Urban growth was largely concentrated in these major cities rather than smaller towns. Mid-sixteenth-century England, by contrast with much of Western Europe, was 'lightly urbanized', with only 5 per cent of its population living in communities of over 5,000 inhabitants (rising to 8 per cent by 1600); whereas France had seven towns of more than 20,000, and a further twenty of 10–20,000 (Clark 2000; Saupin 2002).

These settlements of 5,000 inhabitants and above were the 'chief' towns of Europe; most were set to grow, a few to decline, but no new ones to appear. The typical urban community remained, however, much smaller than this, and urban density was, therefore, much greater than might be presumed. How much greater depends on how towns are defined or, rather, what urban characteristics such settlements displayed. Previously, historians have favoured size (typically over 2,000 inhabitants) or the presence of physical demarcations (principally walls). However, regional variation renders such distinctions problematic. In some places (such as southern France), almost any settlement was walled, whereas elsewhere even quite large towns were not, and in general the need for and function of walls as a means of protection declined over the period. There is now general consensus that a more secure measure to determine where a large village ended and a small town began is economic status. To be categorized as a town, a community must have contained a diversity of trades and manufacture, meaning that the majority of the population was not producing for its own subsistence as agricultural workers. Common occupations included weavers, shoemakers, bakers and smiths. Further characteristics include the acquisition of certain privileges (towns, for example, were often taxed differently from the countryside) and the development of an urban elite.

In definitions of what constitutes an urban rather than a rural community the delineation between the two has not necessarily become sharper. Towns were once

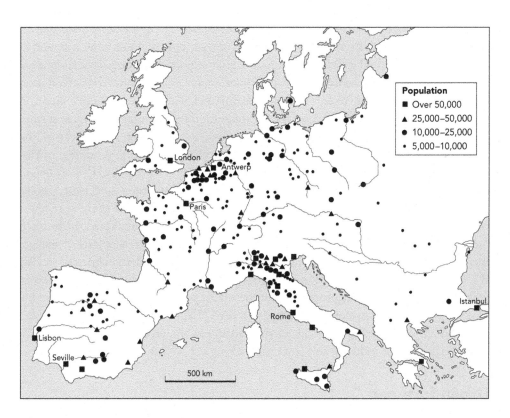

**Figure II.3** Map of main European towns at the start of the early modern period. Pounds 1979, 30.

described as 'non-feudal islands in the feudal seas', implying that their development and nature were quite distinct from the countryside which surrounded them (Postan 1972, 239). On the contrary, it is clear that most towns, even the largest, contained a significant proportion of agricultural workers, who lived in the town but worked in the neighbouring fields or vineyards during the day. The development of market-gardening within town walls suggests that many contained quite extensive land suitable for cultivation (as well as the stimulus given to agricultural output in general by the growth of urban demand). There were all kinds of urban/rural interdependencies, with even the continuing involvement of 'feudal' lords in the governance of some towns. Complicating the picture further was the existence of near-autonomous CITY-STATES, such as those in Italy, parts of the Swiss Confederation and the Empire, which dominated the surrounding countryside. As the early modern period proceeded, urban life drew the traditional rural nobility into towns, attracted by the new theatres and SALONS in the major cities, besides the more obvious pull of the court in princely residences.

As SERFDOM declined in Western Europe, and rural society became less feudal ('Rural society' in Part II), other dependencies developed which were more related to socio-economic change than to urban oppression. Thus, urban / rural relationships should be seen as mutually beneficial, not automatically antagonistic. Towns had an established role in the local economy because of their essential function as a market where PEASANTS could sell their surplus or exchange goods. Nevertheless, there were evident areas of tension, too, especially over grain supply, taxation and the exploitation of the countryside by the town. The relationship was dependent to a large extent on region: factors such as the degree of rural immigration (necessary for towns to sustain and, certainly, to increase their populations due to high urban mortality) or the purchase of rural lands by members of the urban elite. A growing tendency in this period was for closer ties in production through the 'PUTTING-OUT' SYSTEM or PROTO-INDUSTRIALIZATION. This involved the manufacture of certain goods, especially textiles, in the countryside, where labour was cheaper and there were fewer regulations; so merchants – who provided the raw materials and marketed the finished product – were able to prosper from increasing peasant need to supplement meagre incomes at a time of socio-economic adversity ('The early modern economy' in Part II). The development of this system threatened the livelihoods of textile workers, who made up a significant proportion of the urban population, but many were able to adapt and to embrace complementary practices. Thus craftsmen in towns adopted other functions, finishing off goods or specializing in the production of luxuries, for example in the silk industry and stocking-making.

## Urban fortunes

Economic activity differed enormously between towns, according to size, location and type of trade or manufacture. Local, regional and national economies all had a part to play, as increasingly did international networks. With the opening up of trade routes with Africa, Asia and the newly discovered Americas, Europe experienced a shift of emphasis and prosperity away from the Mediterranean towards the Atlantic. While some towns were in a good position to benefit from this trend, others experienced decline. Other factors which affected urban fortunes were the growth of administrative centres and the impact of war (Pollak 2010).

While we see exponential urban growth overall throughout the period – it is estimated that the population of towns doubled between 1500 and 1800 – it is misleading to perceive this as a general, even usual, trend. Some scholars propose different regional timescales (de Vries 1984), others argue that stagnation was more characteristic (Prak 2001). England and the northern Netherlands were thus exceptional and precocious in their development. Contrary to the common perception, urbanization can be seen as a poor indicator of economic development, if we compare Castile and England for instance, suggesting that political protection rather than market pressure was the decisive factor in the growth (and decline) of many an early modern town (Epstein 2001). The continuing significance of certain hindrances to urban growth prevented towns from realizing their full potential (except in the Dutch case): poor infrastructure, especially slow and cumbersome transport of goods by water or road, plus high transaction and customs costs in between (and especially within) countries, among other factors.

The beginning of the period witnessed the growth of the Iberian port cities of Lisbon and Seville due to burgeoning trade with Asia and with the Americas. Complementary, too, was the rise of the French Atlantic ports and, later, Bristol and Liverpool with the increase in the slave trade ('Expanding horizons' in Part IV). This is not to say that Mediterranean trade dried up; Italian ports, especially Venice and Genoa, were still prosperous at least through the sixteenth century, supplemented by the still important Italian banking houses. The southern French port of Marseille was increasingly active in commerce, and the city of Lyon throve, due to its position at the hub of European trade and the development of its banking facilities. The Italian economy was in clear decline in the seventeenth century, as indeed was the prosperity of cities such as Lisbon and Antwerp, as they came to be eclipsed by the growing economic dominance of the Dutch. In particular, there was the spectacular rise of Amsterdam (with its population of over 200,000 c. 1650; Figure II.4) as the great ENTREPÔT or storehouse through which goods from all over the known world would flow. The Dutch increasingly dominated trade routes through the Mediterranean, out to the Atlantic and to the Indies as well as the lucrative carrying trade in the Baltic. They also established financial dominance with the founding of the first national bank in 1609 (the London bank was not established until the 1690s, with Hamburg the only other competitor up to that point). The Dutch were only displaced later in the seventeenth century, principally by England but also by France, which became the dominant economic and political powers of Europe.

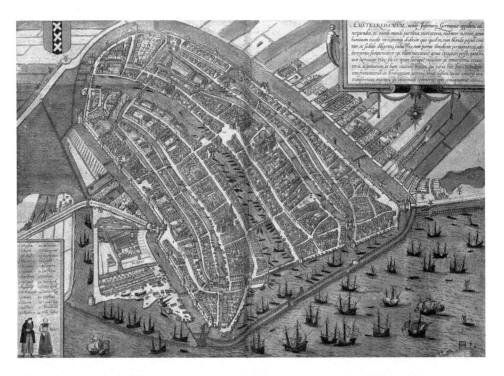

**Figure II.4** This map of Amsterdam, reproduced from Georg Braun and Franz Hogenberg, Civitates Orbis Terrarum (1572), underlines its strategic coastal position and its role as a dynamic centre for mercantile trade. Private Collection / The Stapleton Collection / Bridgeman Images.

It is also important to recognize more subtle developments within regions. The HANSEATIC LEAGUE, a confederation of North European towns such as Lübeck, which in their medieval heyday had dominated Baltic trade, began to decline by 1500. There was a shift of economic prosperity south towards centres like Augsburg and Nuremberg, followed by further readjustments due to the impact of the Thirty Years War (1618–48). Thereafter, the imperial success stories were the strategically placed towns of Hamburg and Danzig, alongside growing administrative centres like Berlin. Such factors also contributed to the rapid growth of Madrid as the established seat of government in Spain in the mid-sixteenth century, displacing older centres in Castile. Similarly, a new administrative rather than commercial centre was established at the Hague in the Netherlands. In France, the population of Paris more than doubled to over 500,000, but just as spectacular was the 'creation' of Versailles from the 1680s. Louis XIV's court was a great consumer, encouraging urban (and rural) growth in its vicinity. Versailles's expansion contrasts with the decline of Prague, as Bohemia was absorbed into the Habsburg Austrian orbit. A different factor underlay the huge growth of Rome: a greater focus on town planning as the period proceeded led to the demolition of medieval walls and the opening up of boulevards. In other, declining towns, populations retreated within their walls.

# Urban society and government

The skylines of early modern European towns were dominated by churches, and their streets by the hubbub of the market-place. Since many were walled there was a clear physical demarcation of urban space which was characterized by narrow streets and open squares. Town life involved collective responsibilities. Within the local parish, town-dwellers participated in devotions and processions. As heads of household within an administrative district, such as a quarter, they would pay tax and serve on the local MILITIA. Their occupation might prompt them to join a guild or confraternity, to live and work alongside their fellow-workers in a particular street or to meet regularly at a particular inn or other meeting-place. Social status was clearly delineated by inclusion in and exclusion from such groupings. Women could join confraternities and some GUILDS and act as heads of household, but they could not serve in the militia or hold municipal office. Citizenship was highly prized but also often restricted to those of a certain status and property, as was the administration of urban affairs (Friedrichs 1995 and 2000; Cowan 1998).

Urban governance was in the hands of a narrow group of officials, often co-opted but sometimes more democratically elected, and usually consisting of a MAYOR and aldermen supported by a wider group of councillors (Box 1). By necessity those who held the top offices had to be wealthy enough to spare the time required by the position. Thus a number of established local families usually dominated the town hall.

Nevertheless, the exact processes of selection and the proportion of the population involved varied from town to town and were jealously defended. This was necessary since most towns had at least a nominal overlord (king, duke, bishop or prince) whose representatives posed a challenge to municipal autonomy and could interfere in issues of precedence and jurisdiction. The main exceptions were Venice and German Imperial Free Cities such as Nuremberg. In the larger towns of early modern Europe many a medieval town hall was rebuilt on a grand scale reflecting a renewed confidence and ambition among its occupants and greater urban prosperity. The inherent economic and political privileges of town life for the elite reinforced civic values and a sense of citizenship which were reflected in civic rituals and ceremonies.

The main responsibilities of town COUNCILS concerned provision for everyday and emergency situations, to avert or deal with crises and to mediate between the interests of overlord and inhabitants. Among the most pressing matters were the provision of grain; measures to prevent the spread of plague (which hit early modern towns on average every 15 years); and the unpredictable incidence of fire and flood or, more unusually, earthquake and volcanic eruption. The most notable instances of these were the Great Fire of London in 1666 (Web resources; Latham 1978) and the Lisbon earthquake of 1755, both of which necessitated considerable urban planning and renewal. In addition, the organization of the local militia, the regulation of crafts and guilds, and the organization of civic events came within the purview of the councillors. They also presided over a number of major social and cultural changes in the early modern period which put growing demands on municipalities. Chief

**Box 1**

**'Concerning the Polity and Government of the Praiseworthy City of Nuremberg, 1516'**

'The supreme political body in our city is the Council. . . . It consists of 42 men, of whom 34 are patricians belonging to the Old Families, and 8 are commoners chosen from the multitude. . . . The government of our city and the common weal rest in the hands of ancient families, people whose ancestors, even back in the earliest days, were also members of the government and ruled the city. Foreigners who have settled here, and common people, have nothing to say, nor ought they to, for all power is of God, and only those may exercise it whom the Creator has endowed with special wisdom. Therefore we admit no one into our Council (excepting the eight commoners already mentioned) whose parents and grandparents did not also sit in the Council. It is true that some exceptions are now being made to this rule, and that some newer residents (but they are men of honest birth and distinguished family) have entered the Council. However, such men may not occupy a position higher than that of Junior Mayor.'

*(Strauss 1976, 58–62)*

The relatively restricted elite involved in urban government – although there is some flexibility towards commoners and foreigners – is evident here, as well as civic pride in the process of election and local traditions.

among these was responsibility for the distribution of poor relief, which became more organized in response to demographic pressures from the 1520s, as well as for educational institutions and for hospitals, all previously the preserve of the Church ('Marginals and deviants' in Part II). The Reformation, and the religious changes which resulted, placed unprecedented strains on municipal governance, as town councils struggled to accommodate confessional diversity and to mediate tensions between the faiths.

Another significant social development of the period, reflected in the growth of urban administrative centres, was a rise in bureaucracy, especially in increasingly centralized states such as France. In many of its larger towns with a significant administrative presence, especially those with sovereign courts or *parlements*, municipal government that was previously dominated by merchants was taken over by the legal elite (Box 2). Equally, manufacturing towns were increasingly transformed into centres of distribution as the 'putting-out' system developed. Elsewhere, where commerce remained of the highest importance, MERCANTILE elites retained their hold, notably in the dominance of the urban patriciates of Venice, Amsterdam, Antwerp and Hamburg (Lindemann 2014). In contrast, in Poland and parts of Eastern Europe, society was increasingly dominated by the 'feudal' nobility and this led to urban stagnation.

The growth in administration was an extension of increasing central authority which has provoked debate about whether the autonomy of municipal institutions was being eroded or enhanced as a result (Benedict 1992). Urban elites found their hands increasingly tied by the encroachment of royal authority, with officials sent in to oversee their activities, from municipal finance to control of the local militia and municipal elections. The reduction of urban autonomy was one of the key concerns of centralizing rulers, who were well aware of the need to curb resistance from towns, as well as to nurture their economic prosperity. The impact on urban culture led to a growing emphasis on law and order. Similarly, religious festivals – which had once served to reinforce civic solidarity, but now provided the opportunity for violent confrontation – were curbed and civic rituals increasingly secularized, reinforcing the authority of both municipality and crown. A further trend in the urban economy was for the greater exclusivity of MASTER craftsmen (who both produced and sold goods) at the expense of JOURNEYMEN (who could only produce, not sell). Entry to masterships, with the status and potential wealth they entailed, was made increasingly

## Box 2

'The town dweller is brought up in complete indifference to the things of the countryside; he scarcely distinguishes the plant that bears hemp from the one that produces flax, and wheat from rye, or either from maslin; he is content to get his food and clothing from them. It's no use talking to most bourgeois about fallow land or saplings, about layered vines or aftermath, if you want to be understood; they don't know what the terms mean. Speak to some of them about yardage, tariffs and taxes, to others about appeal procedure, civil petitions, settlements and summonses. They know society, albeit in its ugliest and least admirable aspects; they know nothing about nature, its origins, its progress, its gifts and its bounties. Their ignorance is often deliberate, and based on their esteem for their own profession and talents. The meanest pettifogger, buried in his gloomy, smoke-blackened study, his mind obsessed with even blacker chicanery, thinks himself superior to the ploughman, who enjoys the open sky, who tills the ground, who sows in season and reaps rich harvests; and if he should sometimes hear talk of primitive men or of the patriarchs, of their rustic way of life and its harmonious order, he wonders how they could have lived in such times, when there were no offices or commissions, no attorneys or Presidents; he cannot understand how people ever survived without the clerk of the court, the public prosecutor and the refreshment-room at the law-courts.'

*(La Bruyère 1963, 'Of the Town', 125–26)*

This biting satire was directed at many groups within late seventeenth-century French society. The passage lampoons the legal elite, an increasingly prominent group within early modern urban society, especially in large towns such as Paris about which the author is writing here.

difficult; it became more expensive, often restricted to the sons of existing masters, and applicants were subject to rigorous moral and religious tests. This resulted in a growing gap between the masters and those they employed, leading to tension and protest. Urban revolts were common in the period, and of concern to the authorities, although they 'took place within the context of traditional power relations' (Beik 1997, 264). The focus of discontent was usually a new or increased levy, or anxiety about the price of grain or bread. The situation was worsened by slumps, especially in the textile industry, and the general economic adversity for craftsmen, particularly in the seventeenth century.

Alongside such developments, towns continued to play a central role in the transmission of ideas because of their dynamic and diverse concentration of commerce, culture and people. Both RENAISSANCE and Reformation movements are traditionally recognized as principally urban phenomena. Alongside courts and the Church, major towns were key centres of artistic PATRONAGE and display, also housing the foremost educational institutions: schools, colleges and universities. The development of print culture had its greatest impact in towns with their higher literacy rates ('From pen to print' in Part V). Theatres and opera houses were established in major centres, attracting a broad cross-section of society. By the eighteenth century, distinctive forms of urban association and sociability had developed, such as COFFEE HOUSES and literary salons, which bolstered the increased focus on the civility of manners (Borsay 1989; 'Enlightenment: England and France' in Part V). Towns were also becoming more politicized with, once again, capital cities such as London and Paris taking the lead in fomenting radical thinking, discontent and even revolution.

## Assessment

What the ups and downs of early modern urban life show us is that both growth and decline were characteristic. The relationships between town and country, and town and crown, provide the essential context for understanding the dynamics of urban development. The impact of economic shifts, locally, nationally and internationally, favoured some towns over others, including those best able to adapt to the changing circumstances of the market. Yet it is also worth remembering that political rather than economic forces were the determining factor in the growth of many early modern European towns. Urban elites developed a dependent but also symbiotic relationship with territorial rulers and took more vigorous measures to curb activities which challenged the prevailing order. Growing prosperity led to greater disposable income and leisure time for some. Socio-economic adversity led to increasing tensions and the marginalization of the poor. Towns were at the forefront of most of the major trends of the period and continued to be the most dynamic component of early modern European society, economically, politically, culturally and socially.

## Discussion themes

1.  Why did some towns flourish in this period while others stagnated?
2.  How were towns governed?
3.  What was distinctive about urban culture?

## Bibliography

### (A) Sources

Bruyère, Jean de la (1963), *Characters (or the Manners of the Age)* [1688], trans. Henri Van Laun, Oxford
Latham, Robert ed. (1978), *The Illustrated Pepys: Extracts from the Diary*, London


### (B) Literature

Barry, Jonathan ed. (1990), *The Tudor and Stuart Town: A Reader in English Urban History, 1530–1688*, London
Beik, William (1997), *Urban Protest in Seventeenth-Century France: The Culture of Retribution*, Cambridge
Benedict, Philip ed. (1992), *Cities and Social Change in Early Modern France*, London
Borsay, Peter (1989), *The English Urban Renaissance: Culture and Society in the Provincial Town, 1660–1770*, Oxford
Clark, Peter ed. (2000), *The Cambridge Urban History of Britain, Vol. II: 1540–1840*, Cambridge
Cowan, Alex (1998), *Urban Europe, 1500–1700*, London
Cowan, Alex and Steward, Jill eds (2007), *The City and the Senses: Urban Culture Since 1500*, Aldershot
Epstein, Stephen R. ed. (2001), *Town and Country in Europe, 1300–1800*, Cambridge
* Friedrichs, Christopher R. (1995), *The Early Modern City, 1450–1750*, London
—— (2000), *Urban Politics in Early Modern Europe*, London
Garrioch, David (2003), 'Sounds of the City: The Soundscape of Early Modern Towns', *Urban History*, 30, 5–25
Lindemann, Mary (2014), *The Merchant Republics: Amsterdam, Antwerp and Hamburg 1648–1790*, Cambridge
* Nicholas, David (2003), *Urban Europe, 1100–1700*, Basingstoke
Pollak, Martha (2010), *Cities at War in Early Modern Europe*, Cambridge
Postan, Michael (1972), *The Medieval Economy and Society*, New York
Pounds, N. J. G. (1979), *An Historical Geography of Europe 1500–1840*, Cambridge
Prak, Marten ed. (2001), *Early Modern Capitalism: Economic and Social Change in Europe, 1400–1800*, London
Saupin, Guy (2002), *Les Villes en France à l'époque moderne (XVIe–XVIIIe siècles)*, Paris

Strauss, Gerald (1976), *Nuremberg in the Sixteenth Century*, Bloomington, Ind.
Vries, Jan de (1984), *European Urbanization, 1500–1800*, London

### (C) Web resources

'A Day in Eighteenth-Century London', in *Norton Anthology of English Literature*:
    <http://www.wwnorton.com/college/english/nael/18century/topic_1/welcome.htm>
'Historic Cities: Maps and Documents': <http://historic-cities.huji.ac.il>
Nevola, Fabrizio and Rosenthal, David, 'Urban Communities in Early Modern Europe
    (1400–1700): A Research Review': <http://earlymoderncommunities. files.
    wordpress.com/2011/12/earlymoderncommunities.pdf>
*The London Gazette*, 3–10 September 1666, 'Fire of London': <http://www.bl.uk/
    learning/timeline/item103652.html>
'The Proceedings of the Old Bailey: London's Central Criminal Court, 1674–1913':
    <http://www.oldbaileyonline.org/>

# Marginals and deviants

*Penny Roberts*

All societies identify as suspect and threatening certain types of behaviour, appearance or lifestyle which differ from the prevailing norms. As a result, associated individuals or groups are marginalized, ostracized or actively persecuted. Although these groups may be quite diverse in the nature of their difference, some common stereotypes recur: their predilection for acts of sexual depravity, criminality and other anti-social behaviour, accompanied by metaphors of pollution and disease (Douglas 1991). From early Christians through the heretical groups of the Middle Ages to the Protestants of the early modern period, religious minorities in Europe were accused of indulging in orgies, ritual violence and abuse of the mainstream faith. Jews and witches faced similar accusations. Above all, such groups or individuals were believed to pose a direct threat to respectable, law-abiding Christian society. Many of these prejudices were a continuation of those of the Middle Ages, although the groups at which they were directed could fluctuate. For instance, Jews had been expelled from several European countries, only to re-emerge in cities like Venice, where they were confined to a circumscribed area known as the GHETTO ('Jews and Muslims' in Part III). With the advent of the Reformation, HERESY entered the mainstream; Protestants and Catholics condemned each other's beliefs while uniting to safeguard society from radicalism, atheism and immorality. At a time when SERFDOM declined in Western Europe, it was reinforced in Central and Eastern Europe; the incidence of slavery in the Mediterranean increased and the transatlantic slave trade began. Rising levels of poverty led to particular concerns about the menace of vagrancy and associated criminality. Prostitution, too, was increasingly criminalized, as were the practices associated with WITCHCRAFT ('Witchcraft and magic' in Part V).

Many large towns in Europe contained foreigners and refugees. Ports and other major trading centres housed communities of foreign merchants. The expulsion of MORISCOS from the Iberian peninsula in the early seventeenth century, the flight of Huguenots from France during periods of persecution and the harassment of radical sects throughout Europe led to new settlements by refugees in areas as far apart as New England and Poland. Although many of these communities were successfully integrated, they still represented a convenient scapegoat at times of crisis. Increasing numbers of vagrants generated a fear of criminal gangs roaming the countryside and posing a threat to property through theft or arson (Roberts in Naphy and Roberts 1997). This prejudice also dogged the movement and settlement of gypsies or Roma throughout Europe. The spectrum of marginalization and active persecution varied according to the relative threat which such groups were believed to pose, in a given place at a given time, to the society in which they lived.

## Dishonourable trades

Not all professional activities were of equal standing in early modern society: at the top of the social hierarchy were merchants, lawyers, doctors and goldsmiths in towns, and substantial free farmers in the countryside. At the bottom were the so-called 'dishonourable trades' such as executioner and skinner (both responsible for the taking of life), grave-digger and latrine-cleaner, plague-worker and prostitute. Their marginalization took the form of ostracism. They could be refused citizenship, membership of GUILDS, medical treatment and entry to social spaces such as inns and bath-houses (although prostitutes regularly frequented these). They were often forced to live in the most insalubrious districts of towns alongside others classified as deviant. Direct economic contact with them was allowed, but no socializing, friendship or intermarriage, because those involved were believed to be tainted by association. In Augsburg, when a young fisherman declared his intention to marry the daughter of a local skinner, both families contrived to keep the lovers apart, but after they both tried to commit suicide they were allowed to wed. As a consequence, the fisherman was ejected from his guild and deprived of his livelihood (Stuart 1999, 1–2). Despite, or because of, their exclusion, 'dishonourable' traders were able to develop their own subculture. Enjoying certain privileges associated with their essential role, and practising social endogamy (intermarriage and occupational heredity), they 'occupied a symbolic position as outsiders' (Stuart 1999, 253).

## The poor

In the Middle Ages poor relief came primarily from private individuals and the Church. In the early sixteenth century municipal authorities began to assume that responsibility by taking over some of the existing institutions, and some have attributed this to the rise of Protestantism. Local studies, however, agree that it was the growing incidence of poverty in early modern towns, rather than religious change, which was the driving force (Pullan 1971). It seems that HUMANIST-inspired welfare concerns were more influential than faith in both Catholic and Protestant contexts, although religion was an important factor in deciding who was worthy of relief. Loaded judgements included distinctions between the deserving and undeserving, as well as between the native and foreign poor, as more systematic official provision displaced more indiscriminate support. In the seventeenth century, a network of workhouses and penal institutions developed in many major European towns, in which troublesome members of society could be locked up, and which would be forerunners of the modern prison and sanatorium (Foucault 1991). At the same time, however, the Catholic Church reassumed some of its responsibility, principally through the efforts of new religious orders such as the Capuchins. Yet this also reinforced the moral distinction to be made between those who were worthy and unworthy of relief, which resulted in the needy being institutionalized alongside criminals. There was a general movement to clear undesirables including prostitutes, vagrants and petty criminals off the streets; or to herd them into particular slum areas of towns. Expulsion from the community was reinforced by more definitive transportation to the newly established colonies in the Americas and, later, Australia.

The institutionalization of workhouses and what might be termed 'community service' (digging and clearing ditches, repairing walls and roads) was a development pioneered in the Netherlands. It soon spread to other European countries as the numbers seeking and in need of poor relief soared. The poor became badged and, therefore, dishonourable members of the community, just as Jews, lepers and prostitutes before them. Badging and distinctive dress, as well as mutilation and branding, ensured that difference and dishonour were recognized. The 'Great Confinement' in houses of correction or BRIDEWELLS suited authorities and elites but also wider society. 'The basic tenets and programmes of any poor relief system reflect the values of the society in which the system functions' (Jütte 1994, 197).

## Medical outcasts

Leprosy had all but disappeared from much of Europe by 1500, but plague was still a regular visitor. Victims of plague were feared, but so too were human agents believed to deliberately spread the disease. In the towns of the western Alps, a number of so-called 'plague spreaders', primarily foreign women who were paid to clean the linen and to clear the houses of the diseased, were executed. Motivated by greed, they were believed to have propagated infection through the use of a special grease (Naphy 2002). Those who we would now classify as suffering from mental illness or a neurological condition were kept hidden away by their families or left to fend for themselves as well as they could on the streets and highways of early modern Europe, alongside beggars, both able and disabled. Epilepsy and depression (or 'melancholy') were associated with demonic possession and subsequently sufferers were subject to a variety of traumatic 'treatments'. Lunacy, although similarly misdiagnosed, was nevertheless admissible as a defence in court. A new challenge was the increasing incidence of syphilis, referred to in much of Europe as 'the French pox', but generally believed to have appeared as a result of contacts with the New World. Correctly diagnosed as a sexually transmitted disease, it provided a further opportunity for moralists to rail against the sins of society, but the stigma attached to it depended largely on the sufferer's social status.

Human curiosities acted as popular forms of entertainment. Fools and dwarfs continued to be a fashionable accessory at many European courts. Monstrous births (of deformed humans or animals) attracted great interest and sometimes public display. Disability and deformity were sources of both repulsion and fascination.

Meaning was sought in why God would have afflicted those who were supposedly made in his image in this way. The sins of the afflicted, or of society more generally, provided the usual answer. Yet as scientific knowledge developed, so too did an interest in understanding as well as observing affliction. Monsters existed in a liminal space between curiosity and prodigy, subject to 'the tolerance conferred by greater scientific understanding of a certain condition, and superstitious horror at that which does not conform to rigid roles of sex, race or species' (Long 2006, 192; Knoppers and Landes 2004).

## Sexual deviants

Whatever the source of difference, sexual deviance was seen as a common characteristic. Lepers and Jews were associated with lasciviousness and Muslims with perverse sexual practices. Protestants claimed that Catholic clergy seduced nuns and female parishioners. Witches were accused of having sexual intercourse with the devil, and vagrants of having many short-lived liaisons. Perceptions of sexual deviance could be very wide-ranging indeed. In theory, any sexual act outside marriage, and even any non-procreative act within marriage, was forbidden by the Church. The position deemed most advantageous for conception, with the man on top, was hierarchically symbolic. Nevertheless, sexual pleasure was allowable and often believed necessary for both parties in order for procreation to take place (which made accusations of rape resulting in pregnancy inadmissible). Sodomy was a term used for a wider selection of activities than simply anal intercourse, including masturbation, oral sex and bestiality. Often, however, only the most heinous and publicly scandalous offences came to trial, and although death by burning was prescribed, judges often handed out lesser sentences. While railed against by moralists, the behaviour of notorious libertines such as the Earl of Rochester or the Marquis de Sade made them into celebrities. Notable too is the commercial success of erotic and pornographic literature in the eighteenth century ('Enlightenment: England and France' in Part V; Figure II.5).

Same-sex activity, although condemned in theory, was often tolerated in practice if it did not outrage public decency (Merrick and Ragan 2000). In the cities of Venice and Florence, distinctions were made between young men for whom such acts could be seen as a passing phase prior to the more 'natural' outlet of marriage, and older men indulging in pederasty (Rocke 1996). For women, an outlet for erotic desire was provided within the special context of nunneries and the delicate constellation of spiritual ecstasy, marriage to Christ and close physical proximity to other sisters (Brown 1986). There was much concern with who took the active (therefore male) and passive (therefore female) role in the relationship. Historians of sexuality are divided over whether there was a distinctive homosexual culture in the pre-modern period, although the so-called molly houses of eighteenth-century London suggest that by the end of our period, at least in a larger metropolis, this was the case. In a criminal case against 'Mother Clap' in 1726, a witness described how he 'found near Fifty Men

**Figure II.5** With its portrayal of power games, pleasure-seeking and sexual conquests among the Parisian elite, the epistolary novel *Dangerous Liaisons* by Pierre Choderlos de Laclos (1782) scandalized and fascinated eighteenth-century readers in equal measure. This illustration by Niclas II Lafrensen depicts an amorous encounter between the viscount of Valmont and the courtesan Emilie. Bibliotheque des Arts Decoratifs, Paris, France / Bridgeman Images.

there, making Love to one another as they call'd it. Sometimes they'd sit in one anothers Laps, use their Hands indecently Dance and make Curtsies and mimick the Language of Women' (Proceedings of the Old Bailey: Web resources). Women only tended to come before the courts due to the scandal caused by a woman subverting the natural order by pretending to be a man. The idea of a woman giving physical satisfaction to another woman threatened masculine superiority. The sexual ambiguity of HERMAPHRODITES, who possessed both male and female genitalia, was viewed as destabilizing if they did not adopt a single gender identity. They could cause all kinds of judicial confusion when they came before the courts (Box 1).

Prostitution, previously the socially acceptable outlet for male sexual energies in particular, was largely driven underground as part of a wider moral agenda during the early modern period. In the Middle Ages prostitutes were frequently taxed according to their trade like any other workers, and many cities even established official bordellos or bath-houses. Attitudes seem to have changed by the mid-sixteenth century, after which prostitutes and their clients had to operate with much more discretion. Even so, known prostitutes were sometimes brought in to judge cases of impotency and even their claims of rape were not dismissed out of hand. Rape in general was a crime extremely hard to prove, and society only took an unambivalent attitude if a young child was involved. The Catholic Reformation spawned a number of religious orders which took charge of rehabilitating repentant prostitutes. The English Society for

**Box 1**

When asked, during a trial before the Inquisition at Toledo in 1587, if s/he had had relations with any other women as if s/he were a man, Elana/Elano de Céspedes answered:

'I've had carnal relations with many other women, especially with the sister of the priest I served . . . . But . . . none of the women I've known was aware that I had female organs, since I was always able to cover them up. My wife María del Caño never knew I had a woman's nature. Even though it's true that many times María desired to put her hand on my shameful parts, I never let her do it, even though she wanted to very much . . . .'

(Kagan and Dyer 2004, 36–59; quotation 48)

After she was arrested for sodomy, the chief accusation against Elana/Elano before the Inquisition was sorcery as well as concerns about bigamy. In her teens s/he had been married to a man and had a child, but had subsequently lived and worked and remarried as a man. The Inquisition ordered that s/he henceforth live as a woman. The case shows the concern of the authorities about sexual ambivalence and the social instability it caused.

the Reformation of Manners undertook its own moral crusade to close brothels and bawdy houses, which became officially prohibited in many parts of Europe (Amster 2007). The authorities were aware that their focus on sexual immorality might also generate prurient interest in the practices they condemned. There was a thin line between descriptions and depictions of illicit behaviour and pornography.

## Criminals

Levels of crime are hard to assess in any age because cases do not always reach the courts or get recorded in other ways. So much harder to quantify is the 'dark figure' of crime in the past before the development of a professional police force. Nevertheless, historians have tried to assess the incidence of violent crime, such as the number of murders per head of population. Interestingly, it seems that property crime and homicide declined between the seventeenth and eighteenth centuries, at least in England (Sharpe 1999). Yet infanticide came to be prosecuted more systematically throughout early modern Europe. Details of criminal trials always give the impression of a violent and lawless society, but both changes and continuities are evident between then and now. Most cases involved petty crime, more men than women were brought before the courts; however, many more crimes commanded the death penalty than now lead to life imprisonment, such as heresy, arson and sodomy. Certain witnesses were seen as more reliable than others, according to gender and social status, and levels of proof were much less than required now. Nevertheless, the flexibility of the courts in deciding sentences more lenient than the law might demand is remarkable (Box 2). From our perspective, it is evident that many designated as criminals were forced to break the law through desperation or coercion. Harsh economic circumstances were often at the source of prostitution, poaching, coin-clipping and pickpocketing. On the other hand, the romanticization of the outlaw's life was a product of the eighteenth century. Notable examples of celebrated careers include the English highwayman Dick Turpin, the German outlaw Johannes Bückler (or *Schinderhannes*) and the Sicilian bandit Rinaldo Rinaldini (Box 3).

A peculiarity of the early modern period was the prevalence of arson scares. Supposed plots were reported in France, Germany and England in the sixteenth and seventeenth centuries, and a composite of vagrants, religious minorities and foreigners

---

## Box 2

'Johanna Lane, Arraigned for picking the Pocket of James Harvey of 3 l. 4s. 10d. but he could not positively swear it; and she bringing sufficient Housholders to vouch her honest course of life, the Jury thought fit to acquit her. 25 Feb. 1685.'

'John Skeldon, of the Parish of Christ-Church, was indicted for the Murder of Williams Douglas, the 13th of February last. John Wells depos'd, That he being with the Deceased, the Prisoner came riding along a full Gallop, about 8 a Clock at Night and the Deceased being a Carman, was leading his Horse, when the Prisoner riding, against him, threw him down, and fell upon him with his Knees against his Breast . . . . The Prisoner call'd several Persons to his Reputation, who gave him the Character of a peaceable inoffensive Person. The Jury found him guilty of Manslaughter. Burnt in the Hand. 26 Feb. 1724.'

*(Proceedings of the Old Bailey; Web resources)*

These two cases reinforce the importance of local reputation as attested to by witnesses for influencing the decision-making of juries.

---

## Box 3

'All Italy speaks of him. The Appenine mountains and the Sicilian vales resound with the name of Rinaldini. It lives in the songs of Florence and Calabria and in the ballads of the Sicilians. From the summit of the Alps to the extremity of the Appenines, men talk of his achievements: and when the garrulous villagers of Calabria assemble in the evening before their doors, every one is ready to relate some adventure of the Valeroso Capitano Rinaldini.'

*(Hinkley 1848)*

This 'Author's Preface' captures the romantic appeal of an oral and musical tradition about a local hero.

were blamed. Arson was categorized as a moral crime, but the principal concern here was the security of the state with fire as a weapon of the enemy. Arsonists and witches have recently been identified as the terrorists of the early modern era (Dillinger 2004). The threat posed to society by such groups, and others perceived not to have the usual investment in the welfare of the community, made gypsies and other outsiders especially vulnerable to criminal accusations. They faced overwhelming pressure to conform; resistance was itself interpreted as an act of wilful disobedience to authority and destructive of the harmony of society.

## Slaves

In most parts of Christian Europe by 1500, slavery had declined rapidly since Roman times, although the system of serfdom had effectively tied much of the PEASANTRY to the land and the service of their lords for centuries. In both Christian and Muslim traditions, enslaving coreligionists was forbidden, but enslaving those of another faith was acceptable. Hence the Ottoman practice of taking slaves as tribute from their European lands to staff the harem and the army. Where Muslim and Christian worlds met, principally in the Mediterranean, the practice of taking captives to use as slaves was commonplace. Thus the slave trade in French, Italian, Spanish, Portuguese, and even English, Irish and Flemish captives to North Africa was brisk. Many were taken at sea along with their ships by Barbary corsairs, but coastal raiding was also effective. There was some enslavement of Muslim captives by Christians, mostly on galley ships, but nothing like on the same scale. Although exact figures are elusive, it is estimated that tens of thousands of Christians were seized and enslaved (Davis 2004, 6). Slaves might be returned to their country of origin, sometimes for a ransom, but this was an elaborate process which often took years of familial pressure on the authorities.

Within Africa itself, slavery had been practised between tribes for centuries. Black slaves were imported to Portugal from the mid-fifteenth century through purchase or kidnap (the enslavement of Moors in the Iberian peninsula was well established). When in the sixteenth century the Portuguese and Spanish colonies in the Americas began to seek slave labour to work on their plantations, traders happily cooperated in meeting this demand through the capture and sale of African slaves. As the trade became increasingly lucrative, white Europeans based in Atlantic ports became keen to profit by providing the ships and processing the slaves. Thus, the eighteenth-century prosperity of ports such as Liverpool and Bristol was based on the black slave trade destined for the sugar, tobacco, rice and cotton plantations of the Americas. 'It was at just about the time when Mediterranean slaving began to falter – around the mid-1600s – that the transatlantic trade really took off' (Davis 2004, xxvii).

The eighteenth century was the heyday or peak of the transatlantic slave trade, and it would prove to be very profitable indeed for the traders and MASTERS. Whereas religion had been the distinguishing characteristic of the Mediterranean culture of slavery, race would characterize that of the Americas. It justified to its perpetrators the harsh and inhumane treatment of the non-white 'other'. Millions of Africans were transported overseas in the most appalling conditions and many died of disease or neglect en route or soon after reaching their destination. The principal demand for slaves came initially from the Caribbean and Brazil and, from the seventeenth century, the southern states of North America. Along with the subjugation of the native peoples in the New World, this trade reinforced Europeans' sense of superiority and entitlement to dominate the global economy. It shaped the imperial mindset with its powerful legacy for the modern age. Although by the end of the eighteenth century the Americas had begun their struggle for independence from European rulers (and the slaves from their masters), their cultures continued (and continue) to be shaped by that same European inheritance ('Expanding horizons' in Part IV; Epilogue).

## Assessment

Much of the official treatment of deviant or marginal groups in the early modern period was a matter of regulation or containment rather than destruction. Thus even a heinous sin like sodomy was more or less tolerated as long as it was kept within certain bounds and did not become notorious or disruptive. We tend to view deviants only through the lens of prosecution and persecution, chiefly because of the sources through which we know about them: judicial records, trials and legislation. Yet marginal groups sometimes played an important social or economic role which allowed for daily interaction and acceptance within the community. Whereas generalized attitudes towards such groups often proved harsh, personal relationships could temper and encourage toleration and protection rather than betrayal. Nowadays, when issues of difference lead to discrimination this prompts the law to step in to protect minorities or vulnerable groups whereas, in early modern times, laws determined the treatment of such groups in the name of protecting society and, by extension, law and order, state and Church. Yet courts could also act judiciously in individual cases when assessing the seriousness of the threat posed.

## Discussion themes

1. Which groups were marginalized in early modern Europe, and why?
2. How harshly did early modern courts deal with deviant behaviour?
3. To what extent did early modern society 'tolerate' deviants?

## Bibliography

### (A) Sources

Amster, Mara I. ed. (2007), *Texts on Prostitution, 1635–1700*, Aldershot
Hinkley, I. ed. (1848), *The History of Rinaldo Rinaldini, Captain of Banditti*, 2 vols, Philadelphia, Pa.

Kagan, Richard L. and Dyer, Abigail eds (2011), *Inquisitorial Inquiries: Brief Lives of Secret Jews and Other Heretics*, 2nd edn, Baltimore, Md.

McCormick, Ian ed. (1997), *Secret Sexualities: A Sourcebook of 17th and 18th Century Writing*, London

Merrick, John and Ragan Jr, B. T. eds (2000), *Homosexuality in Early Modern France: A Documentary Collection*, Oxford

## (B) Literature

Brown, Judith c. (1986), *Immodest Acts: The Life of a Lesbian Nun in Renaissance Italy*, Oxford

Crawford, Katherine (2007), *European Sexualities, 1400–1800*, Cambridge

Davis, Robert C. (2004), *Christian Slaves, Muslim Masters: White Slavery in the Mediterranean, the Barbary Coast and Italy, 1500–1800*, Basingstoke

Dillinger, Johannes (2004), 'Terrorists and Witches: Popular Ideas of Evil in the Early Modern Period', *History of European Ideas*, 30, 167–82

Douglas, Mary (1991), *Purity and Danger: An Analysis of the Concepts of Pollution and Taboo*, London

Foucault, Michel (1991), *Discipline and Punish: The Birth of the Prison*, London

* Jütte, Robert (1994), *Poverty and Deviance in Early Modern Europe*, Cambridge

Knoppers, Laura L. and Landes, Joan B. eds (2004), *Monstrous Bodies / Political Monstrosities in Early Modern Europe*, Ithaca, NY

Long, Kathleen P. (2006), *Hermaphrodites in Renaissance Europe*, Aldershot

* Milner, Stephen J. ed. (2005), *At the Margins: Minority Groups in Premodern Italy*, Minneapolis, Minn.

Naphy, William G. (2002), *Plagues, Poisons and Potions: Plague-Spreading Conspiracies in the Western Alps, c. 1530–1640*, Manchester

Naphy, William G. and Roberts, Penny eds (1997), *Fear in Early Modern Society*, Manchester

Pullan, Brian (1971), *Rich and Poor in Renaissance Venice: The Social Institutions of a Catholic State*, Oxford

Rocke, Michael (1996), *Forbidden Friendships: Homosexuality and Male Culture in Renaissance Florence*, New York

*Sharpe, J. A. (1999), *Crime in Early Modern England, 1550–1750*, 2nd edn, London

Stuart, Kathy (1999), *Defiled Trades and Social Outcasts: Honor and Ritual Pollution in Early Modern Germany*, Cambridge

## (C) Web resources

'The Proceedings of the Old Bailey 1674–1913', HRI Online Publications: <http://www.oldbaileyonline.org/>

# Sickness and health

*Claudia Stein*

Physical pain and suffering count among the most immediate experiences in the life of any human being, past and present. Autobiographical records offer fascinating insights into what early modern contemporaries did when faced with such intense situations. From the notes of the sixteenth-century Cologne city councillor, Hermann Weinsberg (1518–97), for example, we learn that most of the time, he and his wife relied on self-treatment, concocting plasters and syrups after tried and tested family recipes, took medical advice from neighbours, friends and, if too complicated to prepare, bought potions and ointments from the local apothecary shops (Web resources). Weinsberg also turned to the large printed herbal he owned. These often beautifully illustrated self-help manuals became bestsellers in the sixteenth century. Written in the vernacular European languages and aimed at the 'common man', they offered invaluable information on all sorts of cures: the medicinal powers of herbs, plants and minerals, the techniques of distillation, the secrets of chemical and alchemical procedures (Fuchs 1542). Recent scholarship has shown how popular this genre was; Weinsberg's frequent use of his own herbal was clearly not exceptional. He only consulted a 'medicus', an academic physician, if an illness did not pass off easily. But he also asked local surgeons and sometimes an 'empiric' or a local 'root' woman for advice. However, when his second wife fell ill in 1557 none of his own pharmaceutical skills and medical networks were to any avail. After having had her urine expertly examined by three physicians, several rounds of bloodletting, and the obedient consumption of various potions and pills, she died after just two weeks of suffering.

In contrast, the illness of the German knight, poet and HUMANIST Ulrich von Hutten (1482–1523) went on for years, and he suffered greatly according to his treatise from 1519 (English edn 1539, Figure II.6). He had contracted the dreaded FRENCH POX. The pox never claimed as many victims as the PLAGUE (or BLACK DEATH), which, historians estimate, probably wiped out over 25 million Europeans between 1346, when the epidemic first appeared in Europe, and 1720/21, when it mysteriously vanished from the continent (Hatcher 2009). Indeed, the pox was believed to be curable. Nevertheless, the sight of its victims was frightening and Hutten does not spare readers the details of his physical deterioration over the years. Turned into a pile of rotten and stinking flesh, the knight found himself alone because nobody dared or was willing to care for him. Particularly in the early decades after the pox first appeared, he reports, its victims populated the streets of European cities, begging for

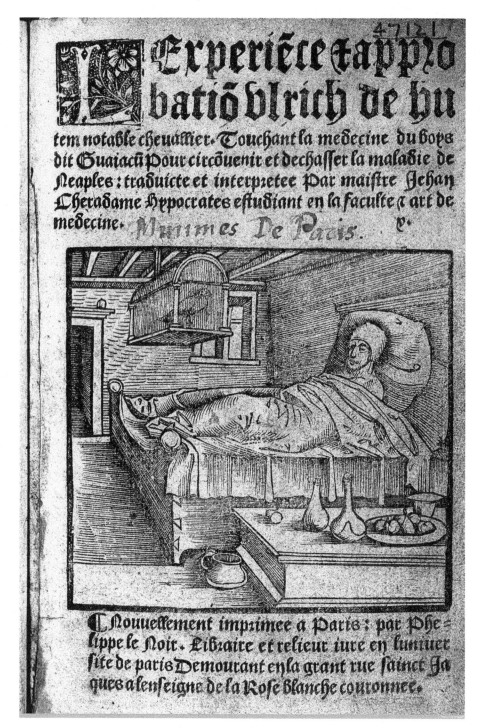

**Figure II.6** The knight Ulrich von Hutten lying in bed, undergoing a treatment with the wood *guaiacum* which involved long periods of extensive sweating in a sauna-type hot room (1519). Wellcome Library, London.

help and presenting a serious health threat to the local population. As none of the existing hospitals, dedicated to the old and chronically ill or to the victims of already well-known infectious diseases such as leprosy or bubonic plague, accepted pox sufferers, special pox institutions were opened. In the Southern-German trading city of Augsburg, treatment – either with mercury ointments or the wood guaiacum, a new drug imported from the New World – was free of charge. It was Hutten's successful cure with the latter, interpreted as a sign of divine mercy, that drove him to pen his treatise. Finally, he rejoiced, there was an alternative to the dreaded mercury. And Hutten knew what he was talking about, having endured such mercury ointments eleven times himself (Box 1).

## Box 1

Mercury was so powerful that it moved the illness to the patient's

'throat and the mouth, from which the disease poured so greatly that all the teeth fell out and one had to worry about the mouth in general. The throat and tongue began to fester . . . incessantly stinking saliva was pouring out of the mouth which polluted everything . . . the entire house was so full of stench that those awaiting to be cured wished to die [rather] than to be cured in that way.'

(Trans. Stein 2009, 35; cf. Hutten 1539 and www.routledge.com/cw/kumin)

How can historians approach such fascinating first-hand reports of physical suffering? How to evaluate early modern explanations of disease causalities, reports of medical diagnosis, and treatment choices? It is interesting that, for a long time, historians of medicine were not particularly interested in such personal accounts, disregarding them as 'curiosities' of a pre-scientific and superstitious age. While celebrating the alleged precursors of modern scientific medicine ('The scientific revolution' in Part V), the medical culture of the 'common man' was simply non-existent to the majority of these elite-focused medical historians (who were often medical doctors themselves). This changed dramatically in the 1960s when social historians, and, a bit later, cultural historians of medicine, 'discovered' the daily lives of popular cultures (Lindemann 2010). Inspired by anthropology, they began to explore early modern medical ideas and practises as expressions of a past and foreign culture whose medical choices needed to be understood in their own terms, rather than measured against modern standards of health and medicine (Stein 2014). Post-modern influences, particularly writings by the French philosopher Michel Foucault (1926–1984), shaped a whole new field of study: the history of the body (Foucault 1994). Scholars working in this area suggested that all human experience, even most intimate human expressions such as physical pain, are relative in time and space.

They always were (and are) socio-culturally constructed. The task of the medical historian is therefore to decipher the rationale behind past expressions of bodily experiences. Why would, they ask, von Hutten willingly submit himself to eleven mercury cures, knowing full well the horrendous effects they would have on his body?

## Micro–macrocosm

In order to understand early modern experiences, we have to go back to classical antiquity. By and large, early modern contemporaries continued to follow the classical medical literature, most importantly the ideas of the physician Galen of Pergamon (129–*c.* 200 CE), himself a follower of Hippocrate (*c.* 450–370 BCE). Based on Aristotle's (384–322 BCE) philosophy of nature, and thus originally pagan, the Hippocratic/Galenic tradition had been Christianized over the centuries and adapted to the idea of a two-folded cosmos, created and ruled by God. Between the body – the 'microcosm' – and the surrounding world – the 'macrocosm' – a close connection was assumed. Indeed, every detail of the microscopic world of the human body was believed to have a corresponding macroscopic counterpart; the body mirrored the God-directed heavenly spheres. The micro–macrocosm idea allowed for the belief that God was able to influence man's individual and collective life, including health and disease, via his 'servants', the stars and planets. Astrologers, whose judgements were taken very seriously by everyone at the time, were busy producing diagrams and horoscopes to calculate the most propitious times for treatment or avoidance of it (Figure II.7) – and they also nailed down the astrological causes for sudden and unexpected epidemics such as the plague or the pox (Kassell 2007).

For early modern Christians, Catholic and Protestant alike, the reason for God's absolute power over the human body was to be found in the Bible. Until man's fall from Grace, so Genesis told them, humans had lived a carefree existence in heavenly paradise, free of all physical suffering. Eve's bite of the apple destroyed all this; not only the right to stay in Eden, but, through her disobedience, the human body became an object of shame and a subject of physical decay and mortality. For all believers bodily suffering was a constant reminder of the Fall that had tainted mankind forever. Disease was thus understood as an immediate reaction of God, his divine punishment (*flagitium Dei*) for human sins.

Nobody therefore regarded illness as random or coincidental. Any bodily harm always had a higher purpose which needed to be deciphered. Individual and public prayers, masses, processions and pilgrimages all remained popular responses to distress and suffering, even after the Reformation (Grell and Cunningham 1993). Yet accepting illness as God's punishment or a test of one's faith did not mean that early modern Christians endured suffering with stoic fatalism and rejected all medical treatment as meaningless. Quite the contrary: it was everyone's duty to look after his or her body (understood as the home of the immortal soul) and to seek medical advice in the event of ill health. Deliberately neglecting one's body and rejecting medical

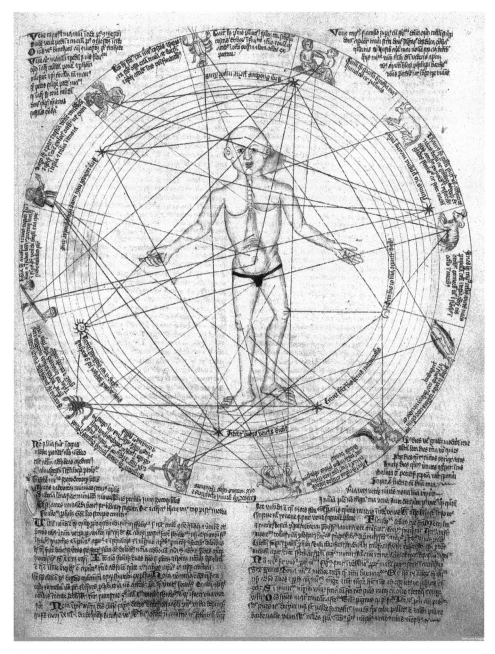

**Figure II.7** Bloodletting or zodiac man, showing the influence of zodiac and its twelve astrological signs on the individual parts and organs of the human body. No therapeutic procedure would be undertaken without astrological considerations (*c.* 1420). Wellcome Library, London.

help was tantamount to wilfully shortening one's life span allotted by God, an almost unsurpassable act of negligence equated with the sin of suicide. So, if medical help was welcomed, on what physiological understanding of the human body was such help based?

## Of complexion and humours

According to Aristotelian and Galenic theory, the human body – as all things dwelling in the sublunary sphere – consisted of the four elements earth, water, fire and air, with their corresponding qualities (dry, moist, hot and cold). Each person was endowed with an innate mixture of these ELEMENTS AND QUALITIES; his or her COMPLEXION, acquired at the moment of conception and kept more or less until death (Siraisi 1999). It was however affected by certain conditions of life and external circumstances. One's youthful heat and moisture, for example, gave way to a general coldness and dryness in old age. Also, women were generally considered colder and moister than men. Environmental and geographical conditions played a role, too. The English as a group were considered colder and wetter than, for example, the Italian or Spanish people due to the general lack of sun and heat on their island.

Closely associated with the concept of complexion was the ancient theory of HUMORS, of which there were also four: blood, phlegm, red or yellow bile, and black bile. Depending on which humour dominated a person's innate complexion, he or she was either sanguine, phlegmatic, choleric or melancholic. Produced from the foodstuff in the stomach, which was then transported to the liver that sent them throughout the body, humors fulfilled two central functions in the body's economy. In the first place, they nourished the individual organs and body parts. Second, collectively they maintained an individual's overall complexional balance. Any alteration of one's innate balance carried the risk of disease (Figure II.8).

To avoid upsetting their complexions, contemporaries relied on ancient advice which preached a regular regiment, including a strict monitoring of the so-called six NON-NATURALS to which the human body was incessantly exposed: air, evacuation and retention, food and drink, motion and rest, sleeping and waking, and the passions. Any alterations of daily habits in relation to these six non-naturals could trigger substantial and potentially dangerous changes in people's naturally balanced complexions. Being exposed to longer periods of cold or wet weather, for example, raised the quantity of wet and cold qualities, which, in turn, might induce wet and cold diseases such as the French pox (Nutton 1983). Food too – each foodstuff was ascribed certain qualities – had to be carefully chosen and monitored to nurture and sustain one's complexion. Everything in moderation, was the general advice given by any medical practitioner.

In the case of illness medical practitioners and their patients had to first trace the exact circumstances of how they fell sick. Every detail of their usual behaviour and the tiniest derivation from it were vital hints as to the causes of underlying illness.

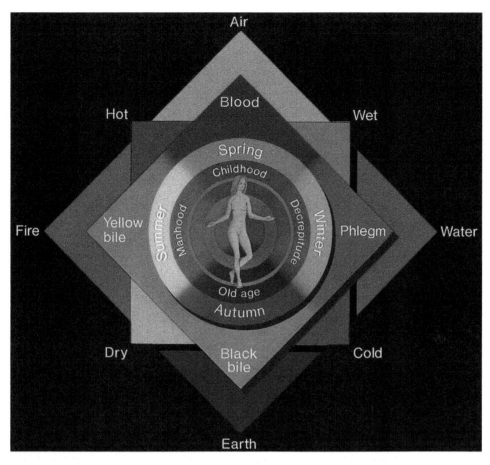

**Figure II.8** The four elements, qualities, humors, seasons and life stages and their interrelations. Wellcome Library, London.

Only if the 'natural causes' of a disease such as the pox were deciphered, a suitable treatment could be suggested.

## Treatment and cure

The first reaction to disease in the early modern period was always to turn to God. Daily prayers were therefore essential for every sufferer. They were also part of routine curative practice in the many charitable institutions for the sick, run by civic communities or by individual donors (Risse 1999). The house rules of the Augsburg civic pox hospital – founded in 1495 and, since the official establishment of the Reformation in the city in the 1530, open to victims of both denominations – ordered patients to pray several times a day in order to speed up their recovery and to thank the founders for providing free cures (Stein 2009).

The physical treatment in such institutions for the poor (more affluent people preferred to be treated in their own homes or booked themselves into a private clinic run by local physicians or surgeons, as Ulrich von Hutten probably did) followed the logic of the theory of humors. The overall aim of all treatment was to bring the individual complexion back to its natural equilibrium. There were various options available to reduce the 'poisonous' matter in the body. First, as the treatment of Weinsberg's wife showed, the contaminated blood in which the four humors were fused could be removed through cupping, bloodletting or purging. While bleeding removed whatever was in the veins, purging (a selected excretion of harmful substances, usually through vomiting and evacuation of the bowels) was directly targeted at specific 'poisons'. But reducing morbid matter, it was believed, could only offer temporary relief. To get rid of a disease, such as the pox, once and forever, its natural causes, that is the qualitative imbalance in the nutritional blood, had to be corrected through carefully targeted remedies. The first priority in choosing any vegetable, animal or mineral remedy was that its qualities should be directly opposed to that of the assumed disease. In the case of the pox, believed to be a cold / wet disease, remedies of a warming, drying and mollifying power were recommended. Mercury, prescribed since antiquity for all kinds of skin affliction, was therefore a perfect choice as it was assumed to be of a hot, even burning and acid quality, ready to dry out the cold and wet disease. Within this logic, von Hutten's aforementioned effects of a mercury cure – copious salivation, diarrhoea, excessive sweating, loss of teeth and all body hair – were explicitly desired by sixteenth-century patients and practitioners alike. They were interpreted as hopeful signs that the disease left the body.

However, in some cases the knife was the only option. Considering that all operations were conducted without anaesthetics and always under the peril of life-threatening infections, the number and variety of procedures that were performed by the surgeons at the time is truly remarkable (Wear 2000). Amputations, head surgeries, all sorts of eye operations or the trussing of bones were daily routine for any skilled surgeon. Patients, however, were understandably reluctant to call them in, even for relatively 'safe' operations such as the 'cutting of the stone', which had been performed with success since antiquity. A great number of sufferers survived this excruciatingly painful procedure (Figure II.9, <www.routledge.com/cw/kumin>).

The survivors of such an ordeal were understandably more than grateful to the Almighty. The London navy administrator Samuel Pepys (1633–1703), for example, who had undergone lithotomy on 26 March 1658 demonstrated his thankfulness by staging an annual banquet for family, friends, and neighbours. From his carefully kept diary, we know that he liked to entertain his guests with the presentation of his stone (apparently as large as the size of a tennis ball!) which he kept in a specially designed case (see yearly entries for 26 March in Web resources). Some contemporaries even felt inspired to express the gratitude and experience in music. A remarkable piece was composed by the French musician and composer Marin Marais (1656–1728). In

**Figure II.9** A depiction of the surgical removal of a stone from the urinary tract, known as 'lithotomy' in 1707. Wellcome Library, London.

his *Tableau de l'Opération de la Taille* (1725), the audience re-experiences audibly each step of the operation. (Web resources).

## The medical market place

Many surviving accounts demonstrate that patients had many options. As today, cities offered more differentiated services than the countryside, but generally early modern Europe supported a wide range of practitioners who met the medical needs of different communities. Not all of the healers chosen were 'professionally' trained; and not all lived from that trade alone. Some practiced only in the spirit of good neighbour-liness, and, as we have seen in the case of Weinsberg, and families possessed a stock of tried and tested recipes that were passed on from generation to generation (Leong 2013, emroc in Web resources). Sufferers could also turn to 'quacks' or 'empirics' who sold their wares and wonder cures on the streets and market squares; even the local executioner was an option, as well as bone setters or Weinsberg's 'root woman'. Patients had no hesitation in mixing and matching. In addition, there were full-time medical practitioners who had undergone a more or less rigorous apprenticeship in a guild system: midwives, apothecaries, surgeons or barber-surgeons (the latter ran the local baths and lived off haircutting, small operations and bloodletting). In terms of medical training as well as social prestige and financial income, academic physicians stood at the top of the professional hierarchy. The difference between them and a surgeon, for example, was that physicians tended not to perform actual operations or dress wounds. Their job was to decipher the hidden causes of diseases, or to use their astrological knowledge to link micro- and macrocosm and, on that basis, suggest suitable medications (Kassell 2007; 'The Casebook Project' in Web resources). Apart from taking the pulse or reading the urine, as in the case of Weinsberg's wife, they left the 'dirty work' to the surgeon who, according to them, needed their advice. As one can easily imagine, this often led to serious tensions between the two groups. Patients from lower levels of society also turned to academic advice but only as a last resort, as the fees of physicians were substantially higher. It is probably safe to say that non-academic practitioners catered for the lion's share of day-to-day medical and surgical care in most communities. And if we include the rising number of military and naval surgeons, they were clearly the most numerous practitioners in both town and country.

## Assessment

Early modern medicine is a fascinating phenomenon, sophisticated in terms of the theoretical understanding of the body and well-equipped to treat its many ailments and diseases. This world shared little with our understanding of the body and medicine. Does this complete 'otherness' give us permission to look down on contemporaries and their beliefs as early generations of historians tended to do? I have suggested a different approach (Stein 2014).

We should try to decipher the logic behind early modern ideas of disease causation, diagnostic procedures and treatments which, at first sight, might strike us as bizarre, indeed perhaps even barbarian. Understandings of the body and its ailments, I have argued, are never universal and transhistorical (not even our own). Any expression of physical experience is relative to its time and culture, and the task and pleasure of an historian is to unravel how earlier generations understood physical suffering and why they expressed their experiences in the way they did.

### Discussion themes

1. Can early modern medicine be considered intellectually 'backward'?
2. Do we experience our bodies today in the same way as early modern contemporaries did?
3. What had to be taken into account when diagnosing disease and suggesting therapy at the time?

## Bibliography

### (A) Sources

Hutten, Ulrich von (1539), *On the Wood Called Gvaicvm*, English edn, London <http://iiif.lib.harvard.edu/manifests/view/drs:6936182$1i>

Fuchs, Hieronymus (1542), *De historia stirpium commentarii insignes (or, Notable Commentaries on the History of Plants)*, Basel: <http://special.lib.gla.ac.uk/exhibns/month/oct2002.html>

### (B) Literature

Foucault, Michel (1994), *The Birth of the Clinic: An Archaeology of Medical Perception* [1963], London

Grell, Ole Peter and Cunningham, Andrew eds (1993), *Medicine and the Reformation*, London

Hatcher, John (2009), *The Black Death: A Personal History*, London

Jones, Colin and Barry, Jonathan eds (1991), *Medicine before the Welfare State*, London

Kassell, Lauren (2007), *Medicine and Magic in Elizabethan London: Simon Forman, Astrologer, Alchemist and Physician*, Cambridge

Leong, Elaine (2013), 'Collecting Knowledge for the Family: Recipes, Gender and Practical Knowledge in the Early Modern English Household', *Centaurus* 55(2), 81–103

Lindemann, Mary (2010), *Medicine and Society in Early Modern Europe*, 2nd edn, Cambridge

Nutton, Vivian (1983), 'The Seeds of Disease: An Explanation of Contagion and Infection from the Greeks to the Renaissance', *Medical History* 27, 1–34

Risse, Guenter B. (1999), *Mending Bodies, Saving Souls: A History of the Hospital*, Oxford

Siraisi, Nancy G. (1999), *Medieval and Early Renaissance Medicine: An Introduction to Knowledge and Practice*, Chicago

Stein, Claudia (2009), *Negotiating the French Pox in Early Modern Germany*, Farnham
—— (2014) 'Getting the Pox: Reflections by an Historian on How to Write the History of Early Modern Disease', *Nordic Journal of Science and Technology Studies* 2(1), 53–60

Wear, Andrew (2000), *Knowledge and Practice in English Medicine, 1550–1680*, Cambridge

### (C) Web resources

'The autobiographical writings of Hermann Weinsberg': <http://www.weinsberg.uni-bonn.de/>

'emroc – early modern recipes online collective': <http://emroc.hypotheses.org/>

'The Casebooks Project: a digital edition of Simon Forman's and Richard Napier's medical records': <http://www.magicandmedicine.hps.cam.ac.uk/>

'Theories of Contagion' from 'Infectious Diseases at the Edward Worth Library': <http://infectiousdiseases.edwardworthlibrary.ie/theory-of-contagion/>

'Tableau de l'opération de la taille', a musical piece composed by Marin Marais (1725): <https://www.youtube.com/watch?v=c2a7ae0oMLU>; cf. article and scores by James L. Franklin in *Hektoen International* (Summer 2012): <http://hekint.org/surgery-note-by-note-marin-marais-tableau-de-loperation-de-la-taille/>

'The Diary of Samuel Pepys', compiled by Phil Gayford: <http://www.pepysdiary.com/>

# The early modern economy

*Steve Hindle*

## Introduction

For analytical purposes, economic activity is often divided into three sectors: agriculture, manufacture/industry and trade/services. For the most part, the early modern economy remained fundamentally agrarian ('Rural society' in Part II). Since the High Middle Ages, of course, towns had become centres of economic differentiation, offering a growing variety of manufacturing crafts regulated by GUILDS and acting as focal points for the exchange of goods with the surrounding country ('Urban society' in Part II). In the sixteenth and seventeenth centuries, however, there was a significant drift of production activities from the highly regulated towns into the countryside where PROTO-INDUSTRIAL manufacture could evolve beyond the reach of the guilds. At the same time, population growth, urbanization and European expansion prompted large-scale increases in the intensity and geographical extent of trade.

This economy can legitimately be described as 'pre-industrial' only when judged by the standard of the vast transformations caused by nineteenth-century factory production. Mechanization was certainly limited and energy supply based on organic and mineral resources. Even so, although European society in the sixteenth and seventeenth centuries might have lacked capital, it emphatically did not lack industry. The most significant example across Europe was the production of textiles, overwhelmingly concentrated in the wood-pasture zones and BOCAGES where pastoral farming could be combined in a dual economy with the processing of fleeces for wool. Other industrial activities were both diverse and regionally specialized: the highland zones saw mining and quarrying; the woods and forests metalwork; and the coasts and ports large-scale fishery and shipbuilding. Where particular mineral resources existed, more specific forms of industrial production developed: the availability of brine, for instance, might provide the basis for dyeing and bleaching wool which later become so fundamental to the chemical industry.

## Agriculture

Although the AGRICULTURAL REVOLUTION, the radical transformation of techniques of cultivation and stock-rearing which made possible the extraordinary population growth of industrializing societies, is classically dated to the eighteenth and nineteenth centuries, there is some evidence of earlier technical progress which has been used to argue for previous agrarian change. YIELD-SEED RATIOS, for instance, improved (and sometimes doubled) across Western Europe between 1500 and 1700. With the advent of new crops in the late seventeenth and early eighteenth centuries, ratios may even have quadrupled. There was also a shift away from the traditional practice of permanent husbandry (arable cultivation), with more progressive farmers learning from their experience of winter pasturing and reverting their arable fields to pasture at five- (or sometimes seven-) year intervals in a practice that became known as 'convertible' or 'up-and-down husbandry' (Broad 1980). Progress of this kind was stimulated by increasing demand in the non-arable sector. Rising population levels across Europe – increasing from perhaps 75 million in 1500 and 100 million in 1600 to 110 million in 1700 and 190 million in 1800 (de Vries 1984, 36; 'Epilogue' in Part VII) – were combined with increasing urbanization and the proto-industrial development of pastoral areas (which stimulated demand for wool, hides and animal fats). The evidence suggests that, broadly speaking, supply was able to keep pace with these rising levels of demand despite the disproportionate growth in the size of the non-arable population. Some European countries, especially those which bordered the Baltic, were exporting grain even in the sixteenth century, which suggests that they had become self-sufficient by then; and even in England, where the growth of the non-arable population was most marked, grain exports were possible by the 1630s. So the evidence of at least some innovation in the agricultural sector is compelling. Hypothetically, there are three mechanisms through which this might have been achieved: the introduction of *additional* factors of production (usually land, capital or labour) in order to increase *gross* output; the development of *more efficient* factors of production (new crops, perhaps, or cheaper labour), which might result in increased output per unit of input; or some combination of the two (though of course increases in gross output will dilute the force of net output). The historical evidence in fact suggests two distinct periods of agrarian change, which were almost certainly the result of shifting levels of demand for agricultural produce.

The period 1500–1650 was one of very significant population increases across most of Europe. Although growth rates varied they were almost universally combined with increasing urbanization. Farmers across Europe were encouraged to boost output dramatically and they did so principally by using additional factors of production. The sixteenth and early seventeenth centuries accordingly saw the more intensive use of land hitherto considered marginal for arable purposes: fens were drained, marshes reclaimed, woodland cleared and the jurisdictional privileges of forests abrogated. This increase in the amount of land under cultivation was supplemented by the large-scale employment of abundant and cheap labour, both in the form of landless wage-earners (paid in cash, usually in arrears, by the day but able to gain regular work only at busy times of the agricultural calendar) and servants in husbandry (usually contracted annually and paid in bread and board). To a limited extent, there is also evidence of the sporadic introduction of new agricultural techniques: the further development of convertible husbandry, the floatation of water meadows and the introduction of new crops and rotation systems, all of them stimulated by the burgeoning literature on agricultural improvement. Since most of these practices were aimed at greater efficiency rather than raising output, however, they remained relatively uncommon at a time when high agricultural prices and low labour costs meant that efficiency savings (which often required expensive investment in the short term) were not a high priority for most farmers.

The period after 1650, by contrast, saw the long period of demographic expansion draw to a close and the stagnation of agricultural demand created a rather different set of priorities for farmers squeezed between increasing labour costs and falling food prices. To maintain, let alone increase, existing levels of production would only glut an already depressed domestic market. One solution, of course, was to funnel grain into exports, and it is generally true that agricultural products took a dramatically increased share of an export market which had traditionally been dominated by textiles in the late seventeenth and early eighteenth centuries (Table II.6.1).

**Table II.6.1** The increasing significance of foodstuffs exported from England, c. 1650–1750

| Product | 1663–69 | 1752–54 |
| --- | --- | --- |
| Woollen cloth (% of total exports value) | 74% | 47% |
| Woollen cloth (values in £s million) | £2.1 | £3.9 |
| Foodstuffs (% of total exports) | 3% | 17% |

Source: Davis 1954; 1962.

Another solution was to diversify, specializing in the production of specific types of foodstuffs for niche markets: the development of market gardening in the English county of Kent or the Dutch province of Holland to furnish fruit and vegetables for the populations of London and Amsterdam offers perhaps the best example of such a strategy. A third was to find ways of farming more efficiently, especially by shedding labour. Indeed the labour productivity of the agricultural sector seems to have increased significantly, at least in England, in the period 1670–1740. It is even possible that this increased efficiency resulted in a rise in output in the years down to 1740 that dwarfed the rates of the late eighteenth century, thought more characteristic of the classic agricultural revolution. To be sure, other factors underpinned agricultural progress in the decades after 1650: there were runs of good harvests in the 1680s, 1730s and 1740s; and rising real incomes stimulated demand for specialized produce such as fodder, fruit and dyestuffs. Overwhelmingly, however, it was efficiency savings in the labour market that enabled farmers to make such headway. After all, the most appropriate response to modest deflation was to farm more efficiently, especially by cutting labour costs. This could be achieved most obviously by hiring farm servants (who could be fed and lodged relatively cheaply when food was inexpensive) rather than wage-earners (who came at a high price when labour was relatively scarce); or more especially by ENCLOSURE, thereby eradicating the common property rights which had characterized the open field system and making economies of scale on holdings which were no longer dispersed across common fields but now concentrated into larger units (Thirsk 1967). Thus it was that the double quickset hawthorn hedge (effectively a form of organic barbed wire) spread across the countryside of North-west Europe in the late seventeenth and early eighteenth centuries. The price for this progress was paid by those smallholders who, unable to find the increased rent payable on enclosed land, were driven into the towns and proto-industrial zones in search of work. To be sure, enclosure of this kind was not unprecedented: small farmers had been carrying it out piecemeal since the demographic contraction of the late medieval period, arousing significant opposition from governments, polemicists and the rural poor (Box 1). But it was the cost-price squeeze of the late seventeenth century that provided farmers with the incentive to shed labour. This became part of a process which – over the course of the eighteenth century – resulted in the expropriation of smallholders and the creation of the ESTATES system which characterized farming until the great depression of the end of the nineteenth century.

## Box 1

'Your sheep . . . which are usually so tame and so cheaply fed, begin now, according to report, to be so greedy and wild that they devour human beings themselves and devastate and depopulate fields, houses, and towns. [Landlords] leave no ground to be tilled; they enclose every bit of land for pasture; they pull down houses and destroy towns, leaving only the church to pen the sheep in.'

(More 1965, 65–67)

A polemical comment on rural developments in Thomas More's famous *Utopia* of 1516.

## Manufacturing and (proto-)industry

Three principal characteristics marked early modern industries (which, unlike their medieval predecessors, were generally located in the countryside). The first was the comparative lack of fixed capital investment. Both coal and iron were relatively expensive; so many industrial processes remained reliant on water power throughout the early modern period. In any case, most industries had no call for such capital. The result was that most industrial activity was small scale: the nail-making industry, for instance, was carried out in numerous household workshops where individual smiths worked with nothing more than a furnace, a hammer and an anvil.

The second was that the pace of technical change was very slow. Techniques were in many respects pre-industrial, almost medieval, in the sense that they were labour- rather than capital-intensive: output could be raised only by increasing the number of workers involved in a particular process. There are, of course, exceptions: blast furnaces, first developed in the Namur region of the Low Countries and spreading subsequently to the Sussex Weald, became common across the Continent after the 1490s; and the technology which made possible the draining of coal mines across Europe was developing by the late sixteenth century (Zell 1994; Levine and Wrightson 1991). But there was no series of technical breakthroughs comparable with those that were to revolutionize the West European textile industry in the late eighteenth and early nineteenth centuries.

The third was that the organization of most industrial production was decentralized. Mining was in this respect the exception that proved the rule, as most industrial processes took place in a large number of geographically scattered and small-scale units (Figure II.10). Although most workers laboured unsupervised in their own homes, they were not generally self-employed. The organization of the textile industry may be taken as typical. For both the purchase of raw materials and the marketing of finished products, domestic producers needed the support of clothiers: entrepreneurs whose circulating capital lubricated what has come to be known as the PUTTING- OUT SYSTEM (Ogilvie and Cerman 1996). Conventionally the clothier would only clean the wool he had bought, but subsequently put it out into domestic production by carders and spinners before redistributing it to weavers, who might be full- or part- time workers but generally received a piece-rate rather than a regular wage. The only significant requirement for fixed capital in the textile industry was the water wheels which powered the mills in which cloth was pounded after being fulled. After the nap was raised and sheared most broadcloth was sold as white cloth to merchant adventurers who would have it dyed in the Netherlands, usually at the metropolitan port city of Antwerp which was both the most important ENTREPÔT in North-western Europe and the hub of a trading network which extended across Europe to the Levant and the Far East. Most cloth was marketed from Antwerp down the rivers Rhine and Elbe. To this extent, small-scale domestic cloth production was linked into a European- wide network of proto-industry in which merchant clothiers organized and financed the manufacture and sale of goods to distant markets. This pattern of domestic pro- duction and international marketing was essentially similar in other industries.

The geographical location of industrial production was determined largely by the availability of labour. In this sense, 'putting out' had its own logic, since labour was the principal cost to the merchant clothiers who organized the system: while raw materials might account for perhaps a third of the costs of cloth production, and carriage for as little as 2 per cent, the remainder (perhaps as much as 65 per cent) was taken up by remunerating the labour force. In this respect, the supply of raw materials was necessary but not sufficient to account for the development of industrial

**Figure II.10** Mining represented an early form of large-scale centralized production. This illustration shows the labour-intensive extraction of precious minerals as well as associated services like market stalls and open-air taverns. Coloured miniature by Jörg Kolber in the *Schwazer Bergbuch*, a description and illustration of the silver and copper mines of Schwaz in the Austrian region of Tyrol (1556), © Tiroler Landesmuseum Ferdinandeum, Inssbruck.

production: in textiles, for instance, wool itself could be easily and cheaply transported, with the consequence that many sheep-rearing areas accordingly lacked a cloth industry, especially if they were sparsely populated. An abundant supply of cheap labour was therefore decisive: hence cloth working came to be located in pastoral areas where the residents were either under- or unemployed, characteristically in those settlements where there was a peculiar concentration of uneconomic smallholdings – a tendency encouraged in those regions characterized by partible inheritance customs in which land was divided equally between the heirs (Kriedte *et al.* 1981, ch. 2). In such circumstances, dual or even multiple employment might develop in which farmers combined the rearing of sheep with the combing and carding of wool or the making of nails and scythe blades. The small farmer who had room for a smithy in his outbuildings might in this way become a linchpin in the nascent cutlery industry. Over time, the existence of a very large pool of landless labour might see the emergence of a proletariat with its own customs and working practices. In turn, some regions became highly dependent on this industrial workforce, especially where (as in the case of coal and iron) the availability of cheap labour was combined with the existence of plentiful raw materials. As mines were sunk ever deeper in the coal fields of late sixteenth-century Europe, the world was gradually turned not so much upside down as inside out.

Trends in industrial manufacture were largely dictated by foreign demand in the distant markets for which many consumer goods were produced. During slumps, disinvestment could be instantaneous, throwing thousands of under-employed weavers out of work altogether. This was particularly true of the production of expensive woollen cloth, for which there was distinctly limited elasticity of demand. Population increase might create a larger need for basic clothing for the common people, but the market for luxury cloth was less subject to ready expansion. Hence the central importance to the European cloth industry of the Antwerp market, whose instability in the mid- to late sixteenth century (due to the tensions between Spain and the Netherlands) caused a collapse in demand for English broadcloth in particular. When the dislocation of the Antwerp market was subsequently compounded by a shift in fashion away from heavier to lighter and more colourful fabrics, which could be produced much more competitively by Dutch producers, the leading sector of the early modern English economy experienced a severe crisis. The textile industry therefore had to diversify into the manufacture of 'new draperies' – light, finished, colourful and above all cheap fabric, the making of which became possible in the Netherlands from the fifteenth century and which was imported to Elizabethan England by Flemish refugees. Where such adaptation proved successful, the textile industry might experience renewed growth, for the new draperies reached a burgeoning market in the warmer climates of Southern Europe where lighter cloth was in huge demand. Overall, the European textile industry is best described as diversifying rather than growing as it matured and developed across the seventeenth century (Berg 1991). Coal and iron, by contrast, were growing apace: output in the Newcastle coal field, driven by demand in the rapidly growing city of London, increased at least tenfold between the 1560s and 1630s. The growth in iron production was less spectacular, despite the fact that output was stimulated not only by domestic consumption but by the demand for ordnance as European states built bigger and more technologically advanced armies and navies ('The theory and practice of politics and government 1500–1800' in Part VI). The late sixteenth century also saw the emergence of new industries, often stimulated by MERCANTILIST attempts to achieve national self-sufficiency in specific products: the first stirrings of small-scale production of such commodities as salt, soap, starch, alum, pins and thread, which subsequently made possible the consumer revolution of the eighteenth century, took place in this period. Yet it is important to remember that they remained local and small scale and did not amount to a revolutionary expansion in an industrial economy still dominated by the extraction of minerals and the processing of organic produce.

The diversification and specialization of industrial activity had very significant consequences for the settlements in which the manufacturing workforce lived. The majority of industrial communities grew increasingly large and densely peopled, as a consequence both of attracting migrants in search of work and retaining those who were born there. Coal-mining areas in particular were notorious for their disproportionate levels of population growth, but areas of textile production also experienced rapid demographic expansion caused both by in-migration and increased fertility, made possible by falling age at first marriage among wage-earning cloth workers (Levine 1984). In turn, manufacturing areas developed a distinctive social structure in which the agricultural population became a minority and the rhythms of the agrarian calendar less significant. The presence of a majority of industrial workers also entailed economic differentiation and social polarization, with fewer resident gentry or nobility and a preponderance of many relatively poor people. Because those who worked in coal, iron or textiles were often landless they could not provide for themselves and became market-dependent not only for the industrial goods which they had a hand in producing, but also for food, which almost invariably had to be imported from arable areas. Industrializing areas were therefore doubly insecure, vulnerable both to trade slumps and to harvest failures. As a consequence, these were often areas of unstable poverty. They could be notoriously volatile at times of unemployment and high prices. It is hardly coincidental that most food riots in Western Europe took place in cloth-producing areas where the workforce kept a vigilant eye on the price of foodstuffs which they could only obtain at what millers and corn-dealers judged to be the going rate ('Popular culture(s)' in Part V). The putting-out system which spread its tentacles into the households of manufacturing districts brought more and more communities into dependence not only on industry but also on the commercial market for those foodstuffs which their ancestors had generally produced for themselves. In turn, the growth of an industrial sector implied that the agricultural workforce would need to become increasingly productive to meet rising levels of demand.

## Trade and services

The basis for European trade was local and regional exchange in thousands of small towns, in which agricultural and manufactured goods were marketed. Alongside, medieval merchants established a flourishing long-distance spice trade, supported by an international financial infrastructure, which led to an early form of commercial CAPITALISM in the leading Italian CITY-STATES ('The Renaissance' in Part V). From the sixteenth century, the discovery of the New World and the desire to exploit its assets shifted the centre of economic gravity from the Mediterranean towards the Atlantic seaboard of the north-west. The symptoms of this early stage of globalization included vast inflows of bullion from the silver mines of Central America; the creation of joint-stock companies like the Dutch EAST INDIA COMPANY (which, by the early eighteenth century, supplied even humble households in North European cities with coffee, tea and other colonial goods); and the creation of national banks ('Expanding Horizons' in Part IV). Still, recent research suggests that the conventional picture of decline in the Mediterranean economy – which found alternative ways to sustain prosperity – may have been overstated (Musgrave 1999, ch. 5).

Early modern expansion, socio-economic differentiation and urbanization thus encouraged the gradual emergence of a consumer society, particularly in England and the Netherlands (Brewer and Porter 1993; 'Epilogue' in Part VII). Alongside this development, there was a major expansion in the provision of services, most obviously by lawyers keen to take advantage of the growing level of dispute in an increasingly contractual society, but also by artists ('Arts and society' in Part V) and leisure providers (taverns, COFFEE HOUSES, amusement parks like Vauxhall Gardens) who were keen to exploit the growing demand for sports, hunting and cultural pastimes among fashionable elites (Arcangeli 2003).

## Assessment

At first sight it is tempting to describe the European economy in 1720 (possibly even in 1800) as 'pre-industrial': most regions of Europe were rural, dominated by aristocratic rentiers and characterized by a manufacturing sector rooted in small-scale artisanal production, with generally low productivity and little market integration. There had, nonetheless, been several key changes during the sixteenth and seventeenth centuries – population growth, urbanization, agricultural innovation, agrarian change, rural (proto-)industrialization, proletarianization, changing patterns of consumption – which might justify the label of an 'early industrial' economy. By 1800, in fact, the European economy was on the brink of a major set of transformations, conventionally referred to as the INDUSTRIAL REVOLUTION, which would bring large-scale mechanization, factory production, a radically new transport infrastructure and novel forms of labour relations. It is thus important to recognize both significant continuities and changes throughout a period which witnessed a transition to 'capitalism' (Braudel 1985). Two key phases can be identified, with the mid-seventeenth century the turning point between a period of rising demand and increasing gross output and one of stagnating demand and increasing labour productivity. Contemporaries themselves were aware that they were living through a period of change and struggled to accommodate the new values of profit and commerce with the conventions of a traditional 'moral' economy. Indeed, it is only because the hammers of change were beating so insistently on the anvils of continuity that it is possible for historians to get a sense of the nature, scale and significance of the transitions through which the early industrial economy was passing.

## Discussion themes

1. How was agriculture organized in early modern Europe?
2. What factors determined the location of industry in this period?
3. What were the most significant changes in the European economy between 1500 and 1800?

## *Bibliography*

### (A) Sources

More, Thomas (1965), *The Yale Edition of the Complete Works of St Thomas More,* *Vol. 4: Utopia,* ed. E. Surtz and J. H. Hexter, New Haven, Conn.

### (B) Literature

Arcangeli, Alessandro (2003), *Recreation in the Renaissance: Attitudes towards Leisure* *and Pastimes in European Culture, 1425–1675,* Basingstoke

Berg, Maxine ed. (1991), *Markets and Manufacture in Early Industrial Europe,* London

Braudel, Fernand (1985), *Civilization and Capitalism, 15th–18th Century,* trans. Siân Reynolds, revised edn, London

Brewer, John and Porter, Roy eds (1993), *Consumption and the World of Goods,* London

Broad, John (1980), 'Alternate Husbandry and Permanent Pasture in the Midlands, 1650–1800', *Agricultural History Review,* 28, 77–89

\* Cipolla, Carlo M. (1993), *Before the Industrial Revolution: European Society and* *Economy 1000–1700,* 3rd edn, New York

Davis, R. c. (1954), 'English Foreign Trade, 1660–1700', *Economic History Review,* 7(2), 150–66

—— (1962), 'English Foreign Trade, 1700–74', *Economic History Review,* 15(2), 285–303

Kriedte, Peter, Medick, Hans and Schlumbohm, Jürgen (1981), *Industrialization before* *Industrialization,* trans. B. Schempp, Cambridge

Levine, David ed. (1984), *Proletarianization and Family History,* London

Levine, David and Wrightson, Keith (1991), *The Making of an Industrial Society:* *Whickham, 1560–1765,* Oxford

\* Musgrave, Peter (1999), *The Early Modern European Economy,* Basingstoke

Ogilvie, Sheilagh and Cerman, Markus eds (1996), *European Proto-Industrialization,* 2nd edn, Cambridge

Thirsk, Joan (1967), 'Enclosing and Engrossing', in: *The Agrarian History of England* *and Wales, Volume IV: 1500–1640,* ed. Joan Thirsk, Cambridge, 200–55

Vries, Jan de (1984), *European Urbanization 1500–1800,* London

Zell, Michael L. (1994), *Industry in the Countryside: Wealden Society in the Sixteenth* *Century,* Cambridge

### (C) Web resources

'The *Schwazer Bergbuch* of 1566', [German] description and illustrations of sixteenth-century mining: <http://www.taurachsoft.at/erzweg/schwaz/bergbuch.htm>

'Trading Places', a British Library online resource: <http://www.bl.uk/learning/hist citizen/trading/tradingplaces.html>

# PART III

# RELIGION

| | |
|---|---|
| 1536 | First edition of Calvin's *Institutes of the Christian Religion* |
| 1536/66 | Helvetic Confessions of the Reformed Church |
| 1541 | Calvin's *Ecclesiastical Ordinances* published |
| 1542 | Re-establishment of the Roman Inquisition |
| 1543 | Martin Luther, *On the Jews and their Lies* |
| 1545–63 | Council of Trent |
| 1546–47 | War of the League of Schmalkalden |
| 1547 | Battle of Mühlberg |
| 1548 | Interim of Augsburg |
| 1549 | Jesuit missionary Francis Xavier arrives in Japan |
| 1555 | Religious Peace of Augsburg |
| 1555 | *Cum nimis absurdum*, papal bull requiring Jews to live in ghettos |
| 1559 | Establishment of the Genevan Academy |
| 1564 | Death of Calvin |
| 1566 | Second Helvetic Confession of the Reformed Church |
| 1568–71 | Revolt of the Alpujarras, Spain |
| 1572 | St Bartholomew's Day Massacre of Huguenots in France |
| 1580 | Book of Concord agreed by the Lutheran Church |
| 1582 | Pope Gregory XIII establishes a new calendar to replace Julian Calendar |
| 1583 | Matteo Ricci mission to China |
| 1598 | Edict of Nantes issued by Henry IV |
| 1605 | Gunpowder Plot in England |
| 1609–14 | Expulsion of Moriscos from Spain |
| 1614 | The Japanese *shogun* (Ieyasu) expels all Christians from Japan |
| 1619 | Synod of Dordrecht by the Dutch Reformed Church |
| 1648 | Peace of Westphalia ends Thirty Years War |
| 1671 | Frederick William I of Brandenburg-Prussia admits fifty Jewish households |
| 1685 | Edict of Nantes revoked by Louis XIV |
| 1689 | Act of Toleration passed by the English Parliament |
| 1700 | Johann Eisenmenger, *Judaism Unmasked* |
| 1702–11 | War of the Cévennes sparked by a Huguenot revolt |
| 1724 | The Chinese Emperor proscribes Catholicism in China |
| 1752 | Britain adopts Gregorian calendar |
| 1789 | *Declaration of the Rights of Man and of the Citizen* |
| 1806 | Napoleon takes measures in favour of Jewish emancipation |

# Church and people at the close of the Middle Ages

*Beat Kümin and Peter Marshall*

## The shape of the Church

The personal beliefs of late medieval Europeans are difficult to gauge: the ordinary people of the period often leave little or no trace of their existence behind them. But we can begin by describing the context in which those beliefs were formed. The Church of the fifteenth century looks, at first sight, like a uniform and well-structured hierarchical institution. The highest position was occupied by the Pope, acknowledged as the successor of the Apostle Peter, to whom Jesus had imparted special authority. He presided over the Church as bishop of Rome, the city in which St Peter had been martyred, following an election by ecclesiastical dignitaries known as cardinals, men chosen by previous popes from the ranks of the bishops (the clergymen in charge of a regional unit known as a bishopric or diocese). Further down the pyramid, the whole territory of Catholic Europe was divided into archbishoprics, bishoprics, archdeaconries and well over 100,000 parishes.

Bishops and parish priests were 'secular' clergymen, because they lived in the world. But alongside the secular hierarchy, the medieval Church had a 'regular' branch: a range of orders of monks, nuns and friars who had taken vows of chastity and obedience and observed a specific rule (Latin: *regula*). Monks and nuns led cloistered lives in communities endowed with pious bequests of landed property. Here they followed an elaborate regime of prayer and worship; friars, on the other hand, depended on voluntary contributions and took a more active part in the spiritual welfare of lay people, especially in towns. Medieval society thus contained within it a large number of professional Churchmen, who collectively formed the ESTATE of the clergy with privileges like immunity from taxation and the right to be judged in separate ecclesiastical courts. Their special status sometimes caused feelings of ANTICLERICALISM.

On the other hand, clergymen were accepted and indeed often honoured, because they were essential for the most important goal of human life: to win salvation (entry into heaven after death). In the later Middle Ages, the nuts and bolts of salvation were hotly debated within an intellectual system known as SCHOLASTICISM, which strove for 'the demonstration of the inherent rationality of Christian theology . . . and the demonstration of the complete harmony of that theology by the minute examination of the relationship of its various elements' (McGrath 2000, 68). The university scholars' arguments about divine GRACE and human powers became increasingly intricate, but the dominant school of thought agreed that the performance of good works could improve an individual's chances of salvation. Specific guidelines were codified in decrees of councils (general assemblies of bishops) and synods (gatherings within particular dioceses). Of key importance was the Fourth Lateran Council of 1215, which ordered all Christians to make confession annually and to receive communion in their parish church (see PENANCE and MASS).

As we move from institutional theory to the level of practical arrangements, the religious landscape starts to become rather more complex. Dioceses, for example, were of vastly different sizes and the structure of divine service ('liturgy') differed from region to region. Relations with political authorities also varied dramatically. In much of central Italy the popes themselves were in charge of secular government, but in the kingdoms of France, England and Castile monarchs gained increasing influence over ecclesiastical appointments and resources, as did some collective bodies like German Imperial Free Cities.

## Parish life around 1500

The influence of the Church in people's lives can hardly be overestimated: its calendar shaped people's perceptions of time and its rites of passage punctuated the journey from cradle to grave. From about 1200, a rather uneven network of parishes served as the principal framework for local ceremonial life in general, and for the administration of the SACRAMENTS in particular (Kümin 1997; Dyas 2010; Figure III.1; 'My-Parish' in Web resources).

Parish membership made a number of demands on the laity. People were expected to know basic prayers like the Our Father and Hail Mary in Latin as well as to memorize the Ten Commandments and the statement of faith known as the Creed. Clergymen exhorted parishioners to avoid the seven deadly sins (lust, gluttony, greed, sloth, wrath, envy, pride) and attend to the seven works of mercy (feeding the hungry, giving drink to the thirsty, clothing the naked, receiving the stranger, tending the sick, visiting prisoners, burying the dead). Everyone was required to attend church on Sundays and major feast days. Only two sacraments were received more than once in a lifetime, giving them a special importance in the lives of the laity. One of these involved confession to a priest in exchange for divine forgiveness of sins (penance); the other was the sacrament of the EUCHARIST in the service known as the MASS.

The mass was the cornerstone of late medieval religion. It was a ritual re-enactment, both of Christ's sacrifice on the cross and of Jesus's actions at the Last Supper, when he gave bread and wine to his disciples telling them, 'this is my body . . . this is my blood'. The faithful believed that at the moment when the priest standing at an altar repeated Christ's words, the bread and wine became the very body and blood of Jesus (TRANSUBSTANTIATION). Worshippers at mass could therefore, in a literal sense, *see* their God, and, at Easter communion, receive Him into their own bodies. The mass was the ultimate good work, and masses could be said for any number of specified intentions. Each parish had its regular high mass, but other specialized celebrations (masses of Our Lady or of the Five Wounds of Jesus) received lay backing too.

The most significant adaptations were requiem masses for the souls of the dead, boosted in number by the belief in PURGATORY – an intermediary place between earth and heaven where flames of fire would cleanse people's souls of any remaining blemishes of sin before they could enter into the presence of God. Crucially, the duration of this (painful) stay could be reduced by mass foundations, good works and pious activities, both during one's own lifetime and by post-mortem initiatives by relatives and friends (Le Goff 1984). Fear of purgatory, or at least a desire to minimize its rigours, prompted intense investment in activities like the maintenance and embellishment of churches and was to a great extent responsible for the flourishing of Gothic art (some 2,000 altar paintings were commissioned in late medieval Tyrol alone). Parishes witnessed a proliferation of CHANTRIES for the souls of specified beneficiaries as well as FRATERNITIES providing funerary rites for their members (Moeller 1972). The latter had a potential to generate subdivisions and frictions within the parish community, but in the case of the *Saint-Esprit* (Holy Spirit) fraternities in rural France practically everybody joined.

**Figure III.1** Parish churches were religious as well as social centres in late medieval communities. This procession of Central European villagers around 1500 neatly reflects the social order: members of the clergy at the front, male householders at the centre, women and children towards the end. The church is by far the largest building and the only one made of stone. 'Village Procession' from Diebold Schilling, *Die Luzerner Chronik* 1513 (Fine Art Facsimile edn, Lucerne, 1977), f. 283r. © Faksimile Verlag Luzern / www.faksimile.ch.

Late medieval churches were multimedia performance centres appealing to all the senses: they provided colourful wall paintings of saints, sung masses with organ music and a smell of incense. This mostly came from lay rather than clerical initiative, particularly through the activities of the elected parish officials known in England as churchwardens (Hanham 1970). Yet the side-effect of directing ever more property into the 'dead hand' of the Church caused concern among secular rulers, while clerical reformers worried about lay piety becoming diverted to marginal cults rather than focusing on the core message of the Scriptures. On the other hand, there was a fifteenth-century trend towards ever-greater concentration on the figure and saving passion of Christ, as exemplified by the large crucifixes dominating nearly every church or the multi-faceted 'blood piety' emerging in theology, art and devotion (Hamm 2004, esp. ch. 1; Bynum 2007).

## Beyond the parish

Religious life was not entirely circumscribed by the boundaries of the parish. Contact with the wider world was supplied by (sporadic) bishops' visitations to check on local conditions and by the activities of Church courts set up to deal with any short-comings, including sexual offences like adultery and fornication. The courts were often perceived as abusing their powers by arbitrary citations, excessive fees and – most threateningly of all – frequent excommunications (removing individuals, if not entire communities, from the sacraments and thus effectively from Christian society as well).

But the world beyond the parish offered enlarged experience as well as repressive discipline. Monastic and mendicant churches were additional focal points for devotion: their incessant round of prayers made them attractive burial locations, particularly for social elites. Nor could parishes match the elaborate liturgical provision in cathedrals, the mother churches of each diocese, where bishops resided. The saints were venerated in parishes, but they were yet more powerful in sites associated with their lives or holding their relics. Large numbers of medieval Christians thus embarked on journeys of pilgrimage to sacred spaces. These might be fairly minor shrines in the vicinity, such as that of St Walstan of Bawburgh in Norfolk (Duffy 2005). More intrepid pilgrims travelled to the sites associated with Jesus's ministry in the Holy Land, to the tomb of St Peter in Rome or to the shrine of the Apostle James at Santiago de Compostela in north-western Spain. The saints were Christian role models, but they were also dispensers of supernatural power, often with their own specialization. St Apollonia could help people with toothache, while the pilgrimage centre of Oberbüren in the Swiss Confederation catered for parents of recently deceased infants hoping for a brief, miraculous revival just long enough to administer the sacrament of baptism (without which children's souls were consigned to limbo, i.e. an ill-defined permanent abode outside of heaven). The phenomenon of pilgrimages was complex: inspired by genuine spirituality, but not free of aggressive and commercial elements either (Box 1).

'In 1516, a learned doctor Balthasar Hubmeier preached so vigorously against the Jews, that with permission of the Emperor, the city council drove them out. Some of the Jews' houses were confiscated by Christians. Others were destroyed like their synagogue. On the place of their synagogue a church dedicated to the Virgin Mary was built. A spontaneous pilgrimage began. All sorts of people came, some with musical instruments, some with pitchforks and rakes; women came with their milk cans, spindles and cooking pots. Artisans came with their tools: a weaver with his shuttle, a carpenter with his square, a cooper with his measuring tape. They walked many miles, but did not tire from the long journey. They all walked in silence. If asked why they were going, they answered: "My spirit drives me there" . . . Thousands came each day to see the miracle . . . the pilgrimage continued for six or seven years, until Dr Martin Luther preached against it.'

*(Dixon and Greengrass, 'The Protestant Reformation',*
*section 02.63; Web resources)*

Contemporary description of the cult of the Beautiful Virgin at Regensburg (southern Germany).

One of the principal objects of pilgrimage was to obtain an INDULGENCE, a document specifying some remission of the 'satisfaction' due for sins, which would otherwise have to be worked off in purgatory. These were theologically sound when combined with proper administration of the sacrament of penance, but became highly questionable when they seemed to be simply sold for money (Swanson 2006).

Pre-Reformation religion is often characterized by historians as a set of practical, problem-solving rituals catering for a largely illiterate population. But this picture needs modification in at least two respects. In the first place, a small, but influential, minority of Christians harboured strong desires for a more personal and reflective spirituality. Inspired by devotional works like the early fifteenth-century treatise *The Imitation of Christ*, this movement known as MYSTICISM strove for more direct contact with God in prayer and for ways to follow Jesus in personal life (Kempis 1997; Van Engen 1988). Second, the advent of the printing press and the steady growth of education, particularly in towns, opened opportunities for closer engagement with the interior side of religion by people of relatively humble status. A very large percentage of early printed works had religious themes, with prayer books, saints' lives and devotional guides becoming increasingly common among laymen's possessions.

## Challenges and pressures for reform

The great variety we have sketched so far is undoubtedly a testimony to the spiritual fervour of the age, but the sheer spectrum of ideas and practices also caused contemporaries considerable unease. There were few if any signs of atheism, i.e. people who did not believe in God at all, but did the faithful receive sufficient guidance about how to worship the divine? Was the Church becoming too preoccupied with defending its privileges and properties rather than propagating the message of the Scriptures? Were there other sources of metaphysical power, beyond the ministrations of the clergy, available to be tapped by the laity? By the fifteenth century, several distinct, if overlapping, movements were posing such questions with an ever-greater urgency. The late medieval Church can only be characterized as a corrupt or decadent institution if we ignore the periodic waves of reformist fervour emanating from within it (Duggan 1978). The scandal of the papal schism of the late fourteenth century (when for nearly forty years at least two rival candidates claimed to be successors of St Peter) led in the fifteenth to the so-called conciliar movement, an attempt to subordinate the Papacy to the authority of regular general councils of bishops and leading Churchmen. The movement in the end split and foundered, but there were other signs of reform from within institutional structures. The perceived laxity of the religious orders led to new foundations, such as the emergence from the ranks of the Franciscan friars of an Observant movement, claiming to observe more strictly the founding ideals of St Francis. The 'revivalist' appeals of some mendicant preachers, like the Italian Bernardino of Siena or the Spaniard Vincent Ferrer, attracted huge audiences.

Some of the most telling internal criticisms of the Church came from HUMANISM, a movement aiming to recapture the wisdom and scholarship of the ancient classical world ('The Renaissance' in Part V). Spreading from Italy to Northern Europe, it obtained a clearer reforming agenda. Christian humanists, the most renowned of whom was the Dutch priest Desiderius Erasmus, disapproved of what they saw as superstitious aspects of popular religion and expressed frustration with clerical abuses such as ignorance, financial greed and absenteeism (affecting 80 per cent of parishes in extreme cases like the diocese of Geneva). Humanists put their faith in the use of pure and instructive religious texts, including satirical works (Erasmus 2003) and scripture itself (Erasmus famously produced his own version of the Greek New Testament in 1516).

Other late medieval critics crossed a line that led the Church authorities to regard them as heretics, false believers who had damned their own souls and threatened those of others. HERESY was spasmodic rather than endemic in the late medieval Church, but it could flare up with considerable force. In the early fifteenth century, the Bohemian priest Jan Hus's denouncements of Church leaders and practices led to his execution as a heretic by the (reforming) Council of Constance (Figure III.2).

Around the same time, followers of the English theologian John Wyclif went beyond attacking popular religion to denounce the authority of the Pope, deny the mass and elevate Scripture as the sole source of religious authority. Known as Lollards, they remained rooted in some parishes of the Midlands and south-eastern England well into the sixteenth century (Box 2).

**Figure III.2** Religious dissent could be a matter of life and death in pre-modern Europe. Despite an invitation to explain his views and assurances of safe conduct, Jan Hus – identified on his hat as a 'leader of heretics' – was burnt for refusing to recant his unorthodox views at Constance in 1415. Engraving from 'History of the Council of Constance' by Ulrich von Richental (c. 1360–1437), published 1483 / Bibliotheque Polonaise, Paris, France / Archives Charmet / Bridgeman Images.

> ## Box 2
>
> 'I . . . willingly acknowledge . . . that I have had in my keeping divers books
> containing heresies and errors against Christian faith and the determination of all
> holy church, which books I have read and declared . . . before many divers persons
> . . . teaching against the blessed sacrament of the altar . . . also against the
> sacrament of confession to priests and penance for satisfaction of sins. . . .. Also I
> have read and declared against our holy father the pope . . . and against the
> veneration and worship of images standing in churches, calling them idols. . . .'
>
> *(Harper-Bill 1989, 115)*
>
> The abjuration of the Lollard John Croft at Hereford in 1505 highlights many of the
> unorthodox views and practices the Church hoped to eradicate. It also points to the
> significance of religious literature and personal bonds within the movement.

In the western Alps, communities of Waldensians, followers of the twelfth-century heretical preacher Peter Waldo, likewise survived through to the Reformation. Ironically, in light of later events, the German territories seem to have been a largely heresy-free zone in the later fifteenth century.

## Assessment

How, then, should the state of the Church on the eve of the Reformation be assessed? Broadly speaking, scholarly interpretations have evolved from an earlier characterization of the period as 'the waning of the Middle Ages', a decline from the spiritual and organizational initiatives of the High Middle Ages (Huizinga 1972), towards a more positive view of a long-term age of reform with many signs of fervent piety and lay assertiveness. Some of the structural problems owed less to excessive papal power than to the increasing hold of lay rulers over ecclesiastical affairs within their dominions. Judgements of monastic life have also changed. Censorious accounts of a religious and moral crisis (based on contemporary visitations and polemical literature) have given way to more differentiated verdicts, distinguishing between different orders and convents. There were many cases of lax discipline, but also of sustained reform initiatives, and the more austere congregations in particular continued to attract much lay patronage. What we can say for certain is that religion was absolutely crucial for people's everyday lives. There was an intensive engagement and investment in approved, orthodox practices, especially the urge to secure salvation through sacraments and good works. But active religiosity was not contained entirely within orthodox structures or kept under tight clerical control. Lay believers could be religious consumers, selecting between different venues, devotions and forms of spiritual guidance, in person or in print. There was also a substantial fuzzy area where Catholic ritual and practice met long-standing 'popular' beliefs in the inherent power of religious objects, rituals and SACRAMENTALS as well as the forms of protective magic practised by village cunning folk (Scribner 1987; 'Witchcraft and magic' in Part V).

Few scholars would now maintain that Catholicism was morally or spiritually bankrupt at the close of the Middle Ages or that the Reformation was in some sense 'inevitable'. Indeed, the current fashion is to emphasize the Church's considerable vitality and flexibility. But this very vitality was in itself a source of instability: pressures for reform were intense, both from within and outside the official Church (Koslofsky 2016). The Church's leadership, from the Papacy downwards, showed little inclination or ability to take control of and direct these pressures. In these circumstances, the danger to the status quo was not too little piety, but too much.

## Discussion themes

1. Should the late Middle Ages be seen as an 'age of faith' or a 'period of religious decline'?
2. Did the late medieval Church meet the needs of the people?
3. Was the emergence of humanism a sign of the Church's weakness or strength?

## Bibliography

### (A) Sources

Erasmus, Desiderius (2003), *The Praise of Folly* [1515], trans. W. H. Gass, New Haven, Conn.

Hanham, Alison ed. (1970), *Churchwardens' Accounts of Ashburton 1479–1580*, Exeter

Harper-Bill, Christopher ed. (1989), 'Documents', in his *The Pre-Reformation Church in England*, London, 97–116

Kempis, Thomas à (1997), *The Imitation of Christ* [1418], ed. B. J. H. Biggs, Oxford

Schilling, Diebold (1977), *Die Luzerner Chronik 1513*, facsimile edn, Lucerne

Van Engen, John ed. (1988), *Devotio Moderna: Basic Writings*, New York

### (B) Literature

Bynum, Caroline Walker (2007), *Wonderful Blood: Theology and Practice in Late Medieval Northern Germany and Beyond*, Philadelphia, Penn.

Duffy, Eamon (2005), *The Stripping of the Altars: Traditional Religion in England c. 1400–c. 1580*, 2nd edn, New Haven, Conn.

Duggan, Lawrence G. (1978), 'The Unresponsiveness of the Late Medieval Church: A Reconsideration', *SCJ*, 9, 3–26

Dyas, Dee ed. (2010), *The English Parish Church Through the Centuries*, USB memory stick, York

Goff, Jacques Le (1984), *The Birth of Purgatory*, London

Hamm, Berndt (2004), *The Reformation of Faith in the Context of Late Medieval Theology and Piety*, Leiden

Huizinga, Johan (1972), *The Waning of the Middle Ages*, Harmondsworth

Koslofsky, Craig (2016), 'Explaining Change', in: *The Oxford Handbook of the Protestant Reformations*, ed. U. Rublack, Oxford, chapter 28

Kümin, Beat (1997), 'The English Parish in a European Perspective', in: *The Parish in English Life 1400–1600*, ed. K. L. French, G. G. Gibbs and B. A. Kümin, Manchester, 15–32

McGrath, Alistair (2000), *Reformation Thought*, 3rd edn, Oxford [4th edn, 2002]

Moeller, Bernd (1972), 'Religious Life in Germany on the Eve of the Reformation', in: *Pre-Reformation Germany*, ed. G. Strauss, London, 13–42

Scribner, Robert W. (1987), 'Ritual and Popular Religion in Catholic Germany at the Time of the Reformation', in his *Popular Culture and Popular Movements in Reformation Germany*, London, 17–47

Swanson, Robert (1995), *Religion and Devotion in Europe, c. 1215–c. 1515*, Cambridge

Swanson, Robert, ed. (2006), *Promissory Notes on the Treasury of Merits: Indulgences in Late Medieval Europe*, Leiden

### (C) Web resources

Dixon, C. Scott and Greengrass, Mark, 'The Protestant Reformation' (TLTP History Courseware Consortium; relaunched 2005): <http://www.albany.edu/jmmh/vol3/creating_cdroms/contents.htm>

'My-Parish', online platform for exchange on parish history, art, heritage and culture: <http://warwick.ac.uk/my-parish>

'Video from a Medieval Mass', featured on *Liturgical Fragments from Denmark*: http://www.liturgy.dk/default.asp?Action=Menu&Item=285>

# The long Reformation: Introduction

*Beat Kümin*

The emergence of rivalling confessions in the sixteenth century has long been recognized as a key process in European history – for many scholars in fact it marks the dawn of a new era ('Introduction' in Part I). In a remarkably short period of time, theological arguments spilled over into the socio-political sphere and gripped large parts of the population, first within the Holy Roman Empire, but soon much further afield. The Eastern Orthodox Church had split from Rome in the High Middle Ages, but for Central and Western Europe the Reformation brought the first experience of formal religious division, leading to centuries of acrimonious conflict, sometimes with repercussions to the present day. There had been reform initiatives and unorthodox movements before ('Church and people at the close of the Middle Ages' in Part III), but they lacked the political backing, mass support and dissemination technology which – together with the spiritual appeal of radically new doctrines – gave the evangelical message such enormous power. What resulted from its stress on individual faith and adherence to the Scriptures was not a 'purified' universal Church (as Martin Luther had originally hoped), but two main branches of Protestantism – Lutheran and Reformed – and a host of dissenting groupings, while Catholicism survived and in turn embarked on a major regeneration programme. All across the confessional spectrum, furthermore, clergymen came to realize that it was relatively easy to alter ecclesiastical structures, but much more difficult to implant new beliefs in people's souls. More and more Reformation historians thus adopt a long-term perspective, with some detecting real grass-roots change only from the late seventeenth century. To mark the Luther quincentenary – 500 years since his *Ninety-five Theses* – a flurry of new biographies and survey works appeared in or around 2017, testifying to the continued significance of the transformations. The following three chapters examine the major confessional contexts in turn. Their emphasis lies on Reformation change in a narrower sense, with the impact on gender relations, unorthodox practices and international politics addressed elsewhere in this volume (See 'Gender and family' in Part II, 'Witchcraft and magic' in Part V and 'Dynastic politics, religious conflict and reason of state *c.* 1500–1650' in Part VI).

# The long Reformation: Lutheran

*Henry J. Cohn*

## Germany – a special case?

In the 'Holy Roman Empire of the German Nation' the Reformation took hold rapidly and with greater early popular support than in other European countries. This head start cannot be explained solely in terms of the charismatic personality of Martin Luther (Figure III.3). In all eras outstanding leaders require favourable conditions to persuade large populations to change their outlook on the world.

In many respects the Church faced the same challenges in Germany as elsewhere: widespread dissatisfaction with the materialism which made it unable to fulfil the spiritual longings of the faithful; incipient nationalism directed against foreigners; and the threat to accepted ideas from Christian HUMANISM, notably through the writings of Desiderius Erasmus (1466–1536) ('The Renaissance' in Part V). Yet certain circumstances in the Empire were exceptional. Its political structure gave opportunities, less common in ordinary monarchies, for the Reformers to receive local protection. The imperial ESTATES – princes, free cities and nobles who stood between the emperor and the ordinary nobles, townsfolk and PEASANTS – enjoyed a partial autonomy which enabled them to introduce the Reformation although Emperor Charles V (1519–58) had condemned Luther's ideas at Worms (1521). During the previous century, and especially after 1500, the Empire experienced more serious peasant uprisings and urban social conflicts than elsewhere. When disturbances multiplied in the 1520s, the Reformation fed off them to gain support. Cultural distinctiveness also favoured the adoption of new ideas. From 1518 the printing press, a mid-fifteenth-century German invention already used for religious books, classical literature and the spread of popular culture, provided pamphlets and broadsheets for disseminating Lutheran teachings ('From pen to print' in Part V). Another such instrument was the sermon: Germany had an especially strong tradition of preaching in the towns and by the mendicant orders (Moeller 1972).

Hostile attitudes towards the Church remained singularly intense while outward signs of religious activity grew. Plentiful new religious endowments, pilgrimages and cults like that of the Virgin Mary were reinforced by thousands of religious GUILDS created by lay people for the care of the poor and sick. Increased reading of the Bible – not available in the vernacular, by contrast, in England – and devotion to private

**Figure III.3** In an imaginary encounter, Luther – dressed as an Augustinian monk – is seen debating with the Pope, a cardinal, a bishop and another monk during the Diet of Worms (woodcut, 1521). Courtesy of the Richard C. Kessler Reformation Collection, Pitts Theology Library, Candler School of Theology, Emory University.

prayer were accompanied by greater belief in miracles and relics. Paradoxically, while ordinary Christians relieved their anxieties about personal salvation by the material means encouraged by the Church, such as paying for MASSES for the dead or buying INDULGENCES, they disliked the growing wealth of the clergy at their expense. ANTICLERICALISM and antipapalism were rife. The Papacy was wrongly believed to be sucking large sums of money from the Empire. There was more substance behind the economic and religious complaints by laymen against the German clergy, whose behaviour was in many instances far from spiritual. The ecclesiastical princes and monasteries owned about a third of cultivated land in the countryside and an even greater share of urban property. The landowning prelates were often the local rulers – a rare combination in Europe – and would bear the brunt of Luther's attack.

## Martin Luther – the message and its dissemination

By 1517 Martin Luther (1483–1546) was a monk of twelve years' standing and a renowned theologian and university professor at Wittenberg in Saxony (Roper 2016, Schilling 2017). His mixed social background helped him to gain wide appeal. Son of a farmer who became a miner and a mother from the upper ranks of small-town society, in 1525 he married Katherine von Bora, a renegade nun of the lower nobility. While studying the Bible, the Church Fathers, the medieval scholastics and late medieval MYSTICISM, he wrestled for years with the fundamental teachings of the Church until matters came to a head in 1517. In the *Ninety-five Theses* his first public dispute with the Church was over indulgences, the sale by the Papacy of remission of penalties imposed by God on souls in PURGATORY. Luther attacked not just papal venality, but the theory behind indulgences that the Pope could make grants to the faithful from the treasury of merits accumulated by Christ and the saints over and above what they had needed for their own salvation. As indulgences were part of the 'works' which, alongside faith, the Church considered essential for salvation, the conflict grew into a fundamental one over the nature of salvation, which Luther insisted was achieved through 'JUSTIFICATION by faith alone'. For him justification was God's gift alone, an act of GRACE making righteous an unrighteous sinner who has faith in Christ. Sinners cannot assist by their own efforts, but may hope that the sacrifice of Christ through His suffering on the cross will earn them pardon. In this 'theology of the cross', Luther now saw God as more merciful than judgemental.

Luther grounded these views in the Bible. Now the most deep-seated disagreement followed, over the nature of authority in the Church. During debates with emissaries from Pope Leo X between 1517 and 1519, Luther successively rejected the authority of the popes, the general councils of the Church and canon law as interpreters of Scripture in favour of the pure Gospel, the Word of God alone. Yet Luther's interpretation of the Bible was selective, in that he and his closest associate, Philipp Melanchthon (in *Loci Communes*, 1521), played down the significance of passages which contradicted their view of justification.

With justification by faith alone were linked other essential beliefs. The PRIESTHOOD OF ALL BELIEVERS expressed Luther's view that all were in direct communication with God, enjoying 'Christian freedom'; priests were not inter-mediaries but ministers appointed to perform certain functions for the community. Catholic commentators on Luther's *Address to the Christian Nobility of the German Nation* (1520) saw this demotion of the priesthood and rejection of the whole apparatus of the Church as Luther's most revolutionary tenet. In the Lutheran SACRAMENT of the EUCHARIST, the faith of the recipient was essential, so that the rite was not a sacrifice but a thanksgiving; lay people were now allowed to receive both bread and wine. Luther decried the doctrine of TRANSUBSTANTIATION, although he did believe in a REAL PRESENCE of Christ. The seven sacraments were reduced to just baptism and the LORD'S SUPPER. Both monasticism, as another form of works, and clerical celibacy were rejected.

Over the next decades these teachings were elaborated in Latin treatises for the benefit of Luther's clerical supporters and to rebut his opponents, as well as for a few educated members of the laity, but his main appeal for ordinary people lay in his parallel programme to Christianize the whole of Europe, to return Christians to the true piety and right living which he contended the medieval church had obscured (Hendrix 2004). He wrote popular pamphlets and published sermons in German, using both the humanist arts of persuasion and earthy language, folk tales and proverbs (Box 1).

Luther's advice for his barber is one example of his guidance on everyday problems of religious and social life: the Ten Commandments, the liturgy and music of services or the proper use of Church property, but also marriage, usury, the education of children and the organization of poor relief. He encouraged neighbourly good deeds, but as the natural outcome of Christian faith and love, no longer as a means to salvation.

**Box 1**

'a good and attentive barber keeps his thought, attention and eyes on the razor and hair and does not forget how far he has got with his shaving or cutting. If he wants to engage in too much conversation or let his mind wander or look somewhere else he is likely to cut his customer's mouth, nose or even his throat. Thus if anything is to be done well, it requires the full attention of all one's senses. . . . How much more does prayer call for concentration and singleness of heart if it is to be a good prayer!'

*(Extract from Martin Luther, A Practical Way to Pray, 1535; Lull and Russell 2012, 36)*

Other Wittenberg university theologians and many clerical and lay preachers helped to disseminate Luther's teachings. The sermon was the prime means of reaching the 90 per cent of the population who were illiterate, alongside other forms of aural and visual communication, such as hymns, ballads, school plays, informal discussions in taverns, and processions. Robert Scribner's brilliant interpretations of woodcut illustrations in single-leaf broadsheets, books and pamphlets illuminate early Reformation mentalities (Scribner 1994; Figures III.4–5). Yet he only claimed that they were the first point of attraction, especially by means of a simplified anticlericalism and antipapalism, but not the principal medium for conveying new doctrine.

**Figures III.4 and III.5** 'Christ Drives out the Money Changers' and 'The Pope Receives Revenues from Indulgences': woodcuts from Lucas Cranach and Philipp Melanchthon, Passional Christi und Antichristi (Wittenberg, 1521). © Private Collection / Bridgeman Images.

More sceptical historians have argued that most woodcuts were too expensive and complex for the illiterate, requiring an ability to read captions, while evidence is slight for reading aloud and explanations by the literate (Pettegree 2005, 104–20). The main purpose of illustrations was to make the messages of the printed word more effective; similarly, Reformation paintings like those of the Cranachs, father and son, were chiefly accessible to the elites. All forms of communication were interconnected, but printed materials were the essential conduit to those who could read and convey 'brand Luther' to others (Pettegree 2015).

## Peasant and urban Reformations

While peasants admired the heroic figure of Luther standing up to Pope and Emperor, and some may have grasped his evangelical teachings, the majority were initially attracted by the social messages read into Luther's writings by Thomas Müntzer and other local religious leaders who mistook Luther's intentions. Slogans like 'the Word of God', 'the LIBERTY OF A CHRISTIAN' and 'brotherly love' were used as ideological justification for throwing off SERFDOM and securing relief from longstanding economic and social burdens. Peasant actions in their revolt of 1524–26 were justified by recourse to 'divine law', the idea – derived from the Zurich Reformer Huldrych Zwingli, not Luther – that social disputes should be resolved by the Bible, not ancient custom ('Riot and rebellion' in Part VI). After their defeat many peasants returned to the practices of Catholicism, from which they had hardly deviated, or, in relatively small numbers, became ANABAPTISTS ('Religious culture' in Part III). The task of truly converting peasants devolved on state churches for the rest of the century and beyond.

The Empire had many large, prosperous towns, especially the imperial cities in the South. The Reformation's advance in Augsburg, Frankfurt, Nuremberg, Strasbourg and the majority of cities was furthered by preachers, humanists, town clerks and lawyers. Geoffrey Dickens credited the cities with saving the Reformation in the 1520s, when few princes supported it and the peasant uprisings had been suppressed (Dickens 1974). Following the German historian Bernd Moeller, he argued that the Reformation was introduced into the cities as a result of popular pressure inspired by preachers, whereas the ruling COUNCILS were a brake on the movement. Moreover, where the urban constitution was more 'democratic', with guild participation alongside the hereditary patriciates, a more Zwinglian rather than Lutheran Reformation was adopted. Only after the Reformation had been introduced did city councils establish a fully-fledged new Church and mould it to reinforce their rule.

Recent research suggests considerable modifications to this pattern. By the 1520s most ruling councillors were sympathetic to reform but cautious about abandoning the Catholic Church for fear of antagonizing the emperor and neighbouring Catholic princes and out of concern for their trade and the preservation of public order. Popular pressure pushed them further and faster on the road to Reformation, but it was a path they would anyway probably have taken. Whether Zwinglian or Lutheran teachings were adopted depended more on proximity to Switzerland and the theological leanings of the urban Reformers than on a city's constitution. Strasbourg, which inclined towards the Swiss position, had earlier admitted guild representatives to its council, but was by now as oligarchically governed as staunchly Lutheran Nuremberg, which had no guilds. Peter Blickle has postulated a 'communal Reformation', a parallel and combined movement of peasants under lordly rule and townsmen under the oligarchs, both seeking control over their own religious institutions until defeated in 1525 / 26 (Blickle 1992). Although similar tendencies were evident, however, cooperation between the two groups was negligible and based on expediency.

The caution of city magistrates meant that urban Reformations were often long drawn out. Wimpfen adopted eight different forms of religious allegiance between 1523 and 1635. The chequered course of the Reformation in Strasbourg only concluded in 1598, when it had become purely Lutheran (Abray 1985). Zwinglian influences declined everywhere in the 1540s, partly because urban rule was becoming more autocratic, but more important were Zwingli's death (1531) and the cities' alliance with Lutheran principalities in the SCHMALKALDIC LEAGUE. Charles V believed that guild participation in government encouraged a rebellious and extreme Protestant outlook. After defeating the Protestants (1547) he introduced the Interim of Augsburg (1548), a compromise between the faiths weighted towards Catholicism. To encourage the southern cities to accept the Interim and resume loyalty to him and to Catholicism, Charles changed the constitutions of half of them to concentrate power on an inner ring of patricians. He had miscalculated, since by now the majority of patricians were Lutheran and few cities returned, as did Augsburg, to Catholicism. Urban 'South German Reformed' influences disappeared, albeit to re-emerge in several principalities after 1555.

## Princely Reformations

The motives of princely rulers are often misrepresented. They did not adopt the Reformation principally to seize church lands or to oppose the emperor. Most were reluctant to cross the emperor unless for strong political reasons, and many delayed in joining the evangelical minority for fear of being outlawed. At the Protestation of Speyer (1529), which gave the movement its name, only six princes and fourteen cities signed a declaration rejecting enforcement of the Edict of Worms against Luther's works.

Religious changes sometimes did serve princely political interests, as in Hesse or Württemberg, but political weapons were also used to serve the genuine religious convictions of princes no less than of town authorities. Like Philip of Hesse, some rulers engaged in theological study. Often it took a change of generation in the dynasty and the influence of women relatives or evangelical advisers before the Reformation was introduced. Elector Frederick the Wise of Saxony moved towards the Lutheran standpoint before his death, but his earlier protection of Luther was of his own subject against the Pope, and any reforming measures from above had to wait until the succession of his brother John (1525–32). John's son, John Frederick (1532–54), was even prepared to sacrifice all to his religious principles. Captured by Charles V at Mühlberg in 1547, he rejected an offer of freedom and restoration to his lands if he converted. Few princes were prepared to be martyrs, but the majority should not be branded as land grabbers. Moreover, the Wittelsbach dukes of Bavaria showed that it was possible to tax the clergy heavily with papal consent, to take control of church administration and to resist the authority of the emperor while remaining staunchly Catholic.

From the 1530s the fate of the Reformation lay with the princes, who governed the majority of the German population and began to accept the Reformation in larger numbers, if only, as in Pomerania, because most of their nobles and towns had already converted. In 1520 Luther had not wanted the princes to control a new Church, merely to initiate reform. By 1525, however, in Saxony as elsewhere the old institutions were collapsing, the income of the Church was draining away and firm control was needed to restore order and provide for the education of clergy, the redirected use of church property and the visitation of the parishes. Only the princes had the authority and bureaucratic means to replace the inactive bishops. These were Luther's prime reasons for turning to the rulers to become 'emergency bishops', not his undoubted concern at the damage wreaked by the Peasants' War. However, rulers had no intention of abandoning their newly found power. Luther became the partly reluctant supporter of state churches, occasionally protesting when rulers instructed the clergy on what they should preach. Rulers used their power to consolidate the Church, but also the Church to consolidate their power. With Luther's blessing bishoprics and monastic lands were incorporated (especially in northern Germany), universities reformed (or newly founded under princely control) and school education, poor relief and the regulation of marriage all became part of the state portfolio.

## Reformation politics

Although until 1530 Charles V was distracted by his wars with France and the Ottomans from devoting sufficient attention to the Reformation in Germany, the complex politics of the Empire contributed as much as foreign wars to his eventual failure to regain the allegiance of the Protestants. For a long time Charles remained undecided between a policy of repression and one of conciliation, the latter inspired by the ideas of Erasmus. In the 1530s the new problem emerged of an armed Protestant League against the Emperor. In addition, many Protestant rulers no longer accepted the decisions of the imperial court on such politico-religious issues as the possession of church lands. Imperial authority was under threat, not just religious unity. Charles had to defeat the League if the title of Emperor was to have significance, but he still did not rely solely on force to achieve a religious settlement. A major aim of the war

(1546 / 47) was to compel the Protestants to attend the Council of Trent, but Charles, unlike the Pope, envisaged genuine discussions with them at the Council, not a mere *Diktat*. Even after defeating them he reverted to attempting a compromise in the Interim, although neither religious party would accept it.

Political factors inclined Charles V towards a peaceful solution between 1530 and 1545. There was no strong Catholic party among the princes to support him. Most bishops feared for their own privileges and would not undertake the Church reforms Charles considered necessary before imposing religious uniformity. Bavaria, the main secular Catholic principality, resisted both any increase in Habsburg power and concessions to the Protestants. For over a decade, a large neutral group of Protestant and Catholic princes, including the majority of the seven electors, twelve bishops and several lay principalities and imperial cities negotiated to bring the extremists to a compromise. They helped to avert war until 1546 and later worked towards a religious peace.

The Peace of Augsburg (1555) was a political solution to the religious problem (Gotthard 2004). The Catholics were the underdogs after Charles V's military defeat in 1552 by the revived Protestants, who frittered away their advantage to benefit selfish territorial interests. It was an archbishop who proposed the main principle of the peace: that each ruler determine the religion of his lands (summarized later as *cuius regio, eius religio*). The treaty did not grant the Lutherans parity with the Catholics, but grudging acceptance. The concessions were limited by the ecclesiastical reservation forbidding conversion of any ecclesiastical principality to Protestantism. The treaty also denied imperial cities the right to introduce the Reformation where not already established. Another imperfection, the omission of Calvinism, was understandable since it had not yet gained hold in any principality. These loopholes left room for the later creation of rival politico-religious parties and eventually the outbreak of the Thirty Years War ('Dynastic politics, religious conflict and reason of state *c.* 1500–1650' in Part VI).

Political factors likewise put a brake on the advances of Lutheranism in Bohemia, Hungary and Poland, but accelerated it in Denmark and other Scandinavian countries. Originally alongside Norway under the rule of the king of Denmark, Sweden / Finland secured independence in 1523 after a revolt under the leadership of Gustavus Vasa, who introduced the Reformation in 1536.

## Assessment: The Reformation – success or failure?

How successful the Reformation proved in changing popular religious attitudes is disputed. Around 1530 Luther and his fellow clergy were optimistic about their mission's success with the next generation influenced by their schooling and CATECHISMS, but thirty years later the Reformers were despondent. Inspections made in the countryside by Protestant rulers confirmed that the clergy's competence had not risen much above the pre-Reformation level, attendance at church was poor and knowledge by the laity of the catechism was rote learning without understanding and quickly forgotten after childhood (Box 2). The towns had preachers and schools of better quality, but the Reformers complained also about the lack of true religion there. Critics have argued that the often anecdotal evidence should not be accepted at face value, and that where visitations were regular they gradually raised the standard of religious observance, as in the villages subject to the city of Strasbourg (Kittelson 1982). On a wider canvas, improvements did occur, as in parts of the Duchy of Württemberg, but the task took most of the sixteenth century.

## Box 2

'Those who come to service are usually drunk. As soon as they sit down they lean their heads on their hands and sleep through the whole sermon, except that they fall off the benches, making a great clatter, or women drop their babies on the floor.'

(Extract from a visitation report from the county of
Nassau-Wiesbaden in 1594; Strauss 1978, 284)

Although the Reformers swept away the Catholic practices they considered harmful, peasants were selective in which Lutheran teachings they adopted. The slow winning of hearts and minds was patchy. Explanations can easily be found. By the later sixteenth century Lutheranism was taken over by Orthodox rigidity with a less human face than in Luther's day. The Lutherans dissipated their energies in doctrinal quarrels and in combating other Protestant denominations and the Anabaptists, failing to concentrate their energies on improving the quality of education and ministers. The Lutheran clergy became a hereditary caste, an academically trained elite with allegiances divided between their employer (the state) and their communities, so that anticlericalism re-emerged. In many regions the territorial nobles, towns and village elites resisted interference by the state and did not fully encourage the new churches. Religious apathy grew wherever the official religion changed several times. An Upper Palatinate peasant complained of having to 'bend like a reed in the wind'. By mid-century the earlier adversity which had spurred Protestant minorities to enthusiasm yielded to indifference under state-controlled religion, with the significant exception of Bavaria and southern German bishoprics where they remained a disadvantaged minority. In the countryside popular belief in SACRAMENTALS, magic and recourse to cunning men and wise women remained stronger than religious doctrine. The Reformation had radically altered the institutions of Church and State, but human nature hardly at all.

## Discussion themes

1.  How much did the Reformation in Germany owe to Luther's personality and ideas?
2.  Did political circumstances help or hinder the advance of Lutheranism?
3.  How popular was the Reformation in the Empire?

## Bibliography

### (A) Sources

Cranach, Lucas; Melanchthon, Philipp (1521), *Passional Christi und Antichristi* [The Passion of Christ and Antichrist], Wittenberg

Lull, Timothy; Russell, William eds (2012) *Martin Luther's Basic Theological Writings*, 3rd edn, Minneapolis

Strauss, Gerald ed. (1971), *Manifestations of Discontent in Germany before the Reformation*, Bloomington

### (B) Literature

Abray, Lorna (1985), *The People's Reformation*, Ithaca

Blickle, Peter (1992), *Communal Reformation: The Quest for Salvation in Sixteenth Century Germany*, London

* Cameron, Euan (2012), *The European Reformation*, 2nd edn, Oxford

Dickens, A. Geoffrey (1974), *The German Nation and Martin Luther*, London

* Dixon, C. Scott (2002), *The Reformation in Germany*, Oxford

Gotthard, Alex (2004), *Der Augsburger Religionsfriede*, Münster

Grell, Ole (2000), 'Scandinavia', in: *The Reformation World*, ed. A. Pettegree, London, 257–76

Hendrix, Scott H. (2004), *Recultivating the Vineyard: The Reformation Agendas of Christianization*, Louisville

Kittelson, James (1982), 'Successes and Failures in the German Reformation', *Archiv für Reformationsgeschichte*, 73, 153–75

* Kittelson, James (1989), *Luther the Reformer*, Minneapolis

Moeller, Bernd (1972), 'Religious Life in Germany on the Eve of the Reformation', in: *Pre-Reformation Germany*, ed. G. Strauss, London, 13–42

Pettegree, Andrew (2005), *Reformation and the Culture of Persuasion*, Cambridge

Pettegree, Andrew (2015), *Brand Luther*, New York

Roper, Lyndal (2016), *Martin Luther: Renegade and Prophet*, London

Rublack, Ulinka, ed. (2016), *The Oxford Handbook of the Protestant Reformations*, Oxford, chapter 8

Schilling, Heinz (2017), *Martin Luther: Rebel in an Age of Upheaval*, Oxford

Scribner, Robert W. (1994), *'For the Sake of Simple Folk': Popular Propaganda for the German Reformation*, 2nd edn, Oxford

Strauss, Gerald (1978), *Luther's House of Learning*, Baltimore

**(C) Web resources**

Dixon, C. Scott and Greengrass, Mark (1997) 'The Protestant Reformation: Religious Change and the People of Sixteenth-Century Europe': <http://www.albany.edu/jmmh/vol3/creating_cdroms/contents.htm>

'Luther at Worms (1521)', Pitts Theology Library – Digital Image Archive: <http://www.pitts.emory.edu/dia/image_details.cfm?ID=4591>

'Project Wittenberg', works by and about Martin Luther and other Lutherans: <http://www.iclnet.org/pub/resources/text/wittenberg/wittenberg-home.html>

# The long Reformation: Reformed

*Penny Roberts*

## The Reformed tradition

When historians of the Reformation refer to the Reformed tradition, they usually mean those movements which emerged in the Swiss Confederation around its dual poles of Zurich and Geneva. While Luther was making waves in Wittenberg, his contemporary and later rival, Huldrych Zwingli (1483–1531), was developing his own challenge to the established Church as principal pastor in Zurich. His more radical and confrontational stance was to shape both the German-speaking and francophone branches of the Reform. Gradually, through preaching and debate, as well as public acts of defiance – eating meat during LENT and advocating the marriage of priests and the destruction of images – Zwingli and his followers won over the municipal authorities and the MASS was officially abolished in Zurich in 1525. As in Germany, there was an evident political dividend to embracing Reformation, since it coincided with the movement for the independence of the Swiss cantons from the authority of the Holy Roman Emperor and, in the case of Geneva, from the overlordship of the bishop of Savoy. Also as in the territories of the Empire, however, not all the cantons were won over to Reformed ideas, including those who disliked Zwingli's opposition to the hiring of Swiss mercenaries to fight in foreign wars on which several areas were economically dependent. Zwingli would die in battle with the Swiss Catholic cantons at Kappel in 1531 (Gordon 2002; Burnett and Campi 2016).

While claiming to have reached his views independently, Zwingli was undoubtedly influenced by Luther's works and freely acknowledged this debt, despite the open and growing hostility between the two camps in the late 1520s. Although they had many beliefs in common, Zwingli felt that Luther had not gone far enough, and so developed more radical views on the SACRAMENTS, ICONOCLASM and the role of secular authority which would later influence Calvin (Boxes 1–2). Tensions came to a head in the only personal confrontation between the men at Marburg in 1529; in contrast to many other points, no compromise could be reached over the EUCHARIST, despite the best efforts of mediators like the Strasbourg reformer Martin Bucer (1491–1551). The damage which the internal squabbles between Lutherans and Zwinglians did to the Protestant movement was a lesson not lost on their successors in the second generation of Reform. John Calvin (1509–64), who trained under Bucer, and Heinrich

**Box 1**

**Lutheran, Zwinglian and Calvinist views on the sacraments and salvation**

For Luther, the SACRAMENTS of baptism and the LORD'S SUPPER were active, i.e. necessary and central to faith and inseparable from the Word. While rejecting Catholic belief in TRANSUBSTANTIATION, he maintained his belief in the REAL PRESENCE in the EUCHARIST during the Lord's Supper. Luther believed that his doctrine of JUSTIFICATION by faith alone allowed for an individual to actively turn to God.

For Zwingli, the sacraments were purely symbolic, neither conferring grace nor imparting faith as Luther claimed; it was the Word that was central. He held the SACRAMENTARIAN view that the Lord's Supper was nothing more than a commemorative, contemplative and symbolic re-enactment. Zwingli maintained that an individual could do nothing to encourage the bestowing of divine favour or damnation (a medieval concept to which Zwingli, and especially Calvin, gave renewed emphasis).

Calvin took a position between these two, although overall closer to Zwingli, allowing for a spiritual rather than real presence during the Lord's Supper. Calvin agreed with Zwingli's views on salvation and upheld DIVINE and ultimately DOUBLE PREDESTINATION, while arguing that good works, godly behaviour and the acceptance of discipline were all necessary outward signs of 'election'. 'For he does not create all in the same condition, but ordains eternal life for some and eternal damnation for others' (McGrath 1988, 91).

**Box 2**

**Lutheran, Zwinglian and Calvinist views on relations between Church and state**

Luther saw Church and state as separate (his doctrine of the two kingdoms), the former dependent on protection from the latter and, therefore, sometimes subordinate to it. He promoted princely or monarchical authority.

Zwingli envisaged a godly magistracy which would assist the ministry in running the Church, merging ecclesiastical and secular authority. Oligarchy was preferred to monarchy.

Calvin retained the idea of godly magistracy but also a separate Church body (the CONSISTORY) who would police the congregation and was not answerable to the secular authorities: 'neither does the church assume anything to herself which is proper to the magistrate, nor is the magistrate competent to what is done by the church' (McGrath 1988, 152). Like Zwingli, he distrusted the tyrannical potential of monarchy.

All were influenced by the circumstances of their ministries: German princely territories, Swiss civic government and an independent city-state. All were forced to contemplate practical situations in which resistance might be justified (Höpfl 1991).

Bullinger (1504–75), Zwingli's successor in Zurich, signed an agreement on that most divisive of issues, the Eucharist, in 1549. Their contribution would consolidate the hold of Protestantism in many areas of Europe just as Catholicism reasserted its claim to supremacy ('The long Reformation: Catholic' in Part III).

## Geneva and Calvin

It was a Frenchman in exile, John Calvin, who was to lead the most successful and expansionist branch of the Reformed movement from his base in Geneva, labelled 'the Protestant Rome' (Gordon 2009). John Knox, the Scottish Reformer, famously described the Genevan Church as 'The most perfect school of Christ that ever was since the days of the Apostles'. However, only recently have the many difficulties Calvin initially faced in setting up his Church been fully examined, not least the opposition from within Geneva itself (Naphy 1994). Calvin's first encounter with the city was in 1536, when he was invited to join his fellow French preacher-in-exile, Guillaume Farel. Yet the problems of working in a faction-ridden city, and the unpopularity of the rigour with which Farel and Calvin imposed discipline on its inhabitants, led to their expulsion in 1538. Calvin then went to work with Bucer in the imperial city of Strasbourg, an experience formative to his later role in Geneva, until he and Farel were invited back by the city COUNCIL in 1541. While factional hostility to the foreign pastors remained (both political and religious opposition which was not easily crushed), the subsequent arrival of mainly French refugees in increasing numbers from the 1540s led to a near doubling of the Genevan population and assured the ascendancy of Calvin and his fellow ministers by the mid-1550s.

Three factors stand out when analyzing the influences upon, and explaining the influence of, Calvin's thought: first, his education and the implementation of doctrine; second, his experience of cooperation and conflict with urban authorities; and, finally, his formation as a religious refugee.

Calvin's education in theology and law in the leading French universities and law schools of his day gave him the RHETORICAL and analytical skills which he later put to good use in his widely circulated sermons. His legal training in particular has been credited with shaping the clear and systematic statements of discipline and exposition of doctrine which characterize his major works. Chief among these was the *Institutes* (or *Institution*) *of the Christian Religion*, rather optimistically dedicated from exile to Francis I of France in 1536, which became a hugely popular and influential guide to a Christian life (Web resources). Here Calvin first expounded his notion of the visible and the invisible Church, that those who God had chosen to save, the ELECT, were known only to Him. Calvin recognized that practical structures were also needed for the Church, as later embodied in his *Ecclesiastical Ordinances* of 1541. This work provided a constitution for the Genevan Church, showing how it was to be organized and its members governed, disciplined and supported, which would become the model for all Calvinist Churches to follow. How to choose and to train suitable pastors was central and, in 1559, the Genevan ACADEMY was specifically set up for this purpose as well as to meet the growing demand for Reformed ministers. To assist the ministry in its duties, lay elders and deacons were also appointed. Together with the ministers, they were to sit on the CONSISTORY, a body which was primarily set up to resolve disputes and to discipline wayward members of the community, thus allowing the Church to regulate both private behaviour and public conduct. Excommunication was the ultimate deterrent, but was rarely applied except in the case of unrepentant or repeat offenders. Discipline was generally accepted as necessary for the maintenance of a godly society, but the Church also provided care for the sick, relief for the poor and support for refugees. Regional and national synods completed the PRESBYTERIAN Church structure. Calvin's insistence on the independence of the Church brought him into conflict with the Genevan authorities, but allowed Reformed Churches to be established even within states where the authorities were hostile or viewed as ungodly. The spread of the Reform was due as much to the Calvinists responding to requests for assistance from fledgling Churches abroad as to a conscious programme of expansion.

It is hard to overstate the importance of Calvin to the formation of the Reformed movement, but it must not be forgotten that Calvinism continued to develop under the guidance of others after his death, primarily his lieutenant in Geneva, Theodore Beza (1519–1605; Diagram III.3.1), and cannot simply be equated with one man's convictions. Equally, the contribution of his contemporary in Zurich, Heinrich Bullinger, was enormous, especially through his declaration of doctrine, the *Second Helvetic Confession* of 1566 – 'the greatest theological work to emerge out of the Swiss Reformation' (Gordon 2002, 182) – which was widely translated and accepted by Reformed Churches across Europe. Acknowledgement of these multiple influences explains historians' preference for the term 'Reformed' over 'Calvinist' for the international movement which Calvin and others propagated.

## The Reformed 'International'

The fact that Reformed Protestantism did not require the goodwill of the established authorities to enable its implementation and spread ensured that it was ultimately a more geographically and numerically successful movement than Lutheranism. While Scandinavia and some German territories continued to embrace the Lutheran Church, outside these regions the Reform's appeal was widespread, even if only among a minority of the people. Protestants in England, Scotland, France and the Netherlands, as well as their coreligionists in Central and Eastern Europe (chiefly Hungary, Transylvania, Poland and some imperial territories like Bohemia), drew inspiration from both Geneva and Zurich. Of course, in many areas the Reformers were building on an already established Lutheran base, as in Hungary, or absorbed 'proto-Protestants' such as the Hussites of Bohemia and the Waldensians (or *vaudois*) of France. Furthermore, the nobility were specifically targeted and their response was vital to

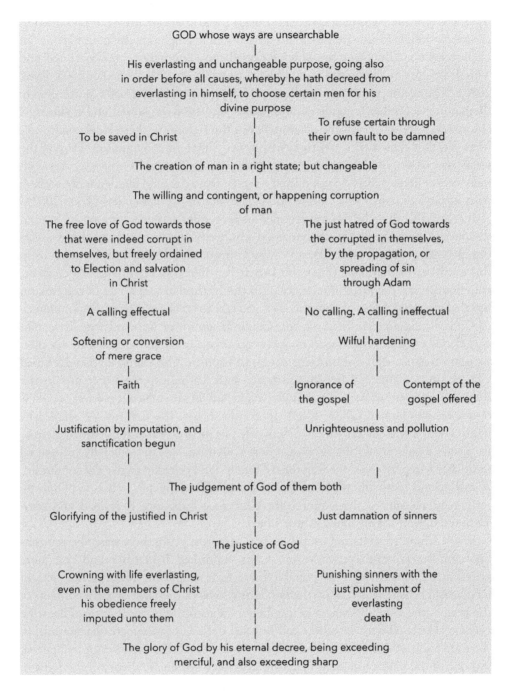

GOD whose ways are unsearchable
|
His everlasting and unchangeable purpose, going also
in order before all causes, whereby he hath decreed from
everlasting in himself, to choose certain men for his
divine purpose

|                                     To refuse certain through
To be saved in Christ           |        their own fault to be damned
|

The creation of man in a right state; but changeable
|
The willing and contingent, or happening corruption
of man

The free love of God towards those                 The just hatred of God towards
that were indeed corrupt in                            the corrupted in themselves,
themselves, but freely ordained                        by the propagation, or
to Election and salvation                                spreading of sin
in Christ                                                  through Adam
|                                                           |
A calling effectual                                    No calling. A calling ineffectual
|                                                           |
Softening or conversion                                  Wilful hardening
of mere grace                                               |
|                                                           |
Faith                             Ignorance of          Contempt of the
|                              the gospel            gospel offered
|                                                           |
Justification by imputation, and                   Unrighteousness and pollution
sanctification begun
|

|                                             |
|         The judgement of God of them both
|                                   |
Glorifying of the justified in Christ    |        Just damnation of sinners
|
The justice of God
|
Crowning with life everlasting,       |        Punishing sinners with the
even in the members of Christ         |             just punishment of
his obedience freely                  |                everlasting
imputed unto them                     |                   death
|
The glory of God by his eternal decree, being exceeding
merciful, and also exceeding sharp

**Diagram III.3.1** Based on an English version of Theodore Beza's 'Table of Double Predestination', this scheme clearly sets out the dual path which the elect and the damned are destined to follow from creation to final judgement, elaborating on Calvin's statement of God's intention. Appropriately, the elect are placed on the right and the damned on the left hand of God.

the success of the Reformed cause. Although it has traditionally been presented as an international movement, historians have begun to emphasize the national or even local character of the Churches which emerged, providing a more 'multinational' and 'pluralistic' picture (Pettegree *et al.* 1994; Scribner *et al.* 1994; Benedict 2003; Ryrie 2006). 'The connections between Europe's Calvinists and Reformed Churches were therefore decentralised, unofficial and could often be disorganised and ineffective' (Murdock 2004, 1). It was the adaptability of the Reform to these local conditions, however, that cemented its position within very different communities. Despite the usual association, of Calvinism in particular, with sophisticated urban centres with high rates of literacy, this did not inhibit its spread into the rural highlands of Scotland with its predominantly oral culture and persistence of popular beliefs (Todd 2002).

It is arguable that the Reform retained its most pure and uncompromised state in the places where the Reformers remained a minority and marginalized group, as did the HUGUENOTS in France (Box 3). Where it was closely allied to the state, as in the northern Netherlands (later the Dutch Republic) and Scotland, by contrast, compromise was the price of its success. In the Netherlands, the fate of the Reform was tied in with political circumstances: the desire to break away from the dominance of Catholic Spain. Ministers of the Calvinist minority were reliant on secular authorities to establish its position as the dominant religion, but failed to get their support on issues such as restricting access to baptism. The Dutch favoured a broad Church and commercial freedom to trade with Catholic powers if it was in the Republic's interests to do so. The Dutch Church's ability to influence matters of policy, therefore, was limited (Duke 2002). In Scotland, too, the Reform was shaped by politics, and it was the nobility which decided its progress (as also in France, despite its ultimate failure, and the Empire, where Calvinism was not officially recognized until 1648). In most cases, the Reformed Church could be modified to local conditions, as in England (with the retention of bishops) or Transylvania (where a pluralistic settlement recognized three Protestant Churches: Lutheran, Reformed and anti-Trinitarian, split largely along ethnic lines).

While Church leaders and secular authorities might clash, there were also tensions between the relative conservatism of the Reformed leadership and the more provocative behaviour of its popular base, for example in carrying out acts of iconoclasm (Figure III.6). In particular, during some of the most divisive conflicts of the period, the Dutch Revolt and the French Wars of Religion, Reformed doctrine became associated with rebellion and resistance. Despite vehement declarations of the need to obey constituted authority, Theodore Beza, Calvin's successor in Geneva, was one of the most prominent figures to develop a systematic theory of the right to resistance by 'lesser magistrates', including nobles and princes as well as high-ranking officials ('Centre and periphery' in Part VI). For Dutch rebels seeking to overthrow Spanish domination, and Huguenot, Scottish and Hungarian nobles fighting against royal forces, such theories provided legitimacy for their cause. In England, too, Puritans enthusiastically opposed the royal supremacy.

'Sire, your most humble and most obedient subjects of the town of Bordeaux and region of the Bordelais, who are of the religion which is called Reformed, remonstrate with you most humbly that even though by your edict for the pacification of the troubles and your declaration thereon you have commanded that everyone should have secure and free access to the places where the exercise of the said religion has been established by your command, and everyone should live in his house unrestricted, without being searched, or molested, or constrained for reasons of conscience, and in order to be better united your subjects should all be received into the administration of towns and communities regardless of religious difference . . . Nevertheless, the town mayor and councillors and other officials and, following their example, several private individuals, disposed to be unruly and disobedient to your commands, imprison, sentence and fine, seize property and otherwise molest the supplicants for things which are permitted by you, and much more that tends to the infraction of your edicts, violation of the protection and assurance which you have given to the supplicants and, consequently, to the subversion of your estate. They beseech most humbly your Majesty to provide for this and to declare your will and intention . . .'

*(Sécousse 1743–45, v. 214–22)*

Despite a reputation for radicalism, French Reformed Churches embraced the royal protection offered to them by successive edicts of pacification during the religious wars (1562–98). The preamble to this petition reveals this, as well as the difficulties for a minority Church of securing its rights under the law in the face of local hostility. It survives in a number of copies in both manuscript and print.

It is with people who fled their native country because of persecution that we find the truly international aspect of the movement, not so much in their integrating with their host countries, since they tended to establish their own communities and churches, known as 'stranger churches', but rather through their contacts with their home countries and other refugees. Calvin himself and his fellow ministers were religious exiles and this inevitably informed their attitude to the movement they had spawned. Strasbourg, Geneva and other francophone centres like Lausanne were magnets principally for French refugees, whereas Emden in northern Germany was favoured by the Dutch, but England also hosted both French and Dutch Churches. Scottish Protestants and Marian exiles, too, sought refuge in a variety of European centres at times of adversity. Exile involved giving up established ties, property and sometimes status, but offered freedom of conscience and a haven from persecution and even death. Calvin viewed exile as the only respectable alternative to martyrdom, condemning those who maintained outward conformity with Catholicism (NICODEMITES). The greatest exception to the influence of established authorities leading to conflict with the Church emerged where both Church and state were newly

Nach wenigh Predication     Das bildent furmen fiengen an     Kay Monstrantz, Kelch, auch die altar     Zerbrochen all in kurtzer stunde
Die Calvinische Religion     Das nicht ein bilde davon bleib sian     Und west sonst dort vor handen was     Gleich gar vil leutten das ist kunde .
                            Anno Dñi.   M.  D.  LXVi     XX   Augusti

**Figure III.6** Iconoclasm, the destruction of images, ranged from clandestine individual acts to officially sanctioned and systematic assault as depicted here. The former were generally condemned as provocative and radical, the latter were encouraged by the state. Destruction of relics and statues in churches, April 1566, engraving by Franz Hogenberg (1535–90), Wars of Religion, France, 16th century / De Agostini Picture Library / G. Dagli Orti / Bridgeman Images.

established, as in New England. Here religious refugees decided the way that society should be structured and organized without having to battle with existing interests. Those unable to move elsewhere, however, had to find strategies to survive as best they could in the face of social hostility and political exclusion.

Those best suited or most adaptable to a life in exile were those with transferable skills, such as printers, merchants and artisans, as well as those who wished to train for the ministry. Protestant educational networks were vital to the international connections of the Reformed movement. Aside from the Genevan Academy, Protestant universities were established at Leiden in the Netherlands and Heidelberg in the Empire in the 1570s, and academies at Sedan and Saumur in France at the turn of the century. Important printing centres were also developed in Geneva and Emden which distributed Reformed literature to the rest of Europe. Trading links were another principal channel for the communication of ideas, and an influx of skilled workers could give a boost to local and national economies, as Netherlandish cloth workers and French silversmiths did in England. Not only did refugees from the largely francophone southern provinces bring skills and wealth to the Dutch economy, they also imported Calvinist beliefs. Military or financial assistance could be sought and given by one Protestant state to another, as by England and the German Protestant princes to the Dutch and French Calvinists whose fortunes in Europe were closely allied. Above all, though, Geneva and other training centres sent out ministers to serve the newly established Churches abroad, gave advice to those setting them up via a vast network of correspondence, resolved their disputes and provided them with funds. Another measure of the movement's success, if also its limits, was that the demand for properly trained ministers soon far outstripped the supply.

## Assessment

The Reformed Churches were essential to the survival and resilience of the Protestant movement in the face of a resurgent Catholicism. Calvin and Bullinger built on the foundations laid by both Luther and Zwingli. They were able to present a more coherent exposition of doctrine and a more practical structure for the survival of the Church and the sustenance of the faithful even within a hostile environment. Reformed Churches were able to adapt successfully to the different local and national circumstances in which they found themselves and became the dominant religious force in the Dutch Republic, England, Scotland, Hungary and Bohemia. Although relations with secular authorities were often strained, the Churches were able to develop independently in cooperation with the state. Even where they failed, as in France, they managed to establish a substantial enough minority to acquire a degree of toleration and legitimacy within the polity (at least up to 1685 and later when restored by the Revolutionaries).

> With Zurich and Geneva offering alternative models of how Church and state fit together, the tradition could appeal both to rulers determined to exercise direct authority over sacred things and to ordinary believers in situations of persecution eager to establish a properly reformed church that could function independently of the state.
>
> (Benedict 2003, 8)

Although far from sweeping all before them, the Churches were able at least to halt the erosion of the first wave of Reform, and to establish a lasting legacy which would be exported to North America.

## Discussion themes

1. Assess the importance of the Swiss Reformation to the spread of Protestantism.
2. What made Calvinism unattractive for some sections of the Genevan population?
3. Why was the Reformed Church the most successful brand of Protestantism in later sixteenth-century Europe?

## Bibliography

### (A) Sources

* Duke, Alastair, Lewis, Gillian and Pettegree, Andrew eds (1992), *Calvinism in Europe, 1540–1610: A Collection of Documents*, Manchester
Höpfl, Harry ed. (1991), *Luther and Calvin on Secular Authority*, Cambridge
Naphy, William G. ed. (1996), *Documents on the Continental Reformation*, London
Potter, G. R. and Greengrass, Mark eds (1983), *John Calvin*, London
Sécousse, D. F. ed. (1743–45), *Mémoires de Condé*, 6 vols, London

### (B) Literature

* Benedict, Philip (2003), *Christ's Churches Purely Reformed: A Social History of Calvinism*, New Haven, Conn.
Burnett, Amy Nelson; Campi, Emidio (2016), *A Companion to the Swiss Reformation*, Leiden
Duke, Alastair (2002), *Reformation and Revolt in the Low Countries*, Hambledon
Gordon, Bruce (2002), *The Swiss Reformation*, Manchester
Gordon, Bruce (2009), *Calvin, 1509–1564*, New Haven
Kingdon, Robert M. (1967), *Geneva and the Consolidation of the French Protestant Movement, 1564–72*, Geneva
McGrath, Alister E. (1988), *Reformation Thought: An Introduction*, Oxford
* Murdock, Graeme (2004), *Beyond Calvin: The Intellectual, Political and Cultural World of Europe's Reformed Churches*, Basingstoke
Naphy, William G. (1994), *Calvin and the Consolidation of the Genevan Reformation*, Manchester
Parker, T. H. L. (1975), *John Calvin: A Biography*, London
Pettegree, Andrew, Duke, Alistair and Lewis, Gillian eds (1994), *Calvinism in Europe, 1540–1620*, Cambridge
Potter, G. R. (1976), *Zwingli*, Cambridge
Ryrie, Alec ed. (2006), *Palgrave Advances in the European Reformations*, Basingstoke
Scribner, Bob, Porter, Roy and Teich, Mikuláš eds (1994), *The Reformation in National Context*, Cambridge
Spicer, Andrew (2007), *Calvinist Churches in Early Modern Europe*, Manchester
Terpstra, Nicholas (2015), *Religious Refugees in the Early Modern World: An Alternative History of the Reformation*, Cambridge
Todd, Margo (2002), *The Culture of Protestantism in Early Modern Scotland*, New Haven, Conn.

## (C) Web resources

Beza, Theodore, 'Must Magistrates Always Be Obeyed as Unconditionally as God?',
   trans. Patrick S. Poole: <http://www.constitution.org/cmt/beza/magistrates.htm>
Calvin, John, *Institutes of the Christian Religion* (1536–59), trans. Henry Beveridge:
   <http://www.ccel.org/ccel/calvin/institutes.titlepage.html>
Dixon, C. Scott and Greengrass, Mark, 'The Protestant Reformation' (Core Resources
   for Historians: relaunched 2005): <http://www.albany.edu/jmmh/vol3/creating_
   cdroms/contents.htm>

# The long Reformation: Catholic

*Anne Gerritsen, Kevin Gould and Peter Marshall*

## Catholic Reformation or Counter-Reformation?

The Catholic Church was deeply troubled by the extent of Protestant successes in the first half of the sixteenth century. By around 1550, Protestantism looked unstoppable, seemingly victorious in Germany, Scandinavia and England, and making serious inroads into France and the Netherlands as well as across the Habsburg lands of Central and Eastern Europe. Yet by the turn of the century, the Catholic Church was resurgent, headed by a revitalized Papacy, its doctrine and practices redefined and its hierarchy subordinate to Rome. This transformation was forged in an extraordinary general council of the Church and implemented by its champions: an invigorated episcopacy and new religious orders. Swaths of land and countless souls lost to Protestantism during the early Reformation period were regained by a pious, disciplined and militant Catholicism during the seventeenth and eighteenth centuries, and new worlds were targeted by missionaries eager to export the 'true faith' across the globe.

Whether this Catholic revival was a direct response to Protestant expansion or instead the culmination of centuries of internal reform is often debated (O'Malley 2000). The nineteenth-century German Lutheran historian, Leopold von Ranke, popularized the influential expression 'Counter-Reformation' (*Gegenreformation*) to express the supposedly negative and reactionary character of Catholic policy in these years. Recent historiography has noted, though, that calls for a *reformatio ecclesiae* – the reformation of the Church in head and members – had been routine in the late medieval period.

## The Council of Trent

As the Lutheran protest gathered steam, secular leaders feared the disorder and disunity caused by confessional clashes, and calls for the Papacy to act more effectively began to mount. Foremost among these voices was that of Holy Roman Emperor Charles V. Charles was aggrieved at the growing challenges to his authority from Protestant German rulers. At the 1521 imperial DIET of Worms, the emperor demanded that a general council of the Church be called as a matter of priority to reconcile the faiths and so end the schism. The Papacy rejected this petition and deflected subsequent calls by procrastinating over feasible locations of any assembly (Charles wanted to host the council in the Empire; the Papacy in the Italian states). But Rome could not deflect such pressures indefinitely, and on 13 December 1545 it convened the nineteenth general council in the Church's long history at Trent, a small northern Italian town, but technically part of the Empire. It soon became evident that the site of the assembly was the only concession Rome was willing to make. The Council's constitution, terms and agenda were all dictated by the Papacy, leaving secular rulers disenfranchised: Charles V failed to secure a forum to restore order to his territories; France railed at papal control of affairs and refused its delegates permission to attend; Spain complained at the prevalence of Italian bishops on the Council; Lutheran delegates who attended the first sessions were undermined and ignored. A general council summoned in the early 1520s might have succeeded in reconciling the Church's critics and keeping them within the fold. But events had moved on. Arguably the Council of Trent came 25 years too late; the medieval Church was now split irrevocably.

The influence of Trent on the fortunes of Catholicism, however, would be profound. The Council met in three sittings: 1545–49, 1551–52 and 1562–63. The early sessions, reflecting the personality of the presiding chair, Paul III, were concerned with combating HERESY rather than healing schism. The Protestant principles of SOLA SCRIPTURA and JUSTIFICATION by faith were formally refuted, and orthodox Catholic tenets such as papal primacy, the authority of tradition, the validity of good works, TRANSUBSTANTIATION and the authenticity of the seven SACRAMENTS were defined and confirmed. The later sessions showed a greater concern with internal reform: every bishopric was ordered to establish a seminary for the training of priests, and bishops were ordered to be personally resident in their dioceses (Box 1). There was intense debate about whether residence was required 'by the law of God', bringing up the question of whether bishops held their office directly from God or only as delegates of the Pope. The decree managed to fudge this crucial theological issue (O'Malley 2013).

The final sessions also confirmed the INDEX LIBRORUM PROHIBITORUM, a creation of one of the most vigorous opponents of Protestantism, Paul IV (1555–59), who had been the architect of the reactivation of the Roman INQUISITION in 1542. Early sixteenth-century popes had feared that a general council would undermine their powers, but in fact papal authority emerged enhanced from Trent. Pius IV (1559–65) confirmed the decrees, but reserved their interpretation to himself and his successors. The next Pope, Pius V (1566–72), carried on the reforming work of the council, standardizing the text of the MASS – the so-called TRIDENTINE rite which remained the standard form until the 1960s. A standardized CATECHISM commissioned by the council was issued in 1566 and a new edition of the Latin VULGATE Bible (declared by Trent the official version) followed in 1592. Many of these reforms were overseen by a new administrative structure, so-called 'congregations' of cardinals, which made the Roman Curia or central administration seem less like a medieval court and more like a bureaucratic state. Fairly or not, the congregation responsible for the propagation of the faith, *Propaganda Fide*, has given the name to a modern term of political manipulation. By the end of the sixteenth century, the authority of the Papacy had been restored in moral as well as institutional terms. Tridentine popes like Pius V, Gregory XIII (1572–85) and Sixtus V (1585–90) were ascetic figures, quite unlike the 'RENAISSANCE popes' of a century before.

---

**Box 1**

'Whereas it is by divine precept enjoined on all, to whom the cure of souls is committed, to know their own sheep; to offer sacrifice for them; and, by the preaching of the divine word, by the administration of the sacraments, and by the example of all good works, to feed them; to have a fatherly care of the poor and of other distressed persons, and to apply themselves to all other pastoral duties; all which (offices) cannot be rendered and fulfilled by those who neither watch over nor are with their own flock, but abandon it after the manner of hirelings; the sacred and holy Synod . . . declares, that all persons who are – under whatsoever name and title, even though they be cardinals of the holy Roman Church – set over any patriarchal, primatial, metropolitan, and cathedral Churches whatsoever, are obliged to personal residence in their own Church, or diocese.'

('Canons and Decrees'; Web resources)

Decree on episcopal residence issued by the Council of Trent (1563).

---

## Diocesan reform and new orders

The reform initiatives originating with Trent would redefine and rejuvenate Catholic doctrine and practice. At the level of the diocese, a new breed of reforming bishops aimed to raise moral and educational standards, while at the same time tightening ecclesiastical discipline and regulating forms of lay piety which had been allowed freer rein in the later Middle Ages. The model was Charles Borromeo, archbishop of Milan (1564–84), whose *Acta Ecclesiae Mediolanensis* [Acts of the Church of Milan] set out an ambitious reform programme (Headley and Tomaro 1988). Here and elsewhere, traditionally strong quasi-independent bodies such as FRATERNITIES and lay devotional groups were subsumed within the revitalized diocese. Religious education in the Middle Ages had been a hit-and-miss affair, but Trent deemed it a parental duty to send children to the parish priest for catechism classes on Sundays and holy days. There was a stronger expectation that all the laity should attend mass on Sundays and holy days, and receive the sacraments – only from their parish priest – at least once a year at Easter. The practice of confession in particular became stricter, with

**Figure III.7** Andrea Pozzo's altar of St Ignatius Loyola at the church of Il Gesù, Rome (1690s), provides an impression of intense engagement with the senses of the worshippers. © Zeno Colantoni, Rome.

the invention (attributed to Borromeo) and rapid diffusion of the secret and secure confessional box. Secular uses of churches and churchyards were discouraged and local religious celebrations banned if they contained 'superstitious' elements of which reforming clergy disapproved. Some have argued that Trent's regulation of lay participation in devotional practices served to extinguish much of the vitality of medieval Christianity (Bossy 1970). But the sheer exuberance and emotional intensity of much of the religious art and architecture of the Catholic reform period points to new possibilities for lay experience of the sacred (Figure III.7).

Promulgating the Tridentine canons across Europe required substantially more foot soldiers than the diocese or parish could muster. Here, newly formed religious orders would prove invaluable, such as the reformed branch of the Franciscans known as Capuchins and the Lazarists founded by the Frenchman Vincent de Paul (1581–1660). During the seventeenth century, Lazarists and other orders undertook regular 'missions' in rural France and Italy, descending in groups on villages to rouse the religious sensibilities of the inhabitants with dramatic processions, religious plays and emotional preaching (Hsia 2005). There was revival among the female as well as male religious. New orders of nuns, such as the Ursulines and Visitandines, were founded to nurse the poor and the sick, though the ecclesiastical authorities became uneasy with the concept of public female ministry, and strict 'ENCLOSURE' was forced on these orders in the course of the seventeenth century ('Gender and family' in Part II).

By far the most influential of the new orders was the Society of Jesus, known as the JESUITS. Founded by the Spaniard Ignatius Loyola (1491–1556) in 1534, the Jesuit order was sanctioned by Paul III in 1540. Loyola was a key figure in the emergence of a militant Catholic Reformation; his *Spiritual Exercises* (1548) both taught a technique of meditative prayer and instilled an unquestioning obedience to the authority of the Church (Box 2). Combining the discipline of the traditional religious orders with a commitment to itinerant activism in the world, the Jesuits excelled in preaching, teaching and missionary activity. They were particularly influential in education. Their first school was opened in 1548, and by 1615 there were 370 such institutions. The Jesuits provided free education to the poor, but also served as educators to the elite (the philosophers Justus Lipsius and René Descartes were graduates of their colleges). Linked to the Pope by a special oath of loyalty, Jesuits would serve as confessors to monarchs and emperors, often arousing jealousy and resentment from fellow Catholics as well as the hatred of Protestants.

## Box 2

'Let the following Rules be observed.

First Rule: All judgment laid aside, we ought to have our mind ready and prompt to obey, in all, the true Spouse of Christ our Lord, which is our holy Mother the Church Hierarchical.

Second Rule: To praise confession to a Priest, and the reception of the most Holy Sacrament of the Altar once in the year, and much more each month, and much better from week to week, with the conditions required and due . . .

Thirteenth Rule: To be right in everything, we ought always to hold that the white which I see, is black, if the Hierarchical Church so decides it, believing that between Christ our Lord, the Bridegroom, and the Church, His Bride, there is the same Spirit which governs and directs us for the salvation of our souls. Because by the same Spirit and our Lord Who gave the ten Commandments, our holy Mother the Church is directed and governed.'

*(Extracts from the Spiritual Exercises of Ignatius Loyola; Web resources)*

## Catholicism goes global

The Jesuits were in the forefront of a crucial development, for it was in the sixteenth and seventeenth centuries that Catholicism (and indeed, Christianity) became for the first time a world religion. Jesuit missionaries, like Franciscan and Dominican friars, followed in the wake of European overseas expansion, linking the spread of Christianity to European attempts to infiltrate and control global networks of trade.

Catholic encounters overseas confronted the Church with serious questions. Were the peoples they encountered to be considered 'full human beings' or 'natural slaves' (as Aristotle had maintained)? What should be done about pagan religions: were they to be rooted out or seen as the building blocks for the construction of new forms of indigenous Catholicism? One Jesuit answer to such questions was formulated by José d'Acosta (1540–1600), who recognized three types of non-Christians. Where the degree of civilization seemed similar to Europe, as in Japan or India, rational persuasion would be used. For peoples without writing systems but with sophisticated political organizations such as the Aztecs or the Incas, a Christian government would be instituted, leaving some freedom of religious choice to the locals ('Europe in 1500' in Part I). Nomadic and semi-nomadic peoples, however, would best be treated as children, with force used to bring about conversion where necessary. Over time, no single solution was accepted, and different circumstances led to a variety of responses and solutions.

The spread of Catholicism to Africa occurred mostly under the auspices of the Portuguese, who were highly ambitious from the late fifteenth century onwards: the lands they aimed to control also included Brazil, Southern Asia, the East Indies and the Far East. The Portuguese considered the Muslim presence in northern Africa the principal obstacle to easy access to the riches of Asia, and alliances with African rulers were formed as part of an anti-Islamic crusade. The conversion of the African continent has been regarded as largely superficial, driven by Portuguese ambitions to control the lucrative trade with Asia. Catholic missionaries toiling away in small enclaves along the trade routes seem to have had little success in reaching the populations inland, and in the exceptional places where Christianity did flourish, it was in a distinctly SYNCRETIC form, characterized by accommodation to African religious practices (Thornton 1984).

From 1498, the Portuguese also had a foothold on the Indian Ocean coast. Settlements remained largely coastal, including bases in Mozambique, Mombasa, Mumbai, Malacca and Macao. The Christian communities on the Malabar coast of India drew members of the religious orders. The Jesuit Francis Xavier, one of the original companions of Loyola, arrived in 1542, and in 1574 Alessandro Valignano settled in Goa, which became the nerve centre for the Asian mission. Xavier is considered one of the greatest Christian missionaries, his frequent letters home stirring interest in Asia throughout Catholic Europe.

Meanwhile, the Spanish were responsible for the mission to the Americas. Franciscans arrived in the Caribbean in 1500, soon followed by Dominicans and

Augustinians, and from there undertook the evangelization of the Americas (McClure 2016). Because of the shortage of priests, members of these orders were initially granted privileges such as administering the sacraments independently from bishops, although this led to later conflicts that marred the success of the mission. In the newly conquered Spanish territories of Mexico and Peru, there was a drive to root out indigenous religious practices. There were spectacular successes for the missionaries, but disappointments too. Many native converts in the Americas practised syncretism, blending elements of the new religion with their own inherited customs, which provoked sporadic crack-downs on 'idolatry'.

From the Spanish base in the Philippine Islands, Jesuits set out to attempt the conversion of Japan and China. When Xavier arrived in Japan in 1549, he sent enthusiastic letters home about the civilized people he had found here. He sought to convert the emperor, but soon realized that actual power had shifted to the individual VASSAL lords, the *daimyo*. The *daimyo*, keen on rituals and outward displays of power, were at first underwhelmed by the impoverished appearance of the humble priests. Only when Xavier made an appearance in magnificent robes did he secure permission to use a BUDDHIST monastery for his preaching. He soon became aware of the high status of Chinese culture in Japan and decided to redirect his efforts there (Box 3 and Figure III.8). The missionaries who followed Xavier to Japan succeeded by the end of the century in creating a thriving local Church, but Japanese Catholicism was all but extinguished by a ruthless persecution in the early seventeenth century (Brockey 2014, pt 2).

## Box 3

'The Japanese have a very high opinion of the wisdom of the Chinese, whether as to the mysteries of religion or as to manners and civil institutions. They used to make that a principal point against us, that if things were as we preached, how was it that the Chinese knew nothing about them? After many disputations and questions, the people of Yamaguchi began to join the Church of Christ, some from the lower orders and some from the nobility. In the space of two months quite as many as five hundred have become Christians. Their number is daily being added to; so that there is great cause for joy, and for thanking God that there are so many who embrace the Christian faith, and who tell us all the deceptions of the bonzes, and the mysteries contained in their books and taught by their sects. For those who have become Christians used to belong, one to one sect, another to another; the most learned of each of them explained to us the institutions and rules of his own way of belief. If I had not had the work of these converts to help me, I should not have been able to become sufficiently acquainted with, and so attack, these abominable religions of Japan.'

*(A letter to the Society of Jesus at Goa, written from Japan by*
*St Francis Xavier in 1551; Web resources)*

**Figure III.8** Painted in Japan by a Japanese Christian identified only as 'the fisherman', St Francis Xavier is wearing the habit and cloak of the Jesuit Order. 'St Francis Xavier', a Japanese painting by 'the fisherman', reproduced from Grace A.H. Vlam, 'The Portrait of S. Francis Xavier in Kobe', *Zeitschrift für Kunstgeschichte*, 42:1 (1979), 48–60. © Kobe City Museum, Japan.

As Xavier states in his letter (Box 3), the Japanese themselves looked to China as the source of civilization, and the Jesuits decided they needed to convert the Chinese first. Francis Xavier never reached China, and the first Jesuits were only allowed entrance there after 1583, when Matteo Ricci moved inland from the Portuguese base on the island of Macao. In line with Jesuit policy, Ricci adopted the dress and customs of the scholarly elites. He wrote learned texts in classical Chinese, and drew attention to Jesuit learning by means of a large map of the world, which featured the Chinese empire near the centre of the map instead of Jerusalem. Ricci set out to convert the Chinese emperor, but only had moderate impact, leaving behind approximately 2,000 Christians at the time of his death in 1610 (Hsia 2010).

The success of the Chinese mission was ultimately severely dented by what came to be known as the Rites Controversy. Ricci and his successors had allowed the Chinese to continue such practices as the worship of Confucius and family ancestors, referring to these as civil ceremonies. The Dominicans and Franciscans were strongly opposed to such accommodationist practices, and the Chinese were disgruntled by these internal conflicts. In 1710, the Pope officially condemned the performance of ancestral rituals by Chinese converts, and when the Chinese emperor became aware of the attempt of a 'barbarian' ruler to outlaw one of the fundamental principles of moral behaviour among his subjects, Christianity was instantly banned in China.

For many Europeans, the huge increase in numbers of Catholic Christians across the globe, with as many as ten million baptized in the Americas alone by 1550, came as a kind of compensation for the losses to the Protestants in Europe and the Turks in the east. In the longer term, the activities of early modern missionaries laid the foundations for dynamic Catholic cultures in Latin America and the Philippines, but in the ancient civilizations of South and East Asia the impact was much more restricted.

## Assessment

Despite Protestant successes, the Catholic Church remained numerically dominant in Europe and managed to reclaim many lost faithful, not least as the result of Habsburg successes in the Thirty Years War. The Council of Trent reaffirmed the power of the Papacy, confirmed Catholic tenets of faith and rejected Protestant theology. The style and substance of Catholicism would remain Tridentine until the Second Vatican Council of the mid-twentieth century. The new orders promoted rigorous devotion for clergy and laity alike, while mystic visionaries such as the Spanish nun Teresa of Avila (1515–82), author of a famous religious autobiography, provided inspiring examples of the inner life of the spirit (Teresa of Avila 1957).

But there were limitations. Trent had placed episcopal reform as the fulcrum of its reform policies, thus reaffirming the medieval pyramidic hierarchy that positioned papal authority at its apex. But Rome no longer received unanimous deference. In Spain, where bishops were often crown officials, the new directions to the episcopate were opposed by Philip II and his lawyers as an intrusion into crown autonomy. Papal supremacy was also less than absolute in France, where Gallican liberties had long allowed the crown to appoint to episcopal office. Some historians have seen the Catholic Reformation as an unprecedented campaign of mass indoctrination, a reform of 'popular religion' as dramatic as that of the Protestant Reformation (Delumeau 1977). Others identify a much slower and more uncertain process, in which crucial reforms like the establishment of diocesan seminaries were frequently long delayed, and in which local communities accepted reforms in an often selective way (Forster 2007). The extent to which the Catholic laity ever became fully 'Tridentized' is also open to question. Unorthodox folk beliefs (about fairies, for example) persisted alongside official Catholicism in parts of rural Spain, Italy and Ireland into modern times, just as elements of non-Christian belief were absorbed into the popular Catholicism of the New World.

Finally, what of the debate over nomenclature? Was this a *Counter-* or *Catholic* Reformation? It is hard to argue with A. G. Dickens's rhetorical observation that it was 'quite obviously both' (Dickens 1968, 7). Yet we need also to recognize that developments within what John O'Malley has argued we should unjudgementally term 'early modern Catholicism' (O'Malley 2000) are not just a matter of narrow ecclesiastical history; they were transformative of the politics and culture of Europe as well as of the wider world.

## Discussion themes

1. Assess the aims and methods of the 'Counter-Reformation Papacy'.
2. To what extent did the religion practised by the Catholic laity change in the sixteenth and seventeenth centuries?
3. What were the principal challenges in establishing Catholicism as a world religion?

## Bibliography

### (A) Sources

*The Catechism of the Council of Trent* (1983), trans. J. A. McHugh and C. J. Callan, Rockford, Ill.
* Miola, Robert S. ed. (2007), *Early Modern Catholicism: An Anthology of Primary Sources*, Oxford
Newitt, M. D. D. (2010), *The Portuguese in West Africa, 1415–1670: A Documentary History*, Cambridge
Teresa of Avila (1957), *The Life of Saint Teresa of Avila by Herself*, trans. J. M. Cohen, London
Xavier, Francis (1992), *The Letters and Instructions of Francis Xavier*, trans. M. Joseph Costelloe, St Louis, Mo.

### (B) Literature

* Bireley, Robert (1999), *The Refashioning of Catholicism, 1450–1700: A Reassessment of the Counter Reformation*, Basingstoke
Bossy, John (1970), 'The Counter-Reformation and the People of Catholic Europe', *P&P*, 47, 51–70
Brockey, L. M. (2014), *The Visitor: André Palmeiro and the Jesuits in Asia*, Cambridge, Mass.
Delumeau, Jean (1977), *Catholicism between Luther and Voltaire*, trans. J. Moiser, London

Dickens, A. G. (1968), *The Counter Reformation*, London

Forster, M. (2007), *Catholic Revival in the Age of Baroque: Religious Identity in Southwest Germany, 1550–1750*, Cambridge

Headley, John M. and Tomaro, John B. eds (1988), *San Carlo Borromeo: Catholic Reform and Ecclesiastical Politics in the Second Half of the Sixteenth Century*, Washington, DC

* Hsia, R. Po-chia (2005), *The World of Catholic Renewal, 1540–1770*, 2nd edn, Cambridge

Hsia, R. Po-chia (2010), *A Jesuit in the Forbidden City: Matteo Ricci 1552–1610*, Oxford

Luebke, David M. ed. (1999), *The Counter Reformation: The Essential Readings*, Oxford

McClure, Julia (2016), *The Franciscan Invention of the New World*, London

O'Malley, John W. (2000), *Trent and All That: Renaming Catholicism in the Early Modern Era*, Cambridge, Mass.

O'Malley, John W. (2013), *Trent: What Happened at the Council*, Cambridge, Mass.

Thornton, John (1984), 'The Development of an African Catholic Church in the Kingdom of Kongo, 1491–1750', *The Journal of African History*, 25, 147–67

Vlam, Grace A. H. (1979), 'The Portrait of S. Francis Xavier in Kobe', *Zeitschrift für Kunstgeschichte*, 42(1), 48–60

Wandel, Lee P. (2007), 'Reformation and the Visual Arts', in: R. Po-chia Hsia (ed.), *The Cambridge History of Christianity*, vol. 6, Cambridge, 345–70

## (C) Web resources

Andrea Pozzo, 'The Altar of St Ignatious Loyola at the Church of Il Gesù, Rome' (1690s), WGA: <http://www.wga.hu/art/p/pozzo/>

'The Canons and Decrees of the Council of Trent', HHTP: <http://history.hanover.edu/texts/trent.html>

'Extracts from the Spiritual Exercises of Ignatius Loyola', IHSP: <http://www.fordham.edu/halsall/source/loyola-spirex.asp>

Jesuit Historiography Online. Open access resource. <http://referenceworks.brillonline.com/browse/jesuit-historiography-online>

St Francis Xavier, 'Letter from Japan to the Society of Jesus at Goa' (1551), IHSP: <http://www.fordham.edu/halsall/mod/1551xavier3.html>

The USF Ricci Institute for Chinese-Western Cultural History <http://www.ricci.usfca.edu/>

# Religious culture in early modern Europe

*Peter Marshall*

## Confessional Europe

The principal outcome of the Reformations of the sixteenth century was that Europeans became, and were to remain, deeply divided in matters of religion (cf. chapters on 'The long Reformation' above). The religious warfare of the later sixteenth and early seventeenth centuries, along with some unpredictable dynastic developments, saw the religious frontiers change several times. But with the conclusion of the Thirty Years War in 1648 the religious map had more or less stabilized. The Italian peninsula, the kingdoms of Spain, Portugal and France, the Southern Netherlands and much of Southern Germany, along with the bulk of the territories governed by the Habsburgs, remained within, or had returned to the Catholic fold. The Scandinavian kingdoms and northern Germany were solidly Lutheran. Reformed or Calvinist Protestantism was dominant in the British Isles (though not Ireland), the Netherlands, and in pockets in Switzerland, France, Germany and parts of Eastern Europe.

As religious divisions had stabilized, they also clarified. In the later sixteenth and seventeenth centuries, all the rival religious groupings made efforts to underline what was distinctive (and uniquely true) about their own version of Christianity. Members of the various churches were now expected to know what their own Church taught, and why the doctrines of the rival Churches were wrong-headed or heretical. The result was a phenomenon known to historians as 'confessionalism' or 'confessional Christianity'. Not to be confused with the Catholic practice of confession to a priest, the process here refers to the adoption, and close identification with, a confession of faith – a defined body of doctrinal propositions. For Lutherans, this was usually the Augsburg Confession of 1530 and the Book of Concord agreed by Lutheran cities and territories in 1580 (Web resources). For Catholics, the Decrees of the Council of Trent fulfilled this function, and for the Reformed, the so-called Helvetic Confessions of 1536 and 1566, as well as the statements of Calvinist orthodoxy agreed at the Synod of Dordrecht in the Netherlands in 1619 (Schilling 1995). Of course, not all lay Christians had a firm grasp of every doctrinal nuance, but increasingly they knew that they were Lutherans, Catholics or Calvinists: 'ordinary people were beginning to own the religious labels' (MacCulloch 2003, 338). Markers of religious difference sprang up in numerous aspects of European cultural life, extending even to the measurement of time. In 1582, Pope Gregory XIII, drawing on the latest scientific advice, decreed a calendar reform to correct the errors of the ancient Julian Calendar, which made the year slightly too long. Catholic Europe rapidly adopted the Gregorian Calendar, but Protestant states held aloof, most abandoning the Julian Calendar only around 1700, and in the case of Britain and Sweden, not till the 1750s. (Orthodox Russia kept the old calendar into the twentieth century.)

Increasing confessionalism was not a purely religious or spiritual phenomenon, but also a political one, linked to the development of European states. From the 1970s, German historians Heinz Schilling and Wolfgang Reinhard developed the concept of 'CONFESSIONALIZATION' to refer to the process by which both Protestant and Catholic rulers sought to create more unified, obedient and 'modern' societies through identifying closely with a particular confession, increasing state control over the administration of the Church, and encouraging a fusion of piety and patriotism among their subjects (Lotz-Heumann 2008).

It is harder to detect a pattern of confessionalization among the Orthodox Churches of Eastern Europe. This is partly because Orthodoxy has always been wary of precise doctrinal formulations, preferring to enshrine its understanding of truth in liturgy,

**Figure III.9** A late seventeenth-century Russian icon of Mary, the Mother of God. Orthodoxy rejects three-dimensional religious imagery as forbidden by the Ten Commandments. 'Bogmater Tichvinskaya' [Tichvine Mother of God] (Russian icon, later 1600s). © Murray Warner Collection of Oriental Art, MWR34.9.

and in the veneration of icons of Christ and the saints (Figure III.9). It is also because in the centuries after the fall of Constantinople in 1453, the ancient heartlands of Orthodoxy came under Turkish rule. The Sultans allowed their Christian subjects freedom of worship, but the PATRIARCH in Constantinople was politically subservient. In these circumstances, the independent Grand Duchy of Muscovy (Russia) became an increasingly important centre of Orthodoxy, and its Tsar was able in 1589 to persuade the Orthodox world to recognize Moscow as the seat of another Patriarch. Although the Orthodox Churches were largely unaffected by the doctrinal controversies of the 'western' Reformations, they manifested their own internal divisions. In the mid-seventeenth century, an attempt by the Patriarch Nikon to bring the rituals of Russian Orthodoxy more in line with those of its Greek counterpart provoked furious resistance from groups of 'Old Believers'. Peter the Great's further reforms in the eighteenth century led Old Believers to regard him as the ANTICHRIST. The religious complexion of Eastern Europe was further complicated from the late sixteenth century by the decision of some Orthodox Churches – in the Ukraine, Romania, Slovakia and elsewhere – to accept the leadership of the Pope. These churches (known to their opponents as 'Uniates') kept, and continue to keep, their traditional forms of worship, and non-Latin customs such as clerical marriage.

## Reform of popular religion

At the heart of confessionalization was something historians term 'social discipline' – a drive by both political and ecclesiastical authorities to regulate more closely the moral and cultural behaviour of ordinary subjects, and get them to conform to official and territorial norms. In the process, local and customary expressions of religious identity – such as the riotous festivity in the carnival season preceding LENT – often came under attack. In this area, recent historians have tended to emphasize not so much the differences between the Protestant and Catholic Reformations, as the similarities of aims and approach: a common drive to require the laity to attend church services, educate them in right belief, particularly through the use of CATECHISMS, and eradicate popular 'superstition'. Both Catholic and Protestant territories witnessed a new emphasis on the education of the clergy as a means of delivering these ends. It has even been claimed that it was only in the era of Reformation and Counter-Reformation that European society, or at least rural society, became meaningfully Christian for the first time, as ancient half-pagan ways of seeing the world were swept aside in a process of parallel 'Christianization' (Delumeau 1977). This may be to take things too far: to deny the label 'Christian' to the popular religion of the late middle ages is to adopt an anachronistic standard of definition ('Church and people at the close of the Middle Ages' in Part III).

The success of reformers in changing popular belief-systems was slow and distinctly patchy. In 1662, a full century after the close of the Council of Trent, a diocesan statute from the Archbishopric of Cologne complained about lay people's trust in astrological predictions, interpretation of dreams, and magical use of amulets, saints' names and relics 'for purposes they could not possess inherently or in accordance with the will of God' (Greyerz 2008, 42–3). In areas affected by the Protestant Reformation, which Max Weber regarded as an agent of modern rationality leading to a 'disenchantment' of the world (Weber 2001, 61), scholars now find a religious culture saturated by the supernatural, alive with signs and portents, and the presence of angels and demons. Officially, mainstream Protestantism held that miracles had ceased in the world after the time of the apostles. But, at both elite and popular levels, the intense Protestant interest in divine PROVIDENCE could serve a very similar function. There is also much evidence of continued reliance on quasi-magical rituals to ward off evil or cure disease, of belief in ghosts and poltergeists, or in the sacred significance of particular times, days or seasons (Thomas 1971; cf. 'Witchcraft and magic' in Part V).

It would be wrong, however, to see the relationship between official Protestantism and popular religious culture as a purely antagonistic one. Protestantism proved capable of generating its own recognizably confessional but genuinely popular forms of religious expression. In seventeenth-century England, for example, strongly anti-Catholic and nationalist sentiments came together in annual popular commemorations of the 1605 Gunpowder Plot. Seventeenth- and eighteenth-century Germany saw much interest in stories about how images of Martin Luther had apparently been miraculously preserved from destruction by fire – an indication of genuine popular regard for the memory of the great reformer, but also of a mindset showing 'unmistakable traces of the Catholic cult of the saints' (Scribner 1987, 328).

## Pluralism and toleration

An almost universal result of the upheavals and vicissitudes of the Reformation was the presence of religious minorities. Such minorities challenged a basic assumption of early modern rulers: that political unity and stability depended on religious uniformity and that God's wrath awaited communities with heretics in their midst. One response to the problem was persecution, most famously perhaps in the St Bartholomew's Massacre of August 1572, in which thousands of French HUGUENOTS were killed with at least the tacit approval of the crown. Persecution was sometimes remarkably successful. The watchfulness of various Catholic INQUISITIONS, for example, ensured that by the end of the sixteenth century, the territories of Italy, Spain and Portugal were largely free of Protestant sympathizers.

Both Catholic and Protestant authorities were hugely intolerant of the free-thinking radicals usually identified by the generic label of ANABAPTISTS. These groups had their origins in Germany and Switzerland in the first phase of the Reformation, but rapidly rejected the leadership of 'magisterial' reformers like Luther and Zwingli in favour of an eclectic theology often rooted in what was believed to be the direct inspiration of the Holy Spirit. The radicals were intensely anti-institutional and anticlerical, and their beliefs often had a sharply ESCHATOLOGICAL edge. It was no accident, however, that they were principally identified by their opposition to infant baptism, for this underlined their rejection of a fundamental principle of early modern thinking, the coexistence and interconnectedness of ecclesiastical and civil society. Membership of Anabaptist groups was on the opt-in principle of adult baptism, and at the same time, believers opted out of the obligations of wider society: they refused military service, for example, and would not take the oaths that under-pinned citizenship, membership of GUILDS, and a host of other social undertakings ('Schleitheim Confession' of 1527: Web resources). These literally anti-social views, combined with the fright caused by a violent takeover of the German city of Münster by Dutch Anabaptists in 1534–35, led to the execution of hundreds of Anabaptists in both Catholic and Protestant areas of Germany, Switzerland and Austria in the mid-sixteenth century. Pockets of the movement survived longer in Eastern Europe, such as the Hutterites – followers of the Austrian preacher Jakob Hutter (d. 1536), who taught the communal ownership of property. In the eighteenth and nineteenth century, these and other Anabaptists emigrated to the United States, where some of their descendants still practice an austere life of separation from corrupting worldly society.

Not all religious minorities could be persecuted out of existence, or driven beyond the boundaries of the state. Some territories attempted to preserve the fiction that only one religion was practised within its boundaries. Religious nonconformists might be tacitly permitted to cross the border on Sundays into a neighbouring state of a different confession, what was called in Germany *Auslauf* (running out). Thus, Lutherans in Habsburg-controlled Silesia could cross for worship into Saxony, while Catholics in the Calvinist Palatinate could attend MASS in the neighbouring bishopric of Speyer. Another expedient was to allow places of dissident worship unofficially, on condition that they gave no indication from the outside of being a church. In Irish towns, for example, unobtrusive Catholic 'mass houses' proliferated in back streets. In the Netherlands, the large minority of Dutch Catholics could worship in clandestine churches or *schuilkerken* – chapels which could be quite elaborate on the inside, but from the street gave the appearance of ordinary merchants' houses (Figure III.10).

In some 'bi-confessional' towns and cities of the Holy Roman Empire – such as Ulm, Donauwörth, Ravensburg and Augsburg – the balance of forces was such that neither confession was able to force the other to go about its business in an underhand and skulking manner. Here, Lutherans and Catholics competed to advertise their presence in the public spaces of the town, using 'multimedia' forms of religious communication, such as singing, processions, satiric rituals and jokes. Possession of a town's most ancient and imposing church was often a source of contention, the solution to which was sometimes to share its use. To the scrupulous, this could seem

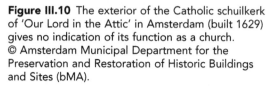

**Figure III.10** The exterior of the Catholic schuilkerk of 'Our Lord in the Attic' in Amsterdam (built 1629) gives no indication of its function as a church. © Amsterdam Municipal Department for the Preservation and Restoration of Historic Buildings and Sites (bMA).

a kind of blasphemy, and the Papacy issued several decrees against the sharing of churches in the early seventeenth century. The practice was nonetheless widespread, though hardly indicative of a modern-style ecumenism: the tightest of civic regulations controlled when and how each confession could use a *Simultankirche*, with the other side looking out for the slightest evidence of infringement.

Religious toleration was normally a characteristic of small or politically fragmented states, but one of Western Europe's most powerful monarchies bucked the trend early. In France, several decades of intermittent religious warfare starting in the 1560s failed either to eradicate the Huguenot minority or to establish it as the majority faith. In consequence, Henry IV issued the Edict of Nantes in 1598, reluctantly inscribing into law the right of Protestants to live and worship peacefully (Box 1). In the following century, the Peace of Westphalia (1648) regulated the coexistence of all three mainstream confessions in the Holy Roman Empire and the English Parliament passed an Act of Toleration (1689), belatedly recognizing the religious pluralism that was a consequence of the upheavals accompanying the mid-century civil wars (Web resources). It allowed Protestant Nonconformists (including the Quakers, who relied on an 'inner light' of religious illumination rather than external authority) places of worship alongside Anglican ones.

It is important to distinguish between toleration and tolerance. The latter is a fundamentally modern attitude, which implies an acceptance of diversity for its own sake, and an attempt to understand opposing points of view. Only few early modern

Box 1

'VI. And in order to leave no occasion for troubles or differences between our subjects, we have permitted, and herewith permit, those of the said religion called Reformed to live and abide in all the cities and places of this our kingdom . . . without being annoyed, molested, or compelled to do anything in the matter of religion contrary to their consciences . . .

'IX. We also permit those of the said religion to make and continue the exercise of the same in all villages and places of our dominion where it was established by them and publicly enjoyed several and divers times in the year 1597 . . .

'XIII. We very expressly forbid to all those of the said religion its exercise . . . in this our kingdom and lands of our dominion, otherwise than in the places permitted and granted by the present edict.

'XIV. It is forbidden as well to perform any function of the said religion in our court or retinue . . . or in our city of Paris, or within five leagues of the said city . . .'

(Edict of Nantes; Web resources)

Henry IV's Edict of Nantes (1598), granting toleration of religion to Huguenots: note the circumscribed and grudging nature of the concessions.

people (like the French theologian Sebastian Castellio or the English philosopher John Locke) advanced such ideas; the vast majority held that there could be only one truth. Dissenters were at best put up with for grudging, pragmatic reasons: because peace was usually seen as preferable to religious civil war. Toleration was a social practice, rather than an attitude of mind (Kaplan 2007) and it did not 'rise' in a straightforward line from sixteenth-century fanaticism towards a more willing and principled acceptance of difference by the later seventeenth century. In some respects, the movement was in the opposite direction. As 'confessional' identities became more developed, communities could move further apart from each other. In the Netherlands, for example, intermarriage between Catholics and Protestants was actually less common at the end of the seventeenth century than at its beginning. Some of the most intense episodes of religious violence and intolerance are also to be found at the end of the seventeenth century and beginning of the eighteenth. In France, the government of Louis XIV brought several years of harassment of the Huguenot minority to a climax with a 'Revocation' of the Edict of Nantes in 1685: Protestant ministers were to leave the country; ordinary Huguenots to adopt Catholicism (though some 300,000 fled into exile over the following decades). Naturally, many conversions were no more than skin deep, and scores were executed as 'relapsed' heretics. In the far south of France, a bitter Huguenot revolt, the War of the Cévennes, was bloodily repressed between 1702 and 1711. Religious violence thus continued to be a feature of Europe in the 'Age of the Enlightenment' (Kaplan 2015). Only towards the end of the eighteenth century did religious pluralism become generally accepted in the major monarchies: the 1770s and 1780s saw legislation granting (some) civil rights to Catholics in England and Prussia, to Huguenots in France, and to Lutherans, Calvinists and Orthodox Christians in the Habsburg territories. These rights often fell short of full freedom of worship, and official intolerance remained the norm in other places, such as Spain.

## New forms of piety

The 'confessional age' saw the establishment of firm religious orthodoxies, and their internalization by many of Europe's peoples, but religious creativity did not come to an end after the first phases of Reformation and Counter-Reformation. In fact, the rigid formalizations of religion within the structures and formularies of the official churches created their own counter-currents: a desire to discover renewed, more spiritual and authentic forms of Christian life. In some Protestant areas this took the form of a conviction that the Reformation had not gone far enough, particularly in transforming lives and morals in a 'godly' direction. In the early seventeenth-century Netherlands, there were repeated calls for *Nadere Reformatie*, or 'Further Reformation', with Calvinist ministers penning tracts advocating more ascetic lifestyles and serious personal piety. In England, the analogous movement is generally known as 'Puritanism'. Puritans disliked many of the ceremonies of the Church of England, which they saw as only 'half-reformed', and they despised the 'profane' culture of the multitude, who frequented alehouses, and played football on the Sabbath. They also practised an intense religious introspection – a regular examination of the state of their souls to convince themselves that they were indeed of 'the ELECT', those God had predestined to eternal life with him in heaven (see Box 2).

In the later sixteenth and earlier seventeenth centuries, Puritanism was largely contained within the Church of England. After the civil wars, Puritans departed to form their own 'Nonconformist' churches, both within England and in its colonies in America. Their departure allowed the Church of England to adopt a more uniformly 'Anglican' character, with unashamed use of some ceremonies and rituals adapted from the medieval church. In the eighteenth century, however, the perceived formalism of Anglican worship led to a further round of religious renewal, the METHODIST movement inspired by the preacher John Wesley (1703–91). Wesley envisaged Methodism as a form of personal evangelical religion to be practised within the Church of England, but by the end of the century, it had developed its own organization and had become a real mass movement, making significant inroads into areas, such as North Wales, that had been little touched by earlier waves of reformation (Hempton 2005).

German Lutheranism was not untouched by calls for spiritual renewal. A feeling that the faith had become ossified, too bound up in formularies and doctrines, was

'Who knoweth how often he doth offend? For my conscience doth chide and accuse me continually, both for sins of omission and sins of commission, not only sins of buying and selling but my sins of omitting of many good duties. . . . And although this accusing conscience is as it were a little hell on earth, that I can be nowhere, nor can go about anything, no not a look nor a thought but still there is a checking or chiding within him [*sic*], yet I see and find abundance of God's mercies to me in this, in that the Lord will not let me sleep and snort in any sin and so go smoothly and quiet to hell (as others do) but my God lays as it were thorns and briars in my way. O great mercy!'

*(Wallington 2007, 165–6; spelling modernized)*

Extract from the diary of the London Puritan craftsman Nehemiah Wallington (May 1642), giving an indication of the fine balance of anxiety and reassurance that pious Puritans found in their religion.

expressed by the Frankfurt pastor Phillip Jakob Spener (1635–1705), who established *collegia pietatis*, regular devotional meetings of the pious, in Frankfurt in the 1670s. Spener's *Pia Desideria* (1675) called for a greater emphasis on the Bible and a practical, individual experience of piety in place of the strict Lutheran orthodoxy with which 'Pietists' were soon in open conflict. PIETISM spread rapidly across the Scandinavian and German Lutheran world. Remarkably, it also achieved a creative synthesis with a surviving fragment of medieval dissident religion. In 1722, a remnant of Hussites from Moravia took refuge with the pietist nobleman, Nikolaus von Zinzendorf, on his ESTATES in Saxony. Zinzendorf reconstituted the group as a community of brothers – the Moravian Brethren. Although formally within the Lutheran Church, the Moravians (like the Methodists whom they influenced) operated as a separate grouping. Filled with a sense of evangelical zeal, they were the instigators of the first concerted Protestant missionary effort of the early modern era, dispatching missionaries in the 1730s to the Caribbean, North America and Greenland. Taken together, Pietists, Methodists and Moravians represent a strong challenge to the view that the eighteenth century saw a universal relaxing of religious fervour, a rationalist religion of the Enlightenment.

The appearance of new religious movements was not confined to the Protestant world. In the seventeenth century, Catholic Europe, and particularly France, was periodically convulsed by the phenomenon of JANSENISM, a kind of 'Catholic Puritanism'. Its origins lay in an attack launched by the Dutch theologian Cornelius Jansen (1585–1638) on the JESUIT Luis de Molina, for teaching that God's fore-knowledge of human good works did not take away their free character, thus granting humans an important role in their own salvation. Jansenism, like Calvinism, had a very negative view of the human capacity for goodness, teaching that God's GRACE was completely unmerited, and emphasizing the need for personal holiness and intense study of scripture and the Church Fathers. Perhaps its most important convert was the theologian and mathematician, Blaise Pascal (1623–62), whose famous *Pensées* contain arguments for faith, as opposed to philosophical reason, as a means of knowing God (Web resources). Politically, French Jansenism tended towards 'Gallicanism', the view that the French Church should be independent in practical matters from the control of Rome. Not surprisingly, popes condemned the movement, and Louis XIV too found it politically suspect. In 1709, direct action was taken against the Jansenist stronghold of Port-Royal, a Cistercian nunnery outside of Paris: the nuns were dispersed, and the buildings razed. A streak of Jansenism nonetheless continued to run through French, and other European Catholicism throughout the eighteenth century (Doyle 2000). Jansenism was too intellectual and too morally austere ever to become a significant popular movement, but its presence serves as a reminder against ever viewing early modern Catholicism as a 'monolith'.

## Assessment: privatization of faith?

There is very little to suggest any process of 'secularization' in Europe before the later eighteenth century, in the sense of a growing indifference about religious truth, or a dramatic social and political marginalization of the Christian Churches. Nonetheless, the role of religion was changing towards the end of our period. The failure of the Reformations to impose or preserve religious uniformity, and the fact, across much of Europe, of practical religious pluralism meant that the confessionalization project – the attempt to make public adherence to a particular form of Christianity into the principal marker of political belonging – was destined eventually to run out of steam. At the same time, social changes, and the desire of educated elites to distance themselves from popular belief and culture, reduced the leverage of shared religious meaning across society as a whole. By the early eighteenth century, fashionable society was exhibiting a tendency to scoff at religious 'enthusiasm', and a scepticism about manifestations of the miraculous or the providential. A few intellectuals were abandoning orthodox Christianity altogether, either for atheism, or for the religious philosophy known as 'DEISM', which denied that God ever intervened in the world He had created. It is possible also that in the course of the eighteenth century, the gradual recession of unpredictable threats to human existence, in the form of famines and epidemic disease, may have blunted a collective obsession with identifying and then carrying out the will of an unpredictable God. In these circumstances, piety gradually became a more private matter, and less a priority for the community's public policy. But as the countless revivals of the eighteenth and nineteenth centuries were to show, religion was a far from spent force in European society as the Age of the Enlightenment dawned.

## Discussion themes

1. What should we understand by the phrase 'confessional Christianity'?
2. How antagonistic was the relationship between reforming movements and popular religious culture?
3. What were the principal obstacles to religious toleration and coexistence in the early modern period?

## Bibliography

### (A) Sources

Wallington, Nehemiah (2007), *The Notebooks of Nehemiah Wallington 1618–1654: A Selection*, ed. David Booy, Aldershot

### (B) Literature

Delumeau, Jean (1977), *Catholicism between Luther and Voltaire*, trans. J. Moiser, London

Dixon, C. Scott (2016), *The Church in the Early Modern Age*, London

Doyle, William (2000), *Jansenism: Catholic Resistance to Authority from the Reformation to the French Revolution*, Basingstoke

Greyerz, Kaspar von (2008), *Religion and Culture in Early Modern Europe*, trans. Thomas Dunlop, Oxford

Hempton, David (2005), *Methodism: Empire of the Spirit*, New Haven

Kaplan, Benjamin (2007), *Divided by Faith: Religious Conflict and the Practice of Toleration in Early Modern Europe*, Cambridge, Mass.

Kaplan, Benjamin (2015), *Cunegonde's Kidnapping: A Story of Religious Conflict in the Age of Enlightenment*, New Haven and London

Lotz-Heumann, Ute (2008), 'Confessionalization', in: *Reformation and Early Modern Europe: A Guide to Research*, ed. David M. Whitford, Kirksville, Mo.

MacCulloch, Diarmaid (2003), *Reformation: Europe's House Divided 1490–1700*, London

Schilling, Heinz (1995), 'Confessional Europe', in: T. A. Brady *et al.* (eds), *Handbook of European History 1400–1600*, 2 vols, Leiden

Scribner, Robert (1987), *Popular Culture and Popular Movements in Reformation Germany*, London

Thomas, Keith (1971), *Religion and the Decline of Magic: Studies in Popular Beliefs in Sixteenth- and Seventeenth-Century England*, London

Weber, Max (2001), *The Protestant Ethic and the Spirit of Capitalism*, trans. Talcott Parsons, Abingdon

**(C) Web resources**

'The Augsburg Confession, 1530': <http://bookofconcord.org/augsburgconfession.php>

'The Edict of Nantes, 1598': <http://www.historyguide.org/earlymod/nantes.html>

'Our Lord in the Attic: Seventeenth-century Catholic clandestine church in Amsterdam': <http://nl.wikipedia.org/wiki/Schuilkerk>

'The Schleitheim Confession' (1527): <http://www.anabaptists.org/history/the-schleitheim-confession.html>

'The Act of Toleration, 1689': http://www.jacobite.ca/documents/1689toleration.htm

'Blaise Pascal, *Penseés*, 1660', in: *Modern History Sourcebook*: <https://sourcebooks.fordham.edu/mod/1660pascal-pensees.asp>

# Jews and Muslims

*Henry J. Cohn*

Jews and Muslims were the largest non-Christian groups with whom Europeans came into immediate contact. Alongside Christian heretics, peoples in distant lands, witches, gypsies and others marginal to society, they were the main representatives of the 'other' against whom both ruling elites and ordinary people defined and distinguished themselves ('Marginals and deviants' in Part II). Because of persecution and expulsions, the members of both these faiths experienced large-scale migration. Medieval Jews had been distributed throughout Europe, with concentrations in the Iberian peninsula and Central Europe. By 1800 the majority lived in Poland or under Islamic rule in the Ottoman Empire. Muslim culture had flourished in medieval Spain, which became the western bulwark of Christian Europe against Islam, but by the seventeenth century the Muslims had been forcibly converted or expelled. On the eastern front, the Muslim Ottomans had advanced into the Balkans, where they ruled over Christians, Jews and immigrant Muslims ('European relations with the Ottoman World' in Part IV; Tolan et al. 2013).

## The Jewish experience

Until the twelfth century, Jews were relatively well integrated into Christian society, especially in Spain and Italy. Instances of violence were short and did not impair the general attitude of coexistence; the undoubted religious antagonisms did not usually interfere with economic and cultural cooperation (Elukin 2007). While Jews often lived in separate quarters in towns, as did many crafts, only in the sixteenth century – beginning with Venice in 1516 – did GHETTOS behind walls emerge, and then by no means everywhere. Points of contact between the Jewish and general populations included not only the ubiquitous peddlers but Jewish physicians, whose services were prized by rich and poor alike. Although not generally allowed to own landed property in the Middle Ages, Jews had engaged in local and long-distance trade and many crafts, as well as the money lending with which they are usually associated (Box 1). Only when the GUILDS became more powerful and popular resentment grew, especially from the BLACK DEATH onwards, were Jews gradually restricted to secondhand trades and lending to the poor. Without political rights, they were nevertheless allowed their own courts and a degree of self-government by elected, though oligarchic, councils (Bell 2008, 95–108). Their exceptionally high degree of literacy meant that some were essential intermediaries in transmitting various classical texts via Arabic

Jews led a separate existence because of the religious requirements of their own faith as well as of the Church. They could not eat meat slaughtered by non-Jewish butchers and they also needed separate bakeries. Among their buildings which have survived the ravages of time, notably in Prague, are synagogues (in the Gothic style of churches), academies of learning as in Troyes, ritual baths for both men and women, and cemeteries with informative tombstones. Jews spoke their own languages, Yiddish or Ladino (local dialects of German or Spanish mingled with Hebrew words), which they then took to Poland and the Ottoman Empire respectively, where Slavic or Arabic/Turkish elements were added (Elukin 2007).

translations. Jews also participated in RENAISSANCE literary, musical and scientific endeavours (Bell 2008, 175–79). A leading Italian philosopher, Giovanni Pico della Mirandola (1463–94), leaned heavily on the MYSTICISM of Jewish Kabbalah. Few Jews published works other than in Hebrew, but Christian scholars studying Hebrew biblical texts were dependent on Jewish translators and interpreters. Jewish culture overlapped with that of European society while not being accepted as part of it.

Papal policy allowed Jews to practise their religion, but restricted their dress and behaviour to separate them from Christians. It was expected that these witnesses-despite-themselves to the truth of Christianity would soon embrace voluntary conversion and herald the Second Coming of the Messiah. However, in late medieval times the attitude of some rulers that the Jews no longer served their fiscal purposes combined with popular economic and religious resentments, themselves fuelled by economic pressures and fierce preaching by itinerant friars, led to expulsions: from England in 1290, France on several occasions until 1394, and thereafter from many cities in Germany. Northern Italy received Jews fleeing from the south of the country and from Germany, while larger numbers left Germany for Poland. Apart from the traditional beliefs of Christianity – that the Jews killed the Saviour and were agents of the Devil – rabble-rousing sermons, folk tales, mystery plays and, later, print spread grotesque false charges that Jews desecrated hosts and killed Christian children to use their blood for ritual or medicinal purposes.

The fiercest persecutions, in the Iberian peninsula, had the widest repercussions. Antisemitic pogroms in Castile and other Spanish kingdoms from the late fourteenth century forced mass conversions. Fears that CONVERSOS (considered genuine Christians whatever the circumstances of conversion) would be influenced by other Jews to become heretics led to the establishment of the Spanish INQUISITION in 1480 to investigate *conversos* suspected of Jewish beliefs and practices and then to the expulsion in 1492 of all Jews who would not convert. Of perhaps 200,000–300,000 remaining Jews, some 100,000 now converted, doubling the number of 'New Christians', whereas outside the Iberian peninsula only handfuls of Jews converted before the eighteenth century. Nearer 40,000 than 200,000 (the figures are much disputed: Kamen 2014, 27–30; Alpert 2008, 28–30) emigrated with great hardship and loss of life to Portugal, North Africa, the Ottoman Empire and Italy, while in the late sixteenth century many moved on to the Ottoman Empire. Already in 1500 Jews had accounted for less than 1 per cent of the European population.

Torture and false testimony were employed in some of the Inquisition's tribunals, so that the true extent of continued Judaizing is hard to gauge. Nevertheless, New Christians and their descendants rose to high office in Church and state and high rank in the nobility, despite a patchy attempt in the sixteenth century to impose 'purity of blood' (freedom from *converso* ancestry) as a condition of office; this early attempt at a racialist policy had limited effect in Castile and none in the Aragonese kingdoms (Amelang 2013, 100–4).

In Germany Martin Luther pronounced on the Jews, but largely as a byproduct of his attack on the Church. His hostility towards Judaism as a legalistic faith which denied the evangelical message of Christ was unwavering, but his views on contemporary Jews switched from condescending benevolence to militant contempt. *That Jesus Christ was Born a Jew* (1523) argued that the Catholic Church had concealed the true Gospel from the Jews, and that once they heard Luther's own teachings they would convert. It soon became apparent that this had not happened. His invective against them escalated until *On the Jews and their Lies* (1543; Web resources) expounded that the Messiah had already come and Jewish teachings were blasphemous. Luther recommended the expulsion of Jews or at least the suppression of their books and right to worship, the burning of synagogues, destruction of their houses, and forced labour for their young. Such measures foreshadowed Nazi policies, but Luther should not be held accountable for the later use of his words to support genocide. His insulting tone towards Jews scarcely differed from that towards his other perceived enemies: the Papacy, the Turks and radical Reformers, or from the general level of sixteenth-century polemics ('The long Reformation: Lutheran' in Part III). Most Christian religious leaders were similarly critical of Jewish beliefs and all pressed for their conversion, with only isolated voices defending their cultural heritage or questioning popular stereotypes. One was the Lutheran Andreas Osiander in 1530: 'Either the Jews are slaughtering innocent Christians most cruelly or the Christians are slaughtering innocent Jews most shamefully' (Kammerling in Bell and Burnett 2006, 236).

Theological arguments rarely influenced the ruling princes of Germany, whether Catholic or Protestant, who tolerated or persecuted the Jews according to the balance of their own economic needs and the pressures of popular and clerical agitation. The Emperor Charles V (1519–58) protected the Jews in the Empire because the Protestant princes and Luther often attacked them, but as King of Spain he supported the work of the Inquisition against *conversos*, as against Muslim converts and Protestants. By 1600 there were fewer cases of blood libel, perhaps because Protestant teaching cast doubt on the attention given to blood in Catholic worship, but the libel was revived in Germany by Johann Eisenmenger's *Judaism Unmasked* (1700) and has reappeared periodically in European countries and the Middle East to the present day (Figure III.11).

The Counter-Reformation Papacy adopted a restrictive policy towards Jews, but failed to implement it effectively. Paul IV's papal bull *Cum nimis absurdum* (1555) aimed at rapid conversions; besides harsh economic restrictions, it required Jews to live in a walled ghetto in Rome. Successive popes and the prelates of Christendom were erratic in enforcing the measure and had little success in extending ghettos to cities outside the papal states. In any case, while ghettos may have produced overcrowding and increased poverty, they also afforded Jews greater protection and helped to foster their communal solidarity. Meanwhile popes often treated MARRANOS – Spanish *conversos* – as renegade heretics subject to the full rigour of the law.

In Portugal the Portuguese and exiled Spanish Jews and *conversos* were able to live relatively unhindered despite the mass forced conversion of 1497 and the establishment of a Portuguese Inquisition (1536). However, once Spain conquered Portugal in 1580, persecution revived there, and New Christians were induced to migrate back to Castile where their commercial skills were appreciated. Despite bouts of renewed pressure, by 1640 (when Portugal regained its independence) Portuguese New Christian agents accounted for half of the extensive war debts of the Castilian Crown. Only new efforts by the Inquisition for the next hundred years impelled many of these *conversos* to join their relatives in southern France, Amsterdam, Hamburg, London, the Caribbean and North America.

The *conversos* were important intermediaries between Christian and Jewish society. The vast majority, especially those forcibly converted in Spain down to the early sixteenth century, were probably absorbed into the Christian faith and did not retain any Jewish beliefs and practices. However, a few of them and a larger number of Portuguese New Christians, who enjoyed long periods under a lax regime, retained vestigial connections with the faith of their ancestors. When they migrated to Venice and other places in Italy, the Inquisition there also investigated tendencies towards Judaizing, but in the more tolerant environment of Protestant Northern Europe they were accepted as part of MERCANTILE society and were able to reconsider their religious allegiance. Often they gradually formed new communities and recovered their knowledge of Judaism. Some had an extensive grasp of both Christian and Jewish culture or, like the renowned philosopher Baruch Spinoza (1632–77; excommunicated by the Jewish community in Amsterdam), were remarkable freethinkers (Kaplan 2007, 319–24). Nevertheless, Portuguese Jews were among the most enthusiastic for the false Messiah Sabbatai Zevi during the years 1665–66. Living in the Ottoman Empire, his claims met with heightened interest – and then revulsion when he converted to Islam – among Christians, Jews and Muslims alike.

For centuries Jews fared best in Poland-Lithuania, where the kings, for their own fiscal advantage, had granted them extensive privileges since the thirteenth century.

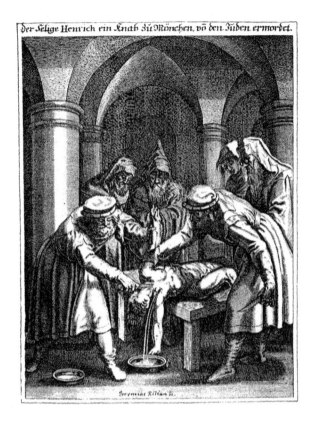

**Figure III.11** This engraving of an alleged ritual killing of a Christian boy by Jews in Munich in 1346 was made as late as 1714 for Matthäus Rader, Bavaria Sancta (German edn, 1714). 'Ritual Killing', Heinz Schreckenberg, *The Jews in Christian Art* (New York, 1996), 274.

From the sixteenth century Jews benefited from the general policy of toleration of faiths, when Poland had six major religious groups. Many of the Polish nobility who employed Jews as ESTATE managers protected them. Jewish numbers increased from about 30,000 in 1490 to 450,000 in 1648. Despite massacres for the next eight years of some 20,000 by Ukrainian Cossacks and others by Swedish and Russian invaders, they numbered *c*. 750,000 by 1750, perhaps half of the world's Jews and 7–8 per cent of Poland's population (Kaplan 2007, 325). In many small towns they formed separate largely autonomous communities parallel with the Christian ones. Their pyramid of elected governing COUNCILS and courts culminated in the national Council of the Four Lands (1580–1764), which represented their interests at the royal court and at parliamentary DIETS (Bell 2008, 106). However, after the late eighteenth-century PARTITIONS of Poland most Polish Jews came under the rule of the Russian tsars, who subjected them to economic restrictions, lengthy periods of military service and heavy taxation.

Meanwhile, from the later sixteenth century the fortunes of the Jews in Western and Central Europe improved somewhat. They may have benefited from European countries concentrating on religious and dynastic wars among themselves. While wars in Eastern Europe against the Ottomans made Jews suspects of treason and subject to temporary expulsions from Vienna and Habsburg, Hungary, scores of Jews were among the cosmopolitan entrepreneurs who financed and supplied the armies of both sides in the Thirty Years War (1618–48). Some developed into Court Jews who in peacetime provided rulers with luxury goods and acted as financial advisers and tax officials. They were also able to persuade rulers to settle small groups of Jews, as in the readmission of Jews to Brandenburg-Prussia in 1671. Popes and kings of England from William III (1689–1702) onwards were among those rulers who relied on Jewish bankers. The enforced migration of many Jews enabled them to play a major role in the international trade of Northern Europe, the Mediterranean and the New World. They were well placed to benefit from the economic advances of the later eighteenth century and to re-enter many manufactures once the hold of the guilds was reduced.

The cultural emancipation of the Jews soon followed, even if political emancipation was delayed beyond 1800. Inspired by the European Enlightenment, the Jewish Enlightenment (*Haskalah*) began in Germany in the mid-eighteenth century and spread eastwards. Jews were encouraged to study secular subjects and European languages, to adopt standard European dress and manners and to enter a wider range of occupations, both professional and commercial. Moses Mendelssohn (1726–89), a Jewish philosopher writing in German, represented Judaism as a non-dogmatic, rational faith open to modernity. He tried to improve the legal situation of the Jews and the relationship between Jews and Christians, arguing for Jewish tolerance and humanity. Jewish women were encouraged to have the same education as men, and some of them were prominent in the cultural SALONS of the eighteenth century. Yet even earlier the memoirs of Glückel of Hameln (1645–1719), a Hamburg business woman and mother of twelve, showed how Jewish women were able, while keeping their separate customs, to participate in the world of commerce (Glückel of Hameln 1962). The normalization of education for Jews was fostered by rulers like Joseph II in his edict of 1782. Governments were anxious to harness the talents of Jews for state purposes. The attitude of the French Revolution was to treat the Jews as citizens without special privileges: 'One must refuse everything to the Jews as a nation, and give everything to the Jews as individuals' (Count of Clermont-Tonnerre in 1789: Kaplan 2007, 329).

## The Muslim experience

In early modern Christendom, contact with Muslims was mainly confined to the lands of the Habsburgs in West and East, although the exceptions included several thousand captured slaves in Italy and c. 250,000 Muslims in Lithuania. Antagonism towards them, unlike that to the Jews, was both religious and military. The last Muslim-ruled outpost in Spain, Granada, was reconquered just before the expulsion of the Jews, and these events can be seen as linked aspects of a drive to ensure the political and religious unity of Spain, although such motives were not evident in statements by the monarchs. The Treaty of Granada (1492) did not require the conversion of the vanquished, but until their expulsion 120 years later Muslims and converted Moors in Spain were regarded as a fifth column aiding the Ottoman foe of Christendom. Granada had 500,000 Muslims, the kingdom of Valencia about 160,000, or 30 per cent of its population, the other regions smaller but substantial numbers (Rawlings 2006, 72–3). Their thrift and sobriety, as well as their living apart, aroused resentment among the populace.

From 1499 royal and clerical pressure to convert was applied, which provoked rebellions. They gave the excuse for a measure in 1502 comparable to that of 1492 against the Jews, though as yet only in Castile, not Aragon with its greater local privileges. The Moors found it more difficult to leave and 50,000 were forced to convert, though most remained Muslim at heart and initially could observe aspects of their traditional culture privately. In 1526 Charles V passed laws attacking their customs, having extended forcible conversion to Aragon, but these measures were not enforced until after 1550, since the Moors contributed heavily to taxation. By 1566, coinciding with renewed Turkish advances in the Mediterranean, 92 per cent of all prosecutions by the Inquisition were against these MORISCOS or Moorish New Christians. (Rawlings 2006, 79). Even so, the forcible nature of their conversion was recognized, unlike in the case of the Jews, and they were initially treated not as heretics but as infidels with whom one should be patient (Kamen 2014, 160–70).

Renewed pressure from 1560 to conform in dress, customs and religious practice led to a major revolt in the largely Moorish mountainous Alpujarras region in Granada (1568–71). Major atrocities on both sides were followed by the resettlement of some 80,000 rebels in southern Castile, where previously the Moriscos had remained quiet. The problem was simply dispersed from Granada to other parts of Spain. In addition, the demographic advance of the Moriscos was seen as alarming. Thereafter the period of tolerance also ended in Aragon and Valencia, but attempts to make the converts into true Christians made little headway, unlike the case of many Jews who had conformed. From 1580 expulsion was discussed but not widely supported in government circles until the measure was passed in 1609. It was then justified on religious grounds but fortuitously helped to divert attention from the humiliating truce of that year with the Dutch rebels ('Dynastic politics, religious conflict and reason of state c. 1500–1650' in Part VI). By 1611 some 300,000 Moriscos had been expelled and over 10,000 were killed in rebellions. Valencia lost nearly one quarter of its population, mostly hard-working farmers valued by their noble landlords as cheap labour, and the economic effects in Castile were also considerable. A few thousand remained or later returned as New Christians, who were eventually left alone. Cardinal Richelieu of France called the expulsion 'the most barbarous act in human annals' (Kamen 2014, 173; Harvey 2005).

In South-eastern Europe the prejudiced view of Muslims which had occasionally surfaced in medieval times was exacerbated by the Ottoman conquest of Constantinople (1453) and subsequent advances through the Balkans, until by 1526 the sultan's forces occupied the greater part of the Hungarian plain. Whereas Islamic territory had receded in the West, it was advancing in the East. The propaganda of

Habsburg clerics and writers on Turkish affairs aimed to reverse this process. Sentiments about the Ottomans were mixed: they were admired as well as feared for their military courage and organization – not least the extensive use of captured Christian slaves – and the absolute power with which sultans like Suleyman the Magnificent (1520–66) raised and financed large armies (Figure III.12). Sultans kept the loyalty of conquered peoples by allowing religious toleration and a degree of self-government; Catholics, who were of the same faith as their Habsburg enemies, might be granted toleration but little autonomy. Commercial ties were eagerly sought with Istanbul by Venice and other trading nations and diplomatic links by all major powers (Goffman 2000).

While popular culture mocked the Turks, the clergy saw them as barbarian non-believers who destroyed and desecrated churches, practised a deviant sexuality and had animalistic customs. There was some justification in the charges of Ottoman barbarity towards soldiers and civilians in wartime as well as of venality and duplicity in diplomatic relations, but Europeans often behaved no better. The Turks had an equally jaundiced view of Christians in a conflict in which each side had both religious and political ambitions to conquer the other (Fichtner 2008, 12–37). Even at the turn of the eighteenth century the Viennese court preacher Abraham a Sancta Clara was not averse to prejudiced ORIENTALIST language (Box 2).

## Box 2

'What is the Turk? . . . He is a replica of the antichrist; he is a piece of a tyrant; he is an insatiable tiger; he is the damned assailant on the world; his cruelty is unlimited; he steals crowns without conscience . . . he is oriental dragon poison; he is the hound of hell unchained.'

(Abraham a Sancta Clara, 'Arise, Arise O Christians to Fight Against Muhammadan Error and [the] Turkish Hereditary Enemy'; Fichtner 2008, 61–62)

However, by now military fortunes had reversed. Already the long-lasting truce after 1606 had allowed Habsburg propaganda to subside from its heights when the sultan threatened Vienna in 1529. The second relief of the besieged city in 1683 brought great credit to the Emperor Leopold I and his European princely abettors. Most of Hungary was then reconquered within a few decades. Hostile opinions about the defeated enemy gave way to others already held by those seeking a more dispassionate view of the Muslim faith and peoples. While the old images did not completely disappear, in the Age of Enlightenment a more factual approach was adopted in assessing an enemy who no longer appeared to have devilish cunning and superhuman powers (Harper 2011). By the late eighteenth century, moreover, Russia had become the common enemy of the Habsburg and Ottoman empires. The Habsburg

**Figure III.12** The army of Suleyman the Magnificent laying siege to Vienna in 1529. TSM H.1524 Siege of Vienna by Suleyman I (1494–1566) the Magnificent, in 1529, from the 'Hunername' by Lokman, 1588 (gouache on paper), Islamic School, (16th century) / Topkapi Palace Museum, Istanbul, Turkey / Bridgeman Images.

lands began to approach other European countries in their trading activity with Istanbul and their taste for coffee and other Turkish exotica. The foundation in 1754 and rapid growth of the Oriental ACADEMY of Vienna boosted scholarly study of the East, which reached a high degree of impartiality in Joseph von Hammer-Purgstall's ten-volume *History of the Ottoman Empire* (1827–35). By contrast, many Western European authors followed Montesquieu's *The Spirit of the Laws* (1748) in employing the stereotype of Oriental despotism to condemn a supposedly corrupt and declining Ottoman Empire (Çirakman 2000).

## Assessment

During the early modern period, changes in political and economic circumstances and the displacement of religious fervour by reason of state in international relations led to the partial abandonment of old stereotypes. The Enlightenment encouraged more favourable attitudes towards both Jews and Muslims, but old prejudices still lurked in dark corners.

## Discussion themes

1. Account for the survival of the Jews as a separate people in early modern Europe.
2. Were Muslims hated mainly for fear of military attacks on Christendom?
3. Were Jews and Muslims 'marginal' to European society?

## Bibliography

### (A) Sources

Glückel of Hameln (1962), *The Life of Glückel of Hameln, 1646–1724*, ed./trans. Beth-Zion Abrahams, London

Schramm, Brooks and Stjerna, Kirsi I. eds (2012), *Martin Luther, the Bible, and the Jewish People: A Reader*, Minneapolis

### (B) Literature

Alpert, Michael (2008), *Secret Judaism and the Spanish Inquisition*, Nottingham

Amelang, James S. (2013), *Parallel Histories: Muslims and Jews in Inquisitorial Spain*, Baton Rouge, La.

* Bell, Dean P. (2008), *Jews in the Early Modern World*, Portsmouth

Bell, Dean P. and Burnett, Stephen eds (2006), *Jews, Judaism and the Reformation in Sixteenth-Century Germany*, Leiden

Çirakman, Asli (2002), *European Images of Ottoman Empire and Society from the Sixteenth Century to the Nineteenth*, New York

Elukin, Jonathan (2007), *Living Together, Living Apart: Rethinking Jewish-Christian Relations in the Middle Ages*, Princeton

Fichtner, Paula S. (2008), *Terror and Toleration: The Habsburg Empire Confronts Islam, 1526–1850*, London

* Goffman, Daniel (2000), *The Ottoman Empire and Early Modern Europe*, Cambridge

Harper, James G. ed. (2011), *The Turk and Islam in the Western Eye, 1450–1750: Visual Imagery before Orientalism*, Farnham

Harvey, Leonard P. (2005), *Muslims in Spain, 1500 to 1614*, Chicago

* Kamen, Henry (2014), *The Spanish Inquisition: An Historical Revision*, 4th edn, London

Kaplan, Benjamin J. (2007), *Divided by Faith: Religious Conflict and the Practice of Toleration in Early Modern Europe*, Cambridge, Mass.

Rawlings, Helen (2006), *The Spanish Inquisition*, Oxford

Ruderman, David (2010), *Early Modern Jewry: A New Cultural History*, Princeton

Schreckenberg, Heinz (1996), *The Jews in Christian Art*, New York

Tolan, John, Veinstein, Gilles and Laurens, Henry (2013), *Europe and the Islamic World*, Princeton

## (C) Web resources

'Internet Jewish History Sourcebook', IHSP: <https://sourcebooks.fordham.edu/
  halsall/jewish/jewishsbook.asp>
Martin Luther (1543), <http://www.jewishvirtuallibrary.org/martin-luther-quot-the-
  jews-and-their-lies-quot>

# PART IV

# THE WIDER WORLD

| | |
|---|---|
| 1324 | First Aztec settlement at Tenochtitlan |
| 1368 | Founding of the Ming dynasty in China |
| 1405–33 | Ming voyages under Zheng He |
| 1415 | Prince Henry captures Ceuta |
| 1434 | Portuguese round Cape Bojador |
| 1453 | Ottoman conquest of Constantinople |
| 1479 | Treaty of Alcáçovas: Portugal recognises Castilian sovereignty over the Canary Islands; Castile cedes rights to navigation, trade and conquest of territory south of the Canaries. |
| 1488 | Bartolomé Dias rounds Cape Horn |
| 1492 | Voyage of Columbus |
| 1494 | Treaty of Tordesillas |
| | Territories in the western hemisphere named 'New World' |
| 1498 | Vasco da Gama arrives in Calicut, India |
| 1500 | Pedro Alvares Cabral arrives in Brazil |
| 1501 | Persian Safavid dynasty founded |
| 1505 | Appointment of a Portuguese viceroy to take charge of the *Estado da India* |
| 1507 | Portuguese conquest of Ormuz |
| 1510 | Afonso de Albuquerque takes Goa |
| 1511 | Albuquerque takes Malacca |
| 1515 | Albuquerque takes Hormuz |
| 1517 | Ottoman conquest of Syria, Egypt and the Hijaz |
| 1518 | Portuguese establish fortified factory at Colombo, Ceylon |
| 1519 | Hernán Cortés enters Mexico |
| 1526 | Founding of Mughal rule in India |
| 1532 | Francisco Pizarro enters Peru |
| 1535–36 | French embassy established at Constantinople |
| 1541 | Ottoman conquest of Buda (Budapest) |
| 1545 | Potosí established as a mining town in present-day Bolivia |
| 1549 | Jesuit missionary Francis Xavier arrives in Japan |

| | |
|---|---|
| 1557 | Establishment of Macao, the Portuguese base on Chinese territory |
| 1559 | Portuguese crown authorizes trade in slaves between Africa and Brazil |
| 1571 | Founding of Manila, capital of the Spanish Philippines |
| 1581 | Levant Company granted charter by Elizabeth I |
| 1583 | Matteo Ricci mission to China |
| 1600 | Foundation of the English East India Company |
| 1602 | Foundation of the *Vereenigde Oostindische Compagnie* |
| 1607 | Jamestown founded by Virginia Company |
| 1614 | The Japanese *shogun* (Ieyasu) expels all Christians from Japan |
| 1620 | New Plymouth colony established by Puritan refugees |
| 1624 | Dutch settlers establish New Amsterdam on Manhattan Island |
| 1625 | English claim Barbados in the name of Charles I |
| 1630 | Massachusetts Bay Company migration to New England |
| | Pernambuco in North-east Brazil captured by the Dutch |
| 1639 | East India Company trading base at Madras (Chennai) – Fort St George |
| 1644 | Fall of the Ming dynasty in China |
| 1652 | First coffeehouse established in London |
| | Dutch colony founded at the Cape of Good Hope |
| 1661 | East India Company trading base at Bombay (Mumbai) |
| 1669 | Completion of the Ottoman conquest of Crete |
| 1699 | Treaty of Karlowitz |
| 1702 | East India Company trading base at Calcutta (Kolkata) |
| 1724 | The Chinese emperor proscribes Catholicism in China |
| 1735 | Qianlong Emperor's reign in China begins |
| 1756–63 | Seven Years War |
| 1757 | Battle of Plassey |
| 1768–74 | Russo-Ottoman War, ending in defeat for the Ottomans |
| 1775–83 | American War of Independence |
| 1776 | American Declaration of Independence |
| 1791–1804 | Haitian Revolution |
| 1793 | English King George III's ambassador snubbed by China |
| 1798–1801 | French occupation of Egypt |
| 1800 | Chinese population estimated at 360 million |
| 1803 | Acquisition of Delhi by the British |
| 1807 | Britain outlaws the international traffic in slaves |
| | Portuguese monarchy flees to Brazil |
| 1808 | Napoleon deposes the Spanish king Ferdinand VII |
| 1839–42 | Opium War |

# Beyond Europe c. 1500

## Anne Gerritsen and Anthony McFarlane

In c. 1500, when Europeans were embarking on transoceanic maritime explorations and overseas conquests, their maps told little of the world's enormous diversity. A myriad of regions lay beyond Europe, each with distinctive forms of agriculture, technology, patterns of trade and religious beliefs. Vast areas of the planet, especially in the Americas, Africa and Australasia, were populated by hunters, food gatherers, herders of domesticated animals and hand cultivators who lived in small communities, often under simple forms of government. In some regions, however, complex societies of great wealth and power projected cultural and political influence over large areas.

The greatest were located in the Eurasian landmass. On its western fringes, Christian Europe was becoming increasingly dynamic and expansive, but the sites of the world's most opulent cultures and strongest states were in the Middle East, India and China. In Africa, many different societies and cultures had emerged across a vast continent, reaching from the Islamic urban civilisations of the north, across the deserts, savannahs and forests of the interior, to the hunters and gatherers of the Kalahari desert in the south. The American continents were a world apart, unknown to peoples on the other sides of the Atlantic and Pacific Oceans. Stretching from pole to pole, with a geographical and climatic range greater than Africa or Eurasia, they were the home of human communities that lived for millennia without interaction with the peoples, flora and fauna of the other continents until the arrival of Europeans (Figure IV).

## The Islamic states of the Middle East

In the eastern Mediterranean and the Middle East, the spread of Islam had provided a powerful unifying force. There were great regional variations within the Dar al-Salam (the House of Islam), but also consistencies throughout the Islamic world, so that the fourteenth-century traveller Ibn Battuta (1304–69) had been able to move from his home in Morocco via Mecca, Persia and southern Arabia, to Afghanistan, India, and China, and find not only familiar religious practices but regular employment as a specialist in Islamic law (Holt et al. 1970).

Around 1500, two great states dominated in the Middle East, one based on Anatolia and the other on Persia. The Ottoman Empire that emerged among the Turks of Anatolia formed the most powerful element. In 1453, Turkish armies under Mehmet the Conqueror had taken Christian Constantinople, the centre of the

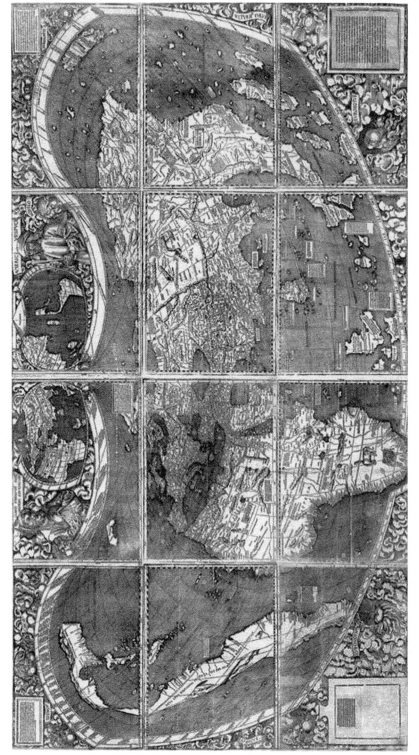

**Figure IV.1** European perception of the world c. 1500.
Source: Martin Waldseemüller, 'Universalis Cosmographia' (1507)

Byzantine Empire, and turned it into the capital – renamed Istanbul – of an expansive Muslim state. Over the next century the Ottomans fast became the greatest Muslim power in the world, as their militaristic monarchy extended its rule to Inner Asia and southwards into Egypt and North Africa, and challenged the powers of Christian Europe (Sidi Ali Reis: Web resources; 'Jews and Muslims' in Part III; 'European relations with the Ottoman World' in Part IV). Ottoman military supremacy was matched by its economic strength. During this early period, the Ottomans controlled the lucrative overland trade via the Silk Routes through Inner Asia as well as the main seaborne trade routes between Europe and Asia, and the wealth from commerce fed the rich material culture enjoyed by the Ottoman ruling elites (Inalcik and Quataert 1994–97).

The other great Islamic dynasty stood on the Ottomans' eastern borders. Founded in 1501 by a people of Turkic descent who settled in Persia (now Iran), the Safavid dynasty lasted until 1736. The Safavids converted from the majority SUNNI tradition to a distinctive variant of Islam known as SHI'ISM. The Shi'a Safavids refused to submit to the Sunni Ottomans and presided over a powerful state and flourishing culture of their own, standing on the crossroads of world trade (Savory 1980). Under Shah Abbas the Great (1587–1629), Persian culture flourished and spread. Shah Abbas had great interest in the outside world: he had Englishmen in his service and collected Chinese porcelain and other luxury goods. The Ardabil shrine in north-west Persia housed his priceless pieces of blue and white porcelain, much of it designed in Jingdezhen in southern China with Persian tastes in mind. The two rugs that graced the floor of the Ardabil shrine further illustrate the cultural prowess of the Safavids (Figure IV.2).

**Figure IV.2** The famous 'Ardabil carpet', made under the Safavids in 1539/40, © Victoria & Albert Museum, London, UK / Bridgeman Images.

## Civilizations and states in South and South-east Asia

The Indian subcontinent encompassed an area as large as that of Europe, with cultures, religions and states that reflected a history of civilizations far older than Europe's. By 1500, India consisted of several strong regional economies with large populations, productive agricultures and sophisticated manufactures, including cotton textiles and luxury goods that were traded throughout the Indian Ocean, the Red Sea, and the Mediterranean. Europeans marvelled at India's artefacts, and had to pay for Indian goods in precious metals, as they possessed little that was comparable to offer in return. The Portuguese who had first arrived on the Indian coast around 1498 had tried to impose Christianity on the local population, but could not compete with the established religious practices associated with Hinduism and BUDDHISM.

Around 1500, the subcontinent was divided into a large number of regional states, many with solid finances, strong armies and, like the kingdoms of medieval Europe, long histories of conflict over territory and resources. However, when Babur of Kabul swept in from Afghanistan in 1526, he founded the Mughal empire, which would subsequently advance southwards and expand into the lands of Hindu princes. The Mughals were henceforth to surpass other Islamic states as their territory and resources expanded during the succeeding centuries. Throughout India, the ruling elite relied on Persian as their shared language, and the social, political and cultural institutions of the Persian Empire entered India, leaving a legacy still visible in the architectural splendour of the Taj Mahal (Robb 2002).

Beyond India, in South-east Asia, various independent kingdoms controlled the territory now occupied by Burma, Malaysia, Thailand, Cambodia and Vietnam. They formed a group of separate states with ethnically diverse populations and distinct languages, but with religious and commercial connections both to the Indian subcontinent and to mainland China. At the crossroads of the Indian Ocean and the South China Sea, the kingdoms in the Indonesian archipelago held major maritime powers, particularly in Java. Around 1500, the port of Malacca was the most striking ENTREPÔT in the region. With a population of around 50,000, it was said to house people speaking 84 languages and acted as a disseminator of Islam, spreading Muslim influence from the Malay peninsula into the islands of the Indonesian archipelago and beyond, to the Spice Islands, Borneo and the Philippines. Here, then, was a vibrant, populous trading area, comparable to the rich MERCANTILE networks of the Mediterranean, the western Atlantic or the Indian Ocean. It was to be a powerful lure to Europeans who wanted the pepper and spices that were key commodities in its trade, and a stepping stone en route to China.

## Ming China

In East Asia, far from the kingdoms of Christian Europe, China constituted a world of its own (Mote 1999). At the founding of the Ming dynasty in 1368, China was the largest unified state in the world. It had a centralized, bureaucratic government that by c. 1500 exercised authority over 155 million people in an area larger than that of the modern United States. At the centre of this bureaucracy stood the imperial throne, occupied by the descendants of the founder of the Ming dynasty, in the Forbidden City in the heart of Beijing. This extensive palace complex was populated by large numbers of women, each of whom could provide the next heir to the throne. To ensure the ritual purity of the line, the emperor was the only male allowed in the palaces after dark; all others were eunuchs who served the emperor in a variety of roles, from cooks and food tasters to powerful political advisers.

Apart from thousands of eunuchs, the emperor was assisted by his civil servants. Men, and only men, were selected for the civil service through a complex set of examinations based on the Confucian classics. A successful candidate started his preparation as a young child by memorizing these texts, then passed examinations at various levels, before finally proceeding to the triennial session of the metropolitan examinations, with a final sitting in the imperial palace, presided over by the emperor. This life-long dedication to learning was theoretically available to every child, but in practice, it was mostly the children of other officials and scholars, and of rich merchants, who found their way into the civil service. By 1500, the spread of wealth had led to huge increases in literacy and in the availability of cheaply printed learning guides and crammers, ensuring fierce competition for places in the examinations. Those who were successful served the emperor in three-year postings throughout the empire, though never in their home county so as to avoid corruption (Figure IV.3, Box 1), while those who failed had to find alternative employment, as tutors, scholars or clerks.

While Confucianism offered clear guidance for the socio-political order, it could not provide answers about the afterlife or the worlds of spirits and ghosts. Buddhism and DAOISM, both complex religious traditions based on canonical texts and presided over by hierarchically organized clerics, coexisted throughout China and offered inspiration and consolation to China's Confucian elites. The vast majority of the

**Figure IV.3** Examination candidates viewing the list of names of those who have passed. Qiu Ying, Guan bang tu (handscroll, c. 1495–1552). © National Palace Museum, Beijing.

- 'From the earliest times great attention has been given to the improvement of agriculture. Indicate the arrangements adopted for that purpose by the several dynasties.'
- 'Different dynasties have since that time adopted different regulations in regard to the use of militia or standing armies, the mode of raising supplies for the army, etc. State these.'
- 'State how the currency of the Sung Dynasty corresponds with our use of paper money at the present day.'

*(Père du Halde in 1575: Web resources)*

Extracts from a Chinese Civil Service Examination recorded by a missionary.

population, however, engaged in SYNCRETIC religious practices known as 'popular religion', centred on local temples where individuals appealed to their deities without the mediating influence of spiritual or political leaders.

Political life focused on the emperor who, according to official RHETORIC, presided over the realm, or 'all under heaven' (*tianxia*). At its centre was China, the central kingdom (Zhongguo) populated by Han Chinese who had the benefit of Chinese civilization; at its peripheries were other, non-Chinese inhabitants of the realm. These were invited regularly to the imperial court to offer tribute gifts in exchange for a vassal-like status and protection.

Away from the official rhetoric and the imperial illusion of Chinese superiority, a thriving cultural and economic exchange characterized relations with the outside world. Inland, the sedentary agriculturalists depended on the horses and hides provided by the migrating steppe populations, and in the coastal regions a vibrant junk trade created complex networks of Chinese merchants throughout East and South-East Asia. In the early fifteenth century, the Ming also looked further afield, sending the Admiral Zheng to sail the oceans in vessels ten times the size of Columbus's ships, carrying thousands of sailors and precious loads into the Indian Ocean as far as East Africa and the Red Sea. This expedition was, however, more concerned to impress others with China's strength than to expand trade or territory. Indeed, at the time when Europe was expanding its external contacts by sea, Ming emperors withdrew from investing in overseas expeditions, preferring to concentrate on defending the inland borders from which threats of invasion had always come. Nevertheless, the imperial court had given up the old aim of reverting to an agrarian society where state revenues came from agriculture. Most of the population was engaged in some kind of trade and the imperial court would soon decide that all taxes had to be paid in silver, a decision that would change not only the nature of trade interactions in China, but the nature of trade across the globe ('Expanding horizons' and 'The global exchange of goods' in Part IV).

## The African world

Africa was a rich complex of societies and cultures, some known to Europeans, others not (Curtin et al. 1995; Iliffe 2007). In North Africa, powerful Muslim states dominated the coastal lands from Egypt to Morocco. In the Sudanic belt of savannah lands that lay between Senegal and the Red Sea, some distinctive states emerged in West Africa during the fourteenth and fifteenth centuries. The main centres of wealth and power were the gold-rich kingdom of Mali, which dominated the region until surpassed by the empire of Songhai at the end of the fifteenth century; their militaristic kings professed allegiance to Islam. A third discrete region was in East Africa, where Islamic influence had spread southwards along the coasts of modern Somalia, Kenya, Tanzania and Mozambique. Merchants from the Arabian peninsula and Persian Gulf traded in iron, gold, cotton, slaves and ivory, and thus connected East Africa to the commercial networks of the Indian Ocean. Porcelain from China, traded throughout the Indian Ocean, also decorated the houses of wealthy merchants on the Swahili coast (Zhao 2015).

The other regions of the continent, deep in Central and Southern Africa, were more isolated and followed an internal dynamic of development based on the growth of societies of iron-working farmers and cattle-grazers. In some places, prosperity promoted by trade in precious metals and other goods provided the basis for the establishment of substantial states. South of the Niger, several new states emerged in the savannah and forest countries, of which Benin is best known, thanks to its famous bronzes. Further south, Zimbabwe was a great royal capital and ceremonial centre that owed its wealth to gold-mining and traded far and wide through the East African ports, the Indian Ocean and China. Africa's coastal regions of course were more outward-looking than the cut-off regions in the interior, but much of Africa's landmass was crossed by trade routes and connected through circulations of natural resources, precious goods and labour. In c. 1500 Arabs dominated the East African coasts, but Europeans were also beginning to make their mark. In the 1480s, Portuguese mariners and merchants were making their first contacts with the civilizations of sub-Saharan Africa, notably with the kingdom of Kongo, a territory that controlled about half a million people and whose kings soon became allies of Portugal.

## The Americas

Of the lands that lay beyond Europe, the American continents were perhaps the most distinctive in 1500. Their peoples were mostly hunters, food gatherers or hand cultivators living in small communities, and some fundamental elements of Old World civilization were absent: native Americans lacked the plough, iron and the wheel, and domesticated animals were rare. However, although vast expanses of both North and South America were devoid of dense populations or urban concentrations, during the fifteenth century the regions now known as Mexico and Peru came under the rule of expansive states created by ethnic groups that were successful in war.

In Mexico, the dominant power in 1500 was that of the Aztecs who, in c. 1324, founded a settlement at Tenochtitlan, in the central highlands, amidst a cluster of competing CITY-STATES (Clendinnen 1991). In 1438, they allied with two neighbouring city-states to defeat their major competitor, Azcapatzalco, then extended their hegemony through Central and Southern Mexico. Their expansion was driven by material and religious imperatives. Tenochtitlan needed resources to sustain its growing population and ruling elites, and Aztec priests demanded thousands of victims for human sacrifice, taken from people captured in war (Box 2).

## Box 2

'Human hearts, torn from sacrificial victims, were needed to keep the sun in motion and blood was required to sustain the fertility of the earth: these were justifications for continuous warfare. All males were trained for combat and successful warriors stood in the first ranks of Aztec society, their prowess calibrated by capture of victims for sacrifice and their prestige displayed in the material rewards they received from tribute payments. The ceremonial human sacrifice that legitimated war among the Aztecs had another function, too. Practised on a grand scale on great occasions, it was a means of intimidating subject peoples and thereby ensuring the continuing flow of tributes to the warriors, priests and lords who dominated the city. These tributes underpinned the growth of Tenochtitlan, which, at its height in 1519, was one of the world's great urban centres.'

*(Clendinnen 1991, esp. chs 4, 10)*

With a population of about 200,000 within its environs, Tenochtitlan was the most spectacular concentration of wealth and power in North America. The city had an impressive array of crafts and its elite had developed a system of pictographic writing which, inscribed on deerskins, recorded tribute payments and events. The social and political order was steeply hierarchical. It was ruled by lords, who chose a male from the royal family to take on semi-divine status as their leader, and enforced by an elite of nobles, priests and warriors. The 'empire' had a special character, however, for the Aztecs did not seek to hold territories or govern peoples conquered in war. They exercised power by intimidation rather than co-optation of the conquered, but their empire was vulnerable to armed opposition. When Spaniards arrived with steel swords, guns and mounted men, they rallied the Aztecs' enemies, defeated warriors armed with only stone age weapons, and summarily crushed the Aztec state.

The disparity between the technology and methods of war found in the Old World with those present in the New World was also evident in the other major American civilization of c. 1500: the Inca Empire that originated in the Andean mountain basins around Cuzco. After c. 1440, the Incas created an empire that extended over 2,000 miles from north to south and at its height held sway over 10–12 million people

(D'Altroy 2002). Their kings were, in theory, all-powerful descendants of the Sun God, holding absolute powers and supported by an aristocracy, an army and a priesthood which organized religious rituals in Cuzco, the 'navel of the earth'. Unlike the Aztecs, the Incas established governments in the territories they conquered but allowed co-operative chiefs of subordinate ethnic groups to share their authority. They also used conquered peoples as allies, distributing goods among communities which accepted Inca rule. Although they lacked a form of writing comparable to those of Eurasia, the Incas had a vital tool for empire in their system of recording and transmitting information by means of knotted strings (*khipus*). Inca rulers professed a 'civilizing mission' designed to bring peace under a benign autocracy, a shared religion and a common language (*Quechua*). Rebellions by subject peoples were not uncommon, however, and, in their search for fresh tributes, Inca kings tended to overstretch their capacities for control. These tensions, combined with the military superiority of the invading Spaniards, were to ensure the collapse of the Inca Empire after 1532 (Cobo 1979).

## Assessment

The world in *c.* 1500 was marked by huge diversity. Some parts were densely populated, urban, outward-looking and materially and culturally rich; other parts were thinly populated by subsistence farmers who eked out a living with meagre resources and little interaction beyond their immediate environment. Many political entities combined both: city-dwellers, especially in rich cities like Lisbon and Venice, lived in a different world from the agricultural labourers of Central and Eastern Europe; Zanzibar on the African coast hosted cosmopolitan merchants, while some of the inland regions of Africa were poor and isolated. In the Americas, 'empires' rested on stone-age technologies that made them into targets for conquest rather than commerce. It was that same diversity between different parts of the world that spurred travellers, merchants, and missionaries on to create and enhance connections between different parts of the world. By 1500, Africa was already connected to Europe, the Indian subcontinent, South-east Asia and China; Chinese merchants travelled as far afield as the African coast, Zoroastrian priests travelled between Persia and India, and Muslim traders and scholars reached all parts of the Indian Ocean network. The world in 1500, thus, was not yet a European world.

## *Discussion themes*

1. How and to what extent were the major civilizations of the world in *c.* 1500 connected?
2. In what senses were the major indigenous states of the Americas comparable to those of Eurasia in *c.* 1500?
3. Was there less potential, around 1500, for overseas expansion in China and India than in Europe?

## Bibliography

### (A) Sources

Cobo, Bernabé (1979), *History of the Inca Empire: An Account of the Indians' Customs and their Origins, Together with a Treatise on Inca Legends, History and Social Institutions* [1653], trans. and ed. Roland Hamilton, Austin, Tex.

### (B) Literature

* Clendinnen, Inga (1991), *Aztecs: An Interpretation*, Cambridge
* Curtin, P., Feierman, S., Thompson, L. and Vansina, J. (1995), *African History: From Earliest Times to Independence*, 2nd edn, Harlow
* D'Altroy, Terence (2002), *The Incas*, Oxford
Holt, P. M., Lambton, K. S. and Lewis, Bernard eds (1970), *The Cambridge History of Islam*, 2 vols, Cambridge
Iliffe, John (2007), *Africans: The History of a Continent*, 2nd edn, Cambridge
Inalcik, Halil and Quataert, Donald eds (1994–97), *An Economic and Social History of the Ottoman Empire*, 2 vols, Cambridge
* Mote, Frederick (1999), *Imperial China: 900–1800*, Cambridge, Mass.
Raychaudhuri, Tapan and Habin, Irfan eds (1982), *The Cambridge Economic History of India*, vol. 1: *c. 1200–c. 1750*, Cambridge
* Robb, Peter (2002), *A History of India*, Basingstoke
* Savory, Roger (1980), *Iran under the Safavids*, Cambridge
Zhao Bing (2015), 'Chinese-style Ceramics in East Africa from the 9th to 16th Century: A Case of Changing Value and Symbols in the Multi-partner Global Trade', in: *Afriques – Débats, méthodes et terrains d'histoire* 6 (2015) <http://afriques.revues.org/1836>

### (C) Web resources

Père du Halde, 'How Chinese Children Learn to Read' (*c.* 1575): <http://www.fordham.edu/halsall/eastasia/1575duhalde1.html>
'Qiu Ying', at China Online Museum: <http://www.comuseum.com/painting/masters/qiu-ying/>
Sidi Ali Reis, *Mirat ul Memalik* [Mirror of Countries] (1557): <http://www.fordham.edu/halsall/source/16CSidi1.asp>
'East Africa and the Indian Ocean: connections, exchange networks and globalisation' (first millennium – nineteenth century): <https://afriques.revues.org/1719>

# European relations with the Ottoman world

*James E. Baldwin*

The Ottoman Empire was one of the great powers of the early modern world, ruling large swathes of Eastern Europe along with much of the Middle East and North Africa, and it played a crucial role in European history. The Ottoman Empire pervaded early modern international relations, it supplied Western Europe with several valuable commodities, and it was a source of fascination for travel writers and their readers. Christian Europeans often portrayed the Ottomans as quintessentially 'other': as exotic, barbarous and intimidating infidels. However, while the boundary between Christianity and Islam was rhetorically formidable, in practice it was surprisingly permeable, and many Western Europeans found much to admire in their eastern neighbour.

The territory the Ottomans ruled was very familiar to Western European imaginations, encompassing regions most Christians considered rightfully their own: the Holy Land, the eastern and African provinces of the old Roman Empire and Constantinople. But while western Christians were expanding aggressively into the Americas and South and East Asia, their conflict with the Ottomans was primarily defensive. From its base in the Balkans and western Anatolia, the Ottoman Empire grew deeper into Eastern Europe for much of the early modern period. The sixteenth century saw the Ottomans conquer Belgrade, Buda and much of Hungary, while reducing Transylvania and Wallachia to vassalage. In the seventeenth century, they captured Crete from Venice and pushed into Poland-Lithuania north of the Black Sea. They even besieged the Habsburg capital Vienna twice: in 1529 and 1683 (Figure IV.4).

Ottoman fortunes started to turn at the end of the seventeenth century. Their failed siege of Vienna in 1683 was followed by a long war with the Habsburgs that ended in defeat. The Treaty of Karlowitz in 1699 marked the first time the Ottomans had formally conceded territory to their Christian neighbours. The first half of the eighteenth century saw a stalemate, with the Ottomans winning and losing territory in several wars with Russia, Austria and Venice. In the second half Ottoman military decline accelerated rapidly, with particularly significant losses to Russia, and the century concluded with France's occupation of the empire's richest province, Egypt. But we should not read back into the early modern period signs of the Ottoman Empire's eventual disintegration. During the sixteenth and seventeenth centuries the Ottoman Empire was one of the strongest powers in Europe. Ottoman-European

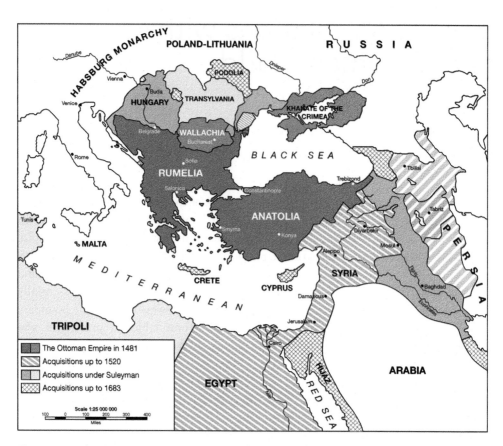

**Figure IV.4** The Ottoman Empire in the seventeenth century.

relations did not consist only of war, however. Several Christian nations forged political alliances with the Ottomans and trade relations were strong even between the empire and its rivals.

## Who were the Ottomans?

The Ottoman Empire originated as a small principality on the Byzantine frontier in the late thirteenth century. The history of its expansion is complex, but two events in particular were crucial in transforming it into a major world empire.

The first was the conquest of Constantinople – the most prestigious city in Christendom, with a glorious imperial heritage – in 1453. To Christians, its fall was a tragedy; in the Muslim world, it was a propaganda coup for the Ottomans. After the conquest, Sultan Mehmed the Conqueror presented himself as both a Muslim Sultan and a new Roman Emperor. The second event was Sultan Selim I's defeat of the Mamluk Sultanate in 1517 and the acquisition of all its territory in Syria, Egypt and the Hijaz (western Arabia). This included the Muslim holy cities Mecca,

Medina and Jerusalem, and from this point on the Ottoman Sultans used the prestigious titles *khadim al-haramayn* (protector of the holy sanctuaries) and, less consistently, CALIPH. The Ottoman Empire united two heritages: it was a Mediterranean and a Muslim power.

Early modern Europeans called the Ottoman Empire 'Turkey' and its inhabitants 'Turks'. This was only partly accurate. The Ottoman dynasty were Turkish Muslims; the other members of the ruling class were of diverse origins. From its earliest days the Ottoman elite drew in Byzantine and Serbian as well as Turkish nobility. Later, it absorbed Albanians, Bosnians, Bulgarians, Greeks, Georgians, Circassians, Abkhazians, Kurds and Arabs, all of whom assimilated to Ottoman high culture. This culture's principal language was Ottoman Turkish. But to be fully literate meant also to read and write Persian, the language of poetry, and Arabic, the language of law and science. The ruling class referred to themselves not as Turks, but as Ottomans. To them, the term 'Turk' referred to a Muslim peasant or shepherd.

A significant source of recruitment for the Ottoman ruling elite in the sixteenth century was the empire's Christian population in the Balkans. A periodic levy of Christian boys from the villages of this region, known as the DEVSHIRME, enslaved selected youths. The boys were converted to Islam and educated at the palace in preparation for a lifetime of military or administrative service. Many joined the Janissaries, the empire's formidable infantry regiment that was the backbone of Ottoman military power. The most talented rose through the ranks to fill the highest positions in the imperial government: many of the Grand Viziers (prime ministers) of the sixteenth century were *devshirme* recruits (Imber 2009, Box 1). In the seventeenth and eighteenth centuries, the *devshirme* faded from prominence, and freeborn Muslims increasingly dominated the ruling class (Tezcan 2010). But slaves of Christian origin – captured in the Caucasus and by Mediterranean privateers – always remained a significant component of the Ottoman ruling class.

The most famous example of the sixteenth century was Sokollu Mehmed Pasha, a Serb from Bosnia who was taken into the *devshirme* at the age of 16. He served as commander of the fleet, led military campaigns to Transylvania and Persia and served as governor of Rumelia (the Balkans), before becoming the last Grand Vizier of Sultan Suleyman the Magnificent in 1565. Sokollu Mehmed Pasha assimilated into the Ottoman-Muslim ruling elite, becoming a patron of Islamic religious institutions. He also remained closely connected with his family and homeland. Some of his family followed him and converted to Islam, others remained Christian. Mehmed was generous in his patronage of all of them, securing relatives appointments in the palace and in the Orthodox Church. Much of Mehmed's extensive philanthropy was directed at Bosnia: the most famous example is the bridge he built across the Drina river in his hometown Višegrad (Figure IV.5). His Serbian heritage could be helpful in the complex politics of the frontier: during the Translyvania campaign, he played on his background to negotiate the defection of Serbian garrisons to the Ottoman side.

**Figure IV.5** Mehmed Paša Sokolovic Bridge on the river Drina. Picture by Jelica18 – own work, CC BY-SA 4.0, https://commons.wikimedia.org/w/index.php?curid=41405926.

The Ottoman Empire's subject population was also diverse. Accurate figures are not available, but Christians were a substantial proportion and may have been a majority before 1517; the Orthodox, Armenian, Coptic, Syriac and Catholic Churches were all represented. Jews made up a much smaller proportion, but were a significant presence in important cities including Constantinople, Aleppo, Baghdad and, in particular, Salonica. The Ottoman Empire was one of the main destinations for the Sephardi Jews expelled from Spain ('Jews and Muslims' in Part III): Sultan Bayezid II issued a proclamation in 1493 inviting them to settle there. These immigrants joined long-established communities of Greek-speaking Romaniote Jews in the Balkans and Anatolia, alongside Arabic-speaking Mizrahi Jews in Egypt, Syria and Iraq (Goldish 2008). Lastly, the Muslim population in the empire was equally differentiated. The largest ethnic groups were Turks, concentrated in Anatolia and the Balkans, Arabs in Syria, Iraq, Egypt and north Africa, and Kurds in eastern Anatolia and Iraq. There were also immigrant Muslim groups such as Circassians from the Caucasus, and indigenous Christian communities that had converted en masse, such as Bosnians and Albanians.

Despite Western European claims of forced conversion, religious toleration was the norm: a striking contrast to most of early modern Europe. The Ottomans placed

**Box 1**

'No distinction is attached to birth among the Turks; the deference to be paid to a man is measured by the position he holds in the public service. . . Those who receive the highest offices from the Sultan are for the most part the sons of shepherds or herdsmen, and so far from being ashamed of their parentage, they actually glory in it, and consider it a matter of boasting that they owe nothing to the accident of birth; for they do not believe that high qualities are either natural or hereditary, nor do they think that they can be handed down from father to son, but that they are partly the gift of God, and partly the result of good training, great industry, and unwearied zeal.'

*(Busbecq 1881, I: 154)*

In this letter, Ogier Ghiselin de Busbecq, Habsburg ambassador to Constantinople (1554–62), contrasted the Ottoman Empire's meritocracy favourably with his own society. As Mehmed's career shows, however, the Ottoman Empire was not free of nepotism.

**Box 2**

'Your Majesty, my Illustrious and Prosperous Sultan, may you be healthy!

Your insignificant, humble servant is a Christian girl from among the inhabitants of Kadıköy, from the Greek people. I attained the divine truth and wish to be honored with the Holy Islam because my parents want to marry me to an unbeliever. I want to be honored with the Holy Islam in your imperial presence. My request is the following:

I plead that, because I accepted the Islamic faith, I be kindly granted my new clothes. The rest is left to the decree of my Illustrious Sultan.'

*(Minkov 2004, 214–15)*

Petition from an Ottoman woman written in 1712.

restrictions on non-Muslim religious practice, limiting the size and number of churches and synagogues, and prohibiting public processions and the ringing of church bells. But within these parameters, Christians and Jews enjoyed freedom of worship; and for most of our period, the restrictions were not zealously enforced. The Ottomans did not compel conversion to Islam, but during the seventeenth century the Sultans increasingly encouraged conversion, paying a one-off benefit in cash or clothing and holding conversion ceremonies (Baer 2008; Box 2).

The Ottoman Empire defined itself as an Islamic state, but Islam was not its only identity. In the mid-sixteenth century, Sultan Suleyman the Magnificent's main antagonist in Europe was Charles V. Their conflict was primarily territorial, with the

Ottomans expanding into Habsburg lands in Hungary, but it was accompanied by much ideological rhetoric. Christian-Muslim holy war was only one dimension of these exchanges. Suleyman and Charles were also competing for recognition as universal emperor, in the context of shared MILLENARIAN expectations. Both identified with common imperial symbols: most obviously Rome, represented by Suleyman's capital

**Figure IV.6** A portrait of Sultan Süleyman the Magnificent wearing the jewel-studded helmet, sharing similarities with both the crown of Charles V and the papal tiara (Italian woodcut, 16th century). The Met, Harris Brisbane Dick Fund, 1942, accession no. 42.41.1.

and Charles's title as Holy Roman Emperor, but also Alexander the Great, the model of a world conqueror for both Muslims and Christians (Ágoston 2007, Necipoğlu 1989). Although the Ottomans are often portrayed as an alien intrusion into Europe, they were in many ways products of the same cultural universe, despite religious differences (Figure IV.6).

## Military and diplomatic relations

Given the Ottomans' spectacular conquests during the fifteenth and sixteenth centuries, Christian Europeans often viewed them with fear. Propaganda portrayed the 'Turks' as cruel fanatics determined to enslave Christians or convert them at sword-point. War was indeed common. In addition to the Habsburgs, the Ottomans fought Venice on numerous occasions; they faced the Portuguese in the Indian Ocean in the sixteenth century; confronted the Polish-Lithuanian Commonwealth frequently during the seventeenth; and in the eighteenth century Russia became their principal enemy. The Ottomans' enemies often drew support from other Christian rulers by using religious rhetoric. The ideal of Christian unity against the Turkish menace was represented in numerous HOLY LEAGUES formed with the blessing of the Pope. The precise make-up differed, but members were typically drawn from among the papal states, Venice, various Italian and German principalities, the Knights of Malta, Austria, Russia and Poland-Lithuania.

Even when not actively at war, Ottoman relations with their Christian rivals were characterized by low-level violence. Raiding across land frontiers was common, while in the Mediterranean Muslim and Christian privateers preyed on the commercial shipping of the other side. Raiding was often carried out by smaller actors who were subjects of the major powers. The 'Barbary corsairs' of Algiers seized ships flying the flags of the Ottomans' enemies; the Tatars of the Crimea raided for slaves in the Polish and Russian Ukraine. Meanwhile, the Knights of Malta, a crusading order under the authority of the Pope, and the Uskoks, Habsburg subjects based on the Dalmatian coast, attacked Ottoman shipping and sold the sailors and passengers into slavery (Bracewell 1992). It was not until the Treaty of Karlowitz in 1699 that the concept of a peace precluding all violence, rather than simply a cessation of active warfare, was agreed by the Ottomans and their enemies. Both sides found this difficult to sell to the frontier populations that made their living through raiding (Abou-el-Haj 1969).

To characterize Ottoman-European relations as one long series of wars would obscure a great deal, however ('Ottoman history podcast' and 'Tozsuz Evrak' in Web resources). For a start, some European countries ignored the rhetoric of holy war and allied with the Ottomans against common Christian enemies. To the French king Francis I, the Ottomans were far less threatening than Charles V, whose territories in Spain, the Netherlands and northern Italy encircled his own. Diplomatic contacts between Francis and Suleyman in the 1520s led to the establishment of a French embassy in Constantinople in 1536 and the basing of an Ottoman fleet in Marseille.

The Franco-Ottoman alliance endured as long as the French monarchy; Napoleon reversed course when he invaded Egypt in 1798 (Isom-Verhaaren 2013). Both England and the Dutch Republic befriended the Ottoman Empire from the late sixteenth century, when they were in conflict with Spain (Brotton 2016). Pragmatic self-interest frequently trumped religious idealism in early modern Europe.

## Trading links

Venice offers a striking example of how pragmatism was compatible with the fevered rhetoric of holy war. As the two leading naval powers in the eastern Mediterranean, the Ottoman and Venetian empires fought six major wars between 1499 and 1718. Nevertheless, Venice was one of the Ottoman Empire's closest trading partners, having dominated trans-Mediterranean trade since the Middle Ages. The *Serenissima* was the only city in Christian Europe with a resident community of Ottoman Muslims, who were all merchants. Many Venetian subjects from its Aegean possessions had family connections within the Ottoman Empire; these people were crucial in lubricating diplomatic and commercial connections (Rothman 2012).

In many ways, trade – rather than religious tension – was the key dynamic in Ottoman-European relations. The Ottoman Empire was the main source for many commodities that were in great demand in Western Europe. Some (like silk, cotton, opium, coffee and carpets) were produced within the empire; others passed through it from further east. Aleppo was one of the termini of the Silk Road from China, while spices from India were shipped to Europe via Egypt ('The global exchange of goods' in Part IV). Most important of all was coffee. Grown in the province of Yemen in southern Arabia, it became embedded in Ottoman urban culture in the sixteenth century, despite a legal controversy about whether it should be prohibited as an intoxicating drink like wine (the jurists ultimately concluded that, as it stimulated rather than disoriented the mind, it was permissible). In the seventeenth century, the practice of coffee-drinking spread to Western Europe, where it proved equally controversial and popular (Box 3). The coffee trade became incredibly lucrative for Ottoman merchants and officials, especially those in Egypt, the key transit point. The empire's hold on the European coffee market was only undermined in the middle of the eighteenth century, when coffee plantations were established in the French Caribbean.

While Western Europeans sought many products available in the Ottoman Empire, they had little to offer in return. Exports consisted largely of paper, tin and cloth, along with a few specialist manufactured products such as clocks. The bulk of Ottoman imports had to be paid for with hard currency, leaving Western Europe with a persistent negative balance of trade. Large chartered companies such as England's Levant Company, granted monopolies in line with the MERCANTILE SYSTEM, consolidated control over Ottoman-European trade during the seventeenth and eighteenth centuries (Masters 1988). This paved the way towards Western Europe's

**Box 3**

'When it is dried and thoroughly boyled, it. . . is good against the small poxe and measles, and bloudy pimples; yet causeth vertiginous headheach. . . occasioneth waking, and asswageth lust, and sometimes breeds melancholly. He that would drink it for livelinesse sake, and to discusse slothfulnesse . . . let him use much sweet meates with it, and oyle of pistachios, and butter. Some drink it with milk, but it is an error, and such as may bring in danger of the leprosy.'

*(Nature of the drink Kauhi 1659)*

Translation of an Arabic treatise on the medicinal use of coffee, published in England in 1659.

economic dominance over the Ottoman Empire, but this was only secured after the INDUSTRIAL REVOLUTION, which flooded Ottoman markets with cheap mass-produced goods, causing the deindustrialization of the Ottoman economy.

Most of this trade was conducted by European merchants who travelled to the Ottoman Empire: many resided for lengthy periods in the main commercial cities such as Constantinople, Smyrna and Aleppo. Apart from the Turkish community in Venice, very few Ottoman Muslims ventured to Western Europe in search of commercial opportunities, chiefly because the bulk of Ottoman trade was internal: the empire ruled a range of geological and climatic zones, and different regions supplied different needs. The Ottomans' external commerce was mainly with countries to the

**Box 4**

'I, who am sultan of the chiefs of sultans and of the grand Khans, who distributes the crowns of ruling CHOSROESES, who curtails the defects of Caesars, who breaks the multitude of Great Kings, I who am hero of water and earth, the shadow of God (may He be exalted) upon the earths, . . . Sultan Ahmed Khan [pronounce:]

You have requested . . . that the merchants [and] servants . . . from the places belonging to [the Netherlands] may come and go with their merchandise in safety and protection to our well-guarded dominions to trade, and that there also be given to them the aforementioned capitulation . . . After this request for benevolence was . . . submitted at the foot of our sultan's throne of felicity, the petitions were met with acceptance . . . The community of merchants of the countries and places belonging to the Dutch provinces may come and go, buy and sell, in our well-guarded dominions.'

*(de Groot 2012, 148–50)*

Capitulation granted to the Dutch Republic in 1612.

east such as India and China. The Ottoman Empire was also a relatively hospitable place for foreign visitors. The government welcomed foreign merchants as a lucrative source of customs revenue. It granted those of favoured European nations CAPITULATIONS, guaranteeing the terms of their residence and trade (Box 4). Merchants found churches to attend in Ottoman cities, and many intermarried with local Christian communities. It was thus much easier for them to reside in the Ottoman Empire than it was for Ottoman Muslims to do the reverse. Some settled permanently, forming a cosmopolitan community of people of mixed Western European and Ottoman Christian heritage known as 'Levantines' in cities on the Mediterranean coast.

## Assessment

Relations between the Ottoman Empire and Europe were close throughout the early modern period. The rhetoric of a titanic struggle between Islam and Christianity was prominent in the politics of both sides, but the actual situation was much more complex. Religious prejudice and hostility was real, but it was often subordinate to geopolitical and commercial interests. While the holy leagues demonstrated Christian solidarity against the Ottomans, European powers that had antagonistic relations with the Habsburgs or the Papacy often befriended the Ottomans, and all parties were keen to maintain profitable trading relations during peacetime. Trade formed a more important dynamic of Ottoman-European relations than war: the empire was a source of many desirable goods, and European diplomacy sought to secure favourable terms for merchants. Only in the second half of the eighteenth century did it become clear to contemporaries that the balance of power, military and economic, was shifting in Western Europe's favour.

### Discussion themes

1. Was there a 'clash of civilizations' between the Ottoman Empire and Western Europe?
2. To what extent was European culture transformed by contact with the Ottomans?
3. How accurate were early modern European portrayals of the Ottoman Empire?

### Bibliography

#### (A) Sources

Busbecq, Ogier Ghiselin de (1881), *The Life and Letters of Ogier Ghiselin de Busbecq*, trans. C. T. Forster, vol. 1, London: <https://archive.org/details/lifelettbusbecq 01forsuoft>

Goldish, Matt (2008), *Jewish Questions: Responsa on Sephardic Life in the Early Modern Period*, Princeton

*The Nature of the drink Kauhi, or Coffe, and the Berry of which it is made, Described by an Arabian Phisitian* (1659), Oxford

## (B) Literature

Abou-el-Haj, Rifaat A. (1969), 'The Formal Closure of the Ottoman Frontier in Europe: 1699–1703', *Journal of the American Oriental Society* 89, 467–75

Ágoston, Gábor (2007), 'Information, Ideology, and Limits of Imperial Policy', in: *The Early Modern Ottomans*, eds. Virginia H. Aksan and Daniel Goffman, Cambridge, 75–103

Baer, Marc David (2008), *Honored by the Glory of Islam: Conversion and Conquest in Ottoman Europe*, New York

Bracewell, Wendy (1992), *The Uskoks of Senj: Piracy, Banditry and Holy War in the Sixteenth-Century Adriatic*, Ithaca, NY

Brotton, Jerry (2016), *This Orient Isle: Elizabethan England and the Islamic World*, London

Groot, A. H. de (2012), *The Ottoman Empire and the Dutch Republic: A History of the Earliest Diplomatic Relations, 1610–1630*, Leiden

Imber, Colin (2009), *The Ottoman Empire, 1300–1650: The Structure of Power*, Basingtoke

Isom-Verhaaren, Christine (2013), *Allies with the Infidel: The Ottoman and French Alliance in the Sixteenth Century*, London

Masters, Bruce (1988), *The Origins of Western Economic Dominance in the Middle East: Mercantilism and the Islamic Economy in Aleppo, 1600–1750*, New York

Minkov, Anton (2004), *Conversion to Islam in the Balkans: Kisve Bahası Petitions and Ottoman Social Life, 1670–1740*, Leiden

Necipoğlu, Gülru (1989), 'Süleyman the Magnificent and the Representation of Power in the Context of Ottoman-Hapsburg-Papal Rivalry', *Art Bulletin* 71, 401–27

Rothman, E. Natalie (2012), *Brokering Empire: Trans-Imperial Subjects between Venice and Istanbul*, Ithaca, NY

Tezcan, Baki (2010), *The Second Ottoman Empire: Political and Social Transformation in the Early Modern World*, New York

## (C) Web resources

'Ottoman history podcast': interviews with historians of the Ottoman Empire: <http://www.ottomanhistorypodcast.com>

'Stambouline': blog on Ottoman art and architecture: <http://www.stambouline.com>

'Tozsuz Evrak: commentaries on fascinating and unusual primary sources': <http://www.docblog.ottomanhistorypodcast.com>

# Expanding horizons

## Anne Gerritsen and Anthony McFarlane

Following Columbus's discovery of America in 1492 and Vasco da Gama's voyage to India in 1498, the centres of Europe's economic and political power shifted, as medieval patterns of trade were supplemented and surpassed by the opening of new oceanic routes for commerce. Reaching into the Atlantic Ocean from Lisbon and Seville, these routes extended to Africa, Asia and the Americas, hugely expanding European economic, political and cultural horizons (Maps 3–4 in the Appendix). This set the scene for empires of a new kind, based on seaborne expansion across the globe rather than overland expansions within the Eurasian landmass.

## Towards the discoveries

The beginnings of Europe's expansion are found in purposes pursued throughout the Middle Ages: curiosity about the world beyond the Continent; the search for trade in high-value Eastern goods (especially spices); the struggle against Islam and desire to recover the Holy Land; the belief that Christians had a providential mission to convert all the peoples of the world. A formative phase came in the late thirteenth and early fourteenth centuries, when European travellers took advantage of the peace imposed by Mongol hegemony in Central Asia and China (c. 1260– c. 1340) to travel east. Merchants and missionaries journeyed along the Silk Road, sojourned in its cities, entered Persia, China and India, and, in so doing, offered tantalising glimpses of the civilisations that supplied the silks, porcelain and spices so prized by Europe's nobles, while also introducing Europeans to Asian peoples who might serve as allies against Islam (Wills 2011). The Black Death, the dissolution of Mongol hegemony in Central Asia, and the revival of Muslim antagonism in Egypt and the Levant severed these connections in the later fourteenth century. However, dreams of Asian commercial and political connections did not disappear (Freedman 2008). Blocked from overland travel, Europeans turned to other means of achieving their goals: Italians from Venice and Genoa sought routes to the Indian Ocean via the Red Sea, while explorations in the near Atlantic gradually strengthened the belief that India and China might be reached by an oceanic route.

These ideas and activities interacted with developments that made oceanic exploration more plausible and attainable. Map-makers' understanding of global geography was enhanced by Latin translations of the ancient geographers Ptolemy and Strabo, and the collation of information from contemporary travels. Gradually,

**Figure IV.7** A full hull model of a Portuguese caravel (c. 1490). © National Maritime Museum, Greenwich, London

medieval cartographers revised thinking about the scale and position of the world's oceans and continents, the connections between them, and the size of the globe, which supported the possibility of seaborne contact with the distant East (Brotton 2012). The potential for oceanic exploration was, moreover, strengthened at a practical, sea-going level by improvements to techniques for long-distance navigation and sailing. PORTOLAN CHARTS entered into wider use both inside and outside the Mediterranean; plus the use of the magnetic compass in combination with charts improved mariners' confidence in the safety of long deep-sea voyages (see Waldseemüller's 1507 map, which included 'America', Figure IV.1). Late medieval developments in ship design also helped. By the end of the fifteenth century, the Portuguese had developed the caravel, a two or three-masted ship which, with its combination of square sails and lateen sails, was capable of oceanic sailing and suitable for exploring shallow waters on African shores (Figure IV.7; Scammell 1981).

Such developments interacted with maritime exploration and provided the means for Europeans to forge new oceanic connections. Unlike the Chinese, who had cut short their oceanic exploration a century before (see 'Beyond Europe, c. 1500' in Part IV), the relatively insignificant monarchies of South-western Europe had ambitions that encouraged them to push at maritime frontiers. Impelled by nobles who sought fame and fortune in crusading wars, the kingdoms of Portugal and Spain stood in the vanguard, competing with each other to champion Christianity against the 'Moors', to find wealth and glory in war, to corner lucrative lines of overseas commerce, and to extend their territorial reach.

## Portuguese expansion in Africa, Asia and America

Portugal is central to any explanation of how and why the Atlantic became a frontier for European expansion, and Prince Henry 'the Navigator' (1394–1460) is a key figure. Driven by personal ambition and religious zeal, Henry seized the Moroccan city of Ceuta (1415), then sought to combine crusade with plunder and commerce by attacking Morocco and probing for weaknesses along its Atlantic coast. His conviction that Africa was as valid for Christian crusade as the Mediterranean was reinforced by the myth of a lost Christian kingdom, known as the land of Prester John, which was believed to lay somewhere behind the Islamic states that stretched from Morocco to the Black Sea. For Henry, Atlantic exploration and a maritime route into Africa promised a convenient way into an alliance with Prester John against Islam (Box 1).

---

### Box 1

'This emperor, Prester John, holds full great land, and hath many full noble cities and good towns in his realm and many great diverse isles and large. For all the country [called] Ind is devised in isles for the great floods that come from Paradise, that depart all the land in many parts. And also in the sea he hath full many isles. And the best city in the Isle of Pentexoire is Nyse, that is a full royal city and a noble, and full rich.'

*(Mandeville 1366, Web resources)*

Account attributed to Sir John Mandeville (1366).

---

The fight against Islam was considered perfectly compatible with the pursuit of material reward, and Henry was interested in finding the African sources of gold and slaves to build a maritime trade in African slaves, for shipment to Portugal and its Atlantic islands ('Marginals and deviants' in Part II). Henry also wanted territory, and expended considerable resources on imposing Portuguese sovereignty over the Canary Islands, Madeira and the Azores, all of which offered opportunities for colonization and, supposedly, evangelization among native peoples. He lost the Canaries to Castile but his development of Madeira provided important lessons in how to organise and profit from overseas colonization, especially when Madeira switched to sugar cultivation using African slave labour. Exploration on West African shores opened new frontiers. In 1434, Portuguese mariners rounded Cape Bojador, allowing Prince Henry to establish the Guinea trade, which made Portugal the leader in both European trade with Africa and the search for a route to Asia. Indeed, returns from the African trade in gold and slaves provided the incentive and the means to keep pushing south in search for a route to India. Bartolomé Dias finally found a way in 1488, when, by rounding the Cape of Good Hope, he confirmed that entry into the Indian Ocean was possible, and thus opened the way to Vasco da Gama's voyage to India a decade later (Russell 2001).

Gama's expedition and those that followed under Almeida and Albuquerque were propelled by the Portuguese nobility's blend of crusading zeal and desire for wealth and glory through war. The Portuguese soon found that their ships' artillery gave them an advantage in battle, and, urged on by the king's messianic dreams of retaking Jerusalem with the wealth snatched from Muslim commerce, expeditions sent by Manuel I (1495–1521) smashed their way into Indian ports and Asian trading systems. In 1510–15, Albuquerque laid the foundations of an empire that had no pretensions to occupy large territories, or to pit Portugal's small population against much bigger states: it was instead built on a network of fortified bases which, when combined with seapower and naval mobility, allowed Portugal to dominate major trade routes. Goa enabled Portugal to enter trade between India and the Levant; Malacca was a base for trade with Indonesia, the Spice Islands, Japan and China; Hormuz controlled routes from the Persian Gulf to the Levant. Another fortified base at Colombo, established in 1518, commanded routes to the Bay of Bengal. By 1550, Portuguese commanders had established an empire of around fifty trading posts between Mozambique in southern Africa and Macao in China, all nominally under the authority of the administrative structure of the *Estado da India*, a system for squeezing profits from lucrative Asian trades by imposing monopolies, peopled by a relatively small diaspora of traders, officials, soldiers and sailors (Boxer 1969). It flourished briefly until, during the early seventeenth century, the Dutch and English seized many of its trading bases and much of its commerce (Box 2).

Africa and Asia were not the only spaces for Portuguese expansion. When sailing to India in 1500, Pedro Alvares Cabral had found territory in the western Atlantic

### Box 2

'The Lusitanian Indian Empire or State, which formerly dominated the whole of the East, . . . gave law to thirty-three tributary kingdoms, amazed the whole world with its vast extent, stupendous victories, thriving trade and immense riches, is now . . . reduced to . . . relics and those but few, of the great body of that State, which our enemies have left us. . .'

*(Boxer 1969, 130)*

The Jesuit Manuel Godinho describing the rise and decline of the Portuguese empire in India as he saw it in 1663.

which he promptly claimed for Portugal under the terms of the Treaty of Tordesillas (an agreement between Spain and Portugal to separate the world into two spheres of influence, divided by a longitudinal line through the Atlantic). While its energies were focused on war and trade in Asia, Portugal did little to activate this claim, but after *c.* 1530 the king made feudal grants to a dozen *donatários* (proprietor lords) in order to stimulate colonial development, while also strengthening the royal presence and ousting French interlopers from 'La France Antartique' at Rio de Janeiro. Under these new conditions, Portuguese immigration expanded, coastal towns were built, agriculture developed, and Brazil was on the way to becoming the world's largest sugar producer and the hub of Portugal's empire ('Europe overseas' in Part IV).

## Spanish expansion in the Americas

Spaniards were also in the vanguard of Atlantic expansion, propelled by religious and material motives similar to those of the Portuguese, their long-standing rivals. After Castile secured the Canary Islands for Spain in 1479, they, too, acquired a growing interest in Atlantic expansion. Hence, when Columbus prevailed upon the Spanish crown to support a westward voyage to reach the shores of Asia, he received a sympathetic hearing.

Columbus used the usual religious rhetoric, promising discoveries that would fulfil the providential purpose of spreading Christianity across the world. However, he supported his proposal with geographical calculations which, by estimating that China was only about 2,500 miles to the west, allowed him to persuade the Catholic Monarchs that 'the Indies' could be reached by sailing directly across the Atlantic (Fernández-Armesto 1992; '1492' in Web resources). On landfall in the Caribbean islands, Columbus therefore believed that he was off the coast of China. This accidental discovery of America expanded European horizons in unforeseen and unintended ways, not least in providing Spain with claims to lands on which it would build an overseas empire of unprecedented size and wealth.

Spanish expansion depended, from its outset, on the use of armed force, which facilitated Spanish exploitation of the Caribbean islands for gold and slaves. The Spanish made sudden, massive gains in the 1520s and 1530s, when they made contact with the Aztecs and Incas. In 1521, Hernán Cortés overthrew the Aztec state and, on the ruins of its capital Tenochtitlán, founded Mexico City, later the capital of the Viceroyalty of New Spain. In 1532, Francisco Pizarro penetrated into Peru and, after killing the Inca king Atahualpa, entered the Inca capital at Cuzco in 1533, where he and his conquistadors established a base for further conquests in South America. The extraordinary windfalls of plunder won by such expeditions attracted waves of Spanish adventurers, traders and settlers, who spread from the core areas of conquest into adjoining regions, where they asserted control over other indigenous peoples.

The Spaniards' astonishing success derived from their daring and determination, and from the divisions among native peoples whom they fought. However, it owed most to their military and biological advantages. Native peoples not only misunderstood Spanish intentions and methods of war, but were also without the weaponry needed to oppose them. Indians had no experience of gunpowder technology, but the Spaniards' chief military advantage came from other battlefield weapons, such as steel swords, steel-tipped lances and horses, which gave them a force-multiplier of extraordinary value: armed men on horseback repeatedly outmanoeuvred and overcame much larger forces. The Spaniards' military superiority was reinforced by a hidden biological weapon: Old World diseases against which the Indians had no immunity. The invaders' germs undermined indigenous resistance both during the conquests and throughout the century that followed. Smallpox, measles, diphtheria, influenza and other Old World diseases swept through native populations with such catastrophic effect that as many as 80 per cent of the Amerindian population in Spanish America died during the century after Columbus's discovery (Figure IV.8).

In addition to their military and biological advantages, Spaniards were able to consolidate their conquest by permanent settlements and systematic exploitation. In highland regions, they found temperate climates that were healthy for Europeans and inhabited by large peasant populations accustomed to rendering tribute to their rulers. The Spaniards also benefitted from the 'Columbian exchange'. Cattle and

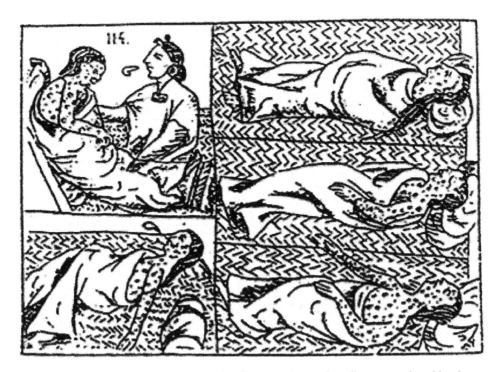

**Figure IV.8** Native American Aztec people of Mexico dying of small pox introduced by the Spaniards, copied from the Codex Florentine, c. 1540 (colour litho) / Private Collection / Peter Newark American Pictures / Bridgeman Images.

horses, sheep and goats, pigs and chickens, none previously known to the Americas, multiplied rapidly; wheat and barley from the Old World provided staples of the European diet, and sugar became a key commercial crop; tobacco, native to the Americas, became an important export across the Atlantic. Over the long term, Europe's farmers gradually absorbed Indian cultigens too: maize (known as 'Indian corn'), potatoes, tomatoes, peppers, squash, common beans and pineapples were among the most notable American crops subsequently cultivated in the Old World (Crosby 1972).

But perhaps most important in economic terms was exploitation of immensely rich silver deposits in Mexico and Peru. Mining towns became growth poles for colonial economies, and precious metals paid for imports from Europe, thus providing new markets for its foods and manufactures. And, as silver production soared, it allowed Europeans to pay for luxury goods from China and other Asian economies, thus sustaining the growth of a truly global commerce ('The global exchange of goods' in Part IV; Box 3).

## Box 3

'. . . [t]here is no gold or silver money in China, but only current weight of gold and silver, and everything is bought and sold by weight; wherefore every man hath a pair of scales and weights in his house, which all are exceedingly perfect. . . For each one laboureth by all means he can to deceive the other, so none do trust the scales and weights of the other, and every one that goeth to buy in the market carrieth a weight and balance and broken silver.'

(Boxer 2004, 128–29)

From an account of China by the Portuguese Dominican Gaspar Da Cruz.

Silver also provided the means for consolidating territorial expansion by political and cultural domination. Revenues from mining and commerce gave the Spanish Habsburgs both incentive and means to create an apparatus of government greater than any seen in Europe since Roman times. These riches also paid for the Catholic Church to pursue a cultural conquest, as its missionaries undertook extraordinary campaigns to convert the Indians, and made a major contribution to spreading Christianity farther beyond Europe than it had ever previously reached.

## Rival empires

The arbitrary Iberian division of the world at Tordesillas did not limit European expansion. Other European rulers quickly challenged such claims, and their subjects joined the surge of overseas exploration and expansion, east and west. During the sixteenth century, Dutch, English and French explorers searched for a north-west passage to China and for rich indigenous civilisations in America, while also plundering Spanish and Portuguese commerce; then, after *c.* 1600, they moved to a new stage, with states supporting private endeavours to challenge Iberian primacy in overseas trade and to establish colonies. The major contenders were the Dutch and English who, backed by growing economies and increasingly ambitious states, fought to share in the gains made by Portugal and Spain.

Rooted in a combination of Protestant animosity against Catholic Spain, political ambition and desire for wealth, Dutch and English overseas expansion spread east and west. Its main vehicle was the joint-stock company, organised for the purposes of private commerce and state power. In Asia, the English operated under the aegis of the EAST INDIA COMPANY (EIC), a joint-stock organisation founded in 1600 with a royal monopoly over English Asian trade, and funded by a large number of merchants and investors ('Trading Places' in Web resources). The Dutch VEREENIGDE OOSTINDISCHE COMPAGNIE (VOC) was established in Amsterdam in 1602 to capitalize on the growing trade in goods from Asia, and, with government approval, expanded rapidly at Portuguese expense (Figure IV.9).

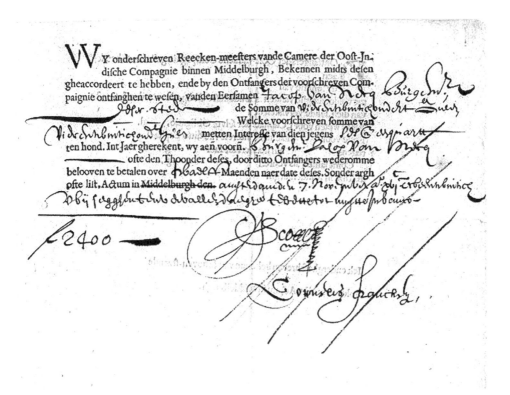

**Figure IV.9** A bond for 2,400 florins issued on 7 November 1623 by the Vereenigde Oostindische Compagnie in its Middelburg chamber, signed in Amsterdam. © Private Collection / Auktionshaus Tschöpe.

The Dutch relied on naval and military force to seize Portuguese trading bases, and concentrated on the spice trades of the Indonesian archipelago, with its capital at Batavia (now Jakarta), while the English, forced from the Spice Islands by Dutch aggression, focused on India (Jacobs 2006). They established trading factories at Surat, Madras, Bombay and Calcutta, and from those ports traded in spices and textiles, and sent ships to China to acquire tea. EIC merchants also used Indian textiles to fund the trade in African slaves that worked on Caribbean plantations. Though less successful than the VOC – which deployed bigger naval forces, had a strategy for expansion, more central direction and larger resources – the EIC nonetheless became a base for empire-building in the later eighteenth century, when the collapse of the Mughal state opened opportunities for territorial acquisition ('Europe and the world, c. 1800' in Part IV).

Dutch and English expansion in the West was driven by much the same combination of commercial and political ambition, and their vehicle was, again, private companies privileged by the state. The *West-Indische Compagnie* (1621), granted the monopoly for trade with the Americas and West Africa, spearheaded Dutch expansion. While at war with Spain, the Dutch invaded Brazil and in 1630–54 occupied valuable sugar plantation regions; they also took lands in the Caribbean and, temporarily, at New Amsterdam (later New York) in North America. The Dutch were, however, no more significant in territorial and cultural terms in America than they were in Asia. Merchants aimed to take over existing trades rather than organising production, and had scant interest in territorial dominion or Christian evangelizing.

English companies, on the other hand, laid the foundations for an American empire, acting on both commercial and religious motives. The Virginia Company established the first English colony at Jamestown (1607) and later turned tobacco into a successful export to Europe. English companies established a colony at Barbados (1625) and later in other Caribbean islands, where they grew tobacco before turning to sugar. The Massachusetts Bay Company founded colonies of a quite different kind in New England, following the example of the Puritan religious refugees who had founded New Plymouth (1620). In 1630, its leaders organised a substantial migration, based on family groups inspired by religious ideals, under leaders intent on founding a New Jerusalem. The English presence was later reinforced by the foundation of colonies in the Middle Atlantic region, which grew strong from agrarian colonisation and trade during the eighteenth century. This contrasted sharply with the French experience. France planted small settlements in Canada and the Caribbean, but was the least successful of the European powers in building a colonial empire overseas (See 'Europe overseas' in Part IV).

## Assessment

In his *Wealth of Nations* (1776), Adam Smith looked back on the voyages of discovery as 'the most important events recorded in the history of mankind' (1976, 560). Though

Smith's statement now seems exaggerated, it highlights the global impact of an overseas expansion that not only altered European configurations of wealth and power, but also generated or accelerated change in the societies most exposed to European commerce and colonisation. American indigenous peoples were most profoundly affected, for they were suddenly thrust into contact with Europeans who introduced deadly diseases, seized their lands, coerced their labour, and imposed alien political systems and cultures. Africa suffered less from European expansion, for, although the communities were disrupted by slaving, the vast African interior remained largely undisturbed. South and East Asian states and societies were also generally secure in their own social and economic systems, cultural codes and religions.

So, while Europeans had made impressive advances outside their world, their expansion did not bring global primacy. Asian societies remained economically and culturally autonomous, and able to compete in military terms. Although Europeans had initiated the maritime expansion that linked continents as never before and created colonies which mobilised new resources, it is important to recognise that the acquisitive power of Asian societies gave them a key role in the emergence of a new system of global trade. Historians have accordingly argued for a 'reorientation' of early modern economic history, away from a Europe-centred view to one which places Asian markets at the core of global development, fuelling the expansion of the maritime trades that energised European commercial CAPITALISM, at least until about 1800.

## Discussion themes

1.  Why were Portugal and Spain leaders in early European expansion overseas?
2.  What part did religious ideals play in European expansion in the sixteenth century?
3.  Can European expansion in the sixteenth century be regarded as the 'first globalization'?
4.  Compare the importance of Europe and Asia in the development of world trade up to *c.* 1800.

## Bibliography

### (A) Sources

Boxer, Charles R. ed. (2004), *South China in the Sixteenth Century, Being the Narratives of Galeote Pereire, Fr. Gaspar da Cruz, O.P., Fr. Martin de Rada, O.E.S.A. (1550–1575)*, reprint of 1953 edn, London
Smith, Adam (1976), *An Inquiry into the Nature and Causes of the Wealth of Nations*, reprint edn, Oxford

**(B) Literature**

Boxer, Charles R. (1969), *The Portuguese Seaborne Empire*, London
Brotton, Jerry (2012), *A History of the World in Twelve Maps*, London
Crosby, Alfred W. (1972), *The Columbian Exchange: Biological and Cultural Consequences of 1492*, Westport, Conn.
Fernández-Armesto, Felipe (1992), *Columbus*, Oxford
Freedman, Paul (2008), *Out of the East: Spices and the Medieval Imagination*, New Haven, Conn.
Jacobs, Els M. (2006), *Merchant in Asia: The Trade of the Dutch East India Company During the Eighteenth Century*, Leiden
Russell, Peter (2001), *Prince Henry 'the Navigator': A Life*, New Haven, Conn.
Scammell, G.V. (1981), *The World Encompassed*, London
Wills, John E. (2011), 'Maritime Europe and the Ming', in: *China and Maritime Europe, 1500–1800*, ed. John E. Wills, Cambridge, 24–77

**(C) Web resources**

'1492: An Ongoing Voyage' (1993), Library of Congress Exhibition: <https://www.loc.gov/exhibits/1492/about.html>
'Auktionshaus Tschöpe', Auction house for old shares and bonds: <http://www.tschoepe.de/auktion51/auktion51.htm>
Mandeville, Sir John, 'Prester John' (1366), in IHSP: <http://sourcebooks.fordham.edu/halsall/source/mandeville.asp>
'The history of the transatlantic slave trade', at International Slavery Museum, Liverpool: <http://www.liverpoolmuseums.org.uk/ism/slavery/> (accessed 16/11/2016)
'Trading Places', British Library website on the East India Company: <http://www.bl.uk/learning/histcitizen/trading/tradingplaces.html>
'Treaty of Tordesillas', National Geographic website: <http://nationalgeographic.org/thisday/jun7/treaty-tordesillas/>

# Europe overseas

*Anthony McFarlane*

One of the most significant long-term effects of Columbus's American landfall in 1492 and Vasco da Gama's voyage to India in 1498 was the dispersion of European peoples across the world. Migration was not a new phenomenon, but transoceanic explorations at that time opened an entirely new chapter. By finding ways across the Atlantic, around Africa and into the Indian Ocean, then farther east to the South China seas, Europeans escaped the confines of the medieval world, and, following new maritime routes, embarked on an unprecedented surge of overseas settlement and empire building ('Expanding horizons' in Part IV).

The movements of European peoples produced many distinctive diasporas, reflecting the varied purposes of migrants, their different social and cultural backgrounds and the diverse physical and human environments into which they moved (Canny 1994). However, one broad distinction stands out: the difference between European patterns of settlements in Africa and Asia from those in the Americas. In the former, Europeans were confined to small areas, often depended on the cooperation of local princes and potentates and had limited cultural impact. The Americas, by contrast, saw the emergence of European colonies built on large appropriations of territory, substantial settlements of migrants, the devastation of native peoples and their cultures as well as the construction of distinctive neo-European societies.

## Europeans in Africa and Asia

The first European settlements in Africa and Asia were the Portuguese FEITORIAS, established to provide bases for exchange, the store of merchandise and repair of ships. The first were installed on the West African coast from the mid-fifteenth century to trade gold, ivory, and slaves, and enter into relations with local powers, such as the Kingdom of Congo. Agrarian settlement was rarely attempted: a royal charter for colonising Angola with Portuguese peasants in 1571, for example, was quickly abandoned in favour of slave trading. Migrants were in fact more likely to assimilate into African societies than impose their own. A striking example is found in the Zambezi region, where Portuguese men took local wives, entered tribal hierarchies and lived according to African norms. Christianity made little headway, hindered no doubt by both the countervailing influence of Islam and the association between Christians and slavery. The only place in Africa settled by European farming families came later, after Dutch settlers started the South African Cape Colony in 1652, cultivating European crops and livestock to supply Dutch ships sailing to Asia, and later importing slave labour to work the land.

Portuguese colonies in South and East Asia were similar, strung out at strategic points from East Africa to the Bay of Bengal, and through the Indonesian archipelago to Macao and, briefly, Japan. This expansion was initially achieved by aggressive maritime warfare, using ships with more effective artillery than those of their adversaries, but in East Asia relied more on diplomacy. Portugal was unable to plant substantial settlements. Its population was too small to supply sufficient numbers, particularly as high rates of mortality from tropical diseases constantly culled its overseas communities. The balance of political power was also invariably unfavourable. The densely-populated realms of South and South-east Asia had high levels of wealth, military strength and political power, and rulers who, though prepared to grant extra-territorial rights to foreign traders, offered no room for substantial colonization. In these circumstances, the Portuguese presence in the ESTADO DA INDIA was always overstretched: by 1600, a century after the first voyages of discovery, there were only about 15,000 Portuguese living in the vast area from East Africa to the Moluccas (Appendix, Map 3). The impact of Christianity was also slight: missionaries never competed successfully with Islam, and made little impression on the adherents of ancient religions such as Hinduism and Buddhism (Russell-Wood 1998).

European settlement in Asia generally followed the Portuguese pattern. The Spanish Philippines were founded in the 1560s using methods of conquest and colonization akin to those used in America, but soon came to resemble Portuguese ENTREPÔTS. When, in the seventeenth century, the Dutch and English followed the Iberians eastwards, they seized Portugal's positions and also followed Portuguese methods ('The global exchange of goods' in Part IV). Relations between Europeans and peoples in the African and Asian regions generally reflected the imbalance in their numbers and power. As female and family migrants were few, male migrants tended to mix with, though not necessarily marry, local women. Indeed, according to scandalised clerics, in Asian towns where female prostitution and slavery were

## Box 1

'I say this of the Portuguese, who have adopted the vices and customs of the land without reserve . . . There are countless men who buy droves of girls and sleep with them all, and subsequently sell them . . . This is carried to such excess that there was one man in Malacca who had twenty-four women of various races, all of whom were his slaves, and all of whom he enjoyed.'

(Boxer 1969, 307–8)

An Italian Jesuit writing from India in 1550.

prevalent, Portuguese settlers readily adapted to a 'harem society', practising polygamy and keeping female slaves for sex (Box 1). In Africa, the Portuguese and later Dutch and English were equally inclined to mix with local women and adjust to local ways. A dominant white elite only emerged towards the end of the eighteenth century, when war among Indian princes generated political instability and, with it, opportunities to divide and conquer. Until then, the principal sites of white settlement overseas were in the western hemisphere. There, in the Americas, Europeans entered a world where their guns, germs and steel allowed them to defeat native peoples and to build colonies based on the appropriation of territory, substantial immigration and the subordination of non-European labour.

## Spanish America

Spain's conquests and early settlements bore the stamp of a Castilian feudal society rooted in medieval traditions of Christian war and territorial conquest against Islamic Spain. Let loose in the Americas, Spanish *conquistadors* pursued wealth and glory, regarding lordship over land and labour as their reward for subjugating native peoples. The crown secured their loyalty through the ENCOMIENDA, thus establishing the first element of a hierarchical society with a highly unequal distribution of wealth and power. The ENCOMENDEROS did not, however, recreate Spanish feudal society, for the monarch decreed that Indians were subject to royal law without seigneurial jurisdiction, and royal officials gradually took over the management of tributary labour.

A remarkable feature of Spanish settlement was its range and depth. The *conquistadors'* plunder of the Aztec and Inca states acted as a magnet to other European migrants, drawing them into the continental interiors, especially to temperate regions with large indigenous populations. There, Spaniards forced Indian peasant populations to provide the goods and labour needed to support Spanish towns and trade; they applied European techniques to mining of precious metals and they appropriated fertile lands capable of supporting European-style agriculture.

As settlements fanned out across the continent, they acted as conduits for an extraordinary transplantation of Spanish culture. Towns stood at the heart of Spanish American societies, reflecting the Mediterranean pattern. They were not fortified strongholds from which to demand tribute and intrude into local trading systems, but economic hubs and administrative centres where Spaniards concentrated political and cultural power. In the ordered grid pattern of their streets, the Mediterranean architecture of their houses, plazas and churches, stores and shops (Figure IV.10 and www.routledge.com/cw/kumin), towns brought Spanish ways of thinking and behaving which, combined with a confident sense of cultural superiority, transformed pre-Columbian America and underpinned Hispanic societies with their own characteristics and identities (Lockhart and Schwartz 1983, Box 2).

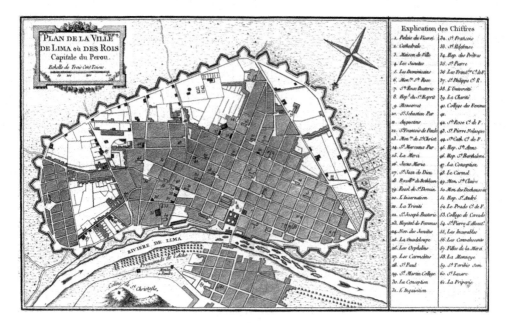

The table at right of the map reads:

Explication des Chiffres

**Figure IV.10** Plan of Lima by Jacques Nicolas Bellin, showing defensive walls built in 1684–87 (1764). Public Domain, David Rumsey Historical Map Collection.

## Box 2

Christian missionaries attempted a parallel 'spiritual conquest' of the Indians. Inspired by millenarian hopes of Christ's Second Coming, they engaged enthusiastically with the enormous task of converting large indigenous communities. They did not succeed completely, as Indians tended to blend their own spiritual beliefs and practices with Christianity, creating a hybrid, 'Indian Christianity' (Mills 1997). Nonetheless, the spread of European religion helped to reconcile Indian communities to Spanish rule, and to bind them to throne and altar. The authorities meanwhile ensured the exclusivity of the Roman Catholic form of Christianity, and the Church became a rich, powerful institution on a par with royal government (Redden 2015; Figure IV.11 and further examples on www.routledge.com/cw/kumin).

Spanish settlement also involved a sexual conquest. Most early migrants were single males who took native women as sexual partners, creating MESTIZO offspring. As people of mixed origins multiplied, the settlers modified their social hierarchy to accommodate local realities. The European 'society of estates' became a 'society of castes', which ranked people according to their ethnic origin and skin colour. People of European descent stood at the top; below them was an increasingly complex spectrum of people of colour, calibrated according to their proximity to Spanish descent. The various sub-groups were free people with some element of white descent

Cathedral "La Paroquia" Guanajuato

**Figure IV.11**
Cathedral
'La Paroquia' at
Guanajuato (photo c.
1905). DeGolyer Library,
Southern Methodist
University.

who generally formed part of Hispanic societies. At the base of the social order we find people who, even when Christians, were regarded as irredeemably inferior: the Indians, who still paid tribute as a mark of conquest, and blacks, who were slaves or descendants of slaves ('New World Orders' in Web resources).

Soon, the majority of whites were born in America and, though these CRIOLLOS attributed their superior status to Spanish descent, they gradually asserted distinct identities. While creole families might hold powerful social positions, Spaniards did not always regard them as social equals, nor did the crown trust them with the highest positions of political power; they therefore cultivated a compensating sense of status, linked to the lands of their birth. Such creole self-awareness did not threaten Spanish rule; if creoles wanted more autonomy, they saw their future within the empire rather than outside it. It was only after 1808, when Spain was plunged into crisis by war and internal revolution, that this 'creole consciousness' shaped Spanish American demands for independence. Until then, while France lost Canada and St Domingue, and Britain lost the United States, Spain's empire remained intact, with territories from California to Cape Horn, a total population of over 13 million people, and a remarkable political stability (Elliott 2006).

## Portuguese America

Portuguese America got off to a slower start than Spanish America. Settlement was slight and transient until the later sixteenth century, when Portuguese planters, following the example set by Madeira and especially the West African island of São Tomé, started to cultivate sugar on the fertile soils of Pernambuco and Bahia, using slave labour imported from Africa.

Sugar was for Brazil's economy and society what silver was for Mexico and Peru: a product of high value that generated networks of transatlantic trade and a source of wealth that attracted thousands of immigrants. Migrants were not hard to find, due to shortages of land and rural poverty in Portugal, and by 1570 more went to Brazil than to 'Golden Goa'. Although many were peasants (mostly males, with few women and family groups), they did not create a neo-European society of family farmers. On the contrary, immigrants avoided manual labour where possible. Indeed, by the end of the sixteenth century, Brazil was becoming a distinctively slave society, in some respects more similar to Portuguese-African São Tomé than to Spanish Mexico or Peru, albeit much richer and more complex.

Brazil's key economic and social institution was the ENGENHO, run by a *senhor de engenho* who controlled large amounts of land and animals, presiding over a largely self-contained community of tenants, workers and slaves. Often enormously wealthy, these landed patriarchs mimicked Portuguese seigneurial style, in an informal aristocracy that dominated local society and government (see plantation image on

www.routledge.com/cw/kumin). They stood at the apex of a social system in which whites occupied the front ranks, followed by free MULATTOS and MESTIZOS, with slaves and Indians relegated to the lowest positions. Weakened by Old World diseases, indigenous communities were largely erased from the coastal regions, with survivors marginalised. Portugal's kings promised to Christianize Indians and slaves, but did less to promote evangelization than the Spanish.

Portuguese Brazil long remained an archipelago of coastal cities, with its main centres in Pernambuco, Bahia and Rio de Janeiro. Some penetration occurred in the south, however, where São Paulo became a spearhead for inland settlement. There, the BANDEIRANTES mixed with Indian women, and their mestizo offspring peopled a vigorous frontier society. Searching for silver and Indian slaves, PAULISTAS found abundant alluvial gold and sparked a gold rush which, in the early eighteenth century, sucked in immigrants and injected new vitality into the Luso-Brazilian economy. This had a tremendous impact on Brazil and its relationship to Portugal, above all through growing imports of African slaves (who made up a third of a population of over three million by around 1800). Brazil had become one of Europe's richest American colonies and, economically, overshadowed smaller, poorer Portugal (Lockhart and Schwarz 1983, Russell-Wood 1998).

## Caribbean plantation colonies

Other variants of European colonisation started later, in regions Spain had neglected. A key area was in the Eastern Caribbean, where English and French settlers established island colonies in the early seventeenth century, producing export crops such as tobacco, indigo, cotton and ginger. These were based on white settlements, as planters and merchants imported indentured workers from their home countries, under contracts for several years' work in return for wages or plots of land. This proved unsustainable, however: few immigrants survived harsh working conditions in tropical climates, and as the white population was unable to reproduce itself, the islands relied on a dwindling supply of replacements from Europe.

Caribbean colonies nonetheless prospered and grew, once Europeans discovered the islands' potential for sugar cultivation and followed the example of Brazil. The trend started in the 1640s, when the Dutch (who held Pernambuco in 1630–54) encouraged sugar production in Barbados. Within a few decades, Barbados's white settler society became a slave society, an example subsequently followed throughout the English and French islands. Everywhere colonies of white settlement were transformed into colonies of black exploitation, in which slaves greatly outnumbered whites. Plantation workers lived short lives, but their population grew constantly, routinely replenished by the expanding African slave trade, which was, like sugar, a source of rich profits (Figure IV.12; Heuman and Walvin 2003; 'Atlantic Slave Trade' in Web resources).

By the mid-eighteenth century, most Caribbean islands were deeply polarised societies. The basic principle of government was to suppress the slaves, who were treated as property, not persons. Little effort was made to Christianize or Europeanize slaves, on the grounds that it might undermine the slave owners' security; slaves were instead left to replicate cultures they brought from Africa. A free coloured population emerged, mainly from concubinage with slave women, and in both English and French islands the mulatto population increased over the eighteenth century (Burnard 2003). They did little, however, to modify the racist social order, for, although most were poor and regarded as inferior, free coloureds tended to identify more with whites than blacks and rarely challenged the bi-racial hierarchy. The major exception was in French St Domingue, where, in 1791, free coloureds inflamed by the rhetoric of the French Revolution demanded civil equality and, when opposed, forged alliances with slave rebels to secure it in the first independent black republic ('The Louverture Project' in Web resources and cf. the Haitian Revolution image on the companion website www.routledge.com/cw/kumin).

On the whole, Caribbean slave societies were built on violence and the threat of violence. Slaves were brutally treated and whites lived in fear of slave insurrection. The Caribbean islands were also exposed to international warfare, as they stood at the crossroads of competing empires. In the later seventeenth century, the BUCCANEERS conducted private wars of plunder, mostly against the Spaniards; during

**Figure IV.12** A generalized view of a 'typical' sugar plantation in the French West Indies, showing the houses of the owner and overseers (surrounded by a fence) on the upper right; the houses of the slaves, 'forming one or two or more streets', on the lower right; sugar cane fields centre and left; the water mill for grinding canes and the boiling house on the lower left; the curing house, where the sugar is dried in pots, on the upper left: 'Encyclopedie, ou Dictionnaire raisonné des sciences, des arts et des metiers', by Denis Diderot and Jean-Baptiste Le Rond d'Alembert, 1751–72 (engraving), Diderot, Denis (1713–84) / Private Collection / De Agostini Picture Library / Bridgeman Images.

the eighteenth century, European wars regularly spilled over into Caribbean waters, where Britain and France sought to capture or destroy the sugar-planting production of their competitors (McFarlane 1994). However, apart from St Domingue, most islands remained under colonial rule until well into the modern era.

## Europeans in North America

During the early seventeenth century, Spain had done little to populate North America outside Mexico; it held Florida, to defend the homeward route of the treasure fleets, but neglected areas further north. It was there, in lands claimed but not occupied by Spain, that other European states attempted to create their own empires, and implanted communities of several different kinds (Kupperman 2000).

France focused on Canada, a vast and ill-defined region peopled by indigenous farmers and hunters. Settlement was always difficult, due to the cold climate and lack of obvious resources, and only weak strands of settlement emerged. One was a line of missions and trading posts, reaching inland from the St Lawrence River, where clerics and traders searched for souls to convert and furs to sell in Europe. The other, more European part of Canada stood on the lower St Lawrence, where the crown planted permanent settlement through a system of *seigneuries* or feudal land grants. Yet this 'New France' grew very slowly. While immigrants were scarce and vulnerable to Indian attack, its richest resource continued to be the fur trade. At the end of the century, the French also occupied Louisiana, but it too was slow to grow: by the mid-eighteenth century, the French population of Canada was no more than 50,000 people, with another 5,000 in Louisiana (Eccles 1972).

Dutch colonisation in North America was transient, and always overshadowed by England. The settlement of New Netherland, established on the Hudson River in 1624, had a population of only about 10,000 people when the English took it in 1664, and at the Treaty of Breda (1667) the Dutch abandoned it in exchange for Surinam (a sugar plantation territory in the Guyanas) and Run, the base for England's nutmeg trade in the Spice Islands. This acquisition confirmed the position of England (and later Britain) as the major colonizing power in North America.

The early Anglo-American colonies reflected different facets of early seventeenth-century England. On one hand, the dissenting Protestant communities who established themselves in New England after 1620 mirrored their founders' desire to reconstruct traditional village societies that were fast disappearing in England itself. The communities established under the aegis of joint-stock companies in Virginia (1607) and Barbados (1625) were quite different: they reflected the more individualistic, materialistic and mobile society that was evolving in England, and developed more dynamically.

In terms of spatial distribution, English settlement in North America resembled Portuguese patterns more than those of Spanish America, for it consisted primarily of agricultural settlements on the fringes of a continent, with ports as the main urban centres. Here, however, the resemblance ends. For, while Brazilian society rested on an export-oriented plantation economy using African slaves, later reinforced by gold and diamond mining, British North America had no mining frontier and became a more richly varied agrarian society. In the north, the New England communities that arose from the idealistic Protestant settlements of the early years became increasingly attuned to a commercial economy, based on agriculture, fur trading, fishing, shipbuilding and maritime transportation. In the south, the settlers of Virginia and Maryland developed tobacco planting using indentured labour, before replacing white immigrant labour with African slaves and opening the way to development of slave-based plantation economies in the Chesapeake region and the Carolinas, producing tobacco, rice and indigo. In the Middle Atlantic colonies (New York, New Jersey and Pennsylvania), another kind of society emerged: here, white family farmers produced temperate crops such as wheat and maize that were increasingly exported to the Caribbean and Southern Europe, and built societies unlike any found in Spanish, Portuguese or French colonies. William Penn, the beneficiary of a land grant from Charles II, for example, created a colony aimed at Protestant refugees from Germany,

Austria and Switzerland as well as Britain; his province of Pennsylvania became renowned as 'the best poor man's country'. Large eighteenth-century waves of immigration into the Middle Atlantic colonies also peopled interior regions, west of the coastal hinterlands, where dispossessed peasants from Northern Britain, Ireland and Scotland intruded into Indian territories, set up family farms and opened new spaces for settlement on a mobile, often violent frontier (McFarlane 1994, 'Colonial America' in Web resources).

Seen as a whole, British North America differed socio-economically from Spanish, Portuguese and French America in several key respects. First, its demographic growth was extraordinarily dynamic. The rate of increase of the white population was particularly notable. From about 26,000 in 1640 it reached around 2.2 million in 1780, reflecting not only high levels of immigration but also strong demographic growth in regions where temperate climes, availability of land and good living standards permitted a high birth rate and low infant mortality. British North America was, secondly, less hierarchical and more open than other colonies of settlement. Wealth was more widely distributed and taxes relatively low; there was no formal nobility, even on the small scale of the Iberian and French colonies; and relatively easy access to land favoured the emergence of a substantial 'middling' class. It was not everywhere a land of opportunity, however: inequalities of wealth widened with commercial development, and Indians and blacks were relegated to inferior and servile positions. Racial mixing was also less widespread than in other colonial societies. In British America, Indians were generally pushed aside, without concern to integrate them into Christian society, and people of Indian-white descent were largely found on frontiers (like the French-American MÉTIS who, as *coureurs du bois*, hunted and traded for furs among Indian allies). There was some mixing between blacks and whites, as slave owners exploited female slaves for sex, but, as slaves were largely segregated on plantations, this did not produce the substantial groupings of free mulattos found in Brazil and parts of Spanish America.

Another peculiar feature of British North America was its diversity of religious belief and practice. In New England, religious groups sought to create a 'godly' society based on autonomous congregations, while in the Middle Atlantic colonies, Quakers, Mennonites, Moravians and others added to a rich variety of Protestant religious practice during the eighteenth century (Bonomi 2003). This pluralism was in marked contrast to Iberian and French America, where religious life was corralled in a single established Church, controlled by an ecclesiastical hierarchy that was intolerant of heterodoxy and strongly supportive of the monarchy. Finally, unlike Spanish and Portuguese dominions, British North America had a system of government that provided for local representation, exercised through elections to provincial assemblies that were regarded as mini-parliaments. Such English 'freedom' bound colonials to Britain, but its defence was also to turn them against British government, leading, as it did in 1776, to the declaration of independence, war against Britain and the foundation of the republic of the United States.

## Assessment

The settlements that Europeans established overseas during the early modern period varied widely in character, but were in different ways enormously significant for both Europe and the regions involved. As the keystones of seaborne empires that reached across the globe, they extended Europe's share of global economic resources; as sources of wealth, they changed the balance of power among the states of Europe (from the spectacular rise of Spain in the sixteenth century to the emergence of Britain as a leading maritime power in the eighteenth); and, as points for settlement, they established economic and cultural connections with powerful long-term repercussions.

These effects were most strongly felt in the regions where early modern Europeans settled permanently. Before Columbus, economic life in the Americas was geared primarily to subsistence production by peasant communities, whose agricultural surpluses supported relatively small groups of artisans, traders and leaders ('Beyond Europe, c. 1500' in Part IV). Europeans transformed this environment: they set up individual landholdings and brought new domestic animals (cattle, sheep and horses) which transformed both farming methods and the means of transport and communication. They also geared their production, where possible, to selling in urban or overseas markets, introducing metal currencies which monetised resources and facilitated commerce.

The social effects of European settlement were equally transformational. Indigenous societies were eviscerated by epidemics and African lives shattered by slavery; European migrants, however, found opportunities to improve their material lives in environments which, for the poor, were often significantly better than at home. And, as settlers and their descendants sought to sustain European ways, they increasingly formed creole communities with identities and aspirations of their own, laying the foundations of the modern states which, during the 'Age of Revolution', were to transform global political geography.

## Discussion themes

1. Explain the character of European colonisation in Asia.
2. Why did Spain create a territorial empire in the Americas?
3. How and why did American colonisation become linked to slavery?
4. What were the similarities and differences between Iberian and British colonization in the Americas?

## Bibliography

### (A) Sources

Diderot, Denis (1762), *Encyclopédie, ou, Dictionnaire Raisonné des Sciences, des Arts et des* Metiers, vol. 1, Paris [digital edn: http://encyclopedie.uchicago.edu]

Geggus, David ed. (2014), *The Haitian Revolution: A Documentary History*, Indianapolis

Kupperman, Karen Ordahl ed. (2000), *Major Problems in American Colonial History*, Boston

Mills, Kenneth and Taylor, William B. eds (1998), *Colonial Spanish America: A Documentary History*, Wilmington, Del.

## (B) Literature

Bonomi, Patricia (2003), *Under the Cope of Heaven: Religion, Society and Politics in Colonial America*, Oxford

Boxer, C. R. (1969), *The Portuguese Seaborne Empire, 1415–1825*, London

Burnard, Trevor (2003), *Mastery, Tyranny and Desire: Thomas Thistlewood and his Slaves in the Anglo-Jamaican World*, Chapel Hill

Canny, Nicholas ed. (1994), *Europeans on the Move: Studies in European Migration, 1500–1800*, Oxford

Eccles, W. J. (1972), *France in America*, New York

Elliott, John E. (2006), *Empires of the Atlantic World*, New Haven, Conn.

Heuman, Gad and Walvin, James eds (2003), *The Slavery Reader*, London

Lockhart, James and Schwartz, Stuart (1983), *Early Latin America*, Cambridge

McFarlane, Anthony (1994) *The British in the Americas, 1480–1815*, London

Mills, Kenneth (1997), *Idolatry and its Enemies*, Princeton

Redden, Andrew (2015), 'Heaven on Earth: Churches in Early Modern Hispanic America', in: *Parish Churches in the Early Modern World*, ed. A. Spicer, London, 243–66

Russell-Wood, A. J. R. (1998), *The Portuguese Empire, 1415–1808: A World on the Move*, Baltimore, Md.

## (C) Web resources

'The Atlantic Slave Trade and Slave Life in the Americas: A Visual Record', ed. Jerome S. Handler and Michael L. Tuite Jr (2015): <http://slaveryimages.org/>

'Colonial America': <http://www.amdigital.co.uk/files/amdigital/Collections/downloads/31f7c433612c4621a7d6890fe655d67a.pdf>

'The Louverture Project' on the Haitian Revolution: <http://thelouvertureproject.org>

'New World Orders: Casta Painting and Colonial Latin America', by Jasmin Ramirez (1996): <http://www.artnet.com/magazine_pre2000/features/ramirez/ramirez12-02-96.asp>

# The global exchange of goods

*Anne Gerritsen and Giorgio Riello*

## Introduction

When Vasco da Gama (1460–1524) and Christopher Columbus (1450–1506) set off on their late fifteenth-century journeys, they were driven by a desire for the rich luxuries that Marco Polo had described in the accounts of his travels to China. Columbus was so convinced he was going to China that he carried with him an annotated copy of Marco Polo's book. In fact, only Da Gama brought a small quantity of goods from Asia back to Europe. By the end of the eighteenth century, however, Europeans could buy goods from all over the world in their local shops, and controlled much of their production and manufacturing in the colonies they had established overseas. Between 1500 and 1800 goods were no longer produced and consumed within a single world region, but were traded across vast distances: crops from the Americas fed peasants in Asia; textiles from India clothed men and women while Asian silks and porcelains graced homes throughout Asia, Europe and the Americas; and the silver extracted from the mines in Spanish America paid for transactions all over the world. More than ever before the exchange of goods acquired global dimensions.

This chapter explores not only the global trade that brought goods to Europe, but also their patterns of consumption: the desire for things, the ways in which they were bought and sold, and the different meanings people assigned to things. This approach to goods draws from the concept of material culture, which sees objects as acquiring different meanings over their lifespan from manufacture and throughout the various contexts in which they play a role (Gerritsen and Riello 2015).

## Sixteenth century: Iberian pioneers

The story of the early modern global exchange of goods begins with the Spanish and Portuguese in the sixteenth century. They embarked on their overseas voyages in the joint service of Church and king, and to some extent all their overseas explorations and exploits were driven by a desire to convert new souls to Christianity. But both the Catholic Church and the king were also interested in the promise of overseas wealth and resources; the sixteenth-century story of Europe's overseas expansion is precisely about the intersection of religious aims and economic opportunities.

From the middle of the fifteenth century onwards, the Portuguese kings, and especially Manuel I (1469–1521), encouraged overseas explorations, and sought to establish a series of dispersed but connected Portuguese strongholds. Manuel oversaw the founding of a base in Brazil after its so-called 'discovery' in 1500 by Pedro Álvares Cabral and the appointment of a viceroy in India in 1505, who was in charge of the Portuguese state in Asia (the so-called 'Estado da Índia'). It was also during Manuel's reign that the maritime routes into the Indian Ocean became firmly established, and certain goods were claimed exclusively for the Portuguese crown. The two items Manuel was most interested in were spices and porcelain, and indeed when Vasco da Gama returned to Lisbon in 1499, he presented Manuel with 'sacks of black pepper, cinnamon and cloves, as well as a dozen pieces of chinaware, the first of 300 million to be shipped to Europe over the next three centuries' (Finlay 2010, 5).

Da Gama was able to bring back a series of gifts, but it proved harder for the Portuguese to secure the quantities of goods that both the king and the market demanded. Porcelain, especially, was in high demand; King Manuel issued a request for pieces of the finest porcelain to be made in China, decorated with his own coat of arms, and with the armillary sphere, an astronomical device that represented the great circles of the heavens used for navigation, that had come to serve as a symbol for Portuguese maritime explorations. A small quantity of such items were indeed manufactured in China in the 1520s and 1530s, but the Portuguese were refused access to the place where these porcelains were made, and the Chinese also resisted Portuguese demands for a foothold on Chinese soil. To gain favour with the emperor, King Manuel sent a Portuguese representative as his ambassador to the Emperor. Previously, Tomé Pires had been based in India and Malacca for several years (Box 1).

---

### Box 1

'Pegu is a kingdom of heathens. It is the most fertile land of all we have seen and known. It is more plenteous than Siam and almost as much as Java. . . . The principal [merchandise] is rice. There comes every year . . . fifteen to sixteen junks, twenty to thirty . . . cargo ships. They bring a great deal of lac [i.e. lacquer], and [BENZOIN, MUSK], precious stones, rubies, silver, butter, oil, salt, onions, garlic, mustard and things to eat like that. . . . There is great profit in bringing rice and lac and all the rest of it from Pegu to Malacca. The chief thing [to bring back] is coarse china of various kinds and ornamented in red, a great deal of quicksilver, copper, vermilion, damask, dark *enrolados* with flowers – which come straight from China for them because they are of no use for others – quantities of tin, and they take an infinity of different kinds of china, seed-pearls, a little gold . . . some cloves, nutmeg, [MACE].'

*(Pires 1944, 97–99; cf. Gordon 2008, 164)*

Tomé Pires' early sixteenth-century description of the Kingdom of Pegu in present-day Myanmar.

**Figure IV.13** Rua Nova dos Mercadores, a street in Lisbon renowned in the sixteenth century for its wealth of goods from Asia (painting, c. 1550–1600). Museu Nacional de Arte Antiga.

Tomé Pires' experience in Asia did not help him; the Emperor refused to receive him, and started a campaign of prosecution and imprisonment of all Portuguese present in China. Eventually, in 1557, the Chinese agreed to the establishment of a Portuguese base on Macao, a small island off the southern coast of China. Most of the Chinese porcelain and silk that was brought back to Europe by the Portuguese was bought at various trading ports throughout South-east Asia, where Chinese junks delivered quantities of goods from mainland China. From their base in Malacca, which the Portuguese annexed in 1511, they extended their power over the Moluccas, also known as the Spice Islands, from where they imported nutmeg, mace and cloves. Over the course of the sixteenth century, Portugal served as one of the most important centres for buying and selling goods from Asia (Boxer 1969). On the Rua Nova dos Mercadores (New Commercial Street) in Lisbon (Figure IV.13), all kinds of luxuries were for sale (Jordan-Gschwend and Lowe 2015).

The Spanish, like the Portuguese, fought for both crown and church; large parts of the Americas became Spanish-America under the dual control of religious institutions and imperial state power. But the Spanish were also after the wealth of goods, and access to Asia was crucial for that. The establishment of a Spanish base in Asia with the founding of Manila in the Philippines in 1571 made this possible. From Manila, the Spanish shipped silks and porcelains across the Pacific Ocean in treasure-laden ships known as galleons. The goods arrived in Acapulco in New Spain, and from there were distributed throughout the Spanish Empire, including Seville in Spain. For 250 years, the Manila galleons crossed the Pacific, bringing a wide range of goods and people from Asia into the Spanish world. In the markets in Acapulco, Mexico City and Lima (now Peru), one could buy gowns and stockings, handkerchiefs and church vestments, all made from the finest Chinese silks, but one could also visit a Chinese barber or buy Chinese medicines (Giráldez 2015, 5).

On their return voyages from Acapulco to Manila, the Spanish ships were heavily laden with the commodity that embedded the exchange of global goods in a single global economic system: silver. There were silver mines throughout New Spain, but the silver mines in the town of Potosí, now in Bolivia, and established in 1545, yielded vast quantities; allegedly around 80 per cent of the silver in circulation between 1500 and 1800 came from the Potosí mines (Flynn and Giráldez 2010). The Spanish wealth generated from these mines came at vast human cost: the indigenous American population and the imported African slaves were exploited ruthlessly, working conditions were abominable, and the incidence of mercury poisoning was very high. But the silver mined and minted into *reales* or 'pieces of eight' in Potosí served as global currency into the nineteenth century. Pieces of eight flooded into China and Japan to pay for the vast quantities of silk and porcelain the Europeans wanted, and went on to become the main currency for the payment of taxes within the Chinese Empire; the Spanish real also formed the basis for the American dollar, and was legal currency in the United States until 1857.

## Seventeenth century: The rise of English and Dutch traders

The global circulation of goods changed significantly around the turn of the seventeenth century with the EAST INDIA COMPANY, VEREENIGDE OOST-INDISCHE COMPAGNIE as well as similar French, Swedish, Danish and Ostend foundations. Over the course of the century, three Anglo-Dutch wars were fought, while in Asia, there were constant clashes over commodities, like spices, porcelain, tea, coffee and textiles, and over key ports such as Ambon, Malacca and Bantam. In fact, from 1660, the Dutch held the MONOPOLY to bring spices back to Europe. They considered the spice trade the most profitable, and invested heavily in gaining exclusive control over the small islands where pepper, cloves, nutmeg and mace grew. Soon Amsterdam became an ENTREPÔT for goods from all over the world (Box 2).

The famous dollshouse, made for Petronella Oortman in the late seventeenth century, and now in the Rijksmuseum in Amsterdam (Figure IV.14), is a replica of a canal house, and shows in minute detail how a wealthy family might have lived in Amsterdam. A closer look at some of the items included in this 'household' shows the extent to which global goods had become part of daily life in Amsterdam. There are Chinese porcelain chamberpots, blue-and-white porcelain jugs in the kitchen, Indian CHINTZES on the beds, Japanese LACQUER cabinets, and African shells in

'There is such abun[dance] of Wheat, Wine, Hemp, Flax, Wood and Spices, [it is]
as if all other Provinces of the world were emptied of their wealth, to make
*Amsterdam* a publick treasury of all they produce. . . . When I saw the Store-
houses, and Magazeens reaching at a great distance, from the East-India House,
full of Spices, Silk, Stuffs, Purcelane, and what ever China and the Indies afford
that is most rare, I thought Ceylon had sent thither all its Cinamon, the Moluccas
al their Cloves, the islands of Sumatra and Java, all their Spices, China all its rich
stuffs; Japan its excellent works of several kinds, and the rest of the Indies its
Pepper and Silk.'

*(Olearius 1669, 230; cf. Corrigan, van Campen and Diercks 2015, 124)*

The German adventurer Johann Albrecht von Mandelslo (1616–44) describes the riches
of seventeenth-century Amsterdam.

**Figure IV.14** Anonymous, Dollshouse of Petronella Oortman (*c.* 1686–*c.* 1710). H 255 cm ×
W 190 cm × D 78 cm. Amsterdam, Rijksmuseum, BK-NM-1010.

the cabinets. The goods for sale in Amsterdam may have come from all over the world, but by the time they were integrated in domestic spaces like this canal house, they had become part of the seventeenth-century Dutch world. By 1620 the Dutch Company was already importing 63,000 pieces of Chinese porcelain a year and over the course of the seventeenth and eighteenth centuries pieces of porcelain were traded to Europe in their millions (Gerritsen and Riello 2015). Probate inventories (lists of belongings compiled at the time of death of their owner), paintings and prints also show the profusion of Asian goods to be found in Dutch domestic interiors.

Asia was not the only area of the world with which Europe traded. Over the course of the seventeenth century a flourishing exchange emerged between Europe and the Americas ('Europe overseas' in Part IV). The British colonies in the Americas (including the West Indies), for example, became large purchasers of woollens and linens, metalware and other manufactured goods produced in the British Isles. Attempts at creating new trade routes can be seen also in the creation of the Muscovy Company for the trade between England and Russia and the Levant Company for trade with the Ottoman Empire. The seventeenth century saw a reconfiguration of global trade away from the Mediterranean and Southern Europe and towards both the Indian and the Atlantic Oceans.

## Eighteenth century: expansion and competition

The amounts of Asian goods imported into Europe expanded dramatically over the course of the eighteenth century. The European companies traded in porcelain, furniture, precious and semi-precious materials and stones and artefacts made of lacquer. Textiles, however, formed the bulk of their trade, accounting for up to 70 per cent of all cargoes that reached London and Amsterdam (Riello 2009, 264). Millions of pieces of Indian CALICOES and chintzes were traded to Europe every year and were used first as soft furnishings to adorn interiors and later as cloth for shirts, petticoats and underwear. In one of Molière's plays a French bourgeois gentleman, Monsieur Jourdain, decides to don an informal robe (called BANYAN, Figure IV.15) made of imported Indian calicoes: 'I had this printed cotton made up', says Monsieur Jourdain, 'my tailor told me that people of quality wear them in the morning' (Riello 2009, 271).

In the early eighteenth century the Dutch and English were joined by French traders. The French East India Company, established by Colbert in the 1660s, expanded its activities especially in India. After the battle of Plassey in 1757, Britain secured control over key textile-producing areas in India, thus expanding the supply of cloth even more. The importation of large quantities of Asian goods – and especially Indian textiles – generated protests among European manufacturers keen to protect their markets. They demanded and obtained the banning of the importation, sale and weaving of Indian cottons and Chinese silks in France (1686), England (1701 and 1721) and most other European states with the exception of the Dutch Republic.

**Figure IV.15** The loosely cut style of this banyan was based on that of the Japanese kimono. Its cloth was produced on the Coromandel coast of India and the garment was possibly tailored in the Netherlands (c. 1750). London, Victoria and Albert Museum, T.215–1992.

They argued that excessive importation damaged the work opportunities of the poorer in society and that Asian goods had to be paid in bullion (silver) thus diminishing the wealth of the nation. But despite these attempts at banning imports, textiles from India continued to be highly prized (Box 3).

Protected from competition and with easy access to the American and African markets, European entrepreneurs developed imitations of Asian products. Cotton textile production, a sector practically unknown in Europe until the late seventeenth century, developed into the largest industry in England and in other countries in continental Europe by the end of the eighteenth century. Copies of Asian goods such

**Box 3**

'The beautiful and delicate MUSLINS from Dacca [. . .] have again directed attention in some measure, towards that peculiar district and branch of industry in Bengal to which we are indebted for productions so exquisite and so costly. It is admitted on all hands, that the finest of the Dacca muslins exceed anything which can be produced by the looms of Europe: and when the Manchester manufacturer described them as "the merest shadow of a commodity" he pronounced, in fact, the highest eulogium which they could receive, and indicated in a few words the deficiencies of the English when compared with the Indian manufacture of Muslins.'

(Anonymous, 1851, 130; cf. Berg 2015, 119–20)

as Indian cottons, Chinese porcelains and Japanese lacquer were invented; in the 1730s, for instance, the Martin brothers in Paris perfected a new recipe for lacquer, the famous *Vernis Martin* that was more similar to Oriental lacquer than anything that could be produced previously. In the eighteenth century, completely novel goods created by new inventions appeared, as did the application of new technologies inspired by goods from Asia. These rarely required enormous financial investment, thus making it easier for everyday consumer goods to be replaced on a regular basis.

Consumers in Europe benefitted from a variety of commodities coming not just from Asia but also from the Americas. At the end of the seventeenth century, coffee was still a costly stimulant, but by the end of the eighteenth, it had become a common beverage: in 1785 nearly half of all working-class homes in Paris owned a coffee pot. Tea from China had also become a widely popular beverage especially in England. Hot drinks, and especially chocolate, made from cocoa cultivated in the Americas, required large amounts of sugar, another commodity from Asia that in this period came to be cultivated in plantations in the Americas. The manufacture and trade of tropical produce as well as the import of raw materials such as cotton and indigo connect the history of global trade to that of slavery and plantation.

## Assessment

Between 1500 and 1800 the exchange of goods became global, and European consumers could buy goods from all over the world. At the beginning of the period, goods from Asia were seen as exotic luxuries for kings and noblemen; by the end of our period, silks and porcelains had come within the reach of orphans in Amsterdam or the descendants of slaves in New Spain. The impact of this development was huge: the African slave trade and the sugar and cotton plantations throughout the Americas were closely related to the almost insatiable desire for global goods. In early modern Europe, the demand for Asian goods vastly outstripped supply, and new commodities were manufactured to make up for this shortfall. Arguably, the textile manufacturers and potteries of Central and Northern England that drove the Industrial Revolution did so because of the competition with Asian goods. In sum, global goods transformed the early modern world.

## Discussion themes

1. How important was the Spanish exploitation of the silver mines in Peru for European history?
2. Why did the Dutch concentrate so heavily on spices?
3. Which global commodity transformed European life to the greatest extent?
4. Was Europe central to the global exchange of goods?

## Bibliography

### (A) Sources

Anonymous, (1851), 'Review of *A Descriptive and Historical Account of the Cotton Manufacture of Dacca, in Bengal, by a former Resident in Dacca* (London: Mortimer, 1851', *The Athenaeum*, November 1, no. 1253, 130– 40

Olearius, Adam (1669), *The Voyages and Travells of the Ambassadors Sent by Frederick, Duke of Holstein, to the Great Duke of Muscovy and the King of Persia*, 2nd corrected edn, London

Pires, Tomé (1944), *The Suma Oriental of Tomé Pires: An Account of the East, from the Red Sea to Japan, Written in Malacca and India in 1512– 1515*, trans. Armando Cortesao, London

### (B) Literature

Berg, Maxine (2015), '"The Merest Shadows of a Commodity": Indian Muslins for European Markets 1750–1800', in: *Goods from the East, 1600–1800: Trading Eurasia*, ed. idem, Basingstoke, 119–34

Boxer, C. R. (1969), *The Portuguese Seaborne Empire, 1415– 1825*, New York

Corrigan, Karina, van Campen, Jan, and Diercks, Femke, eds (2015), *Asia in Amsterdam: The Culture of Luxury in the Golden Age*, Salem

Finlay, Robert (2010), *The Pilgrim Art: Cultures of Porcelain in World History*, Berkeley

Flynn, Dennis Owen and Giráldez, Arturo (2010), *China and the Birth of Globalization in the 16th Century*, Farnham

Gerritsen, Anne and Giorgio Riello, eds (2015), *Writing Material Culture History*, London

Giráldez, Arturo (2015), *The Age of Trade: The Manila Galleons and the Dawn of the Global Economy*, Lanham, Md.

Gordon, Stewart (2008), *When Asia Was the World*, Cambridge, Mass.

Jordan-Gschwend, Annemarie and Lowe, K. J. P., eds (2015), *The Global City: On the Streets of Renaissance Lisbon*, London

Riello, Giorgio (2009), 'The Globalization of Cotton Textiles: Indian Cottons, Europe, and the Atlantic World, 1600–1850', in: *The Spinning World: A Global History of Cotton Textiles, 1200–1850*, ed. idem and P. Parthasarathi, Oxford, 261–87

### (C) Web resources

'The Atlas of Mutual Heritage', featuring information on the Dutch East / West India Companies: <http://www.atlasofmutualheritage.nl/en/>

'Global Commodities: Trade, Exploration and Cultural Exchange': <http://www.global commodities.amdigital.co.uk/>

'Commodity Histories', a forum for research exchange: <http://www.commodity histories.org/>

# Europe and the world, c. 1800

*Anne Gerritsen and Anthony McFarlane*

In our initial survey of the situation around 1500, we found a polycentric world, where Europe was one of a number of Eurasian regions with potential for further development and expansion, though it was then outshone in wealth, power and cultural achievement of the Islamic realms, India and China. If we now ask how much had changed by *c.* 1800, we find a world where Europe had gained a new prominence. For, since 1500, Europe had been a key area of change in the early modern world, as the expansion of overseas commerce and territory started in the 'Age of Discoveries' enlarged its economy and enhanced the power of its states. The greatest change was the creation of a Euro-Atlantic world of trade and settlements which provided Europeans with the precious metals needed to break into Asian trading systems, new lands to farm, and a novel form of production in the slave-based plantation economies. Europe's first 'globalisation' did not, however, bring global dominance. For much of the seventeenth and into the eighteenth century, European population growth was slow, agricultural and industrial productivity low, and consumer markets insufficiently dynamic to drive internal development. Moreover, much of the wealth generated by Europe's expansion was expended on courts and aristocracies, government and ecclesiastical bureaucracies, and on wars between European states. And, although European commercial expansion stimulated innovation in trade, shipping and finance, it did not open substantial markets for European products in the rich Asian economies. Europe's merchants took Asian goods for European consumers, mostly in exchange for American bullion, rather than selling European products to Asians, and they relied on the tolerance of local rulers to carry on their business. For most of the period, then, Europe was caught in what John Darwin has called an 'early modern equilibrium', where its wealth and power were counter-balanced by rich and powerful states in other regions, notably the Ottoman Empire, Mughal India and China (Darwin 2007). This balance started to shift in the eighteenth century, however, as the tempo of economic, social and cultural change accelerated in Europe. By 1800, the world was on the cusp of a new phase of development, in which Europe moved to a new plane of power, pioneered by British industrialisation. What, then, were the new patterns of power in *c.* 1800, and how had they come about?

## China

During the eighteenth century, China still displayed characteristics evident in c. 1500: it was a great power resting on a highly productive economy, managed by a centralised state, and was largely impervious to European influence. Under the MANCHU, Chinese territory had been expanded significantly, and now included Outer Mongolia, parts of Inner Asia and the Tibetan highlands. Agricultural developments had made tremendous population growth possible, and although precise figures for the rate of that eighteenth-century growth remain elusive, the estimate of 360 million Chinese in 1800 is widely accepted. Great wealth and effective government were reflected in China's cultural lustre. Under the Qianlong emperor (1735–99), the state embarked on a number of vast cultural projects, including the anthology known as the Four Treasuries, which was to include China's entire literary heritage. Books and manuscripts from the whole realm were gathered at the capital, housed in a special pavilion, reviewed by teams of scholars and copied into the 36,381-volume anthology, excluding all texts deemed unsuitable or unorthodox. The project presented its imperial sponsor with an opportunity to gain legitimacy and to weed out any remaining opposition among the population.

The cultural brilliance of the eighteenth century would not continue, however, nor would China's splendid isolation. In 1793, when Qianlong snubbed King George III's ambassador, Chinese intellectuals had very little interest in Europe, and China's government, focused on maintaining an internal balance of power and defending its northern borders against invading nomadic troops, neglected to build naval forces. This vulnerability to Western maritime threats was revealed by the Opium War of 1839–42, when Britain used the opium trade to prise open Chinese markets and thereby started a new era in China's relations with the outside world (Mote 1999; Box 1).

---

### Box 1

'Our dynasty's majestic virtue has penetrated unto every country under Heaven, and Kings of all nations have offered their costly tribute by land and sea. As your Ambassador can see for himself, we possess all things. I set no value on objects strange or ingenious, and have no use for your country's manufactures. This then is my answer to your request to appoint a representative at my Court. . . . It behoves you, O King, to respect my sentiments and to display even greater devotion and loyalty in future, so that, by perpetual submission to our Throne, you may secure peace and prosperity for your country hereafter.'

(Emperor Qian Long, 'Letter to George III' 1793; Web resources)

This letter reveals the emperor's attempt to fit the British demand into the Chinese vision of foreign affairs, based on the premise of Chinese superiority.

## The Islamic world

By 1800, the world of Islam remained rich and culturally impressive, but had stopped expanding for some time. Its main political base in the west, the Ottoman Empire, was still large and powerful, but undoubtedly in retreat. Since the sixteenth century, successive conquests had enlarged Russia's revenues, strengthened its armies and underpinned missionary enterprises which spread Russian influence (Khodarkovsky 2002). In 1780, the balance of power between the Ottomans and Russia shifted decisively when Russia seized the Crimea and ended Ottoman dominance in the Black Sea. Ottoman realms in Africa and the Eastern Mediterranean were also threatened, as Napoleon showed with his extraordinary project for taking Egypt in 1798. Though unsuccessful, it reflected the vulnerability of a state structure which posed problems for the longer term: it was not clear, for example, whether successions could be resolved without the bloody removal of a candidate's potential opposition (often including kin). There were social problems too. The state segregated slaves and women and tended to suppress opposition. It had also rejected printing and the use of vernacular languages for official communications, making it more difficult for those outside the privileged social and political elites to become active participants and contributors ('European relations with the Ottoman world' in Part IV).

The other great Islamic power in the Middle East, the Safavid regime in Iran suffered more dramatic difficulties: its collapse in the early eighteenth century was mirrored in the decline of urban civilization and the arts, and brought the fragmentation of the empire into warring local polities. However, just as Iranian power seemed about to dissolve, a new military leader rebuilt it: having recovered lands lost to the Ottomans and Russia, Nadir Shah took the throne in 1736, and moved on to conquer Delhi, capital of the Mughal empire in 1739.

## South Asia

Mughal power had been an important element in the equilibrium of the early modern world, and its vicissitudes during the eighteenth century had global ramifications. Under Mughal rule, North India had flourished and, although the Mughals stopped short of imposing the kind of political and cultural unity that the Ming achieved in China, the Indian subcontinent was one of the world's most economically dynamic regions, open to international trade in a way that China was not. Cotton textiles were central elements, and India became the world's largest textile producer, exporting to the Middle East, Africa and Europe. Mughal rule was, however, destabilized by rebellion and warfare during the eighteenth century, leading to the decentralization of power and opening opportunities for others to expand their influence and territory.

For the British, who had lost the American colonies, India offered a new frontier for imperial expansion (Bayly 2004). The EAST INDIA COMPANY pushed outwards from Bengal, seeking trade and revenues to finance its forces, and Britain gained a growing share of the wealth of South Asia. It took control of the entire Coromandel Coast and part of the Malabar Coast north towards Goa, and acquired the northern regions up to Delhi (which would follow in 1803). Further north in the Gujarat, the British also held cities like Surat and Bombay, and coastal regions from which the Indian Ocean could be controlled. The India that emerged around 1800 was a place full of contradictions. Built on the foundations of Indian society, with its range of religious and spiritual practices, distinctive social structures, regional differentiations and material and economic prowess, it was beginning to take a form shaped by the British: not only were the rule of law and administration, the economy and the infrastructure largely created by the British, but also the ways in which Indian history was told, Indian languages were understood and Indian art was practiced (Metcalf and Metcalf 2002).

## Africa

In Africa, the interior remained largely untouched by outsiders, but the coasts had seen a considerable expansion of European trading settlements, including the Spanish and the Portuguese, the French and the British, the Danish and the Dutch. It was on the coastal fringes that African societies were most exposed to currents of overseas trade. The West African coast saw the growth of European exports of slaves into the Atlantic trade in return for firearms, alcohol and various consumer goods, while the east coast exported slaves, gold and ivory via the merchant networks of the Indian Ocean. Throughout western and equatorial Africa, local power rested on access to trade commodities such as palm oil, gum-senegal and peanuts. Scarce resources were fiercely contested between communities separated by ethnicities, religion (Muslim or non-Muslim), farming style (nomadic or sedentary), and status (merchant or princely). In the interior of southern Africa, farming villages and chiefdoms also struggled for control over water, land and hunting stock, in conflicts intensified by the loss of manpower through the slave trade and the gradual militarization of society.

By the eighteenth century, Africa's most significant contribution to world trade was through the commodification of its people. In the early modern period, nearly eight million Africans were transported into slavery. Some went to the Old World (Europe, Atlantic islands and São Tomé) but the vast majority went to the plantation agricultures of the Americas (where Brazil and the Caribbean took the largest share; Curtin *et al.* 1995; Table IV.6.1).

## The Americas and the Atlantic economy

The most singular feature of global change after 1500 was Europe's development of settlement, trade and slavery in the Americas ('Europe overseas' in Part IV; Box 2). Europeans and their descendants set up an export-oriented plantation agriculture,

**Table IV.6.1** Slave imports 1451–1810

| Importing region | 1451–1600 | 1601–1700 | 1701–1810 | Total for region | % |
|---|---|---|---|---|---|
| Old World | 149,900 | 25,100 | – | 175,000 | 2.3 |
| Spanish America | 75,000 | 292,000 | 578,600 | 945,600 | 12.3 |
| Brazil | 50,000 | 560,000 | 1,891,400 | 2,501,400 | 32.6 |
| British N. America | – | – | 348,000 | 348,000 | 4.5 |
| British Caribbean | – | 263,700 | 1,401,300 | 1,665,000 | 21.7 |
| French Caribbean | – | 155,800 | 1,348,400 | 1,504,200 | 19.6 |
| Dutch Caribbean | – | 40,000 | 460,000 | 500,000 | 6.5 |
| Danish Caribbean | – | 4,000 | 24,000 | 28,000 | 0.4 |
| TOTAL | 274,900 | 1,340,600 | 6,051,700 | **7,667,200** | 100 |
| % | 3.6 | 17.5 | 79 | (early mod. total) | |

The slave trade peaked in the eighteenth century, but continued well into the 1800s. Overall more than ten million Africans may have been displaced (Curtin 1969, 268).

imposed their languages, religion, cultures and forms of governance, and created new social hierarchies from peoples of different race and colour. The cultural effects were also far-reaching, for, having learned that they could dominate Americans and people taken from Africa, Europeans came to regard themselves as superior and to see the subordination of non-Europeans as a 'civilising mission'. And, last but not least, transatlantic connections produced economic innovations which brought Europe's first 'globalization' ('The global exchange of goods' in Part IV).

## Box 2

### The impact of slavery

The forced migration of millions of slaves from Africa to the Americas (Table IV.6.1; Eltis 2001; Figure IV.16) was a crucial feature of global economic and social transformation in the two centuries before 1800. Although historians no longer accept that the trade in slaves and sugar was the primary source of capital for the industrialization that underpinned Britain's emergence as a world power in the nineteenth century, it is clear that the slave trade and the systems of production and trade that rested on slave labour played a highly significant part in European, especially British, economic development during the seventeenth and eighteenth centuries, as well as inflicting social damage in several regions of Africa. Slavery underpinned the development of American export agricultures which, from the later sixteenth century onwards, supplied Europe with sugar and tobacco, and by 1800 were diversifying into other plantation crops such as coffee, cotton and rice, all of which generated substantial mercantile profits as well as expanding the European habits of consumption that characterized the eighteenth-century 'industrious revolutions' of North-western Europe and North America, and drove further expansion of trade and manufacture (De Vries 1994).

Trade in slaves and sugar was not only one of the keystones of a burgeoning Atlantic economy, creating rich commercial flows between Africa, the Americas and Europe, and generating commercial capital and taxes. It also promoted the ability of Europeans to project power globally, as their frequent internecine struggles for overseas resources and oceanic trades forced European states to develop the technological, financial and tactical means of waging expensive, long-distance wars. Wars in the Caribbean, fought mainly between Britain and France to protect their huge investments in sugar and slaves, played a particularly prominent part in stimulating the development and deployment of armed naval power. This struggle for maritime superiority was turned to other uses too. During the late eighteenth and into the nineteenth century, both British and French navies explored and established new colonies in the Pacific and supported the expansion of commerce and conquest in Asia ('European politics from the Peace of Westphalia to the French Revolution c. 1650–1800' in Part VI).

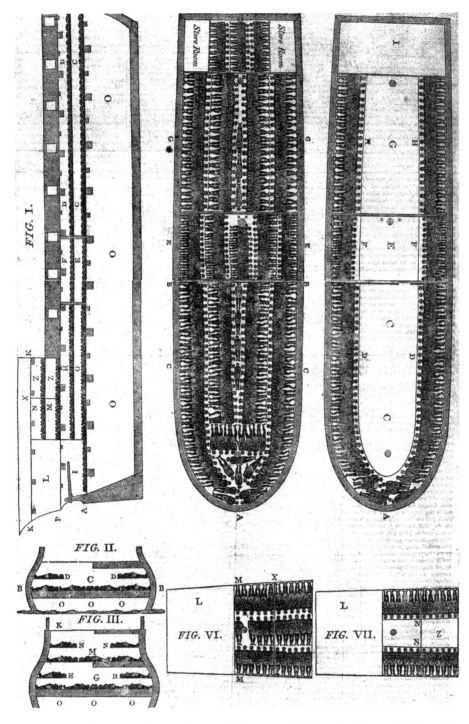

**Figure IV.16** The Slave Ship 'Brookes', publ. by James Phillips, London, *c.* 1800 (wood engraving and letterpress), English School (19th century) / Private Collection / © Michael Graham-Stewart / Bridgeman Images.

## Repercussions in Europe

The repercussions of early modern Europe's expansion overseas were most apparent in struggles for territory and resources in the Americas, particularly during the later eighteenth century. In the Seven Years' War (1756–63) Britain took Canada from France; in the American war of independence (1776–83) France and Spain helped Britain's North American colonials to secede from the British monarchy, which was replaced by the United States. From 1789 the French Revolution brought even greater instability into Europe's Atlantic world. First, France's empire began to disintegrate during the 1790s, when slave rebellion in Saint-Domingue (France's richest colony) led to the creation of independent Haiti. Then, during the Napoleonic wars (1793–1815), the empires of Spain and Portugal came under attack. In 1807–8, Napoleon's invasions forced the Portuguese monarchy to flee to Brazil and completely collapsed the Spanish monarchy at its centre, casting both empires into crises which led to their dissolution in the 1820s.

The transformation of the Euro-American political landscape was paralleled by changes in economic and social life. Rapid demographic and economic growth, the strengthening of state and nation, the political revolutions and cultural trans-formations which have been described in other chapters, meant that the lives of Europeans in 1800, whether they were millworkers in Lancashire, glassmakers in

**Figure IV.17** Global trade in consumer goods like tea, coffee and porcelain enriched the lives of Europe's 'polite society' towards the end of the early modern period. A Family of Three at Tea, c. 1727 (oil on canvas), Collins, Richard (fl.1726–32) / Victoria & Albert Museum, London, UK / Bridgeman Images.

Murano, farmers in Poland or shipbuilders in Porto, were very different from the lives of their equivalents in 1500 ('Epilogue'). Much of that change was to do with global connections. The influx of tea and porcelain from Asia, sugar and coffee from the Americas, peoples from Africa, and the development of ideas, philosophies and literatures that exalted European values, thoroughly changed the European world (Figure IV.17). Not only had Europeans become richer and more intent on consumer comforts, but they had learned that they could establish empires overseas, assert their dominion over other peoples, and, by accumulating knowledge, improve their mastery over the material world.

## Assessment

There are many different ways to account for the great changes to Europe's place in the world that took place between 1500 and 1800, depending on the perspective taken and the questions asked. One approach is to ask why and how Europe rose to power while the rest of the world stagnated. This 'rise of the west' argument usually begins with fifteenth-century developments, where RENAISSANCE scholars searched for new horizons, scientists discovered new ways of measuring and mapping the world, and shipbuilders experimented with new techniques ('The Renaissance' and 'The scientific revolution' in Part V). From that followed a curiosity about what the wider world might have to offer, a desire to improve knowledge about the realms that lay beyond what was immediately familiar and to gain access to the fabled goods such as gold, spices, sugar, dyestuffs, textiles and precious metals which that world was said to hold. Once galvanised, these ambitions drove Europeans to compete for commerce and colonies, to establish maritime empires, and to project their religion and values across the world.

Others take a less economistic view. Eurocentric scholars argue that cultural superiority was based on the continent's rational and scientific thought that emerged during this transition from the Middle Ages to the modern era (Landes 1998). One might look specifically towards religious motivations; the desire to push back the Muslim threat, combined with a newer, post-Reformation desire to claim back the souls lost to Protestantism through conversion of the heathens that populated the rest of the world ('The long Reformation' in Part III). The (presumed) European dominance in 1800 is then demonstrated by pointing to superiority in military terms over the Amerindian empires in the Americas, in naval terms over the Arab empires, and in commercial terms over all of Asia. The European powers, it seems, had the political, organizational and financial skills, with just the right combination of central control and mercantile autonomy, to make the most of their resources, both domestically and across the globe.

More recently, such views of European excellence and superiority have been challenged. Rather than assuming that Europe began to forge ahead, leaving the rest of the world behind after 1500, many scholars now take a different view. There is, first, some scepticism about the potency of the European advance after 1500. It is of course true that Europeans achieved remarkable things: they turned the oceans into highways for trade, through which Europe not only enlarged its share of global resources but also extended the reach of its society and culture. The creation of the Euro-Atlantic colonial world represented the first step towards 'globalization' by linking Europe, Africa, Asia and the Americas in networks of commerce, settlement and government. However, impressive though they were, these achievements did not guarantee that Europe's economic trajectory would diverge from that of comparably rich societies in Asia and lead to global dominance. To understand why it did, we must adopt the wider outlook of 'global history', which, rather than seeing the world from a European perspective and isolating factors for its rise, aims to understand global economic and cultural connections. Maxine Berg, for example, has shown how the influx of luxury goods from Asia impacted on European manufactures (Berg 2004).

The work of Kenneth Pomeranz deserves special mention. Pomeranz drew on a wide range of economic source materials to compare in great detail the economic circumstances under which peasants worked in Britain, China and India. On the basis of the cost of living, the price of grain and land, he argued that the experience of the peasantry in those three places had important similarities before the latter half of the eighteenth century, and that the subsequent DIVERGENCE derived from the 'accident' of their geography more than being the inevitable outcome of a superior culture and physical environment. He points, for example, to the advantage that Britain derived from having coal located close to places where it could be used for industrial development, compared to China, where northern coal was very far from the hub of economic development in Southern China. He also stresses the accidental nature of historical developments: when China decided around 1400 to rely on silver as the basis for its monetary system, and began to convert all tax payments in kind and all labour duties to payment in silver in the 1570s, a global network was set in motion that delivered silver from the mines in Peru and Mexico to China. Most of the profit from the silver trade was made by Europeans: the mine owners of Spanish America, the European shipping merchants who transported silver via Manila or Europe to Asia and the European traders who benefited from the lucrative exchange rates, driven up by China's insatiable demand for silver. European success in exploiting this trade explains the divergence better than any inherent European superiority (Pomeranz 2000). Since Pomeranz's important work, scholars have moved beyond the singular focus on economic divergence, and explored the multiple and diverse ways in which early modern European history is entangled in global developments (Parthasarathi 2011; Werner and Zimmermann 2004; Vries 2009).

The world in 1800 was evidently a very different place from that world in 1500, with Europe now emerging as the major economic and political force behind global developments. As the economic rewards of Atlantic commerce and colonization grew, so the leading colonial powers engaged in increasingly intense warfare to defend and extend their possessions overseas. From their competition, new patterns of power emerged, with Britain in the vanguard. At the end of the Napoleonic wars in 1815, Britain was fast becoming an industrial economy capable of competing for consumers in markets throughout the world, and, freed from war in Europe, was able to embark on a new era of economic and political expansion, with the foundations of a 'second empire' laid in India. With this went the new economic theory of free trade, expressed in Adam Smith's famous work *The Wealth of Nations* (1776), which argued that freedom to produce and trade was the key to prosperity and human happiness. The British became increasingly committed to this doctrine and, as well as freeing markets at home, sought to open new markets overseas, sometimes using threats and force to do so.

Thus, the first European empires of the Americas were overtaken by new empires in Asia and Africa, and Europe's economic, political and cultural influence spread throughout the globe at an accelerating rate during the nineteenth century. Another major mutation of the world order was under way, moving from the Eurasian equilibrium of the early modern period towards global dominance by European powers, led by Britain.

## Discussion themes

1. How comparable were the lives of Europeans to their equivalents in other parts of the world in 1500? And in 1800? How can we make such judgements?
2. To what extent do global connections explain the transformations of the early modern period?
3. Is 'divergence' a useful concept for describing the different trajectories of Europe and Asia in the early modern period?

## Bibliography

### (A) Sources

Eltis, David et al. eds (1999), *The Transatlantic Slave Trade: A Database on CD-Rom*, Cambridge

Smith, Adam (1976), *An Inquiry into the Nature and Causes of the Wealth of Nations* [1776], reprint edn, Oxford

### (B) Literature

Bayly, Christopher (2004), *The Birth of the Modern World, 1780–1914*, Oxford

Berg, Maxine (2004), 'In Pursuit of Luxury: Global Origins of British Consumer Goods in the Eighteenth Century', *P&P*, 182, 85–142

* Bernier, Olivier (2000), *The World in 1800*, New York

Curtin, Philip D. (1969), *The Atlantic Slave Trade: A Census*, Madison, Wis.

Curtin, P. et al. (1995), *African History: From Earliest Times to Independence*, 2nd edn, Harlow

Darwin, John (2007), *After Tamerlane: The Rise and Fall of Global Empires, 1400–2000*, London.

De Vries, Jan (1994), 'The Industrial Revolution and the Industrious Revolution', *Journal of Economic History*, 54, 240–70

Eltis, David (2001), 'The Volume and Structure of the Transatlantic Slave Trade: A Reassessment', *William and Mary Quarterly*, 3rd Series 58, 17–46

Khodarkovsky, Michael (2002), *Russia's Steppe Frontier: The Making of a Colonial Empire, 1500–1800*, Bloomington, Indiana

Landes, David (1998), *The Wealth and Poverty of Nations: Why are Some so Rich and Some so Poor*, London

Metcalf, B. D. and T. R. (2002), *A Concise History of India*, Cambridge

Mote, F. W. (1999), *Imperial China 900–1800*, Cambridge, Mass.

Parthasarathi, Prasannan (2011), *Why Europe Grew Rich and Asia Did Not: Global Economic Divergence, 1600–1850*, Cambridge

Pomeranz, Kenneth (2000), *The Great Divergence: China, Europe, and the Making of the Modern World Economy*, Princeton, NJ

Vries, Peer ed. (2009), 'Global History', *Österreichische Zeitschrift für Geschichtswissenschaft* 20(2), 1–202

Werner, Michael and Zimmermann, Bénédicte eds (2004), *De la comparaison à l'histoire croisée*, Paris

### (C) Web resources

'Internet East Asian History Sourcebook', IHSP: <http://www.fordham.edu/halsall/eastasia/eastasiasbook.html>

'The Making of the Modern World', Goldsmith-Kress Library of Economic Literature: <http://gdc.gale.com/products/>

Qian Long, 'Letter to George III' (1793), IHSP: <http://www.fordham.edu/halsall/mod/1793qianlong.html>

# PART V

# CULTURE

| | |
|---|---|
| 1633 | Galileo's trial in Rome |
| 1637/ 1644 | Publication of Descartes's *Discourse on Method* and *Principles of Philosophy* |
| 1640 | *Parlement* of Paris forbids prosecutions for witchcraft within its jurisdiction |
| 1645–47 | Matthew Hopkins's witch hunt in Essex and East Anglia |
| 1649 | 'Commonwealth sale' of art in England |
| 1660 | The Royal Society founded in London |
| 1666 | Académie des Sciences founded in Paris |
| 1682–1725 | Reign of Peter the Great of Russia |
| 1687 | Publication of Newton's *Philosophiae naturalis principia mathematica* |
| 1692–93 | Salem witch trials |
| 1726 | Publication of Jonathan Swift's *Gulliver's Travels* |
| 1748 | Publication of Montesquieu's *The Spirit of Laws* |
| 1751–72 | Publication of the *Encyclopédie* |
| 1759 | Publication of Voltaire's *Candide* |
| 1762 | Publication of Jean-Jacques Rousseau's *Of the Social Contract* |
| 1762–96 | Reign of Catherine the Great of Russia |
| 1765–90 | Reign of Joseph II, Holy Roman Emperor |
| 1776 | Publication of Adam Smith's *The Wealth of Nations* |
| 1781 | Publication of Immanuel Kant's *Critique of Pure Reason* |
| 1789 | Publication of Emmanuel Sieyes' *What is the Third Estate?* |
| 1791 | Publication of Thomas Paine's *Rights of Man* |
| 1792 | Publication of Mary Wollstonecraft's *Vindication of the Rights of Women* |
| 1793 | Opening of the Louvre Palace, Paris, as a public art gallery |

# The Renaissance

*Humfrey Butters*

In 1861 Jacob Burckhardt, a professor at Basel University, published a work entitled *The Civilization of the Renaissance in Italy*. It was a brilliant essay in the comparatively new genre of cultural history and has a good claim to be the most influential study of its subject ever written. Although many of the views to be found in it are no longer accepted, its fundamental premise, that RENAISSANCE Italy was the birthplace of the modern world, still retains some of its appeal, if in diluted form, for many scholars. Burckhardt's interpretation of the Renaissance, therefore, serves as a useful introduction to a discussion of the subject.

## A new era?

Burckhardt began by asking the question why the Renaissance was in origin an Italian phenomenon, and by finding the answer in the unusual political conditions obtaining in the peninsula: unlike northern states such as France or England, Italy was not subject to one monarch, and its northern and central regions were mostly governed by a collection of fiercely competing CITY-STATES. Italian social structure was equally marked by openness and fluidity, with talent and ruthlessness rather than noble origins providing the keys to success. In this secular and individualistic world the Renaissance SIGNORI, such as the Este of Ferrara or the Sforza of Milan, constructed their states like artworks and found natural allies in writers and artists keen to bolster the authority of generous PATRONS. The Renaissance ('rebirth') certainly involved the revival of classical literature and art, but it was the marriage of this with 'the genius of the Italian people, which achieved the conquest of the Western world' (Burckhardt 1960, 104). For Burckhardt modernity, which for him involved realism, individualism and a secular worldview, was born in Renaissance Italy.

## Political life

Burckhardt treated the Renaissance as a crucial period in European history, radically different from the Middle Ages and far more than a stage in the development of the arts and of literature. Other historians have tended to see it as a cultural movement. In trying to decide which of these perceptions is the more accurate, it is appropriate to start where Burckhardt started, with Italian political life. He was right to find this odd and unusual, but failed to identify the true nature of its singularity: the revival of the city-state form that had characterized the ancient world. We can speak of the cities of Northern and Central Italy as city-states thanks to the degree of independence that they won for themselves and their possession of a territory beyond their walls. Only a few cities in Northern Europe, mostly in the Swiss Confederation and the German lands, could claim a similar status. This is not the sole weakness in his account: by choosing to devote most of his attention to the fourteenth and fifteenth centuries he neglected what was the golden age of the Italian city-states, from 1075 to 1300. This was the period in which the COMMUNES, or city-state republics, broke free from imperial or papal rule and, in practice if not fully in theory, became self-governing; and it was also the era when they produced the most striking innovations in government and administration, establishing their own bureaucracies, courts of law, systems of public finance, armies and statutes. Nowhere else in Europe at this time was public regulation developed as ambitiously as it was by the governments of the Italian communes, which produced a multitude of provisions embracing almost every area of life: city planning and maintenance, communications, production and exchange, social welfare, religious and moral behaviour and family life (Jones 1997, 401–2; 'The theory and practice of politics and government 1500–1800' in Part VI). In the extent of popular participation in government that they permitted and the importance of the role that they assigned to electoral procedures, they had few if any rivals before the French Revolution.

The *signori* who overthrew many of these republican regimes, mostly in the period 1250–1325, reduced popular participation to the minimum, but in most respects proved themselves to be far removed from the radical innovators envisaged by Burckhardt. They were content, indeed, to leave in place large parts of the governmental and administrative structures they had inherited. Paradoxically, therefore, in point of 'modernity' the medieval Italian communes score higher marks than the Renaissance despots, and there can be little justification for speaking of a 'Renaissance state' (Butters 2005, 133–38). It is true that by the fifteenth century six large 'regional' states had emerged as the major powers in Italy, but the process of territorial accumulation that had produced this outcome started long before 1300.

One reason for the 'conservatism' of the *signori* was that they were almost all drawn from the Italian nobility. This was a further error Burckhardt committed: he failed to perceive the vital role played by noble families in Italy's economic, social and political life. One of the distinguishing features of Italy's great families was that, while maintaining substantial ESTATES outside the city walls, they tended to live in cities and, not infrequently, to engage in MERCANTILE activities. This was one of the reasons why the communes had the political will and the economic and military resources to break free from subjection to Pope or Emperor; but it also serves to explain why so many of them failed to survive into the late Middle Ages, for what destroyed them were party conflicts and feuds in which nobles played a salient role. The *signori* were invariably leaders of parties, rather than merely talented individuals in the Burckhardtian mould, and, as such, they were fully aware of the need to keep their followers, particularly their noble followers, happy. Even in the surviving republics like Venice and Florence political life was dominated by the old families. The *signori* were well aware that their survival depended on the support of the noble families of their dominions, and to secure it they dispensed patronage in the form of tax relief and of grants of office, lands and pensions. In this respect they resembled the rulers of Northern Europe. Precisely because these nobles came mostly from families that had been prominent in earlier centuries, it makes little sense to speak of 'Italian *Renaissance* society', sharply distinct from what had preceded it. This latter conclusion is confirmed by an analysis of the Italian economy.

## Economic developments

In the period between 1000 and 1300 Europe underwent a commercial revolution in which the leading role was played by Italians. It is hardly an exaggeration to say that with their innovations in banking, accounting, company structure, insurance and commercial law, they invented commercial CAPITALISM. In Italy as in Northern Europe, merchants acquired a respectability and a social and political prominence denied them in the ancient world, in whose literature they were usually treated as vulgar or venal ('Europe in 1500' in Part I). Long before the Catholic Church banned the lending of money at interest, Aristotle had condemned it as unnatural; and when ancient Rome's greatest satirist Juvenal remarked: 'Everything in Rome has a price tag', his purpose was not to comment favourably on the virtues of a free market. As Karl Marx perceived, most of the city-states of classical ANTIQUITY were run by landowners, not by merchants.

These revolutionary changes, however, did not merely help to usher in a very different sort of world from that of classical Antiquity, they preceded the period normally associated with the Renaissance; and although there were economic developments in the fourteenth and fifteenth centuries, they were not so striking as to entitle the historian to conjure up a 'Renaissance economy'. Even as momentous an occurrence as the BLACK DEATH can be seen as accelerating existing trends rather than creating new ones.

If, for the reasons given above, a 'Renaissance state', a 'Renaissance economy' or a 'Renaissance society' are not useful categories, it follows that one cannot single out the Renaissance as a historical period clearly distinguished from what preceded and followed it. It remains to be seen, nonetheless, whether it should be characterized as a cultural period or as a cultural movement, and in deciding this question it is necessary to consider what Renaissance authors thought of themselves and of the age in which they lived.

## Medieval and Renaissance culture

It was Petrarch (1304–74), the most influential HUMANIST, or classical scholar, of the fourteenth century, who first referred to the period that stretched from the ancient world to his own day as a 'Dark Age'; and many years later the historian Flavio Biondo (1392–1463) adverted to it as the 'Middle Age'. Petrarch also suggested that a new era might be dawning in which the darkness would be left behind and the 'radiance' of Antiquity rediscovered, a notion energetically promoted by his followers. These usages are clearly significant for two reasons: logically a Renaissance or rebirth presupposes some sort of cultural death, such as Petrarch's Dark Age; and by coming to identify that Dark Age with the Middle Ages, Petrarch's followers invented modern chronology, with its three principal divisions: the ancient world, the Middle Ages and the modern period. The humanists spoke of themselves as 'moderns', but 'modern' is what philosophers call an 'indexical' term, whose reference depends on the context in which it is uttered, and their 'modernity' was certainly not ours, nor was it Burckhardt's.

To take seriously the metaphors of darkness and light would be to accept humanist polemic at its face value. Petrarch's charge that the culture of his own day was cut off from that of the ancient world was completely false. Latin was, after all, the language of the medieval Church; and a crucial element in the medieval educational system comprised the liberal arts, whose roots were in classical Greece. At a medieval university, moreover, studying law normally involved the study of ROMAN LAW; studying philosophy or theology usually entailed acquiring at least some sort of acquaintance with Aristotle's works, in translation; and studying medicine gave the student the chance to draw upon the ancient Greek medical texts, also in translation. Medieval poets and historians constantly turned to classical models, and the greatest poetic masterpiece of the Middle Ages, *The Divine Comedy*, was profoundly influenced by the poetry of Virgil, Rome's supreme epic poet.

## Humanism

How, therefore, did Renaissance writers and artists differ from their medieval predecessors? Burckhardt and those influenced by him laid stress on the Renaissance 'discovery' of man, contrasting the secular interests and outlook of Renaissance Italians with the other-worldliness of medieval attitudes. But the distinction is quite artificial, being based, at least in the case of some authors who have drawn it, on a fundamental misunderstanding of the term 'humanism'. A modern 'humanist' is someone who has a set of humane values, normally secular, based on a particular conception of man and of his potential; *humanista* in fifteenth-century Italian, by contrast, denoted a teacher of the humanities, the *studia humanitatis*, a particular set of studies based on grammar, RHETORIC, poetry, history and moral philosophy. One reason why humanists did not have a new philosophy of man is that they were not essentially philosophers at all, but rather classical literary scholars who occasionally dabbled in philosophy (Kristeller 1961). The discipline that principally served to define them was Rhetoric. It was studied in the Middle Ages as one of the seven liberal arts. The humanists often referred to themselves as *oratores*. When they addressed issues in moral philosophy, what they produced, in the main, was not markedly original, in part because the principal classical works from which they took their ideas, those of Aristotle, Seneca and Cicero, had been thoroughly discussed in the Middle Ages. It is idle, moreover, to try to associate humanism with any particular doctrine, because humanists can be found as advocates of princely rule or republican government, the active life or the contemplative, the dignity of man or the misery of human exist- ence, Protestantism or Catholicism. Sometimes, indeed, simply to show off their rhetorical skills, they defended first one side of a case and then the other. It is true that some of them made little or no reference in their writings to the Christian tradition; but others were Churchmen and addressed Christian subjects. In many ways, the humanists produced a far less uniformly secular body of writings than did the twelfth- and thirteenth-century Italian rhetoricians, the *dictatores* (Black 2001, 3). Machiavelli (1469–1527) certainly attacked Christian morality as a guide to govern- ment in *The Prince*, but he was a profoundly unusual and original humanist (Hooker et al.: Web resources).

In the period between 1350 and 1600 SCHOLASTICISM, often with a strong Aristotelian emphasis, continued to be prominent in the universities, despite the attacks on it by the humanists. In the course of the fifteenth century, however, partly thanks to the influence of Byzantine scholars teaching in Florence, the study of Platonism and neo-Platonism came to be fashionable, though its principal advocates, Ficino and Giovanni Pico della Mirandola, tended to regard the humanists as superficial.

In the sphere of education, too, the humanists were less novel in their approach than they claimed: the leading modern authority on Italian education in the fourteenth and fifteenth centuries has concluded that in most important respects the principal Latin grammars of the fifteenth century, Guarino's and Perotti's, resembled those of their fourteenth-century predecessors, and that the fundamental discipline in fifteenth-century grammar schools was what it had been for a long time, philology in its various branches, such as grammar and rhetoric, rather than moral philosophy (Black 2001, 80–1).

## Philology and the fine arts

For these reasons the Renaissance cannot be classed as a cultural period, sharply distinct from the Middle Ages. But it was certainly a serious cultural movement. The contributions of Renaissance humanists to classical scholarship were considerable: they discovered or rediscovered works of Latin authors either unknown to, or little

> **Box 1**
>
> In a letter of 5 February 1486 to Ercole d'Este, Duke of Ferrara, Lorenzo de' Medici, the leading figure in the Florentine government, made the following request:
>
> 'Your Excellency has in his library a work by the historian Dio, *De Romanis historiis*, which I should very much like to see, both because of the pleasure and consolation that I derive from history, and because Piero my son, who has a certain acquaintance with Greek literature, has urged me to procure for him this author's work, which, he understands, is very rare in Italy.'
>
> (*Medici 2002, 165*)

studied by, medieval scholars. In the second place some of them applied themselves to the study of ancient Greek, which few medieval scholars had mastered (Box 1).

Third, the best of them greatly improved the study and editing of classical texts in both Latin and Greek, and Lorenzo Valla's application of these new approaches to the New Testament strongly influenced Erasmus and, even more importantly, Luther. Fourth, they began the critical study of the physical remains of the ancient world.

But it was as *promoters* of classical education that the humanists had their greatest impact. The crucial breakthrough they made was to convince Europe's upper classes that true gentlemen, like those who figured in Cicero's and Quintilian's works on rhetoric, needed to be trained in the classics. The idea was vigorously promoted by Florentine patricians like Palla Strozzi and Niccolò Niccoli in the early fifteenth century, and in the course of the next hundred years spread throughout Europe (Black 2001, 93). It is to be found in Castiglione's *Book of the Courtier*, perhaps the sixteenth century's most influential work on courtly behaviour, which takes the form of a dialogue (Box 2).

The humanists were fortunate that their campaign coincided with and was greatly helped by the invention of printing; but they themselves played an important part in another fifteenth-century innovation, the public library.

In the course of the fifteenth century humanism began to spread north of the Alps: to England, with figures such as Tiptoft and Grey, to Germany, where Rudolf Agricola made major contributions to the humanist reform of logic and Johannes Reuchlin pioneered the study of Hebrew by Christian scholars, and to France, with Jacques Lefèvre d'Etaples. In the early sixteenth century Erasmus of Rotterdam (1477–1536) became active, both as a classical scholar and as a critic of contemporary abuses, lay and ecclesiastical (Bainton 1969). His friendship with Thomas More (1478–1535) was punningly referred to in his satire *In Praise of Folly*, since the Greek word for folly is μωρία ('moria'). More's own attack on the ills of society, *Utopia*, was published in Louvain in 1516, thanks in part to Erasmus's good offices (Brown 1999, 83).

**Box 2**

Count Lodovico da Canossa, one of the speakers in Castiglione's dialogue, says of the good COURTIER:

'I would have him more than passably learned in letters, at least in those studies which we call the humanities. Let him be conversant not only with the Latin language, but with Greek as well, because of the abundance and variety of things that are so divinely written therein.'

(Castiglione 1959, 70; see also 'Courts and centres' in Part VI)

But beyond the contribution of path-breaking individuals there was that of institutions: schools whose curricula reflected the humanist programme began to be founded, such as St Paul's in London or St Lebwin's in Deventer where Erasmus was educated. Until the last century a classical education was thought essential for England's upper classes.

Although a serious interest in 'NATURAL PHILOSOPHY' was not a necessary characteristic of Renaissance humanism, being indeed more commonly found among medieval intellectuals, the astronomer Copernicus and the anatomist Vesalius, whose discoveries transformed their respective subjects, were both classical scholars with a profound respect for ancient Greek thought ('The scientific revolution' in Part V).

But the Renaissance was not merely a movement claiming to revive and study the written culture of classical Antiquity; in sculpture and architecture the relics of the ancient world also served it as models to emulate. The pointed arches and high windows of the Gothic style were replaced by classical columns, arches and pediments. When Raphael designed the Villa Madama in Rome for Pope Leo X's family (Figure V.1), he used his knowledge of Vitruvius's *Ten Books on Architecture* and of the letters in which the younger Pliny spoke of his own villas; and in a letter about the project he employed Plinian vocabulary to describe it (Jones and Penny 1983, 226–34). In the *Lives of the Most Excellent Painters, Sculptors and Architects* by Giorgio Vasari (1511–74), moreover, there are frequent approving references to the skill with which the subjects of his biographies imitated ancient works of art. Vasari took this as evidence of how 'modern' they were, a clear sign of how dramatically his version of 'modernity' differs from our own (Vasari 1987). For him and his contemporaries, even our modern notion of art might have seemed arcane, since in the sixteenth century the Italian word *arte* meant 'skill', 'craft' or 'discipline'. But fifteenth- and sixteenth-century architects went far beyond a slavish copying of ancient buildings, and Filippo Brunelleschi's discovery of perspective enabled fifteenth-century painters like Masaccio to treat pictorial space in a manner undreamt of by ancient ones (Figure V.2; Gombrich 1950, 163–65; 'Arts and Society' in Part V).

**Figure V.1** In his design of the loggia for the Villa Madama, built by the Medici family in Rome around 1520, Raphael followed architectural models from Antiquity. Interior of the loggia of the Villa Madama in Rome, designed by Raphael around 1520, Villa Madama, Rome, Italy / Bridgeman Images.

**Figure V.2.** Tommaso Masaccio's fresco The Trinity, painted in the church of Santa Maria Novella, Florence, provides a very early example of the use of perspective. The Trinity, 1427–28 (fresco) (post restoration), Masaccio, Tommaso (1401–28) / Santa Maria Novella, Florence, Italy / Bridgeman Images.

## Assessment

Burckhardt's dramatic and memorable study of the Italian Renaissance was based on a peculiarly nineteenth-century version of modernity, secular and individualistic, which not merely led him to miss some of Italy's principal features between 1200 and 1500, but would have profoundly puzzled those Italians who, in that same period, referred to themselves as 'moderns' when comparing themselves with the 'ancients'. If he had been, as he later became, more sensitive to the claims of economic history, he would have seen the importance of Italy's contribution to the development of commercial capitalism, whose practices, in the main, the great authors of the classical world would have disdained; and he might even have appreciated the irony of the fact that some of the profits of those selfsame practices were used to finance a cultural movement that proclaimed its commitment to the revival of classical values. But there was a further irony: from the fifteenth century onwards that movement acquired its

European significance from the fact that it won over a group whose social and political significance far outweighed those of merchants: the landed nobility, whose ideal representative was the gentleman rather than Burckhardt's heroic individual.

## Discussion themes

1. Was the Renaissance more a period than a movement?
2. Assess the significance of Renaissance humanism.
3. How far was Burckhardt justified in locating the birth of the modern world in Renaissance Italy?

## Bibliography

### (A) Sources

Castiglione, Baldesar (1959), *The Book of the Courtier* [1528], trans. C. Singleton, New York
Medici, Lorenzo de' (2002), *Lettere*, IX (1485–86), ed. H. C. Butters, Florence
Vasari, Giorgio (1987), *Lives of the Artists* [1550], trans. G. Bull, London

### (B) Literature

Bainton, Roland (1969), *Erasmus of Christendom*, New York
Black, Robert (2001), 'Introduction' and 'Humanism' in: *Renaissance Thought: A Reader*, ed. idem, London, 1–20, 68–94
* Brown, Alison (1999), *The Renaissance*, London
Burckhardt, Jacob (1960), *The Civilization of the Renaissance in Italy* [orig. edn 1860], trans. S. Middlemore, London
Butters, Humfrey (2005), 'La storiografia sullo stato rinascimentale', in: *Il Rinascimento Italiano e l'Europa, I: Storia e storiografia*, ed. M. Fantoni, Vicenza, 121–50
Gombrich, Ernst (1950), *The Story of Art*, New York
Hale, John (1993), *The Civilization of Europe in the Renaissance*, London
Jones, Philip (1997), *The Italian City-State 500–1300*, Oxford
Jones, Roger and Penny, Nicholas (1983), *Raphael*, New Haven, Conn.
Kristeller, Paul (1961), 'Humanism and Scholasticism in the Italian Renaissance', in: his *Renaissance Thought: The Classic, Scholastic and Humanist Strains*, New York, 92–119, 150–63

### (C) Web resources

Hooker, Richard, Brians, Paul, Hines, Richard and Law, Richard, 'Italian Renaissance' (1996–99): <http://richard-hooker.com/sites/worldcultures/REN/CONTENTS.HTM>

# Arts and society

*Luca Molà*

## The role of the artist

Throughout the early modern period the formation and methods of what we today call 'artists' remained steeped in medieval artisanal tradition. The various skills required for the trade of painter, from the mastering of TEMPERA and FRESCO TECHNIQUES to the preparation of different types of colours, are best described in *The Craftsman's Handbook*, a manual written by the Italian artist Cennino Cennini in the late fourteenth century. Training usually started at an early age, when a boy entered the shop of a MASTER to begin his apprenticeship. After years of learning the secrets of the craft, first simply grinding pigments and then slowly progressing through the preparation of the wooden panels or canvases to the painting of some minor details, apprentices reached the rank of master on completion of an original high-quality work. In most European cities, GUILDS – commonly dedicated to St Luke the Evangelist, who had allegedly painted an image of the Virgin – controlled their entire professional careers. Statutes and officers regulated all aspects of production and organization, just as in bakers', butchers' or carpenters' guilds (Cole 1983).

In Northern Europe, artists' guilds survived well into the seventeenth century. In Italy, by contrast, the rediscovery of classical culture in the RENAISSANCE resulted in a more distinctive role of the artist. This trend can be traced back to 1434, when the HUMANIST and architect Leon Battista Alberti arrived in Florence, the city from which his family had been exiled for political reasons. Full of admiration for the seemingly unattainable models of Greek and Roman ANTIQUITY, he nonetheless marvelled at the degree of refinement that the arts had reached among Florentines. When he published the first theoretical treatise on painting (*De Pictura*, soon translated from Latin into the vernacular) the following year, Alberti praised in particular the achievements of the architect-engineer Filippo Brunelleschi. In the 1420s, the latter had accomplished the technological feat of covering Florence's cathedral with a dome the size of Rome's Pantheon, one of the most awe-inspiring buildings from Antiquity. Alberti also provided the first detailed description of linear perspective, another recent discovery by Brunelleschi. This rational method of spatial measurement permitted the realistic representation of a three-dimensional space on a two-dimensional surface, a technique that was to dominate western painting for centuries (Figure V.2, page 237). By rooting the work of painters in mathematical and geometrical expertise, Alberti helped to raise the status of artists from that of mechanics to that of intellectuals, freeing them from the stigma of manual labour and putting their work on a par with that of poets, musicians and philosophers (Blunt 1956).

Indeed, working at Italian courts, top-ranking artists found not only profitable employment, but also an avenue to improve their social standing through frequent contacts with princes and COURTIERS. Andrea Mantegna, painter to the dukes of Mantua, acquired noble status and great wealth in the late 1400s, while Raphael gained the friendship of several popes and members of the Roman elite a few decades later. After 1530, Emperor Charles V granted his court painter Titian rewards, titles and high respect: during a visit to the artist's workshop, for example, Charles humbled himself by picking up Titian's paintbrush. A further step in the glorification of painters and sculptors was Giorgio Vasari's *Lives of the Artists* in 1550. This collection of biographies delineated the historical evolution of Italian art from the early fourteenth-century revival accomplished by Giotto to the unsurpassable attainment of Michelangelo, the embodiment of the 'artist as genius', capable of equal excellence in painting, sculpture and architecture (Barker *et al.* 1999; Trevor-Roper 1991). Michelangelo became president of the first ACADEMY of Art in Florence, a government-sponsored establishment founded in 1563 to provide artists with theoretical knowledge in geometry and mathematics. Similar institutions followed in Rome (1577), Bologna (1582) and Paris (1648), starting an academic artistic tradition that by the eighteenth century had spread to most European capitals (among others Berlin, Vienna, St Petersburg, Madrid, Copenhagen and London) (Goldstein 1996).

Outside the male-dominated world of academies, some limited room for expression opened up for female artists from the sixteenth century. The Italian Sofonisba Anguissola, of noble descent, became a celebrated painter. Employed by the Spanish court in 1559–73, she inspired other women to pursue careers as engravers, portraitists and even sculptors. In Northern Europe, Caterina van Hemessen from Antwerp worked as painter for Mary of Hungary, Charles V's sister, while Levina Teerlinc obtained the title of 'king's paintrix' from Henry VIII and served no fewer than four English monarchs. In the seventeenth century, Artemisia Gentileschi reached celebrity status, enjoying a refined lifestyle and contacts with members of the high nobility and leading intellectuals like Galileo Galilei. Even so, women were judged to have less artistic ability than men: sufficient for copying from nature, but lacking the creative genius for complex religious, historical or mythological scenes. Early modern audiences primarily appreciated them as painters of people, flowers and animals. Given contemporary gender roles, furthermore, self-portraits of female artists often included symbols of chastity, virtue and modesty (Chadwick 2002).

## Patronage, collections and power

From the late fifteenth century, some women also acted as PATRONS of the arts. The most famous example is Isabella d'Este, daughter of the Duke of Ferrara and wife of the Duke of Mantua. A veritable trendsetter for noble elites, she created her own *camerino* [treasure chamber] with precious objects ranging from CAMEOS and jewels to medals and ancient sculptures. To satisfy her cravings, she issued famous artists like Leonardo da Vinci with detailed requests (Cole 1995). Isabella recognized the growing significance of art in European court culture, where distinction came to depend on ever more complex criteria of taste and refinement. By the early seventeenth century several princes and courtiers possessed large collections of paintings and sculptures, composed of both the works of Renaissance masters – whose value had steadily increased – and those of contemporary artists. Connoisseurship and the capacity to discriminate in artistic matters became new attributes of nobility, adding a cultural dimension to their traditional sources of power.

Following Isabella's lead, the Gonzaga dukes of Mantua amassed one of the richest and most renowned art collections in Europe. Lacking in political power, but endowed with great dynastic ambitions, they used artworks to boost their international prestige. In 1627–28, during a period of financial difficulties, Duke Vincenzo II sold many of his best pieces to Charles I of England for the fabulous sum of £30,000, more than the king's annual landed revenue. This was the largest art transaction that Europe had ever seen and it provoked outrage: the citizens of Mantua complained about the humiliating loss of lustre, while English bankers had to divert money destined for the support of French Huguenots at La Rochelle. Charles's agents Nicholas Lanier and Daniel Nys, early representatives of a new early modern profession, played fundamental roles in the transaction. As international art dealers, they acted diplomatically, and at times illegally, to secure the best masterpieces for their clients. Indeed, it was mostly these agents who satisfied the craze for art collecting, especially in England, where it gripped not only the royal family but also leading courtiers. The king's favourite George Villiers, Duke of Buckingham, built up a collection of four hundred paintings and one hundred statues in just five years (Box 1). However, following the establishment of a republic in 1649, the Puritans saw such collections as symbols of Catholic culture and disposed of the royal possessions in the so-called Commonwealth sale: around 1,570 paintings oiled the wheels of the international art market, to the joy of dealers acting for private collectors and other crowns, especially the Spanish (Brown 1995). This 'cannibalization' of an enemy's cultural patrimony was by no means unique. During the bitter religious struggles of the first half of the seventeenth century, conquests of cities or territories commonly resulted in the confiscation and relocation of art treasures. In 1648, for example, Queen Christina of Sweden may have ordered her army to hasten the attack on Prague to secure Rudolph II's famous art collection before the signing of the Peace of Westphalia ended the Thirty Years War (Trevor-Roper 1970).

During the early modern period, therefore, paintings and sculptures joined buildings as elements of political propaganda. In the sixteenth century, Duke Cosimo I de' Medici of Florence, founder of an upstart dynasty with a MERCANTILE background, maintained several artists to create an aura of magnificence and promote Medici power

'Sometimes, when I am contemplating the treasure of rarities which your Excellency has in so short a time amassed, I cannot but feel astonishment in the midst of my joy, for out of all the amateurs and princes and Kings, there is not one who has collected in forty years as many as your Excellency has collected in five. Let enemies and people ignorant of paintings say what they will, they cannot deny that pictures are noble ornaments, a delightful amusement . . . Our pictures, if they were to be sold a century after our death, would sell for good cash and for more than three times what they cost. I wish I could only live a century, if they were sold, in order to be able to say to those facetious folk who say "it is monny cast away for bobbles and shadows". I know they will be pictures still when those ignorants will be lesser than "shadows".'

(Denvir 1988, 175)

Letter of the art dealer Balthasar Gerbier from London to the Duke of Buckingham, February 1624.

abroad. Similar policies were pursued elsewhere. In the 1630s, the count-duke of Olivares, first minister to King Philip IV, hoped to revive Spanish fortunes through an ambitious plan of artistic renewal. The construction of the Buen Retiro palace, adorned with hundreds of artworks, on the outskirts of Madrid signalled the crown's power, wealth, taste and cultural discernment to both courtiers and foreign visitors. The centrepiece was the famous Hall of Realms, where a carefully selected range of paintings – portraits of royals on horseback, images of Spanish victories, crests of the various realms of the kingdom – projected the image of a victorious king and a united monarchy (Brown and Elliott 2003). Following the threat of the *Frondes* in the 1650s, France embarked on an even more impressive image-building campaign for the Sun King Louis XIV. A committee of architects and artists, headed by the Minister of Finances Jean-Baptiste Colbert, devised a multimedia campaign – featuring medals, portraits, engravings, equestrian statues, etc. – to disseminate an idealized heroic image of the French monarch throughout the realm. The apex of glorification came with the construction of the palace of Versailles outside Paris, a gigantic project mobilizing enormous resources and all the arts. This royal residence set new standards and provided a model for Peter the Great of Russia and many other eighteenth-century princes (Burke 1992; 'Courts and centres' in Part VI).

## Art and religion

The arts played a crucial role in the confessional age. Following Pope Gregory the Great's saying that religious art was 'the bible of the illiterate', Catholics enhanced the visual element of their faith by multiplying images of Christ, the Madonna and the saints in their places of worship. Catholic churches became ever more grandiose and ornate, with marble and other precious materials used to glorify God and inspire awe among the congregation. By the seventeenth century the new BAROQUE style symbolized Rome's renewed claims to universal power ('The long Reformation: Catholic' in Part III, esp. Figure III.7, page 127). At the same time the Counter-Reformation Church tried to control religious art more closely. In an attempt to prevent heretical, pagan or secular overtones, the Council of Trent issued a decree on sacred paintings in 1563, which assigned supervisory powers to local bishops. Decency was another concern, to the point that the nude figures in Michelangelo's *Last Judgement* in the Vatican (painted in the 1530s) were retouched to cover their intimate parts with pieces of clothing (Blunt 1956, ch. VIII).

In marked contrast, Protestants gave absolute priority to the preaching and reading of the Scriptures. Partly in reaction to what they saw as 'superstitious' uses of images in the late Middle Ages, Calvinists in particular whitewashed, removed or destroyed the frescos, paintings and statues present in their churches, together with all other Catholic paraphernalia. Even though Luther himself had been moderate on the issue of religious art, stating that it was admissible if it did not result in idolatry, an ICONOCLASTIC movement developed in most Protestant countries, causing the violent destruction of religious art by official order or at the hand of angry masses. Paradoxically, images retained an important role as a tool of popular propaganda during the early Reformation, when huge numbers of broadsheets, pamphlets and woodcuts satirized the Papacy (Koerner 2003; 'The long Reformation: Reformed' in Part III, esp. Figure III.6, page 120).

## The art market in the Dutch Republic

The Protestant ban on the representation of divine subjects proved particularly important for the artistic development of the Calvinist Dutch Republic, the rising economic power in seventeenth-century Europe. In this thriving industrial and mercantile society, demand for pictures came from almost all quarters, including traders, artisans and even rich PEASANTS. As we know from many extant household inventories, families commonly invested between three and 10 per cent of their capital in paintings. This 'democratization' of buying and collecting fostered the production of a wide range of secular art, from land- and townscapes to scenes of everyday life (such as in the famous masterpieces by Johannes Vermeer), moving well beyond conventional Italian genres (Alpers 1983). Still lifes, in particular, became one of the hallmarks of Dutch painting: frequently depicting local and exotic foods, Chinese porcelain, refined glasses and silverware on tables covered with rich fabrics or oriental carpets, they represented the wealth of the United Provinces and the amazing variety of goods obtained through global trade. Unlike other European painters, Dutch artists did not wait for commissions, but produced work serially, often specializing in a single genre to improve efficiency and reduce costs. Painting thus turned into an industry, catering for an anonymous market with a high degree of technical innovation. In Amsterdam paintings were sold in public houses and even used as prizes in lotteries aimed at members of the lower sort (North 1997; Figure V.3, page 245; 'Popular culture(s)' in Part V).

## Art, science and global exchange

A distinctive trait of Dutch, Flemish and Northern European art was the detailed, almost 'photographic' representation of reality (often in combination with symbolic messages). The faithful depiction of flowers, plants and insects, so commonly found in still lifes, was soon put to the service of scientific discovery. Scholars investigating the flora and fauna of Europe, America, Africa and Asia relied on the skills of artists to produce ever more differentiated herbals and zoological treatises. Some painters embarked on long voyages overseas to draw animals and plants from life and in their natural environment, others worked from imported specimens. Supported by the Dutch government, the painter-entomologist Maria Sybilla Merian and her daughter Dorothea travelled all the way to the South American colony of Surinam in 1698 to study local insects and flowers. After years of field work, they published *Metamorphosis Insectorum Surinamensium* – a book with a lasting influence on the field of scientific illustration – in 1705 (Chadwick 2002, 133–37). Printing fostered new forms of collaboration between the sciences and the arts (Ellenius 1985). The success of Andreas Vesalius's revolutionary work on anatomy, *De humani corporis fabrica* (1543), depended in large part on its startling engravings of the human body, while the expansion of geographical knowledge owed much to colourful maps produced in Italy, Germany and the Dutch Republic with the help of professional painters. From the late sixteenth century, the achievements of applied technology, too, were disseminated through heavily illustrated texts, so-called *Theatres of Machines*. Printed in large sizes and resembling today's coffee-table books, they showed the components and mechanisms of both real and fantastic machines (mills, pumps, industrial implements, etc.) for the delight and pleasure of princes and the learned public (Keller 1978).

This combination of artistic endeavour, natural science and technology is particularly prominent in the *Wunderkammern* [Chambers of Wonder] established all over Europe (and especially in the many principalities of the Holy Roman Empire) between the sixteenth and seventeenth centuries. Composed mainly of strange and unusual objects created by nature (*naturalia*) or man (*artificialia*), these eclectic collections aimed for an encyclopedic illustration of the wonders of the universe in a microcosm. Select visitors admitted to see these collections encountered all kinds of marvellous things: unicorn horns, coconuts and exotic shells mounted on precious metals; minerals, fossils and corals; models of machines and so on. Items in *Wunderkammern* were often meticulously categorized according to their material, provenance or function, as in the celebrated collection of the Habsburg Archduke Ferdinand II

**Figure V.3** This painting shows the early modern interest in the accumulation of artworks and the collection of luxury goods, which was now felt to be a sign of social distinction. The Sense of Sight, 1617 (oil on panel), Brueghel, Jan (1601–78) and Rubens, P.P. (1577–1640) / Prado, Madrid, Spain / Bridgeman Images.

at Ambras (Tyrol), where each cupboard contained a specific class of objects. These ancestors of modern museums distinguished themselves by an almost anthropological interest in artistic and utilitarian artefacts produced by distant civilizations (Impey and MacGregor 2001). The large presence of *exotica* from all corners of the globe, ranging from Aztec feather garments via Canadian canoes to bejewelled Ottoman weapons, testifies to the fascination that foreign lands and markets exerted on the European imagination (Box 2).

Cross-cultural artistic contacts date back to at least the fifteenth century. In a diplomatic move to end a protracted conflict in 1479, the Venetian government sent one of its best painters, Gentile Bellini, to portray Sultan Mehemed II and members of the Ottoman court in a western style, while Sultan Suleyman the Magnificent showed interest in European art in the sixteenth century ('Jews and Muslims' in Part III). Later on, JESUIT missionaries in Asia grasped the potential of images to break linguistic barriers, supporting their religious endeavours by importing engravings of European art as well as illustrated treatises on art and architecture. This resulted in a hybrid visual culture, in which Indian or Japanese artists adapted European elements and Christian symbols to their own traditions. Spending 49 years under three emperors of the Qing dynasty at the Chinese court (1715–64), the Italian artist Giuseppe Castiglione laid the foundations for a distinctive Sino-European style. As chief architect for a set of new buildings in the rococo style with European tapestries, clocks, furniture and paintings, he achieved a remarkable blend of artistic traditions, mixing

**Box 2**

'[In Brussels] I saw the things which have been brought to the King from the new land of gold [Mexico], a sun all of gold a whole fathom broad, and a moon all of silver of the same size, also two rooms full of the armor of the people there, and all manner of wondrous weapons of theirs, harness and darts, wonderful shields, strange clothing, bedspreads, and all kind of wonderful objects of various uses, much more beautiful to behold than prodigies. These things were all so precious that they have been valued at one hundred thousand florins. All the days of my life I have seen nothing that has gladdened my heart so much as these things, for I saw amongst them wonderful works of art, and I marveled at the subtle *Ingenia* [ingenuity] of men in foreign lands. Indeed, I cannot express all that I thought there.'

*(Stechow 1966, 100–1)*

On a visit to the Netherlands in August 1520, the German Renaissance artist Albrecht Dürer was deeply impressed by Charles V's New World treasures.

European perspective and shading with Chinese materials and giving the emperor enough western realism to delight him, but not so much as to disconcert him. During the same century, Cantonese workshops produced large numbers of Chinese water-based paintings on paper specifically for the European and American markets, where owners of town and country houses frequently decorated one room in an oriental style. These images depicted plants and flowers, but also the various stages of ceramics, silk and tea production, providing European elites with an idea of how their favourite exotic products were made (Clunas 1987).

By that point, in fact, the import of luxury goods from the east had long played a fundamental role in western consumer habits. In the seventeenth century, for example, the demand for porcelain grew to unprecedented levels. A single ship of the Dutch or English EAST INDIA COMPANY returning to Amsterdam or London could carry over 100,000 pieces of porcelain, which flooded the European markets to cater for both the upper and the middle classes (Fig IV.17, page 222). Whereas the techniques of Chinese porcelain manufacture remained undiscovered until the early 1700s, many other Asian luxuries – silk cloth, glass, metalworks, etc. – were successfully copied and even improved upon by Europeans. Until about 1750 there was no clear borderline between such items (together with tapestry, jewellery and a myriad of other products appreciated not just for their material value, but also the skills required for their production) and what we today class as 'fine arts'. During most of the early modern period collectors acquired all sorts of luxury goods, from clothing and gilded mirrors to expensive furniture, all of which bestowed as much social recognition and distinction on their owners as pictures or statues.

# Assessment

The relentless struggle of Renaissance painters, sculptors and architects to raise their social standing by stressing the intellectual dimensions of their work gradually transformed them from craftsmen into artists. Some, like Leonardo, Titian and Michelangelo, acquired celebrity status. By the seventeenth century, the growing importance of collecting among princes and nobles stimulated a lively international art market (Fantoni *et al.* 2003), while in the Dutch Republic paintings appealed to almost all ranks of society, fostering a deep interest in extra-European cultures. Finally, in the last decades of the eighteenth century, two distinct fields emerged: the 'minor' or 'decorative' arts, manufactured by artisans, imitating traditional models for a specific and practical purpose; and the 'fine arts', created by artists and aimed exclusively at the aesthetic enjoyment of the upper classes. These works of 'Art' were now completely detached from their original contexts and appreciated as outstanding examples of human creativity. They came to be displayed in public museums like the gallery opened at the Louvre by the French Revolutionary government in 1793 (Shiner 2001). The study of the arts, therefore, provides us with important clues about the professionalization, commercialization and cultural evolution of European society in the early modern period.

## Discussion themes

1.  In what ways can the analysis of the arts help us to explain early modern change?
2.  How important was the role of the arts in creating and propagating the image of a ruler?
3.  What were the preconditions for the development of an art market in early modern Europe?

## Bibliography

### (A) Sources

Denvir, Bernard ed. (1988), *A Documentary History of Taste in Britain*, vol. 1, London
Holt, Elizabeth ed. (1981–82), *A Documentary History of Art, Vol. 1: The Middle Ages and the Renaissance; Vol. 2: Michelangelo and the Mannerists. The Baroque and the Eighteenth Century*, Princeton, NJ
Stechow, Wolfgang ed. (1966), *Northern Renaissance Art, 1400–1600: Sources and Documents*, Englewood Cliffs, NJ

### (B) Literature

Alpers, Svetlana (1983), *The Art of Describing: Dutch Art in the Seventeenth Century*, Chicago

Barker, Emma, Webb, Nick and Woods, Kim eds (1999), *The Changing Status of the Artist*, New Haven, Conn.

Blunt, Anthony (1956), *Artistic Theory in Italy, 1450–1600*, Oxford

Brown, Jonathan (1995), *Kings and Connoisseurs: Collecting Art in Seventeenth-Century Europe*, New Haven, Conn.

Brown, Jonathan and Elliott, John H. (2003), *A Palace for a King: The Buen Retiro and the Court of Philip IV*, revised edn, New Haven, Conn.

Burke, Peter (1992), *The Fabrication of Louis XIV*, New Haven, Conn.

Chadwick, Whitney (2002), *Women, Art and Society*, New York

Clunas, Craig ed. (1987), *Chinese Export Art and Design*, London

Cole, Alison (1995), *Virtue and Magnificence: Art of the Italian Renaissance Courts*, New York

Cole, Bruce (1983), *The Renaissance Artist at Work: From Pisano to Titian*, Boulder, Colo.

Ellenius, Allen ed. (1985), *The Natural Sciences and the Arts: Aspects of Interaction from the Renaissance to the Twentieth Century*, Uppsala

Fantoni, Marcello, Matthew, Louisa c. and Matthews-Grieco, Sara F. eds (2003), *The Art Market in Italy, 15th–17th Centuries / Il Mercanto dell'Arte in Italia, secc. XV–XVII*, Ferrara

Goldstein, Carl (1996), *Teaching Art: Academies and Schools from Vasari to Albers*, Cambridge

Impey, Oliver and MacGregor, Arthur eds (2001), *The Origins of Museums: The Cabinet of Curiosities in Sixteenth- and Seventeenth-Century Europe*, London

Keller, Alex (1978), 'Renaissance Theaters of Machines', *Technology and Culture*, 9, 495–508

Koerner, Joseph Leo (2003), *The Reformation of the Image*, Chicago

North, Michael (1997), *Art and Commerce in the Dutch Golden Age*, New Haven, Conn.

* Shiner, Larry (2001), *The Invention of Art: A Cultural History*, Chicago

Trevor-Roper, Hugh (1970), *The Plunder of the Arts in the Seventeenth Century*, London

Trevor-Roper, Hugh (1991), *Princes and Artists: Patronage and Ideology at Four Habsburg Courts, 1517–1633*, revised edn, London

### (C) Web resources

'Mark Harden's Artchive': <http://www.artchive.com/ftp_site.htm>
WGA

# From pen to print: a revolution in communications?

*Mark Knights and Angela McShane*

Today's digital media have transformed the lives of people across much of the world. Digitized images, text and sound mean that we have new ways of accessing what we want to learn about or enjoy, and the range of things we can know about has expanded. Yet the book you are reading is testament to the long reach of another technology that had a similarly transformative effect in the early modern period: print. The printing press was one of three inventions – alongside gunpowder and the compass ('The theory and practice of politics and government 1500–1800' in Part VI; 'Expanding horizons' in Part IV) – that seemed to revolutionize society. The politician, intellectual and essayist Francis Bacon claimed that 'these three have changed the whole face and state of things throughout the world' (Bacon 1620, Bk. I, cxxix). In this chapter we will consider Bacon's claim in relation to the invention, development and significance of printing and its role in two broader developments: first, the 'communications revolution' of the early modern period and, second, the intellectual, religious and cultural changes of the RENAISSANCE, the Reformation and Enlightenment.

## Communication media and the coming of print

Medieval society used a wide range of interconnected oral, written and visual media. Face-to-face exchange predominated, but many individuals and institutions kept records, while scribes produced multiple copies of old and new texts, not only theological works (although they formed the majority), but also literary classics, medical treatises, legal documents and writings related to government business. It was a visual world, too, where symbols, rituals and ceremonies pervaded religious and political interaction. Painted and sculpted images conveyed ideas and told stories, both before and after the Protestant Reformation, when churches, civic buildings and homes all over Europe were highly decorated inside and out with images and objects depicting aspects of everyday life and religious belief. Printing added to this web of communicative practices, building on older technologies like the 'codex' or book form (which had largely, though not completely, replaced rolls), paper-making and fixed

**Figure V.4** Beginning of Jerome's Epistle to Paulinus from the Gutenberg Bible of 1454–55 (vol. 1, f. 1r). Note how Gutenberg produced pages that replicated, as far as possible, typical scribal productions of the period: © British Library Board. All Rights Reserved / Bridgeman Images.

inks. MOVABLE TYPE in clay, wood and metal had been invented centuries before in China (between 1041 and 1234), and we know that books were printed in the east as early as 1377. But the extensive and systematic exploitation of this technology occurred first in fifteenth-century Europe, perhaps because it was a technology better suited to the more restricted alphabets of the west than to the hundreds of characters required for Chinese printing. The breakthrough came in the 1440s when Johannes Gutenberg combined three innovations: a way of producing movable metal type, a new kind of oil-based printer's ink and the wooden hand press. Cumulatively, these led the way to the mass reproduction of books and a myriad of other printed goods such as pamphlets, pictures, tables, maps, ballads, etc.

A defining moment was the production of the 'Gutenberg Bible' at Mainz in 1454–55, the first major book printed in the west (of which 48 of the *c.* 180 original copies still survive; Figure V.4 and Web resources). As Gutenberg's example suggests, printers and booksellers (the early modern equivalent of publishers) were important players in the story of the creation of a market for print (Pettegree 2002).

The expansion of the printing industry was rapid. By 1500 there were more than 1,000 printing shops across Europe, including William Caxton's printing press in England, set up in 1476. Their number and output also increased over time, though this was uneven throughout Europe and often depended on the degree of press freedom that governments and Churches allowed as well as on the vigour of religious, political and cultural debate. In England, some 400 titles were published by the first decade of the sixteenth century; 6,000 in the 1630s; 20,000 (after the temporary collapse of governmental control) in the 1640s; 21,000 (after pre-publication censorship was finally abolished in 1695) in the 1710s and 56,000 by the 1790s (Raven *et al.* 1996, 5; Houston 2002, 175). In Germany the Thirty Years War curbed book production: 1620 levels were not achieved again until 1765, but thereafter output became buoyant, with two-thirds of the 175,000 titles published in the eighteenth century produced in its last third. In France, where censorship was stronger, the number of titles increased less dramatically, from just 500 in 1700 to 1,000 per year by the Revolution of 1789; and in eighteenth-century Russia the figure only reached 250 titles a year in the 1780s (Blanning 2002, 140–42; Box 1).

## Box 1

Estimates of European book production:

| | |
|---|---|
| Before 1500 | 20 million copies |
| 1500–1600 | 150–200 million copies |
| 1700–1800 | 1,500 million copies |
| | *(Houston 2002, ch. 8)* |

The figures in Box 1 are necessarily imprecise, since evidence about print runs is fragmentary. Two or three hundred copies of a title may have been quite common, though larger runs were printed for controversial or best-selling items, and books were also reprinted if there was demand. For example, Italian, German and French towns produced between them vast numbers of schoolbooks, especially works by Ovid, Virgil, Terence and Horace, in pocket-size formats. Fourteen thousand copies of Virgil's *Aeneid* were produced in the 1490s alone, while between 1469 and 1599 approximately 1,125,000 were printed (Wilson-Okamura 2010). Books catered for many different markets. There were expensive large (folio) editions sold in bookshops but also cheap print, such as ballads, that could be hawked around by pedlars and achieve widespread dissemination ('English Broadside Ballad Archive' and Meertens, 'Ballads': Web resources; cf. Salzberg 2014). The book trade was also innovatory, developing new genres such as the periodical, which flourished in the seventeenth and eighteenth centuries. In France there were 15 periodicals in 1745 but 82 by 1785; in Germany we can trace 58 journals up to 1700 but an incredible 1,225 new ones in the 1780s alone (Blanning 2002, 158–59). Thus the printed word became widely accessible, assisting (and reflecting) an increase in literacy (Box 2).

## Box 2

A popular German novel, set in the period of the Thirty Years War and published in 1668, explained how print itself impacted upon literacy: the hero Simplicissimus describes how he was taught to read by his hermit mentor:

'Now when I first saw the hermit read the Bible, I could not conceive with whom he should speak so secretly . . . when he laid it aside I crept thither and opened it . . . and lit upon the first chapter of Job and the picture that stood at the head thereof. [When the hermit explains the nature of the image and the 'black lines' on the page Simplicissimus demands to be taught to read. He explains how the hermit wrote out for him] an alphabet on birch-bark, formed like print, and when I knew the letters, I learned to spell, and thereafter to read, and at last to write better than could the hermit himself: for I imitated print in everything.'

(Grimmelshausen 1989, 21)

Simplicissimus's story shows how both pictures and words could act to spread knowledge among all kinds of people, and how the form of printed letters began to affect how people wrote. It also reminds us that learning to read came before learning to write. In the early modern period, reading was increasingly considered an essential skill, for religious as well as social purposes. It is now thought that while the ability to read was reasonably widespread, and augmented by illustrated texts and communal reading practices, the ability to write was much less prevalent, since it took a long time to learn and was only necessary for those who needed to write for their trade.

Literacy rates were on the rise, albeit with significant social, regional and gender variations (Houston 2002). During the century between the 1680s and 1780s, literacy rates in France increased from 29 per cent to 47 per cent for men, and from 14 per cent to 27 per cent for women. In German-speaking countries, the rise was from 10 per cent of the adult male population in 1700 to 25 per cent in 1800 (Blanning 2002, 112–13). Such rates were achieved much later in Eastern and Southern Europe, but earlier in England, where male literacy ran at 30 per cent in 1640 and 45 per cent by 1715, and even higher in London, where under 10 per cent of males were illiterate by the 1720s (Cressy 1980, Table 7.3). The rise in literacy, along with the rise in print, fostered the emergence of a reading public that consumed print in a variety of ways (Sharpe 2000; Raven *et al.* 1996). We can detect active and reflective readers, who scribbled notes and comments in the margins of their books; but we also know that reading was considered a sociable rather than a solitary affair (at least until notions of privacy gained sway in the eighteenth century), with material read out aloud to companions. As the amount of print available increased (particularly in metropolitan areas), so reading for some changed from an intensive experience of a few texts to an extensive one, sampling many. Above all, perhaps, print became a form of entertainment as well as a means of disseminating information.

But did all this amount to a print revolution?

## The case for a 'printing revolution'

In an influential text that held sway for over twenty years – and which continues to reverberate – Elizabeth L. Eisenstein argued that the development of printing marked a shift from old production methods, which had relied upon hand-written copies, and that the 'transforming powers of print', via the technology of the press, permitted a fixed and reliable mass replication of texts, images and symbols (Eisenstein 1979). Her thesis has since been challenged in several respects, so here we will consider the various arguments in some detail.

Eistenstein's key themes were that the printing press brought about:

- *Standardization*: the ability to reproduce the same text over and over again was important for the acquisition of new knowledge, e.g. in astronomy, since a 'single text might enable scattered observers to scan the heavens for the same signs on the same date'.
- *Diffusion and dissemination of knowledge*: the massive growth in the numbers of books and other forms of print led to increasing scholarly exchange, facilitated by related institutions like libraries and book fairs.
- *Preservation of texts*: print was 'the art that preserved all other arts', allowing the accumulation of texts, data and opinions with a potential to destabilize the established order (Eisenstein in Grafton *et al.* 2002).

These features, Eisenstein argued, created a new 'print culture' in Europe, which changed the early modern world by shaping the processes we call the Renaissance, Reformation and Scientific Revolution. She pointed out that printing brought new occupational groups (such as printers, publishers and booksellers); gatherings of authors and readers in printing shops; and new marketing and manufacturing techniques. As it was easier to move books than people, these new products – she suggested – transcended geographical borders and limitations of travel. This greatly assisted the gathering and dissemination of knowledge in the 'scientific Renaissance' ('The scientific revolution' in Part V).

Historians of the Reformation have also noted the importance of print. Scholars such as Robert Scribner (1981) see the press as intrinsic to the dissemination and contestation of the Protestant Reformations ('The long Reformation: Lutheran' in Part III, esp. Figures III.3–5, pages 103 and 105). Cheap print, such as ballads and primers, could be used to inculcate piety or, as in the case of visual satires, to ridicule religious opponents. Print allowed the religious debates to be played out to a wide audience and to reflect and shape its thinking (Box 3). Sometimes the link between print and Protestantism was clear: the decision of Sweden's new King Gustavus Vasa to bring about a Lutheran Reformation led to the setting up of a Swedish publishing trade for the first time.

## Box 3

In his *Book of Martyrs*, the English Protestant John Foxe saw printing as part of the onslaught on Catholic superstition and ignorance:

'hereby tongues are known, judgement increaseth, books are dispersed, the Scripture is seen . . . times be compared, truth discerned, falsehood detected . . . and all . . . through the benefit of printing. Whereof I suppose, that either the pope must abolish printing, or . . . he must seek a new world to reign over: for else as this world standeth, printing will doubtless abolish him.'

(1583 edn, 707; Web resources)

In Catholic territories, by contrast, Eisenstein argued, scientific advance was hampered by the papal INDEX LIBRORUM PROHIBITORUM (Web resources; 'The long Reformation: Catholic' in Part III). This listed titles forbidden to be printed or read by Catholics and it came to include many scientific books, such as works by Galileo and Brahe. Yet, even in Catholic countries, print fed the imaginations of those relatively low down the social scale. Perhaps the most famous example is Menocchio, a sixteenth-century Italian miller, whose private reflections on what he read were exposed by the INQUISITION and revealed a world of heretical belief (Ginzburg 1980).

Another intellectual development in which print arguably played an essential role is the Enlightenment ('Enlightenment: England and France' in Part V). Like the 'scientific revolution' and the Protestant and Catholic Reformations, the Enlightenment thrived on the dissemination of ideas and challenges to existing authorities. In the mid- and later seventeenth century it played a very significant part in the intellectual ferment of two British revolutions (Zaret 2000). The massive expansion of print in the eighteenth century, which affected Catholic as well as Protestant countries, allowed the circulation of ideas and knowledge as a collective and even pan-European phenomenon. Although states increased their power and ability to clamp down upon dissidents, intellectuals could bypass state censorship and disseminate their ideas by taking advantage of improved travel and communications systems and the international print trade. The Enlightenment PHILOSOPHE Voltaire, for example, after an early spell in prison for libel in 1718, took to living near Switzerland so that he had access to publishers and printers who were free from French government censorship. In addition to the growth of communications between scholars, intellectuals and political and religious radicals across the Atlantic world, the market for pirate or cheap copies of texts became common. The multi-volume ENCYCLOPÉDIE was reproduced in unofficial editions that collectively ensured a far greater and wider impact than the 'officially' produced original would ever have done alone. Thus the French Revolutionaries looked back to the *philosophes* and their popularizers as precursors who had helped lift the veil of ignorance and tyranny. Robert Darnton argues that cheap print, even the semi-pornographic books of eighteenth-century France, played a key role in carrying Enlightenment ideas (Darnton 1995). Moreover, Enlightenment print was also at the heart of a growing European and American sociability that had political and cultural repercussions: contemporaries shared their reading in clubs, COFFEE HOUSES and SALONS, spreading ideas that chipped away at the established order. Another consequence was that such 'print communities' facilitated the emergence of national identity, especially in states such as the Dutch Republic, Spain, France and Britain, by helping to foster similar imaginative boundaries and shared national cultures. In Britain, for example, the 'news revolution' promoted by the flourishing of periodicals after governmental control on them lapsed in 1695 may have helped to strengthen ties, or a sense of 'imagined community' (Anderson 1983).

Print, then, was arguably part of a revolution in science, religion and ideas; it helped create revolution in seventeenth-century England and bring down the ANCIEN RÉGIME in France. And it led to cultural transformations across Europe.

## The case against a 'print revolution'

Reluctant to place so much emphasis on one new technology, some scholars perceive a wider early modern communications revolution (Behringer 2006). An item of print only had impact once it was disseminated and that relied on improvements in marketing but even more fundamentally in the means of transport. Over the early modern period space and time shrank, as better roads, ships, canals and postal services improved communications. The Habsburgs developed a postal system in the early sixteenth century; and by the end of the eighteenth century there were about 2,500 postal stations in Germany and France. Travelling time between towns was cut dramatically. Thus, whereas in 1500 it took 30 days to go from Hamburg to Augsburg, by 1800 this had been cut to just five for postal couriers (Behringer 2006, 364). News – both manuscript newsletters and then printed newspapers – flowed along such routes; indeed, it depended on them. Without these developments in transport infrastructure the impact of the 'print revolution' might have been rather more restricted.

Historians have also argued that the revolution from a hand-written (scribal) and oral culture to a print culture has been exaggerated (Crick and Walsham 2004, 'Introduction'). Workshops of late medieval scribes had already created large numbers of books and manuscripts that proliferated across Europe. Indeed, whereas for Simplicissimus the character of print shaped the way he wrote, scribal practices and styles could in turn influence print which aped letter forms or imitated manuscript formats. Nor was scribal production suddenly replaced by printing. Hand-written copies of texts continued to flourish at least until the late seventeenth century, especially where censorship restricted the activities of authors and publishers. For much of the early modern period a literate, rather than a print, culture was what mattered, with a key divide between those who possessed or had access to texts and could read them, and those who did not.

Just as scribal practices remained vibrant, oral culture was not undermined or even replaced by 'print culture' ('Popular culture(s)' in Part V). Rather, print and oral culture existed in mutually reinforcing and stimulating ways: what was talked about found its way into print, and what was printed was talked about. Indeed, periodicals aimed at the middling sort – such as the *Tatler* – appeared with the specific intention of providing men and women in taverns, markets, clubs, salons and coffee houses with topics of conversation, and learned journals like the Royal Society's *Philosophical Transactions* stimulated debates all over Europe.

The case for a print revolution argues that it was instrumental in spreading knowledge and information. Yet it can be argued that print spread disinformation. Contemporaries used print but they also distrusted it. This was less the case in the scientific and cultural worlds but more so in the religious, political, social and economic arenas. Far from verifying and establishing 'truth' and 'reason', print could be used to distort and invert them. Paradoxically, then, although print 'fixed' texts, it could unfix truth. Indeed, partisans of all stripes believed their rivals engaged in deliberate attempts to mislead readers. In those circumstances, traditional forms of gauging credit – for example, through social or religious status – remained highly important. Distrust was further boosted by the ubiquitous anonymity of the medium – almost half the number of titles had no attributed author – which apparently allowed writers to lie without fear of reprisal (Figure V.5). The developing nature of the book trade also encouraged the more disreputable end of the trade, especially in France and England, whereby the eighteenth century a 'grub street' of impoverished authors, printers and publishers readily invented stories or took both sides of an argument in order to stoke the public appetite. As Filippo di Strata put it: 'The pen is a virgin, the printing press a whore' (Brooks 2005, 4). Print was a business, like any other, that pandered to markets. The profits were as much financial as cultural or intellectual.

Nor, it could be argued, was the print revolution necessarily one that undermined the Ancien Régime; indeed, it could even support and strengthen the role of authoritarian governments. The type of print products available remained surprisingly

**Figure V.5** This anti-cavalier broadside ballad was published, probably with parliamentary approval, in 1642 at the outset of the English Civil War and as part of the enormous printed propaganda campaigns that broke out from 1640. An attack on the pillaging behaviour of cavalier soldiers, copies could be sent all over the country by post and they could be pasted onto whipping posts in market-places, on church doors and on the walls in alehouses – in any place where both cavaliers and roundheads could see them. Image taken from *The English Irish Souldier with his new discipline, new armes, old stomache, and new taken pillage: who had rather eate than fight.* [A satire, in verse.] Originally published/produced in London, 1642. © British Library Board. All Rights Reserved / Bridgeman Images.

traditional. Theological debate kept a high profile in the output of the eighteenth century, for all the so-called secularizing tendency of the Enlightenment. Printed satire may have helped to delegitimize notions of a sacred monarchy or an unquestioned Church, but religious texts, sermons, schoolbooks, proclamations and government apologists served to defend it. And print could enhance and enforce authority within the state. Bureaucratization, centralization, more effective fiscal powers, militarization and the defence of ideologies of order were all facilitated by better communications. Moreover, the financial revolutions of the eighteenth century, which saw large amounts of private money invested in governmental debts and loans, relied to an important extent on information being available to investors via the newspapers and other forms of print. Indeed, the activities of the state stimulated printed news: the 'coranto', an early form of newspaper, which developed at the beginning of the seventeenth century in the Netherlands, from an earlier French example, concentrated entirely on foreign affairs and European conflicts (Davies and Fletcher 2014).

Finally, even if there was a print revolution in the sense of the greater production and availability of the press, it is hard to establish a clear correlation between text and action. Because propaganda was available, does that guarantee that its message would be followed? Was the French Revolution the result of the Enlightenment and the Enlightenment the result of the press?

## Assessment

It is certain that distribution and accessibility of texts increased Europe wide from the fifteenth century onwards. Historians and literary scholars have pointed to revolutions not just in reading habits and print formats but also in religion, science, politics and wider cultural belief-systems that seem attributable to the press. Yet how far they actually were remains hotly contested. On the one hand, there are many who see the press as truly instrumental in fostering a religion of the word, such as Protestantism; as disseminating ideas that both spread a rebirth of classicism and undermined the established order; and as contributing to the state and national identity as well as to a culture of entertainment and new forms of writing. On the other hand, there are scholars who stress that print did not provoke a radical break with the past and that its impact was often dependent on other technologies, especially transport. Far from undercutting an oral and literate culture, print merely reinvigorated it in different ways; print was not always available, especially among the poor and less well-off; print did not fix truth and reason but promulgated lies, propaganda and polemical irrationalities as one author railed against another. Moreover, the correlation between text and behaviour is uncertain.

Yet these are not mutually exclusive interpretations. We might simply want to build important caveats into our analysis of the transformative power of print. Indeed, in this respect it is helpful to think of the ways in which modern digital technologies coexist with older ones, are taken up at different rates with varying degrees of enthusiasm and foster new ways of thinking and behaving. When we evaluate such questions we are thrown back to problems faced by those who lived in the early modern period. Do changes in communicative practices change the way we think and what we say? Should we embrace transforming technologies or be sceptical about them or both? Are there justifiable limits on the freedom of expression or publishing copyright? How do we discern lies and misinformation, and what can we do about them? These are early modern questions that have a twenty-first-century urgency.

## Discussion themes

1. Is the term 'print revolution' misleading?
2. Did changes in communicative practices change belief and behaviour in early modern Europe?
3. Was print necessarily subversive of authority?

## Bibliography

### (A) Sources

Bacon, Francis (1620), *The New Organon: Or True Directions Concerning the Interpretation of Nature*, London

Grimmelshausen, Johan Jacob (1989), *Simplicissimus* [1668/69], trans. S. Goodrich, Sawtry

### (B) Literature

Anderson, Benedict (1983), *Imagined Communities: Reflections on the Origin and Spread of Nationalism*, London

Behringer, Wolfgang ed. (2006), 'Communication in Historiography', special issue of *German History*, 24(3)

Blanning, T. C. W. (2002), *The Culture of Power and the Power of Culture: Old Regime Europe 1660–1789*, Oxford

Brooks, Douglas A. ed. (2005), *Printing and Parenting in Early Modern England*, Aldershot

Cressy, David (1980), *Literacy and the Social Order: Reading and Writing in Tudor and Stuart England*, Cambridge

Crick, Julia and Walsham, Alexandra eds (2004), *The Uses of Script and Print, 1300–1700*, Cambridge

Darnton, Robert (1995), *The Forbidden Best-Sellers of Pre-Revolutionary France*, London

Davies, Simon F. and Fletcher, Puck, eds. (2014), *News in Early Modern Europe: Currents and Connections*, Leiden

* Eisenstein, Elizabeth L. (1979), *The Printing Press as an Agent of Change: Communications and Cultural Transformations in Early Modern Europe*, 2 vols, Cambridge

Ginzburg, Carlo (1980), *The Cheese and the Worms: The Cosmos of a Sixteenth-Century Miller*, Baltimore, Md.

* Grafton, Anthony, Eisenstein, Elizabeth L. and Johns, Adrian (2002), 'AHR Forum: How Revolutionary was the Print Revolution', *American Historical Review* 107, 84–128

Houston, R. A. (2002), *Literacy in Early Modern Europe*, 2nd edn, London

Howsam, Leslie ed. (2015), *The Cambridge Companion to the History of the Book*, Cambridge

Pettegree, Andrew (2002), 'Printing and the Reformation', in: *The Beginnings of English Protestantism*, eds P. Marshall and A. Ryrie, Cambridge

Raven, James, Small, Helen and Tadmor, Naomi eds (1996), *The Practice and Representation of Reading in England*, Cambridge

Salzberg, Rosa (2014), *Ephemeral City: Cheap Print and Urban Culture in Renaissance Venice*, Manchester

Scribner, Robert (1981), *For the Sake of Simple Folk: Popular Propaganda for the German Reformation*, London

Sharpe, Kevin (2000), *Reading Revolutions: The Politics of Reading in Early Modern England*, New Haven, Conn.

Wilson-Okamura, David S. (2010), *Virgil in the Renaissance*, Cambridge

Zaret, David (2000), *Origins of Democratic Culture: Printing, Petitions and the Public Sphere in Early Modern England*, Princeton, NJ

## (C) Web resources

'English Broadside Ballad Archive', University of California, Santa Barbara: <http://ebba.english.ucsb.edu/>

Ettinghausen, Henry (2015), 'How the Press Began: The Pre-Periodical Printed Press in Europe' <http://www.janusdigital.es/anexos.htm>

'The Gutenberg Bible' (c. 1454), British Library: <http://www.bl.uk/treasures/gutenberg/homepage.html>

'Index Librorum Prohibitorum' (1557– ), IHSP: <http://www.fordham.edu/halsall/mod/indexlibrorum.html>

'John Foxe's *Book of Martyrs*', Humanities Research Institute, Sheffield: <http://www.hrionline.ac.uk/johnfoxe/>

Meertens Instituut, 'Broadside Ballads': <http://www.geheugenvannederland.nl/?/en/collecties/straatliederen>

Pettegree, Andrew et. al., 'The Universal Short Title Catalogue': <http://www.ustc.ac.uk/>

# The scientific revolution

*Claudia Stein*

The term 'scientific revolution' refers to a period stretching roughly from 1500 to 1700. Its beginning is generally associated with the works of the astronomer Nicolaus Copernicus (1473–1543) and the anatomist Andreas Vesalius (1514–64) and its climax with the English EXPERIMENTAL PHILOSOPHER Isaac Newton (1643–1727). While the precise nature of developments is a matter of debate, all scholars agree that it is a key moment when a specific way of looking at the natural world – what we call 'modern science' – began to take shape.

Although very familiar to us today, the term was only coined in the 1940s by historians and philosophers interested in the history of the sciences (Box 1). With the term 'revolution', they emphasized the idea of a sudden and dramatic change in the way Europeans understood the physical world in the early modern period. But what exactly *did* change? For these scholars, most of them champions of intellectual history, the change manifested itself in the way people were *thinking* about nature. For them, the most important element of scientific endeavour was 'thought': bold, logical, objective, abstract and predominantly male. Their writings hailed the so-called scientific revolution as the triumph of a fearless, rational mind over the superstitious and backward reasoning of the dark Middle Ages.

Since the 1970s, however, this heroic view of the scientific revolution has come under attack. Scholars felt increasingly uneasy with the very idea of the scientific revolution as a singular and discrete event. Medieval historians, for example, have shown that their period was certainly not characterized by ignorance and scientific backwardness. On the contrary, they argued, medieval philosophers provided the foundation for the scientific revolution. Following these claims, John Henry argued that no single coherent cultural entity called 'science' underwent revolutionary change in the sixteenth and seventeenth centuries, simply because the modern notion of 'science' only emerged after 1800 (Henry 1997, 4). Before that date, it is now agreed, the natural world was approached with the intellectual and practical tools belonging to a scholarly tradition best described as NATURAL PHILOSOPHY (Dear 2001, 199).

Natural philosophers were not concerned with discovering new things but aimed at *explaining* the entire existing system of the world. Their knowledge and practices covered such diverse fields as navigation, mining, medicine, botany, pharmacology, geology, alchemy, astronomy, but also philosophy, theology and law. Henry therefore warned that the scientific revolution must not be seen as a revolution in science, but

**Box 1**

The monograph *The Origin of Modern Science* by the English philosopher of history Herbert Butterfield, first published in 1949, probably contains the most celebratory assessment of the scientific revolution:

'Since that revolution overturned the authority in science not only of the middle ages but of the ancient world – since it ended not only in the eclipse of scholastic philosophy but in the destruction of Aristotelian physics – it outshines everything since the rise of Christianity and reduces the Renaissance and Reformation to the rank of mere episodes, mere internal displacements within the system of medieval Christendom.'

*(Butterfield 1957, viii)*

as a set of dramatic transformations moving natural philosophy towards our modern concept of science. Particularly striking is the increased use of mathematics and measurements to obtain a more precise idea of how the world and its parts work. Moreover, natural philosophers began to trust observations and personal experiences more than ancient texts and, where necessary, embarked on specifically conceived experiments to gain a better understanding of nature's secrets.

Historians also reassessed the socio-cultural context in which scientific practices developed. The long-cherished image of the lonely male investigator of nature, obsessed with his work and immune to any worldly temptations, came under increasing attack. Equipped with methods from neighbouring disciplines like sociology or anthropology, historians began to investigate the context of early modern science. They tried to see the world through the eyes of their historical actors and asked, for example, how their scientific enterprise was shaped by institutions such as the early modern PATRONAGE system or the etiquette of court culture. Feminist scholars demanded a place for women in the heroic accounts of the scientific revolution. Why is it, they asked, that hardly any women featured in the many histories of the scientific revolution? What are the socio-cultural reasons for their invisibility? As a result of subsequent investigations, we now know more about the activities of women as independent researchers (e.g. the German painter and botanist Maria Sybilla Merian, 1646–1717), as patrons (e.g. the English natural philosopher Margaret Cavendish, 1623–73) or as matrons of an early modern 'scientific' household (e.g. Jane Dee, 1555–1605, wife of the court physician John Dee, 1527–1608), and how significant they actually were for the development of modern science (Davis 1995; Schiebinger 1989; Harkness 1997).

Despite these recent debates, many historians still speak of a 'scientific revolution', since natural philosophers themselves, particularly those of the seventeenth century, believed that they were doing something radically new and different from their predecessors. Peter Dear has argued that the term should be reserved for the seventeenth century, when there is overwhelming evidence for the desire to break with previous conceptions and practices. Natural philosophers of the sixteenth century, in contrast, merely sought to 'correct' mistakes and 'renew' ancient wisdom. This phase, personified by Nicolaus Copernicus and Andreas Vesalius, may be best conceptualized as a 'scientific renaissance' (Dear 2001).

## The scientific renaissance

After his university studies Nicolaus Copernicus worked as an administrator on ESTATES belonging to the Catholic Church in Poland. His real passion, however, was mathematics and astronomy and every minute he could spare was devoted to the investigation of the cosmos. A reclusive scholar, his findings were only published in 1543, the year he died. In this famous book, *De revolutionibus orbium coelestium* (On the Revolution of the Celestial Spheres), Copernicus put forward his observation that the sun was the centre of the universe, with the earth and planets orbiting around it. This HELIOCENTRIC view turned the prevailing understanding of the cosmos – based on a stationary spherical earth at the centre and heavenly bodies in orbits around it – upside down. The GEOCENTRIC view of the cosmos was based on the 'bible' of astronomers at the time, the *Almagest*, written by the Greek astronomer Claudius Ptolemy (after 83–161). Ptolemy, whose intellectual framework derived from the writings of his compatriot Aristotle (384–322 BCE), believed in the existence of a two-sphered cosmos: the terrestrial sphere composed of the four elements, earth, water, air and fire, on the one hand; and the surrounding celestial sphere consisting of only one element, aether, on the other. According to Aristotle, the terrestrial sphere between the earth and the moon (also called the sublunar sphere) was characterized by constant change, generation and corruption; the celestial sphere above the moon (or supralunar sphere), however, by perfection and complete harmony – a place where nothing came into being or ceased to exist (Figures V.6–7, page 264).

By challenging these ancient and ultimately pagan ideas Copernicus entered dangerous territory, because over the centuries they had been assimilated into the teaching of the Church. According to the latter the earth at the centre of the universe was God's creation and anybody who questioned this view was a potential heretic. Copernicus was well aware of the controversial content of his work, although he did not consider it a 'revolutionary' break with the magical, irrational past, as many historians have argued. In the preface, which is dedicated to Pope Paul III (1534–49), he explained how he wished his findings to be understood. Copernicus first complains about the terrible state of astronomy. His explicit aim was to improve the situation by scrutinizing the views of all ancient philosophers and astronomers. From the point of view of a 'modern' scientist, this sounds distinctly odd, but for sixteenth-century university-trained academics like Copernicus it was essential to find ancient precedents for their positions. Whoever presented work as 'innovative' was unlikely to be taken seriously. Innovations – in our sense of the word – were considered trivial and

**Figures V.6–7** From the sixteenth century, scholars like Copernicus replaced the traditional geocentric view of the cosmos (on the left, with the earth at the centre) by a heliocentric model (right, with the sun [sol] at the centre). Diagrams for the cosmos according to Petrus Apianus, Cosmographia (Antwerp, 1539), and Nicolaus Copernicus, De revolutionibus orbium coelestium (Nuremberg, 1543). From: http://ads.harvard.edu/books/1543droc.book.

insubstantial. 'Real' and 'truthful' knowledge could only be found in ancient literature and intricate philosophical debate.

By advocating a return to ANTIQUITY, Copernicus supported the intellectual programme of HUMANISM, the great cultural movement of his time originating in fourteenth-century Italy. The principal objective of humanists (most of whom taught classical literature and RHETORIC at the universities) was to reinvigorate their own society through the practices of the ancients ('The Renaissance' in Part V). Renewal was their watchword and also the aim of Nicolaus Copernicus's study of the universe. He hoped to restore and correct ancient astronomical practice. A like-minded personality was the anatomist Andreas Vesalius, another key figure in the history of the scientific RENAISSANCE. Born in Brussels in 1514 and trained as a physician at various European universities, Vesalius not only sympathized with humanist ideals but also possessed outstanding technical skills. He was widely renowned for his art of dissection, a practice effectively non-existent in universities at the time. Medical teaching there relied almost entirely on the interpretation of ancient texts. Flamboyant and happy to challenge more conservative colleagues, Vesalius propagated a return to practical anatomy to check whether the ancient medical writers, in particular the Roman physician Galen (129–c. 200), had been correct in their descriptions of the human body. The fruit of his work was a lavishly illustrated book, *De humani corporis fabrica* (On the Fabric of the Human Body), published in 1543 (the same year as Copernicus's treatise). For the first time in the history of western medicine, the human body was shown realistically ('Arts and society' in Part V; Figure V.8).

Again, however, one should be careful not to project modern understanding of science onto the past and praise Vesalius as a radical liberator from the shackles of the medieval past. It is more appropriate to see *De Fabrica* as the work of an ambitious

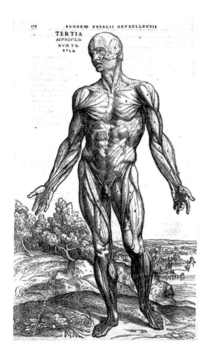

**Figure V.8** The 'Third Muscle Man' is one of the many striking anatomical illustrations in Vesalius' *On the Fabric of the Human Body* of 1543

**Box 2**

Vesalius's rhetoric in his introduction to *De Fabrica* (dedicated to the Holy Roman Emperor Charles V, ruled 1519–58) is very similar to that of Copernicus and reveals his true ambitions. Having deplored the decline of medicine since Antiquity, Vesalius asserts how in the present age:

'things have taken a turn for the better, and medicine, along with other studies, has begun so to come to life again and to raise its head from profound darkness that in several universities it has, beyond all argument, come close to recovering its former glory.'

(Vesalius 1998, f. Ii)

humanist (Box 2). Vesalius wished to contribute to the revival of Antiquity and desired to restore the kind of medicine that Galen had championed, but not by uncritical reverence of the latter as the ultimate authority. In his dissections Vesalius found many errors in Galen's work. This is not surprising, since Galen never dissected humans, only apes. Nevertheless, while acknowledging inaccuracies, Vesalius still upheld Galen as the model to be emulated. He was satisfied to correct Galen without undermining his broader physiological or pathological views. Like Copernicus, Vesalius did not seek to shake the foundations of antique knowledge, only to cleanse them of error.

However, by about 1600, the ambitions of those interested in the physical world had changed. Nothing distinguishes the 'new science' of the seventeenth century more clearly than its proponents' claim that it was 'new'. Natural philosophers increasingly aimed for a clean break with the past. Although ancient texts continued to be enormously important, they no longer served as signposts to a lost golden age, as in the sixteenth century.

## Scientific revolution

In April 1633, the papal court in Rome initiated a trial whose outcome was anxiously awaited by many involved in the investigation of nature all over Europe. The defendant was the Florentine Galileo Galilei (1564–1642), a natural philosopher, mathematician and author of *The Dialogue Concerning Two Chief World Systems* published a year earlier. In his work, Galileo discussed Copernican and Ptolemaic ideas of cosmology. A close reading of the text had convinced the papal authorities that it represented a vigorous attempt to establish the physical reality of the heliocentric Copernican system and to ridicule the Church's beliefs in the geocentric Ptolemaic cosmos. Galileo had supported his bold claims by brand-new 'discoveries' made with an improved telescope. He had observed, for example, that the ancient astronomical theory, according to which no changes occurred in the heavenly sphere, was flawed. Galileo's daily observations had revealed blemishes and irregularities on the surfaces of the sun and moon, from which he had deduced that changes *did* occur in the celestial sphere and that the Aristotelian doctrine of the heavens must be wrong. This claim was absolutely unacceptable for the Church whose entire body of teaching relied on Aristotelian premises. It thus comes as little surprise that the trial in 1633 ended in Galileo's defeat. He had to publicly refute Copernican ideas, *The Dialogue* was prohibited and its author condemned to life imprisonment in his own house, where he died in 1643. It was only two centuries later, in 1831, that *The Dialogue* was taken off the Church's INDEX LIBRORUM PROHIBITORUM.

Galileo's trial in Rome was *the* hot topic among Europe's natural philosophers. One in particular was extremely disturbed by its outcome, the Frenchmen René Descartes (1596–1650). Descartes was in fact so terrified by the verdict that he decided to leave his Catholic homeland for the Protestant Low Countries, where the intellectual climate, he felt, was less restrictive. In retrospect, he was probably right, because his aims were even bolder than those of Galileo: Descartes aimed at a radically new philosophy capable of replacing the Aristotelian paradigm. The 'Cartesian system' was part and parcel of a larger attempt to rethink the universe, a so-called 'mechanical philosophy' which became one of the most influential concepts of the seventeenth century. Indeed, by the end of the 1600s it had replaced Aristotelian ideas about the functioning of the physical world.

Descartes's ambition was to build this system on a foundation of certainty. He aimed at explanations of natural phenomena that could never be challenged. But how could absolute certainty be established? Descartes devised an ingenious intellectual strategy to test the truth value of natural knowledge. In a first instance, he doubted everything that was regarded as certain knowledge in his time and discussed the proposition from all possible angles. Nothing survived this rigorous test. Descartes then wondered whether any true and certain knowledge existed at all. He finally came to the conclusion that the only thing that could never be doubted was his own existence and his capacity for critical thought. The result of his reasoning is reflected in his famous sentence: 'Je pense, donc je suis' (or 'Cogito ergo sum', in part IV of his *Discourse on Method*: Web resources). Descartes's belief in the ability of the human mind to solve and explain anything also shaped his ideas about the functioning of the natural world. In his famous books *Discourse on Method* (1637) and *Principles of Philosophy* (1644), he tried to convince his readers that all physical phenomena could be explained by mathematical and mechanical concepts. In his view, the natural world worked like machinery, in the sense that change was brought about by (and could be explained in terms of) the intermeshing of bodies, like cogwheels in a clock. Descartes also applied his mechanical model to animals and human beings, which he imaged as complex automata or machines based on hydraulic systems, and he distinguished sharply between mind and matter, i.e. the body.

CARTESIANISM – as his mathematical view of the world soon came to be known – did not have the same sweeping success in England as it had on the Continent. This is mainly due to the development of a strong mechanistic 'experimental philosophy' in England, a type of investigation of the natural world that relied on gathering facts from experimental and observational work. One of the most important contributions to the understanding of the human body resulted from such experiments: the circulation of blood 'discovered' by the physician William Harvey. In his treatise *Anatomical Exercise on the Motion of the Heart and Blood in Animals* (1628), Harvey argued for the first time that the human heart serves to pump blood continuously around the entire body. While the ancient medical literature spoke of two independent circuits, Harvey argued that the arterial and venous systems were two components of one larger circulatory system. His hypothesis could not, of course, be demonstrated by simply opening a living animal body. To prove his claim, Harvey devised numerous experiments on a wide variety of animals and human beings over the course of a decade.

Harvey was just one of a large number of 'experiment enthusiasts' in seventeenth-century Britain and although these men faced much criticism, their methods soon prevailed. Experiments were about discovery, about finding new things, and that was exactly what many people found so fascinating about them. The greatest practitioner of experimentation was without doubt Isaac Newton. In 1703, he became president of the Royal Society, an institution – still in existence today – founded in the early 1660s as an association of like-minded individuals created to conduct experimental and natural historical enquiry on an organized basis. Newton contributed several new theorems and methods to mathematics, including differential calculus. But he also made important findings in physics. He showed, by experiment, the compound nature of white light and figured out a theory of colours. At the same time he solved the puzzle of the force of gravity. The latter theory, elaborated in Newton's celebrated *Philosophiae naturalis principia mathematica* (Mathematical Principles of Natural Philosophy, 1687), was entirely based on experimental observation and led him to the formulation of the three laws of motion, the basis of Newtonian mechanics as well as modern engineering.

Galileo, Descartes, Harvey and Newton would have been unable to pursue their interests without the support of a patron. Seventeenth-century universities offered no support to those interested in these new experimental approaches to investigate nature. A patron could be either a wealthy and noble individual such as the Grand Duke of Tuscany Cosimo II de' Medici, who sponsored Galileo's enthusiasm for astronomy, or an institution such as the Royal Society in the case of Newton ('Courts and centres' in Part VI). However, this does not make the investigation of nature in the early modern period an entirely elitist enterprise. Recent studies have identified other 'homes' where knowledge about nature was produced and exchanged such as private alchemical laboratories, museums or botanical gardens (Moran 2005; Findlen 1994; Spary 2000). An increasing research focus is also how these new ideas about nature could be disseminated and how they were adopted (and often reshaped) by people of lower social standing (Eamon 1994; Fissell 2004).

## Assessment

By the time of Newton's death in 1727, educated Europeans looked at the natural world in a strikingly different way from their ancestors around 1500. While Copernicus and Vesalius had hoped to 'correct' ancient wisdom and adjust their own findings to it, French Cartesians and English experimental philosophers such as Harvey or Newton in the seventeenth century were primarily concerned with discovering new things and with the control of the natural world. Yet even though the ways Europeans thought about nature and its exploration changed beyond recognition during the period of the scientific revolution, one component remained the same: investigating nature always involved God ('Religious culture in early modern Europe' in Part III). Even Newton, the celebrated perfectionist of experimental philosophy, a cool and abstract thinker, understood his endeavour as being a service to the Almighty. There were no atheists among the natural philosophers of this period. They all saw themselves as part of God's governed universe and never doubted its creator.

## Discussion themes

1. Is 'nature' a given entity or a social construct?
2. What is the difference between 'scientific renaissance' and 'scientific revolution'?
3. What did the 'scientific revolution' overthrow?

## *Bibliography*

### (A) Sources

Apianus, Petrus (1539), *Cosmographia*, Antwerp
Newton, Isaac (1687), *Philosophiae naturalis principia mathematics*, London
Vesalius, Andreas (1998), *On the Fabric of the Human Body* [1543], trans. William
Frank Richardson, San Francisco

### (B) Literature

Butterfield, Herbert (1957), *The Origins of Modern Science, 1300–1700*, New York
Davis, Nathalie Zemon (1995), *Women on the Margins: Three Seventeenth-Century Lives*, Cambridge, Mass.
Dear, Peter (2001), *Revolutionizing the Sciences: European Knowledge and its Ambitions, 1500–1700*, Basingstoke
Eamon, William (1994), *Science and the Secrets of Nature*, Princeton, NJ
Findlen, Paul (1994), *Possessing Nature: Museums, Collecting, and Scientific Culture*, Berkeley, Calif.
Fissell, Mary (2004), *Vernacular Bodies: The Politics of Reproduction in Early Modern England*, Oxford
Harkness, Deborah E. (1997), 'Managing an Experimental Household: The Dees of Mortlake and the Practice of Natural Philosophy', *Isis*, 88, 247–62
* Henry, John (1997), *The Scientific Revolution and the Origins of Modern Science*, London
Kusukawa, Sachiko (2012), *Picturing the Book of Nature: Image, Text and Argument in Sixteenth-Century Human Anatomy and Medical Botany*, Chicago
Moran, Bruce (2005), *Distilling Knowledge: Alchemy, Chemistry and the Scientific Revolution*, Cambridge, Mass.
Nummedal, Tara (2007), *Alchemy and Authority in the Holy Roman Empire*, Chicago
Schiebinger, Londa (1989), *Has Mind No Sex? Women in the Origins of Modern Science*, Cambridge, Mass.
* Shapin, Steven (1996), *The Scientific Revolution*, Chicago
Spary, Emma (2000), *Utopia's Garden: French Natural History from Old Regime to Revolution*, Chicago

### (C) Web resources

Copernicus, Nicholas (1543), *De revolutionibus orbium coelestium*: <http://ads.harvard.edu/books/1543droc.book/>
Descartes, René, *Discourse on Method* (1637): <http://www.earlymoderntexts.com/assets/pdfs/descartes1637.pdf>
'The Galileo Project': <http://galileo.rice.edu/>

'Scientific Revolution', IHSP: <http://www.fordham.edu/Halsall/mod/modsbook09.asp>

Vesalius, Andreas (1543), *De corporis humani fabrica libri septem:* <https://www.nlm.nih.gov/exhibition/historicalanatomies/vesalius_home.html>

'Virtual Library for the History of Science, Technology & Medicine': <http://vlib.iue.it/history/topical/science.html>

'Wellcome Images': <http://wellcomeimages.org/>

# Witchcraft and magic

*Penny Roberts*

Magical beliefs and practices permeated early modern European society. It was widely believed that some individuals could perform incredible acts by harnessing the power of supernatural forces. Most people had recourse to 'white' magic at some time in their lives in order to ensure the welfare of loved ones, livestock or crops. It was also understood that such powers or 'black' magic could equally be directed to do harm. This 'magical' worldview encompassed other commonly held beliefs: in prophecy, divination and astrology, the operation of divine PROVIDENCE and the possibility of demonic possession (Thomas 1971; Wilson 2000). The mental construction of such beliefs affected intellectuals and PEASANTRY alike in their understanding of how God and the devil operated in the world. Sorcery or demonic magic became associated with witchcraft by the end of the Middle Ages, and the Church and DEMONOLOGISTS came increasingly to attribute all magical acts to the agency of the devil. Those who were believed to have conspired with him were labelled witches and prosecuted as such. The sharp rise in prosecutions for witchcraft between the mid-sixteenth and mid-seventeenth centuries has long been a source of popular fascination and, in recent decades, has generated much historical debate. However, the fact that its perpetrators became a judicial target in the early modern period has proved difficult to explain. Theories encompass wider patterns of socio-economic, political, intellectual and cultural change as well as religious reform.

## The rise in prosecutions

Although a widespread belief in the existence of witchcraft predated the early modern period, a notable intensification in prosecutions for it occurred during the century *c.* 1560–1660. However, early estimates of hundreds of thousands brought to trial across Europe have been exaggerated and are not sustained by recent research. In fact, isolated trials and executions, although more frequent than before, continued to be the norm in most countries. Exact figures are difficult to obtain because of the patchy survival of sources (not least because some were burned along with the condemned witch), but those trial records that do survive can be extremely detailed. Early estimates were extrapolated from the more sensational and exceptional cases which involved greater numbers (but perhaps only 10–20 per cent of the total), yet even the reassessed figures are shockingly high (one recent estimate being 110,000 prosecutions and 60,000 executions: Levack 1995, 25) for a crime that most people now do not believe to be possible, let alone worthy of capital punishment.

The rise in prosecutions varied according to time and place and was dependent on a number of regional variables (Table V.5.1; Figure V.9, page 274). Some areas were prone to mass trials, principally parts of the Holy Roman Empire, especially the south-west, while in others these were much less common, as in France and England. The role of certain individuals, usually judges, in particular regions proved crucial in a number of instances, notably Matthew Hopkins in Essex in the 1640s and Nicolas Rémy in Franche Comté at the end of the sixteenth century (Rémy 1930). The differences in the intensity of prosecution between countries has led historians to downplay the notion of a European-wide panic. Spain, Italy and Russia all experienced only relatively brief and low-key prosecutions. In Spain and Italy this was undertaken by the INQUISITION, which was more concerned with enforcing orthodoxy than locating diabolism and required a higher standard of proof than accusations of witchcraft could provide. Salem was the only 'big' case in New England and, for all its notoriety, only resulted in nineteen executions in 1692.

England's apparent leniency has been explained by its peculiar legal system which treated witchcraft as a felony rather than a HERESY (so that witches were hanged rather than burned as elsewhere) and forbade the use of torture, reducing the likelihood of confession and the incrimination of others which commonly lay behind mass convictions on the Continent (Macfarlane 1978). The contrast with Scotland, with its Continental-style use of ROMAN LAW, interrogation and torture (and greater number of prosecutions), supports this. Yet even in France, which is often contrasted with England, remarkable restraint was exercised by the judges of the leading sovereign court, the *Parlement* of Paris, which had jurisdiction over much of France. It was in the borderlands of Lorraine and Franche Comté (only incorporated into the kingdom under Louis XIV), Normandy, the Pyrenees and the far north-east, unstable and further away from central control, that the number of executions was significant. The sensational cases of possessed convents, such as Loudun in the 1630s, were again exceptional. The restraint of judicial processes in parts of Germany, notably Rothenburg, Nuremberg and the Palatinate, reinforces the variety of practice in the Empire as well as suggesting that 'areas which did not experience large-scale witch-hunts may well have been the early modern norm rather than the exception' (Rowlands 2003, 2).

Across Europe, the average estimate that only 40 to 50 per cent of those who came to trial for witchcraft were actually executed does not suggest that the judgements were driven by panic. Indeed, the leniency or caution of the judges in these cases is impressive in contrast to the zeal we might expect to rid society of witches. This contrast is even more pronounced if we consider the conviction rate for similar 'moral' crimes which were increasingly prosecuted in this period. In percentage terms, there were twice as many convictions for plague-spreading as for witchcraft in the city of Geneva. Infanticide (an almost exclusively 'female' crime) resulted in the execution

**Table V.5.1** Percentage of defendants at witchcraft trials actually executed

| Location | Executed (%) |
|---|---|
| Pays de Vaud | 90 |
| Imperial free cities | <50 |
| Channel Islands | 46 |
| Poland (1701–50) | 46 |
| Moscow (17th century) | 32 |
| Essex | 26 |
| Geneva | 21 |
| Poland (16th century) | 4 |

This table illustrates both the national variation but also the general pattern of 40–50 per cent of accused witches executed. Note the contrast between sixteenth- and eighteenth-century Poland (Scarre 1987, 30).

of the vast majority of those accused; 70 per cent before the Paris *Parlement* which had only a 20 per cent conviction rate for witchcraft (Soman 1978). This was despite the fact that every effort was made to load the case against accused witches by allowing the usually inadmissible testimony of women, children, felons and those with a vested interest in the outcome. Combined with the use of interrogation and torture to extract confessions, such practices underline the status of witchcraft as an exceptional crime. In places where prosecution was more intense, such as in Lorraine or Trier and Würzburg in Germany, mass trials led to a conviction rate of some 90 per cent. The sporadic pattern of prosecution, and the very real fear of witches, should not detract from the tragic outcome of such trials (Box 1).

## Explanations

Historians have sought to rationalize the actions of those responsible for the prosecution of supposed witches, both accusers and judges, and to explain the remarkable rise and just as rapid decline in that prosecution in the context of early modern beliefs and circumstances. Some relate it to centralization processes (state building) and the authorities' quest for greater social discipline. The most prominent explanations, however, encompass religious fervour, reactions to disaster and crises, the refusal of charity, changes in the legal system, a heightened awareness of the devil's agency, an alliance of elite and popular beliefs, misogyny and regional difference.

The coincidence, more or less, of the rise in prosecutions with the Protestant and Catholic Reformations is worthy of note. However, this was not so much because Catholics accused Protestants and vice versa in an outburst of confessional hostility,

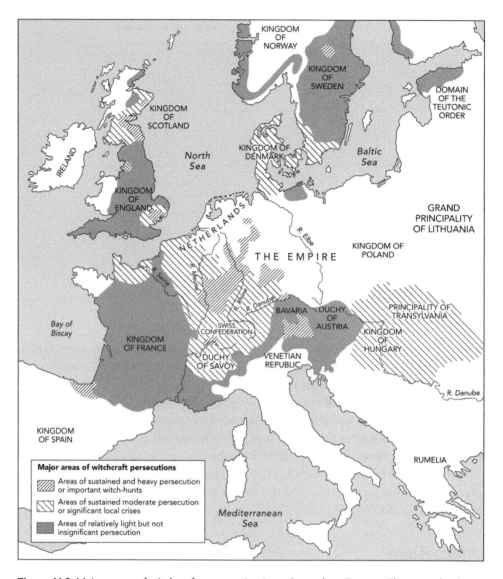

**Figure V.9** Major areas of witchcraft persecution in early modern Europe. The map clearly shows the variegated intensity of prosecutions. The densest were concentrated in pockets of the Holy Roman Empire, Scotland and the Swiss Confederation. It also suggests that the English rate of prosecution was far from unique, being on a par with that in France, Austria and Sweden. 'Major Areas of Witchcraft Persecution in Western, Central, and Northern Europe', reproduced from Robin Briggs, Witches and Neighbours: The Social and Cultural Context of European Witchcraft (London: Blackwell, 1996), xi.

but because both movements encouraged the condemnation of witchcraft as a sin against God and Christian society (although this view predated the CONFESSIONAL age). Since it was generally held to be impossible to acquire supernatural powers by natural means, it was logical to assume that the devil was involved in all forms of magic, however benign, as outlined in the Bible (Clark 1997). Popular acceptance of this viewpoint was nevertheless far from assured. It is a paradox that the Reformations perpetuated superstitions which they condemned in the context of the suppression of popular religious beliefs and practices. For contemporary scholars, the apparent increase in diabolical activity appeared to presage, and was explained by, the Last Days as foretold in Revelation. Interestingly, increased reports of werewolf sightings and other forms of demonic possession and shape-shifting occurred in the same period, suggesting a wider anxiety about the present danger posed by the devil.

---

**Box 1**

Two typical cases brought to trial:

1. In 1587 in the town of Rothenburg, an imperial city in South-central Germany, a six-year-old boy and his mother were brought before the courts to answer claims that they had flown at night to a witches' dance with a 'black, horned man'. Despite the fact that he was below the age when his testimony was supposed to be credible, the boy Hans was the main focus of the interrogation, but inconsistencies in his story led the judges to dismiss the case (although not before the accused had been subjected to torture) (Rowlands 2003, 81–101).
2. In 1596 in the Duchy of Lorraine, on the imperial border with France, a woman claimed that another, with whom she had a long-running enmity, had sent her a poisoned pear via her husband. When the fruit turned black and was found to be full of grease, she threw it into a field where a sow and her piglets ate it and all soon died (Briggs 1996, 114).

The involvement of children was not unusual, nor was the leniency of judges even in Southern Germany. Poison by (diabolically procured) grease or powder was a common, almost mundane accusation. Neither case suggests the traditional depiction of a witch-hunt or craze of panic proportions resulting in mass executions.

---

A rise in prosecution rarely seems to have responded to a particular catastrophe; indeed, some argue that a lack of crisis was more conducive, when authorities were not otherwise distracted by war or famine. Europe had been through worse with the BLACK DEATH and subsequent epidemics in the fourteenth century. Wider socio-economic difficulties throughout the period probably provide better grounds because of the instability they brought; however, the areas most affected were not necessarily those which experienced the highest rate of witchcraft trials. The coincidence of accusations of 'weather magic' in Central Europe with a prolonged drop in temperature, labelled by historians the 'Little Ice Age', is more substantive (Behringer 1995).

The conjuring of hailstorms in particular threatened crops and, therefore, the welfare of the community. There is a correlation here too with the association of the witch with sterility, whether human or agrarian, going against the natural (particularly female) instinct to nurture (Roper 1994). The inversion of societal norms was a common motif in witchcraft accusations: the individuals concerned overturned the moral and spiritual order as well as expectations of neighbourliness.

Several historians have argued for the importance of neighbourly relations in accusations (Thomas 1971; Briggs 1996). They assert that worsening economic circumstances made people more reluctant to give to the poor who were increasingly perceived as a threat and a problem ('Marginals and deviants' in Part II). Furthermore, a decline in almsgiving accompanied the institutionalization of poor relief which exonerated individuals of responsibility. However, the refusal of charity led to resentment and ill-feeling and in turn to the guilt of those who turned the needy away. Any subsequent misfortune could then be attributed to the malice of the offended party, leading to an accusation of witchcraft (and the assuaging of guilt). The malicious acts thus procured were known as MALEFICIA and – as practical proofs that witchcraft had taken place – were lent great weight by the people and the judges. Witchcraft provided both an explanation and a remedy (through counter-magic or trial) for the misfortunes people experienced, and therefore such accusations constituted both a rational and a reasonable response in their own terms. It was personal interactions within local communities which led to accusations, which may reflect a growing unease and insecurity at a time when antagonisms were increasing and customary bonds were breaking down.

Greater centralization of the legal system in territories such as the Empire and France may have eased the process of accusation and prosecution by removing the penalty for bringing a wrongful case, opening up the system for those who wanted to bring suspect witches to account. The reinvigoration of Roman law in much of Europe was central to the process of witchcraft investigation (Levack 1995). Recourse to the law became a substitute for local grievance solving. Again, though, it is worth emphasizing that prosecutions were not lightly brought. Judges required a number of witnesses to support the accuser and a substantial case history of misdemeanours. This explains why many of the accused were relatively old, having built up a reputation over a lifetime (Briggs 1996). Communities often preferred to wait until other avenues had been explored before bringing outsiders in, disliking external interference, the costs of litigation and the local rifts which a prosecution could cause. Possible retribution from the accused's relatives (or the accused themselves) if the prosecution failed was a further deterrent, a fear firmly wedded to the belief in the supernatural powers of the supposed witch. But it was not only the people who embraced the reality of witchcraft; so too did the elite, the intellectuals and judges who were the driving force behind the prosecution.

Demonology rose to prominence in the fifteenth century and was propagated via a number of printed pamphlets and tracts. The widely distributed *Malleus Maleficarum* of 1486 (Krämer and Sprenger 2007; Web resources), written by two Dominican inquisitors, established the standard checklist of witch stereotypes, particularly the association with women and their diabolical (often sexual but always blasphemous) pact with Satan. The advent of print assisted the widespread dissemination of these and other ideas ('From pen to print' in Part V). Witches were depicted as enemies of society who needed to be destroyed, and who met together to indulge in unspeakable acts: denigrating the host, eating babies, copulating with the devil and rendering men impotent. By prosecuting them, judges were believed to be saving not only society but also the soul of the accused if they were prepared to confess and repent. It is indeed remarkable how often the accused came to believe in their own guilt (occasionally thanking the judges for their concern) and produced elaborate confessions, even when a minimal amount or no torture at all was used. Such admissions in turn reinforced the belief of the judges in the justice of what they were doing, and reveal a shared culture or mental world between popular and elite.

Although the diabolical pact was high on the intellectual agenda (whereas accusers tended to focus on *maleficia*), in practice there was more overlap between popular and elite attitudes than this suggests. Judges lent great weight to the harmful acts of which the witch was accused in making their judgements, alongside the location of the devil's mark as 'proof' that a pact had been made. Popular beliefs also contained some elements of diabolical involvement, as accused witches confessed to encounters with dark strangers, attendance at SABBATS and plotting the downfall of their enemies (Figure V.10). The extent to which elite diabolism was grafted onto the popular imagination as a result of suggestive questioning during trials, as some historians have suggested, is uncertain.

Should prosecutions be interpreted as a war on women? An estimated 80 per cent of those accused of witchcraft were women, which has been equated to a hate campaign by an increasingly misogynistic and PATRIARCHAL society (Table V.5.2). However, the remaining 20 per cent indicates that this was a gender-related rather than gender-specific offence, and there were fluctuations (Larner 1984). In some areas, such as Normandy and Russia, the majority of those convicted were men and, in general, men were more likely to be executed if accused (Apps and Gow 2003). Furthermore, many of the witnesses who testified against female witches were women, and the sporadic nature of the prosecutions makes a coordinated campaign to target women implausible. Nevertheless, the imbalance remains and needs to be explained. The general consensus is that women were disproportionately associated with witchcraft because of traditional perceptions of their susceptibility to sexual temptation, inconstancy, gullibility and deceitfulness. In a world governed by polarities, women were automatically correlated with these negative traits (Clark 1997). The predominantly female domestic roles of childrearing, treating the sick and food preparation also made them suspect when people, especially children, or livestock fell ill or died (circumstances which were at the centre of many witchcraft denunciations). It may be that some women resorted to magic in order to acquire power,

**Figure V.10** This graphic depiction of a sabbat includes various themes relating to diabolical witchcraft: unbridled sexuality (female nakedness, presence of a goat, phallic objects); sorcery (preparation of a potion, flight); and inversion (sitting backwards, female sexual dominance, unnatural practices). The Witches at the Sabbath, after Hans Baldung Grien, illustrated in a history of magic published late 19th century (litho), Baldung Grien, Hans (1484/5–1545) (after) / Private Collection / The Stapleton Collection / Bridgeman Images.

to pretend to a status within the community otherwise denied them; to make themselves feared. If so, socio-economic circumstances probably drove them to it. A declining economic situation meant that single women struggled to survive, becoming more reliant on communal support and increasingly marginalized (the category most associated with, though not necessarily the most typical of, those accused of witchcraft).

In Cambrésis those making the accusations were people of property and status who targeted the poor and defenceless in their community. However, most historians have found that the accusers were often of a similar status to those they accused, and that accusations served as a marginalizing device. Only occasionally did scares lead to mass prosecutions affecting groups throughout society, even reaching as far as the judges themselves and territorial rulers in Germany in the early seventeenth century (as at Würzburg in 1629).

## Reasons for the decline in prosecutions

Explanations for the decline in prosecutions ought to respond to these arguments, reflecting change as well as new developments. The initiative for the decline as well

**Table V.5.2** The proportion of women among defendants at witchcraft trials

| Location | Women tried (%) |
|---|---|
| Basel | 95 |
| Essex | 92 |
| South-west Germany | 82 |
| Venice (Inquisition) | 78 |
| Geneva | 76 |
| Castile (Inquisition) | 71 |
| Freiburg (Switzerland) | 64 |
| Moscow (17th century) | 33 |

This table shows how characteristic it was, with few exceptions, for defendants at trials to be female (Scarre 1987, 25).

as the rise is attributed to the judges, the elite, for their actions were decisive in bringing legal prosecution to an end. For the people the 'reality' of witchcraft continued to function much as before as an everyday hazard within their communities. Key factors were the triumph of scepticism and changing circumstances.

The elite fascination with witchcraft is reflected in the writings of famous people of the day, from the political theorist Jean Bodin in his *Démonomanie des sorciers* (1580: Web resources) and James VI of Scotland and I of England in his *Daemonologie* (1597). Like Bodin, James initially advocated the harshest punishment for witches, but later became renowned for his scepticism and refutation of judicial prosecution. Sixteenth-century authors Michel de Montaigne, Reginald Scot and Johann Weyer were in the minority in upholding a consistently sceptical approach: 'After all, it is to put a very high value on your surmises to roast a man alive for them' (Montaigne 1987, 1169). Weyer concluded that the devil was more than capable of undertaking acts of *maleficia* without human agency and claimed that diabolical influence lay behind the accusations of witchcraft (Weyer 1991). Only gradually would such views gain ascendancy. The early Enlightenment's encouragement of a more rational, less fearful view of the world (and the potential of evil forces within it) provided a coherent intellectual context for increased scepticism (Davies and de Blécourt 2004). This was confirmed by the increasing diagnoses of accused witches, and those who claimed that they were possessed as a result of their magic, as mentally unstable and confused individuals. Thus, we might conclude that judges ceased to believe in witchcraft, that it became an impossible crime.

However, it was not necessarily the case that judges no longer accepted the influence of the devil and the reality of witchcraft; in fact, there is plenty of evidence that they continued to do so. Their increasing scepticism was instead related to their ability to prove the guilt of those accused and a judgement that it was better not to condemn the innocent. This trend is revealed in the policies of the courts. The *Parlement* of Paris, for instance, introduced the automatic appeal of all witchcraft cases from the French provinces in 1624, so that it could keep a check on lesser courts' activities, and in 1640 forbade the prosecution of witchcraft cases altogether (a position not officially decreed by the crown until 1682). The revelation of abuses and abusers within the system, and growing concerns about the use of torture, led to such reconsiderations of the judicial position on witchcraft. Practical experience thus played a major part in persuading the elite that witchcraft prosecution was not an effective means of justice or for dealing with the forces of evil. Judgement of such individuals was to be left to God.

The encouragement of denunciations in fact provided a greater opportunity for disorder, with popular justice being meted out to witches and occasional scares. So if the intention of the elites was to eliminate deviants in the interests of order and conformity, prosecutions proved counter-productive. By the end of the seventeenth century, it is arguable anyway that the socio-economic crisis and other causes of instability had peaked and, thus, provided a less compelling context for accusations. Nevertheless, although in most parts of Europe prosecutions had fizzled out by the early eighteenth century, in Poland they intensified.

## Assessment

The rise in the prosecution of witches in early modern Europe was the result of growing concerns about order and conformity which targeted non-Christian and disruptive elements. Socio-economic crisis resulted in greater insecurity which led to the need to seek scapegoats by marginalizing certain individuals. This in turn fed on traditional misogyny and the popular belief in the battle between good and evil in the world. Intellectuals developed a coherent context for increased diabolical activity as a threat to society based on biblical exegesis. Judicial authorities provided accusers with the legal means and encouragement to bring accusations to the courts as a final resort, rather than sorting them out within, or expelling the offender from, the community. This resulted in elite interference in local tradition and custom which was enthusiastically embraced, producing a pattern of prosecution which was regional rather than national or international in character. Once judges withdrew their support because of increased scepticism and concerns that prosecutions were not serving their intended purpose, they ceased. Witchcraft accusations provide an interesting example of the overlap of popular and elite attitudes working together in a common cause for more than a century. Witchcraft prosecutions were, therefore, far from an aberration in terms of the prevailing beliefs, both intellectual and popular, of their day, and have a great deal to tell us about the early modern worldview.

## Discussion themes

1. Does regional variation make it impossible to generalize about reasons for the rise in European witchcraft prosecutions?
2. Were the European witch-hunts primarily a war against women?
3. Why did the legal pursuit of witches seem to make less sense in 1720 than in 1500?

## Bibliography

### (A) Sources

James VI (1597), *Daemonologie*, Edinburgh

Kors, A. C. and Peters, E. eds (2001), *Witchcraft in Europe, 400–1700: A Documentary History*, revised edn, Philadelphia, Pa.

Krämer, Heinrich and Sprenger, James (2007), *Malleus Maleficarum* [1486], ed. P. G. Maxwell-Stuart, Manchester

Montaigne, Michel de (1987), *The Complete Essays* [1592], trans. M. A. Screech, London

Rémy, Nicolas (1930), *Demonolatry* [1595], trans. E. A. Ashwin, London

Scot, Reginald (1972), *The Discoverie of Witchcraft* [1584], ed. Montague Summers, New York

Weyer, Johann (1991), *De Praestigiis Daemonum* [1563], Binghampton, NY

### (B) Literature

Ankarloo, Bengt and Clark, Stuart eds (1999), *The Athlone History of Witchcraft and Magic in Europe*, 6 vols, London

Apps, Laura and Gow, Andrew (2003), *Male Witches in Early Modern Europe*, Manchester

Behringer, Wolfgang (1995), 'Weather, Hunger, Fear: The Origins of the European Witch Hunts in Climate, Society and Mentality', *German History*, 13, 1–27

Behringer, Wolfgang (2004), *Witches and Witch-Hunts: A Global History*, Cambridge

\* Briggs, Robin (1996 [2nd edn, 2002]), *Witches and Neighbours: The Social and Cultural Context of European Witchcraft*, London

Clark, Stuart (1997), *Thinking with Demons: The Idea of Witchcraft in Early Modern Europe*, Oxford

Davies, Owen and de Blécourt, Willem eds (2004), *Beyond the Witch Trials: Witchcraft and Magic in Enlightenment Europe*, Manchester

Larner, Christina (1984), *Witchcraft and Religion: The Politics of Popular Belief*, Oxford

\* Levack, Brian P. (1995 [4th edn, 2016]), *The Witchhunt in Early Modern Europe*, London [with companion website]

Macfarlane, Alan (1978), *Witchcraft in Tudor and Stuart England: A Regional and Comparative Study*, London

Oldridge, Darren (2002 [2nd edn, 2008]), *The Witchcraft Reader*, London

Roper, Lyndal (1994), *Oedipus and the Devil: Witchcraft, Sexuality and Religion in Early Modern Europe*, London

Rowlands, Alison (2003), *Witchcraft Narratives in Germany: Rothenburg 1561–1652*, Manchester

Scarre, Geoffrey (1987), *Witchcraft and Magic in Sixteenth- and Seventeenth-Century Europe*, Basingstoke

Sharpe, James (1997), *Instruments of Darkness: Witchcraft in England, 1550–1750*, London

Soman, Alan F. (1978), 'The Parlement of Paris and the Great Witch Hunt (1565–1640)', *SCJ*, 9, 31–44

Thomas, Keith (1971), *Religion and the Decline of Magic*, London

Wilson, Stephen (2000), *The Magical Universe: Everyday Ritual and Magic in Pre-Modern Europe*, London

**(C) Web resources**

Bodin, Jean, *De la demonomanie des sorciers* (1580), excerpts in HHTP: <http://history.hanover.edu/texts/bodin.html>

Gifford, George, 'A dialogue concerning witches and witchcraftes' (1593), excerpts in HHTP: <http://history.hanover.edu/texts/gifford.html>

Goodare, J., Martin, L., Miller, J. and Yeoman, L., 'The Survey of Scottish Witchcraft 1563–1736' (2003): <http://www.shca.ed.ac.uk/Research/witches/>

'The Witch Persecutions at Bamberg' excerpts in HHTP: <http://history.hanover.edu/texts/bamberg.html>

# Popular culture(s)

*Bernard Capp*

## Introduction

In January 1525 a dozen youths roamed through the streets of Boersch, in Alsace, with a drummer and piper, knocking on doors and demanding money and food for their 'king'. It was a traditional, festive custom. But when the canons of St Leonhard's turned them away empty-handed, the youths became abusive, threatening revenge. Several weeks later, at Easter, a large crowd sacked the foundation and destroyed its images. Some defecated on the altar while others poked fun at religious ceremonies in an impromptu mummers' play (Scribner 1987, 75–76). The episode illustrates well the ambivalent nature of many popular traditions, and the uneasy relationship between the popular and elite worlds.

## Definitions and debates

'Popular culture' is a problematic term, and both of its components have provoked heated debate. In this chapter it is taken to denote those beliefs, values, customs and practices that were distinct from the culture of the 'elite' or 'learned' minority. We should recognize, however, that many important features of early modern culture were shared by most people at every social level. Catholic kings and PEASANTS alike venerated saints and visited shrines. Aristocrats and peasants held broadly similar views on gender relations and accepted a broadly hierarchical view of the political and social order. COURTIERS and artisans together thronged the playhouses of Elizabethan and Jacobean London and together enjoyed the crude pleasures of the cock-fight and bear- and bull-baiting. Cultural divisions certainly existed within every society and so, increasingly, did cultural conflict, with repeated attempts by the Church and state to reform or suppress popular practices and beliefs deemed profane, disorderly or superstitious. But we should also be sensitive to overlap and exchange, in both directions, between different cultural worlds.

Two influential studies published in the 1970s, by Robert Muchembled and Peter Burke, painted a sharp binary division between elite and popular culture. Muchembled described a process of ACCULTURATION in France, an alliance between the Catholic Reformation Church and the state to strengthen their control by rooting out profane and superstitious customs and imposing the culture of the elite upon the whole population. The reformers sought to eradicate the 'folkloric' elements of traditional Catholicism, reform the parish clergy and place local religious confraternities under firm control (Muchembled 1985). Peter Burke, surveying the whole of Europe in a pioneering and influential work, offered a rather different picture. Burke posited a medieval culture that had embraced the whole of society, except a tiny handful of learned schoolmen or theologians. During the early modern period, by contrast, the elites gradually withdrew from much of this traditional world, a process encouraged in different ways by Renaissance HUMANISM, the Protestant and Catholic Reformations, and the Enlightenment. The RENAISSANCE and Enlightenment promoted the values of reason and civility, or politeness, and all waged war on 'superstition', disorder and excess ('The Renaissance' and 'Enlightenment' in Part V). Religious reformers sought to improve clerical standards and separate the sacred world from the profane; Catholics wanted to ban rowdy festivities from the church and churchyard, while Calvinists tried to suppress them altogether. Burke presented these developments as a war between 'Carnival' and LENT, Carnival standing for the rough, earthy and boisterous celebration of life and the senses, Lent for the new values of civility, restraint and discipline – a war that ended with the triumph of Lent (Burke 1978).

In recent years many scholars have questioned such a stark binary division, stressing instead cultural continuities, interaction and diversity. Instead of viewing cultural change simply in terms of acceptance or resistance, Roger Chartier has emphasized the need to see how each element was used, understood and 'appropriated' by different communities (Chartier 1987). The cult of saints continued to flourish in Catholic lands, if now more closely supervised. In Lutheran Germany, where saints disappeared, the figure of Luther himself took on some of their attributes, with stories telling how his picture had remained unharmed by fire, sweated blood or tears, and even worked miracles. Moreover, such reports were fostered by educated clerics, realizing perhaps that they needed to work within the grain of traditional beliefs rather than trying to destroy them (Scribner 1987, 323–53). In England, where the intervention of saints in people's daily lives was also swept away, a belief in God's PROVIDENTIAL direction of human affairs took its place, reflected in the widespread conviction that God rewarded virtue and punished the wicked in this life as well as the next. Such developments have led historians to speak increasingly of 'post-Reformation' rather than 'Protestant' beliefs ('The long Reformation' in Part III). For their part, Puritan ministers complained bitterly about what they dismissed as the 'country divinity' of most villagers, who after endless sermons still failed or refused to absorb the doctrine of salvation by faith alone, and remained convinced that heaven was a reward for all who lived a decent life. Lutheran ministers made similar complaints, and Catholic missionaries in the more remote parts of France, Spain and Italy found the peasantry equally resistant to new Catholic Reformation teaching. We should not conclude, however, that ordinary folk were always passive or traditionalist in their thinking. The Italian miller Menocchio drew on his limited reading and fertile imagination to

> **Box 1**
>
> 'When man dies he is like an animal, like a fly, and . . . his soul and everything about him also dies.' – Menocchio
>
> 'He is always arguing with somebody about the faith just for the sake of arguing – even with the priest.' – A neighbour on Menocchio.
>
> *(Ginzburg 1992, 2, 69)*
>
> The Italian miller Menocchio (burned at the stake 1599/1600) reminds us that unlearned people could also think for themselves, though not without risk.

devise a new cosmology, which eventually brought him to the stake (Ginzburg 1992; Box 1). Many other men and women fashioned personal beliefs from the mélange of religious ideas in circulation, especially in Reformation Germany and revolutionary England.

## Popular culture – or cultures?

While Burke stressed the conceptual value of an elite/popular division, he also acknowledged and explored the diversity of popular cultures or subcultures, a theme which almost all historians now emphasize. In very broad terms we can distinguish between a Southern European culture, centred on the outdoor world of processions and parades, and with tight restrictions on women's freedom, and the more indoor, less exuberant culture of the north. We can also distinguish between rural and urban cultures (and between the rural cultures of mountainous or pastoral regions and those of the arable plains). Urban culture developed its own character, focused on the GUILDS and associations of JOURNEYMEN and apprentices. Beyond that, many occupational groups developed their own subcultures and language, most strikingly in the case of sailors and soldiers. All that suggests we would often do better to speak of 'cultures' in the plural.

Other historians have pointed to distinctive cultural traits found among the so-called 'middling sorts' – merchants, professional men and increasingly substantial farmers (English yeomen and French *laboureurs*) (Barry and Brooks 1994). Such groups cannot easily be labelled either 'elite' or 'popular', neither can we simply place them at some point between the two. The values of sobriety, moral rigour and hard work appealed more readily to the merchant or lawyer, for example, than to the often quarrelsome and spendthrift nobility. Proverbial sayings such as 'drunk as a Lord' and 'to swear like a Lord' suggest that respectable, middling-sort culture might stand equally distant from the worlds of both the disorderly poor and the profligate rich.

Most scholars have agreed with Burke in stressing the importance of cultural interchange, with some features (such as chivalric tales) descending from the elite to the popular and others (dances and songs) moving in the opposite direction. In Shakespeare's *Hamlet*, the aristocratic Ophelia sings snatches from popular songs, while the French writer Rabelais wove popular tales into his comic epic *Gargantua*.

## Orality and print

Most people were illiterate in 1500, and literacy rates improved only slowly, especially in Southern Europe and among women. For centuries the cultural world of the majority rested on the spoken word. The young picked up skills from their parents or employers and absorbed values and beliefs, both secular and religious, from what they saw and heard in the home, at church and in the street. Inevitably the invention of print brought changes ('From pen to print' in Part V). First in Germany and then throughout Western Europe, the printing presses generated books, short pamphlets, cartoons and ballads in ever-increasing numbers. Many were illustrated with woodcuts, which reinforced the message and made print more accessible to unlearned readers. Ballads, set out in simple verse and designed to be sung to popular tunes, were a multimedia form, combining print, image and music. The spread of print encouraged greater literacy, especially in North-western Europe, which in turn further stimulated the growth of the press. Oral communication remained fundamental, of course, and printing did not necessarily pose a threat to the old order. Very often censorship and market forces persuaded publishers to issue material that was safe and traditional. Many of the early best-sellers were deeply conservative works like *The Golden Legend*, stories of saints' lives and miracles. The *bibliothèque bleue*, the popular fare which flourished in seventeenth- and eighteenth-century France, was almost wholly conventional, much of it focused on popular piety or stories of legendary heroes such as *Pierre of Provence* or *The Four Sons of Aymon*. Most of the black-letter ballads and chapbooks that flourished in England were equally conservative. Ballads told of royal coronations, love stories, drunken revelries, murder, monsters and adventures at sea. Many chapbooks, short and simple prose works, resembled the French material, while astrological almanacs (calendars with other information and lore related to the stars) were also generally bland, as in France – until the English Revolution. But from the 1640s English almanacs took on a very different character, offering rival political, religious and social views that reflected the divisions within society and encouraged a wider political awareness. That sudden shift reminds us of print's radical potential, even if it was one only occasionally realized. Something similar had happened much earlier in Germany, the Netherlands and Switzerland: pamphlets, many with scabrous woodcuts, played a vital role in spreading the Protestant message in the 1520s and undermining the authority of the Catholic Church. The spread and success of the Protestant Reformation owed much to a powerful alliance between powerful preachers and pamphleteers ('The long Reformation: Lutheran' in Part III). Similarly the radical movements in mid-seventeenth-century England, and the Parisian *Frondes*, would have been impossible without a large reading public ready to devour cheap pamphlets, newspapers and satirical verses. John Bunyan, the radical sectarian whose visionary *Pilgrim's Progress* was to remain a best-seller for two centuries, embodies the transforming potential of print; his story-telling flair had developed from the chapbook adventures he had loved as a child. But Bunyan also complained that many adults continued to prefer simple ballads and chapbooks to the Bible and other more serious publications.

The English antiquarian John Aubrey, writing in the late seventeenth century, thought that print had almost driven out the world of folk tradition. He was exaggerating. Adam Fox has shown how the relation between orality and print was far more complex. Very often an 'oral tradition' can be shown to have originated in some printed ballad or story; sometimes the process went in the other direction; and sometimes stories or songs moved to and fro between the oral and written traditions (Fox 2000). Moreover, readers might appropriate printed texts for their own use, as when the Derbyshire yeoman Leonard Wheatcroft drew on printed verse-miscellanies to woo his future wife (Houlbrooke 1986, 15, 55–60, 68–70). Print could enrich as well as undermine traditional oral culture.

## Popular sociability

How did popular ideas and values find expression in social behaviour? To answer that we must enter the alehouse and tavern, where men (and less often women) gathered to drink, play games, talk, gossip, sing, gamble and tell jokes (Kümin and Tlusty 2002; 'Drinking Studies Network' in Web resources). In Germany and France women gathered at the well or washing-place and also in evening 'spinning-bees' devoted to work and gossip. Everywhere we find the working year punctuated by holiday festivities. In 1500 the church was at the heart of this popular sociability, centred on the Christian year and the celebration of the local patron saint, with processions and feasting. This tradition survived, especially in Catholic lands, alongside more secular festivities characterized by singing, dancing, feasting, sports and drinking. All these activities had an appeal across the whole social range, though there were clear social as well as geographical features; thus football, popular in England from medieval times, was always primarily a plebeian sport. In Southern and Central Europe, the festival world revolved around carnivals, which in Venice and many other cities featured huge, rowdy processions with men and women in costume or cross-dressed, heaping abuse on magistrates and bishops, singing bawdy songs, feasting and drinking. It was a period of semi-licensed and often violent disorder, a world turned briefly upside down. Whether carnivals helped preserve social hierarchy, by providing an outlet for popular resentments (the 'safety-valve' theory), or threatened it, remains debatable and perhaps unanswerable. For carnival was an ambivalent occasion, viewed nervously by magistrates who recognized how easily festive disorder might spill over into serious violence. Occasionally that happened, most notably in the French town of Romans in 1580, when local elites interpreted festive licence as a serious threat and responded by massacring the revellers (Le Roy Ladurie 1980). Earlier, over 20 German carnivals in the 1520s and 1530s had turned into anti-Catholic parades, reflecting and helping to promote the advance of early Lutheran movements (Scribner 1987, 71–102).

## Popular political culture

Despite occasional outbursts, most ordinary people throughout Europe appear to have broadly accepted the traditional political order. The accession day of England's Queen Elizabeth was still celebrated long after her death. The execution of Charles I was deeply unpopular, and in the 1650s all parties acknowledged that a free popular vote would quickly restore the monarchy. Charles II's return in 1660 sparked such frenzied excess that the king himself had to urge restraint. In France, Henry IV became a popular folk-hero, and when Queen Christina of Sweden announced her decision to abdicate in 1654, the Marshal of the Peasants' Estate in the *Riksdag* made an emotional plea for her to reconsider. It would be wrong, however, to see popular political culture wholly in terms of deference and loyalty. Parish officers, bailiffs and tax officials often faced abuse and physical violence from ordinary men and women, and magistrates too encountered scornful defiance. Elizabeth Smith, who ran a London brothel, told a magistrate bluntly in 1653 that 'she did not care a fart for never a justice in England' (London Metropolitan Archives, MJ/SR/1108/160).

More important than truculent individuals was the widespread belief that rulers had obligations towards the common people, as well as rights over them ('Centre and periphery' in Part VI). This deep-rooted concept of reciprocal obligations should not really surprise us, for it also underpinned ideas about family life and religion too; most Christians worshipped God in the hope of rewards in this life or the next, ideally both. In the political sphere, this mentality helped trigger petitions and protests over changes to land usage, such as ENCLOSURES and fen drainage, or food supplies. A 'bread riot' might occur in England or France after a poor harvest, when local people saw grain being carried away to be sold abroad or in some distant city. The rioters would stay the grain, demanding that it be sold locally. They were also trying to force local magistrates to intervene, using the riot to remind them that they were failing in their duty. Very often the move succeeded, for though magistrates might briefly arrest a few leading rioters, they generally took the remedial action the protesters had demanded. Similarly in enclosure riots, the protesters believed they had a moral and legal right to defend traditional rights of access to common lands and were sometimes eager to see the issue brought before a law court. If that did not happen, they might wear the landlord down by tearing up hedges and fences faster than he could replace them, forcing him to abandon the project or compromise. Women often played a prominent part in such episodes, which made it easier for magistrates to agree to the demands without losing face. To give way to a crowd of armed men would look like weakness, whereas accepting women's demands could be presented as Christian compassion. But tolerance went only so far. Magistrates responded positively to the

**Figure V.11** Hudibras, a Puritan, is shocked to encounter a rowdy procession, with an unruly woman beating her feeble husband who sits behind her spinning (i.e. doing women's work). Note the 'rough music', and the petticoat and smock carried as trophies. The couple at the window are probably the targets of this ritual humiliation. Hudibras Encounters the Skimmington, engraved by T.E. Nicholson, in 'Hudibras', by Samuel Butler (1612–80) from 'The Works of Hogarth', published 1833 (litho), Hogarth, William (1697–1764) (after) / Private Collection / Photo © Ken Welsh / Bridgeman Images.

demands of Ann Carter, who led a grain riot at Maldon (Essex) in March 1629, but when she led another, larger and more threatening riot in May that year she was promptly arrested, tried and hanged (Thompson 1991, 185–351; Walter 2006, 14–66).

This sense of the community's right to intervene when magistrates had failed to act can be found in many other contexts throughout Europe. It underpinned the protests in Germany at the demands of oppressive landlords, which swelled into the great Peasants' War of 1525 ('Riot and rebellion' in Part VI). It is evident too in the apprentices' Shrovetide riots in early Stuart London, which generally took bawdy-houses as their targets. While the rioters enjoyed their festive violence, they could point to bawdy-houses as scandalous places which the magistrates themselves should have suppressed. This kind of 'community justice' can be seen too in the ritual punishment of those breaching accepted social behaviour, as in the French CHARIVARI or English SKIMMINGTON. The usual targets were wives who beat their husbands and remarrying widows or widowers. In France such rituals were often organized by village youth groups or urban 'Abbeys of misrule' (20 in sixteenth-century Lyon alone), with their own officials and structures. Thus a woman who beat her husband might find a crowd of young men parading outside her house, banging pots and pans ('rough music'), with figures facing backwards on an ass to represent the offending couple (Davis 1975, 97–123; Ingram 1984, 79–113; Figure V.11 and Box 2).

**Box 2**

'[300–400 men came one day] some like soldiers . . . and a man riding upon a horse, having a white night cap upon his head, two shoeing horns hanging by his ears, a counterfeit beard upon his chin made of a deer's tail . . . [and outside the victims' house] the gunners shot off their pieces, pipes and horns were sounded, together with lowbells and other smaller bells, . . . and rams' horns and bucks' horns, carried upon forks, were then and there lifted up and shown.'

(Ingram 1984, 82)

A skimmington, with 'rough music' at Quemerford, near Calne, Wiltshire, in 1618. The main target, Agnes Mills, was beaten up as well as humiliated.

Such rituals were designed to shame or frighten victims into more appropriate behaviour, but there was always the risk that they would degenerate into serious violence, as occasionally happened. Like attacks on bawdy-houses, these shaming rituals symbolized a public cleansing or purification, and this feature was even more evident in the religious riots of sixteenth-century France. Catholics and Calvinists both accused the rival community of polluting society and religion, blaming magistrates for their failure to act. Local people, many of them youths or mere boys, accordingly took on the task themselves, with Calvinists destroying and desecrating holy objects and Catholics killing and mutilating the 'polluters' themselves (Davis 1975, 152–87). French riots over bread supplies were about retribution, the verbal or physical humiliation of those held responsible, as much as about securing access to the grain (Beik 2007, 78–94).

## Assessment: change over time

Cultures are always evolving, both internally and in response to outside pressures and influences. Thus by the mid-eighteenth century, 'rough music' in England was often directed at men who beat their wives, rather than vice versa, a reflection of changing values. While change often came slowly, especially in more remote rural areas, the popular cultural world of 1800 differed considerably from that of 1500. Belief in astrology, WITCHCRAFT and magic, for example, formed part of the shared culture of the sixteenth century; by 1750 such beliefs had been abandoned by the elite and the middling sort, surviving only as a strand of popular culture, especially among women. Religion itself exercised a weaker hold, at least in much of the Protestant north. As church attendance dropped, ministers complained that Sundays and religious festivals were treated simply as holidays. We should not exaggerate such trends, however; religion maintained its grip in much of Southern Europe, and even in the north new movements such as METHODISM proved that the religious spirit remained very much alive ('Religious culture in early modern Europe' in Part III).

Finally, the spread of literacy and the huge growth in printed material of all kinds had brought another major cultural shift. Printed ballads, chapbooks and almanacs constituted a print culture that was commercially driven, a 'mass culture' rather than one genuinely 'popular'. Such had been the case ever since printing began, of course, and it is worth noting that this market was highly sensitive to consumer choice; people bought only what they liked. Even in France, where most popular literature was blandly conservative, the eighteenth century saw the emergence of many 'forbidden best-sellers' – illicit pieces, either politically subversive or sexually explicit. Print helped to make possible the French Revolution – just as the popular 'culture of retribution', seen in earlier crowd violence, found new forms of expression in the violence of the Revolutionary era (Beik 2007, 94–110).

## Discussion themes

1. Did changes in popular culture(s) over this period owe more to internal dynamics or to outside pressures?
2. 'Popular culture' or 'popular cultures'?
3. How far did the spread of print influence popular culture?

## Bibliography

### (A) Sources

Butler, Samuel (1726), *Hudibras*, London
Houlbrooke, Ralph ed. (1986), *The Courtship Narrative of Leonard Wheatcroft, Derbyshire Yeoman*, Reading


### (B) Literature

Barry, Jonathan and Brooks, Christopher eds (1994), *The Middling Sort of People: Culture, Society and Politics in England 1550–1800*, Basingstoke
Beik, William (2007), 'The Violence of the French Crowd from Charivari to Revolution', *P&P*, 197, 75–110
* Burke, Peter (1978), *Popular Culture in Early Modern Europe*, London
Chartier, Roger (1987), *The Cultural Uses of Print in Early Modern France*, Princeton, NJ
Davis, Natalie Zemon (1975), *Society and Culture in Early Modern France*, Stanford, Calif.
Fox, Adam (2000), *Oral and Literate Culture in England 1500–1700*, Oxford
Ginzburg, Carlo (1992), *The Cheese and the Worms: The Cosmos of a Sixteenth-Century Miller*, Harmondsworth
Harris, Tim ed. (1985), *Popular Culture in England c. 1500–1850*, Basingstoke

Ingram, Martin (1984), 'Ridings, Rough Music and the "Reform of Popular Culture" in Early Modern England', *P&P*, 105, 79–113

Kümin, Beat and Tlusty, Anne eds (2002), *The World of the Tavern: Public Houses in Early Modern Europe*, Aldershot

Le Roy Ladurie, Emmanuel (1980), *Carnival in Romans*, London

Muchembled, Robert (1985), *Popular Culture and Elite Culture in France 1400–1750*, Baton Rouge, La.

* Reay, Barry (1998), *Popular Cultures in England 1550–1750*, London

Scribner, R. W. (1987), *Popular Culture and Popular Movements in Reformation Germany*, London

Thompson, E. P. (1991), *Customs in Common*, London

Walter, John (2006), *Crowds and Popular Politics in Early Modern England*, Manchester

## (C) Web resources

'Bodleian Library Broadside Ballads': <http://ballads.bodleian.ox.ac.uk/>

'Drinking Studies Network', interdisciplinary network connecting researchers of drink and drinking cultures: <https://drinkingstudies.wordpress.com/>

'Early Modern Broadsides' [Single-leaf prints from the early modern period]: <https://www.digitale-sammlungen.de/index.html?c=sammlung&projekt=1046961503&l=en>

# Enlightenment

*Colin Jones*

## What was 'enlightenment'?

'Was ist Aufklärung?' ('What is enlightenment?') asked the German philosopher Immanuel Kant (1724–1804) in 1784 in a reply to an open enquiry launched by a Berlin newspaper. It was a rhetorical question: he had an answer. Enlightenment, his pamphlet stated, was 'man's release from his self-incurred immaturity'. For Kant, the prime agent of 'release' was human reason. 'If it is now asked whether we live in an *enlightened age*, the answer is: No. But we do live in an age of *enlightening*' (Eliot and Stern 1979, ii. 250, 253).

Kant's well-known opinion is valuable for highlighting key features of the intellectual and cultural movement in eighteenth-century Europe known as the Enlightenment. First, it was a phenomenon of which he and contemporaries were aware and which was a subject of public debate. It was not, in other words, a trivial issue; nor was it a subsequent invention by historians ('The scientific revolution' in Part V). Second, the use of human reason to produce beneficial change lay at the heart of the movement. Third, enlightenment was a process rather than a finished good. Indeed, for Kant it was more than a process, it was a project still under way. He was well aware that established authority did not always like the answers that human reason produced. One needed moral courage as well as intellectual capacity in order to undertake the work of human enlightenment. The watchword for any 'enlightener' should be, Kant concluded, the Latin injunction *sapere aude* [dare to know!].

In this chapter, we shall use Kant's argument as the framework for understanding the European Enlightenment in the eighteenth century. We shall focus first on the notion of human reason as an agent of change, highlighting the development of scientific method as a means of understanding the world. We shall go on, in the second section, to discuss the social and intellectual ways in which individuals reasoned. Kant's discussion, for example, was carried in a newspaper, and the easy and open communication this exemplified was crucial to the Enlightenment process. In the third section, we shall examine the politics of enlightenment, noting some of the difficulties the Enlightenment faced, and why 'daring' was a key component in the enlightener's intellectual toolbox. Finally, in the concluding section, we shall examine some problems to do with enlightenment – where 'daring' fell short of the mark, who was left out as well as who was included in the process, and who might have felt that the 'enlightening' process, far from representing human emancipation, was irrelevant or even repressive.

Throughout we shall focus on the intellectual, ideological, philosophical and scientific backbone of the movement within Europe. It is important to note that the Enlightenment also had powerful artistic and cultural dimensions. Enlightenment philosophers and scientists rubbed shoulders with composers such as Bach, Haydn and Mozart; painters such as Gainsborough, Constable, Reynolds, Hogarth, Boucher, Greuze, David, Friedrich and Goya; and poets such as Pope, Johnson, Gray, Goethe, Schiller, Wordsworth and Coleridge. In addition, we need to bear in mind that the movement transcended European frontiers. Enlightenment was to be found on the American continent, most notably in the British colonies to the north, but also in French, Hispanic and Dutch zones of influence. Enlightenment was evident too in the ongoing work of European discovery and exploration. The traveller's tale – which might be a scientific report on local flora and fauna, an account of a religious mission, a utopian tale or the fictional setting for a novel – was a genre found at every level of the Enlightenment (Figure V.12).

## Reason and science

The notion of light embedded in the word enlightenment is present in most European languages – German's *Aufklärung*, for example, is matched by the Italian *illuminismo*, while in French the Age of Enlightenment was *le siècle des lumières* ['the age of lights']. In all cases, the light was the light of human reason, figured as dispelling the forces of darkness (prejudice, superstition, ignorance, etc.). Human reason, it was held, operated through the scientific method pioneered in the previous century. Enlightenment thinkers eschewed A PRIORI (that is, derived from first principles) thinking, rejected scriptural revelation and valued inductive, empirical approaches. Their heroes were seventeenth-century English figures: arch-empiricists Francis Bacon (1561–1626) and John Locke (1632–1704) and, especially, Isaac Newton (1643–1727). Newton was the patron saint of Enlightenment. His law of gravity demonstrated reason's capacity for unlocking the secrets of the natural world. Post-Newton, the universe could be viewed more as a precise mechanism strictly observing general rules than as an unintelligible, divinely inspired mystery. The laudatory couplet by Alexander Pope (1688–1744), intended as Newton's epitaph in Westminster Abbey, caught the Enlightenment mood – and metaphor – exactly: 'Nature and nature's laws lay hid in night. God said, "Let Newton Be" and all was light' (1730).

The scientific revolution of the seventeenth century had achieved breakthroughs in the 'hard sciences', notably astronomy (Galileo Galilei, Newton), chemistry (Robert Boyle), physics (Newton) and biology (William Harvey). This kind of research continued and prospered in the Enlightenment. The Swedish natural historian Linnaeus (1707–78), for example, devised modern botanical nomenclature,

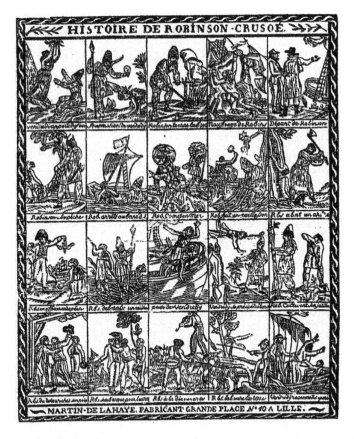

**Figure V.12** Daniel Defoe's Robinson Crusoe (1719–21) used a fictional account of shipwreck to explore key facets of human nature as well as humankind's relations with the natural world and exotic 'others'. It was translated into numerous European languages. Histoire de Robinson Crusoé (woodcut, Lille, c. 1810). © Musée des Civilisations de l'Europe et de la Méditerranée, Paris, Réunion des Musées nationaux / Jean-Gilles Berizzi.

the comte de Buffon's (1707–88) *Natural History* was an impressive and enduring summation of the human and animal worlds, while in the 1780s Antoine Lavoisier (1743–94) and Joseph Priestley (1733–1804) effected a 'chemical revolution' with the discovery of oxygen and other gases. Yet what was also striking about the Enlightenment was the parallel effort to adapt scientific method for 'softer' forms of knowledge focused on the human rather than the natural world. Tellingly, the Enlightenment supplied many foundational figures in what became the social sciences – economics (François Quesnay, Adam Smith), linguistics (Jean-Jacques Rousseau), history (Giambattista Vico, Voltaire, William Robertson, Edward Gibbon), politics (Montesquieu, Rousseau, Edmund Burke – and the French Revolutionaries) and so on. The spirit of the age was opposed to excessive specialization. 'Enlighteners' saw themselves as all-round NATURAL PHILOSOPHERS – the French term PHILOSOPHES was widely used – with a purview over all forms of knowledge.

The yardstick for the validity of reasoned knowledge was social utility and collective happiness. New knowledge was thus potential power – power to produce a rational and therefore (it was thought) contented and prosperous world. Contributors to the great multi-volumed 'Bible of Enlightenment', the ENCYCLOPÉDIE, edited by Denis Diderot (1713–84) and Jean-le-Rond d'Alembert (1717–83), were aware of this stirring venture. Diderot claimed that the aim of the *philosophe* enterprise, as expressed through the *Encyclopédie* was to

> collect knowledge disseminated around the globe; to set forth its general system to the men with whom we live, and transmit it to those who will come after us, so that the work of preceding centuries will not become useless to the centuries to come; and so that our offspring, becoming better instructed, will at the same time become more virtuous and happy, and that we should not die without having rendered a service to the human race.
>
> (*Encyclopédie*, vol. 5, 636: Web resources)

Put this way, the Enlightenment was a secular mission dedicated to the improvement of humanity (Figure V.13).

Like the scientific revolution, the Enlightenment tended to be unpopular with the Churches. The Enlightenment narrative of progress, provocatively expressed by Edward Gibbon (1737–94), blamed the Church for crushing the Graeco-Roman heritage and blocking out the light of reason until the RENAISSANCE. The Enlightenment campaigner Voltaire (1694–1778) used his famous watchword, *écrasez l'infâme* (crush infamy), most powerfully against ecclesiastical misuse of power – as with miscarriages of justice like the Calas Affair (1762–65), in which he orchestrated a European protest movement against the wrongful execution of a French Protestant. The *philosophes* were harder, however, on the Church than on God. Outright atheists had rarity value in the Enlightenment. Recent work by the historian Jonathan Israel has alerted us to the existence across Europe of small groups of thinkers who adhered to the rationalist materialist conception of the world championed by the Dutch philosopher Baruch Spinoza (1632–77). These figures – including Diderot and d'Holbach – adhered to atheism, although prevailing political arrangements made it dangerous for them publicly to avow such a belief (Israel 2001). In general terms, however, most eighteenth-century scientists worked on the DEIST assumption that the universe was the work of a benevolent deity. Newtonians imagined a watch-maker god, who was content merely to observe the mechanical exactness of his creation. Later in the century, Rousseau (1712–78) attacked the watch-maker God idea, insisting on an intuitive sense of human rapture in the face of divine creation. But in most of Europe he was pushing at an open door: despite often strong reservations about the clergy, most individuals involved in the Enlightenment subscribed to a natural theology which sought to reconcile science and faith rather than prise them apart. The *Spectacle of Nature* by the Abbé Noel-Antoine Pluche (1688–1761), an

**Figure V.13**
Charles-Nicholas Cochin's frontispiece for the *Encyclopédie* utilized the foundational metaphor of Enlightenment so as to highlight the work's underlying mission. Crowned Reason and Philosophy unveil naked Truth, as the light of Reason pours through the receding clouds of ignorance and fanaticism. Engraved frontispiece to Denis Diderot's *Encyclopédie*, Paris, 1751–80. / Photo © Granger / Bridgeman Images.

immensely popular work of natural history, was grounded in a PROVIDENTIALIST deity who offered the natural world to the human gaze as 'sugar-coated spectacle' (Stafford 1994, 234).

## The public world of Enlightenment

The Enlightenment – like the *Encyclopédie* – was a collective venture. Seventeenth-century scientists producing knowledge which seemed to threaten the status quo –

as, for example, Galileo's 'heretical' views on the cosmos – had been relatively isolated and could be picked off and silenced by established authorities. The Enlightenment, in contrast, was a group project and produced new knowledge as a social and interactive enterprise. The Royal Society in London (1660) and the Académie des Sciences in Paris (1666) provided the template for scientific sociability, establishing protocols of evidence, networks of information and methods of scientific legitimation ('Courts and centres' in Part VI). The ACADEMY style of group science was widely diffused throughout Europe, and as the century wore on widened its remit: by the 1780s, learned societies were as likely to be discussing the relief of poverty or hospital hygiene as devising chemical experiments or adding to botanical classifications.

No academy worth its salt was an island unto itself. Intra-institutional sociability was matched by inter-institutional exchange. Efficient and improving communications – another factor enjoyed by the Enlightenment but not the scientific revolution – provided its infrastructure. The findings of one academy could be transmitted swiftly to dozens of its peers – especially now that the postal service made correspondence an effective and everyday activity. Shorter journey times helped in this: road improvement and canal-building were passions of the age, contributing to the notion of news as current affairs. Book production soared over the century, but readership grew even faster as a result of the emergence of a strong newspaper press, facilitated by improvements in literacy levels. The transformation of communications made the Enlightenment a 'virtual community' in some ways like the internet of the twenty-first century – albeit dependent not on digital technology but on the humbler methods of road and water transport.

Besides the scientific academy, the other two most characteristic forms of Enlightenment sociability and knowledge production were the SALON and the COFFEE HOUSE. Both were widespread throughout urban Europe, but were held to have their most brilliant incarnations in Paris, the city that prided itself on being the unofficial capital of the Enlightenment. This claim, though disputed, was supported by the development of the French language as the *lingua franca* of Enlightenment Europe (Mercier 1999). Salons, usually presided over by witty, intelligent women from wealthy backgrounds, brought together the (largely male) elites from the social, political, cultural and intellectual worlds, providing a forum for discussion grounded in an atmosphere of polite worldliness. COFFEE HOUSES were altogether more relaxed and informal. They highlighted how closely the world of intellectual exchange was linked to commercial exchange: tobacco, tea and sugar, alongside coffee, had once been exotic but were now everyday colonial products consumed there alongside newspapers, news, ideals, opinions, gossip and jokes (Ellis 2004; Box 1).

Many other forums of intellectual exchange and sociability developed too as vectors of Enlightenment: freemasonic lodges, for example, political clubs, philan-thropic groupings, Vauxhall and other public gardens, theatres, conservatoires, libraries, reading clubs, taverns, inns and brothels. In the supremely self-conscious discourse of Enlightenment, such sites were figured as so many points of light, whose

'The fine Gentleman . . . rises late, puts on a Frock . . . and leaving his Sword at Home, . . . goes . . . to some Coffee-house, or Chocolate-house, frequented by the Person he would see; for 'tis a Sort of Rule with the English, to go once a Day at least, to Houses of this Sort, where they talk of Business and News, read the Papers, and often look at one another without opening their lips; and 'tis very well they are so mute; for if they were as talkative as the People of many other Nations, the Coffee-houses would be intolerable, and there would be no hearing what one Man said, where there are so many. The Chocolate-house in St. James's street, where I go every Morning, to pass away the Time, is always so full that a Man may scarce turn about in it. Here are Dukes, and other Peers, mixed with Gentlemen; and to be admitted, [one] needs nothing more than to dress like a Gentleman.'

(Pöllnitz 1737, ii. 462–63)

This account by a German visitor to London strikes a jaundiced but revealing note. Coffee houses were part of everyday urbane sociability and keeping in the swim.

combined effect was to produce a radiant collective opinion whose influence could only be socially beneficial (Jacob 1992). The Renaissance had developed the idea of fame and reputation resting on 'opinion', but it was really the Enlightenment which put the notion of 'public opinion' on the map. It was increasingly strongly valorized as a kind of supreme tribunal of human rationality. As the Genevan Jacques Necker (1732–1804), finance minister to France's Louis XVI, expressed it, public opinion had become 'an invisible power that, without treasury, guard or army, gives its laws to the city, the court and even the palaces of kings' (Baker 1988, 193; cf. Van Horn Melton 2001).

## The politics of Enlightenment

Necker's view of public opinion was rose tinted. In fact, many of those who praised the impartiality and rationality of public opinion were themselves keen to influence and shape it. Many *philosophes* envisaged social progress working by a trickle-down from themselves to the rest of society. Jonathan Israel has recently sought to establish the existence of a pan-European movement of 'radical enlightenment' based on the materialist ideas of Spinoza, and favouring atheism, republicanism and democracy (Israel 2011). But his view has failed to attract much support. Certainly, the vast majority of Enlightenment thinkers were not advanced democrats in any sense: 'the public' were routinely differentiated from 'the people'. Most writers viewed the latter as little better than 'the mob' and regarded the humanization of the lower classes as an extremely long-term project.

Scepticism about the slow pace of trickle-down Enlightenment led to consideration of alternative strategies for producing a rational and happy world. Some French *philosophes* followed Montesquieu, for example, in calling for a mixed and balanced polity on the English constitutional model, with separation of powers producing some of the effect that 'public opinion' could have in restraining 'despotic' tendencies in rulers. Others looked upwards for inspiration, towards rulers who might be won over to the cause of Enlightenment and could be trusted to put its precepts into effect. Voltaire's brilliant career as an Enlightenment writer and battling *philosophe* ran in counterpoint with increasingly unavailing (and pathetic) efforts to inveigle himself into favour with King Louis XV, then with Frederick II ('the Great') of Prussia. Telling truth to power could turn sycophantic and demeaning. The point was all the sadder in that in France, elective home of Enlightenment, writers risked imprisonment, exile and financial ruin for criticizing Church or state. The spectre of the Bastille was in the back of the mind of every *philosophe* who 'dared to know'.

The *philosophes* were encouraged in their efforts to act as advisers to enlightened rulers by the fact that a generation of European monarchs either exhibited interest in the idea of the Enlightenment or else put into effect reforms which formed part of the Enlightenment credo. Historians have come to call this phenomenon ENLIGHTENED DESPOTISM or ENLIGHTENED ABSOLUTISM (Blanning 1970). They were strongest in the east – notably Frederick II of Prussia (ruled 1740–86), Catherine II ('the Great': ruled 1762–96) of Russia, Joseph II (ruled 1780–90) of Austria – and in the south – especially Charles III of Spain (ruled 1759–88), José I of Portugal (ruled 1750–77) and Duke Leopold of Tuscany (ruled 1765–90). This geography is revealing: it coincided with a geography of economic and political underdevelopment (in the east) or stalled development (notably in formerly dynamic northern Italy) ('The early modern economy' in Part II). These regions lacked the growing urban orientation, burgeoning commercial CAPITALISM and emergent entrepreneurial and middling classes of North-west Europe. Outside this North-western corner of Europe, covering England, France and the Low Countries, Enlightenment tended to be top-down and state driven. It was also less audacious in Catholic states in Southern Europe because of the continuing strength of the Catholic Church. For many individuals in these regions, the eighteenth century was less an age of Enlightenment than an age of post-Tridentine CONFESSIONALIZATION ('The long Reformation: Catholic' in Part III).

Rulers drew on the Enlightenment for a variety of reasons. First, continuing the patronage of science begun in the seventeenth century, they looked for scientific and technological innovation to promote the economic diversification of their largely rural, PEASANT-based, 'backward' economies. The royal academies they sponsored were more likely to be concerned with improvements in military technology and hardware than in philosophical niceties; and the schools they instituted had a strong technical orientation. Second, as this suggests, rulers picked and chose among Enlightenment ideas, systematically selecting policies which strengthened the state. Thus the religious toleration upon which Frederick the Great insisted allowed him to attract to Prussia skilled industrial workers of every imaginable religious background. Third, 'enlightened despots' exploited the favourable publicity which the *philosophes* gave them in western Enlightenment circles. Enlightenment was sometimes little more than an ideological smokescreen for policies that politically attuned western intellectuals would have vigorously denounced had they been applied in the west. The ideological mileage which Catherine the Great got from proposed 'enlightened' legislative reforms in 1767, for example, far outweighed any substantial reform attempted, let alone achieved.

## Enlightenment tensions

Leading *philosophes* such as Voltaire, Diderot and Kant presented the Enlightenment as a unified and collective campaign for the promotion of reason as a means of achieving a virtuous and happy society. Yet one only has to scratch the surface to see the gaps and flaws in this perspective. The Enlightenment loved a good scrap. The *philosophes* were rarely happier than when they were fighting – among themselves as well as against the Enlightenment's enemies (Figure V.14, page 303). The vagueness of their united goal meant that the strategies for human emancipation that they advocated were infinitely various.

Outside North-western Europe, Enlightenment was for the most part a power strategy aimed at fulfilling very traditional political aims. In Catherine the Great's Russia, for example, flirtation with the language of Enlightenment did not preclude the empress from massively extending SERFDOM (Box 2). In Southern and Eastern Europe, the level of engagement with social groupings outside the traditional elite was very small, but even within more 'advanced' North-western Europe it was far from extensive. Mass society would be a creation of the late nineteenth and twentieth centuries. The lower orders within most of Europe must have felt that the Enlightenment had little to do with them, or indeed that it was part of some overall strategy of more effective social control (Foucault 1977). This was even more the case with indigenous peoples outside Europe subjected to the outreach of European power.

Closer to home, it was moot whether the Enlightenment was a good thing for women either. The greater freedom of the public sphere offered women opportunities for participation in the Enlightenment project that many gladly took up. Salon hostesses (Madame de Geoffrin, Madame Necker), female scientists (Madame du Châtelet), writers (Mary Wollstonecraft, Olympe de Gouges), painters (Madame Vigée-Lebrun, Angelica Kauffmann) and others contributed to the eighteenth century's cultural efflorescence (Schiebinger 1989). But such women also had to deal with a line of thinking – represented most powerfully by Rousseau – which held that their sex was biologically and socially equipped only for reproduction and household sociality. Domestic ideology and the notion of 'separate spheres' shaped their future (Knott and Taylor 2005; 'Gender and family' in Part II).

## Assessment

Among historians, the jury is still out on the meaning and value of the Enlightenment. The German philosopher Jürgen Habermas's highly influential work represents one end of the spectrum. For Habermas, the emergence of a 'bourgeois public sphere' which bade to break asunder the court-based cultures of the early modern state, establishing a zone of open, rational debate, gives an emancipatory, almost Kantian glow to the Enlightenment (Habermas 1989). At the other extreme, Michel Foucault's similarly influential writings provide a pessimistic gloss: the knowledge which the Enlightenment engendered was put to use in overarching strategies of social discipline (Foucault 1977). Feminist and post-colonial scholars have tended to fall in behind Foucault rather than Habermas (Goodman 1994). Perhaps one of the most regrettably persistent myths of the Enlightenment portrays the movement as a single, homogeneous bloc.

### Box 2

#### Joseph II and the contradictions of enlightened despotism

'Here Lies Joseph, Who Failed in All He Attempted.'

The epitaph which Holy Roman Emperor Joseph II (ruled 1765–90) is alleged to have provided for himself is a tombstone monument to 'enlightened despotism'. An avid reader of Voltaire and the encyclopédistes, Joseph was won over body and soul to the notion of social justice implicit in Enlightenment thinking. He spent the first 15 years of power chafing at the bit as subaltern ruler to his mother, the highly pragmatic Maria Theresa (ruled 1740–80). As soon as she died, he launched a spate of radical reforms. Criminal law was revised on rational lines and the death penalty abolished. Censorship was lifted and freedom of opinion was accompanied by religious toleration. The Catholic Church became another target, especially forms of worship that Joseph judged to be irrational (numerous saints' days, baroque rituals, etc.). German was imposed as the administrative language of state. Joseph also attacked FEUDALISM on the land, bade to equalize taxation and removed numerous institutional checks to central authority. Yet he proved an enlightened young man in too much of a hurry. By the last years, the range and the speed of his reform agenda had triggered revolts by provinces resisting centralization, by nobles protesting his tax and institutional reforms, by polyglot subjects irritated at his promotion of the German language and by a Catholic populace who jibbed against his allegedly 'rational' religious measures. By the time of his premature death, he was already clipping the wings of his own ambitions and rescinding many reforms. The process was taken further by his successor, Leopold II, who as duke of Tuscany (1765–90) had been even more 'enlightened' in his policies than Joseph. Now, however, the Revolution of 1789 in France had tolled the knell of enlightened despotism and frightened rulers who had hitherto privileged enlightened reforms turned towards outright reaction (Blanning 1970).

**Figure V.14** Enlightened sociability – commonly associated with sobriety, the reading of newspapers and polite conversation – was by no means devoid of heated debates and 'uncivil' behaviour. 'The coffeehouse mob'. A large group of men in a coffee house. / British Library, London, UK / © British Library Board. All Rights Reserved / Bridgeman Images.

The unifying discourse of Enlightenment is not the best guide to how Enlightenment actually worked out in the different terrains on which it engaged. In some sense, however, contemporary disagreements form a substantial legacy: for the Enlightenment gave western society both an apprenticeship in collective rational debate within the world of modernity and an awareness of the limits of that debate.

## Discussion themes

1. In what ways did the Enlightenment build on the achievements of the scientific revolution?
2. Who sought to enlighten whom in the Enlightenment, and for what purposes?
3. Why did the Enlightenment require 'daring' (Kant)?

## *Bibliography*

### (A) Sources

Eliot, Simon and Stern, Beverley eds (1979), *The Age of Enlightenment*, 2 vols, London

Mercier, Louis-Sébastien (1999), *Panorama of Paris* [1781–88], ed. Helen Simpson and Jeremy D. Popkin, University Park, Pa.

Pöllnitz, Karl Ludwig (1737–38), *The Memoirs of Charles-Lewis of Pollnitz, being the observations he made in his late travels*, 4 vols, London

Ward, Ned [Edward] (1710), *Vulgus Britannicus, or the British Hudibras*, 5 parts, London

### (B) Literature

Baker, Keith M. (1988), *Inventing the French Revolution*, Cambridge

Blanning, Timothy C. W. (1970), *Joseph II and Enlightened Despotism*, Harlow

Chartier, Roger (1993), *Cultural Origins of the French Revolution*, Ithaca, NY

Edelstein, Dan (2002), *The Enlightenment: A Genealogy*, Chicago

Ellis, Markman (2004), *The Coffee House: A Cultural History*, London

Foucault, Michel (1977), *Discipline and Punish: The Birth of the Prison*, London

Goodman, Dena (1994), *The Republic of Letters: A Cultural History of the French Enlightenment*, Cambridge

Habermas, Jürgen (1989), *The Structural Transformation of the Public Sphere*, Cambridge

Israel, Jonathan (2001), *Radical Enlightenment: Philosophy and the Making of Modernity 1650–1750*, Oxford

Israel, Jonathan (2011), *Democratic Enlightenment: Philosophy, Revolution, and Human Rights 1750–1790*, Oxford

Israel, Jonathan (2014), *Revolutionary Ideas: An Intellectual History of the French Revolution from The Rights of Man to Robespierre*, Princeton

Jacob, Margaret (1992), *Living the Enlightenment: Freemasonry in Eighteenth-century Europe*, Oxford

Jones, Colin (2002), *The Great Nation: France from Louis XV to Napoleon*, London

Knott, Sarah and Taylor, Barbara eds (2005), *Women, Gender and Enlightenment*, Basingstoke

Porter, Roy (2000), *Enlightenment: Britain and the Making of the Modern World*, London

Schiebinger, Londa (1989), *The Mind Has No Sex? Women in the Origins of Modern Science*, Cambridge, Mass.

Stafford, Barbara (1994), *Artful Science: Enlightenment Entertainment and the Eclipse of Visual Education*, Cambridge, Mass.

Van Horn Melton, James (2001), *The Rise of the Public in Enlightenment Europe*, Cambridge

## (C) Web resources

ECCO

'Scottish Enlightenment': <http://www.bbc.co.uk/history/scottishhistory/enlightenment/
features_enlightenment_enlightenment.shtml>

'The Encyclopedia of Diderot and D'Alembert Collaborative Translation Project':
<http://www.hti.umich.edu/d/did>

# PART VI
# POLITICS

| | |
|---|---|
| 1485 | Henry Tudor defeats Richard III of England at Bosworth Field |
| 1494–1559 | Italian Wars |
| 1520–21 | Revolt of the Comuneros in Spain |
| 1522 | Francis I of France authorizes sale of public offices |
| 1524–26 | Peasants' War in Germany |
| 1528 | Publication of Baldassare Castiglione's *The Book of the Courtier* |
| 1530 | Imperial Police Ordinance enacted in Germany |
| 1532–39 | Legal foundations of the Henrician Reformation of the Church in England |
| 1536 | Pilgrimage of Grace in northern England |
| 1549 | Kett's Rebellion in Norfolk, England, 'Prayer-Book Rebellion' in the south-west |
| 1568–70 | Rebellion of Moriscos in Granada |
| 1572, 1597/ 1601 | Poor Laws enacted in England |
| 1576 | Publication of Jean Bodin's *Six Books of the Commonwealth* |
| 1598 | Publication of Robert Barret's *The Theorike and Practike of Modern Warres* |
| 1614–15 | Last French Estates General before the Revolution |
| 1637 | *Nouveaux Croquants* rural protest in France |
| 1637–40 | Scottish Prayer Book Rebellion |
| 1639 | Nu-Pieds rural protest in France, Rebellion in Scotland |
| 1640 | Catalonia and Portugal rebel against Spanish rule |
| 1641 | Rebellion and massacre in Ireland, not crushed until Cromwell's invasion and reconquest, 1649 onwards |

| | |
|---|---|
| 1642–60 | Civil Wars and Interregnum in England |
| 1647 | Masaniello leads anti-Spanish revolt in Naples |
| 1648 | Uprising in Moscow against taxation |
| 1648–59 | Franco-Spanish War |
| 1649 | Execution of Charles I and abolition of monarchy |
| 1652–54/ 1665–67/ 1672–74 | Anglo-Dutch Wars (England vs United Provinces) |
| 1653–59 | Oliver Cromwell, Protector (1653–58), Richard Cromwell (1658–59) |
| 1660 | Restoration of the Monarchy in England |
| 1672–78 | Dutch War (France vs United Provinces) |
| 1683–99, 1716–18 | Austrian alliance vs the Turks (Austria vs Ottoman Empire) |
| 1685 | Duke of Monmouth executed after failed attempt to overthrow James II of England |
| 1688–89 | 'Glorious Revolution' overthrows James II |
| 1689–97 | Nine Years War (England, Austria, Spain, United Provinces, Savoy, Brandenburg-Prussia vs France) |
| 1698 | Whitehall Palace in Westminster is destroyed by fire |
| 1700–14 | War of the Spanish Succession (France, Spain vs Britain, United Provinces, Austria, Prussia, Portugal) |
| 1700–21 | Great Northern War (Sweden vs Russia, involving Poland, Denmark, Ottoman Empire, Britain) |
| 1714 | The House of Hanover replaces the Stuarts as Britain's reigning dynasty |
| 1716–18 | War of the Quadruple Alliance (France, Britain, United Provinces, Austria vs Spain) |
| 1727–28 | Anglo-Spanish War |
| 1733–38 | War of the Polish Succession (Russia, Austria vs France, Spain) |
| 1736–39 | Austro-Russian–Turkish War (Russia, Austria vs Ottoman Empire) |
| 1739 | War between England and Spain ('Jenkins's Ear') |
| 1740–48 | War of the Austrian Succession (Prussia, France, Spain vs Austria, Britain, United Provinces, Russia) |

| | |
|---|---|
| 1741–43 | Russo-Swedish War |
| 1756–63 | Seven Years War (Prussia, Britain vs Austria, France, Russia, Sweden) |
| 1768–74 | Russo-Turkish War (Russia, Egypt vs Ottoman Empire) |
| 1773–75 | Pugachev's Cossack Rebellion, Russia |
| 1775–83 | War of American Independence (American colonies, France, Spain, United Provinces vs Britain) |
| 1776 | Declaration of Independence by Britain's American colonies |
| 1778–79 | War of the Bavarian Succession (Prussia vs Austria) |
| 1787–92 | Ottoman War (Russia, Austria vs Ottoman Empire) |
| 1788–90 | Russo-Swedish War |
| 1789 | The French Revolution begins with the storming of the Bastille |
| | Promulgation of the Declaration of the Rights of Man |
| 1792 | Deposition of Louis XVI |
| 1792–1802 | War with Revolutionary France (France vs Spain, Britain, Prussia, Russia, Austria, Portugal, Ottoman Empire, United Provinces) |
| 1793 | Execution of Louis XVI; introduction of LEVÉE EN MASSE |
| 1793–94 | The Terror |
| 1794 | 9 Thermidor coup |
| 1795–99 | The Directory |
| 1797 | France conquers Venice |
| 1799 | Advent of Napoleon Bonaparte as First Consul |
| 1806 | Holy Roman Empire dissolved |
| 1812 | Napoleon invades Russia |
| 1815 | Final defeat of Napoleon at Waterloo |

# (A) Surveys

The study of 'politics' encompasses all norms, values and activities relating to the government of people and territories. Usually placed at the beginning of general surveys, it concludes our examination of early modern history – not to downplay the significance of this 'classic' topic, but to allow a better understanding of the socio-economic, religious and cultural parameters of political life. The following chapters are grouped in two complementary sections: first, survey essays on political theory / practice and the broad chronology of principal conflicts and events; second, thematic accounts of locales, warfare, discontent and revolution.

# The theory and practice of politics and government 1500–1800

*Humfrey Butters*

## The states

In this period states came in more than one form but monarchy was predominant ('Europe in 1500' in Part I; 'Periodical Historical Atlas: Web resources). Republican regimes could, however, be found, for example in cities belonging to the German Reich, in Swiss cantons, and in Italy. Until the Reformation neither those who governed or administered these states, nor those who produced theoretical accounts of their activities, saw themselves as licensed to produce radically novel views of the aims of government or the bases of political authority. Novelty might be acceptable, but it had to be novelty within long established and revered bodies of thought. The principal sources of political ideas were three: Greek and Roman political thought, particularly the works of Aristotle and Plato, Cicero and Seneca; ROMAN LAW, as set out in the great sixth-century compilation, commissioned by the Emperor Justinian (Figure VI.1), the *Corpus Iuris Civilis* (Body of Civil Law), and as interpreted by the jurists who expounded that seminal collection of texts; and, finally, the principal monuments of the Christian tradition, that is, the Bible, canon law and the writings of the Fathers of the Church, especially St Augustine. With the help of these 'authorities' rulers, administrators and polical theorists were able to develop workable concepts of the state, sovereignty and political representation (Guenée 1971; Skinner 1979).

This does not mean, however, that the views expressed in these magisterial works all cohered around a single and harmonious vision. Nothing, for example, could have been further from Aristotle's assertion that the social and political life of the city-state was natural to man than St Augustine's conviction that Church and State were God's bridles for sinful man, which had to be obeyed. Even within a single authority it was possible to find differing verdicts upon crucial issues such as the best form of government: Aristotle and the Bible, for example, could be and were used to defend both monarchy and republicanism, although in neither was a defence of the modern form of democracy to be found. Before and after 1500 theorists were perfectly aware that sharply conflicting viewpoints could be found in the great classical and Christian

**Figure VI.1** The Emperor Justinian (ruled 527–65), who ordered the Corpus Iuris Civilis to be compiled, is depicted here in a mosaic in the Basilica of San Vitale in Ravenna, the seat of his government in Italy. Emperor Justinian's vault, detail from Emperor Justinian with his entourage, mosaic, northern wall of apse, Basilica of San Vitale (UNESCO World Heritage List, 1996), Ravenna, Emilia-Romagna, Italy, 6th century / De Agostini Picture Library / A. De Gregorio / Bridgeman Images.

texts, and that was one reason why medieval thinkers had laid such emphasis upon the need for correct interpretations of them. But even of a single work different interpretations might be offered, a fact that led one medieval author to stress that 'authority' had a 'waxen nose' (Grossi 2006, 162).

Such differences of interpretation had major practical consequences in political life. The pope, for example, as bishop of Rome, based his authority over the Catholic Church on Christ's charge to his apostle Peter, later first bishop of Rome (Box 1).

### Box 1

'And I say also unto thee, That thou art Peter, and upon this rock I will build my church; and the gates of hell shall not prevail against it. And I will give unto thee the keys of the kingdom of heaven: and whatsoever thou shalt bind on earth shall be bound in heaven: and whatsoever thou shalt loose on earth shall be loosed in heaven.'

(Matthew, XVI, 18–19)

Lay Catholic rulers accepted this claim, but were less convinced by the pope's further contention that as vicar (representative) of Christ he could depose sinful monarchs or intervene in other ways in the government of states. Members of the

Greek, Russian or Protestant churches naturally rejected all such papal claims, while agreeing that worldly authority ultimately derived from God, for the Bible said it did.

Augustine, despite his reluctance to condone resistance to rulers, was quite capable of distinguishing just ones from tyrants, and in the *City of God* he declared that without justice states amounted to nothing more than organized brigandage (St Augustine 1950). Justice was one of the four 'cardinal virtues' and the quintessentially political one. In the *Digest*, one of the texts that made up the *Corpus Iuris Civilis*, the third-century jurist Ulpian, influenced by Aristotle, gave the following definition of it: 'Justice is a fixed and perpetual intention of according each what is due to him' (1988, I. I. 10). The ruler's principal tasks were to do justice and maintain peace, and to acquire the financial means necessary, by a judicious admixture of force, prudence and goodness.

It is not hard to account for the importance accorded by political thinkers in a Christian Europe to the great Christian texts, but in Italy, from the twelfth-century onwards, a rather different tradition developed, associated with the study of rhetoric ('The Renaissance' in Part V), distinguished by the fact that writers who belonged to it drew more heavily upon classical authorities than upon Christian ones. Machiavelli's works represent both the highest point reached by this tradition and, in some respects, a decisive break with it. His shocking denial that it was always prudent or safe for a ruler to follow the dictates of Christian morality caused his works to be placed on the INDEX LIBRORUM PROHIBITORUM (Box 2).

## Box 2

Machiavelli summarized his radical views in *The Prince* (1513):

'It is essential to realise this: that a prince, and above all a new prince, cannot practise all those things which gain men a reputation for being good, as it is often necessary, in order to keep hold of the state, to act contrary to trust, contrary to charity, contrary to humanity, contrary to religion.'

(Machiavelli 1998, 97)

Prior to the Reformation no classical political theorist was more influential than Aristotle. Machiavelli, for example, fully accepted his judgment that while monarchy and republicanism were both defensible forms of government, one should always consider what sort of constitution was best suited to a particular type of society. This is why Machiavelli devoted one work to monarchies (*The Prince*) and another to republics (*Discourses*). It was also thanks to thirteenth-century translations of Aristotle's *Politics* that the adjective *politicus* became fully established in political language, its principal meanings being 'of the *polis* (city or state)', 'pertaining to the constitution (form of government) of the *polis*', or 'of the polity' (Aristotle's term for acceptable popular government). Later it came to denote constitutional as opposed to absolute government (Rubinstein 1987).

Roman law was of crucial significance for the theory and practice of government, before and after 1500, in the first place because in many European countries (but not England) it was the foundation of secular law, and it also had a notable influence upon the development of canon law, the law of the Catholic Church. Secondly, lawyers who had studied it at university played a cardinal role in the administration of Church and state. Since its revival in the twelfth century lawyers and rulers had derived from Roman law some of their main ideas about the state, sovereignty and political representation. The two fundamental tenets of monarchical ABSOLUTISM, that the prince's will has the force of law and that the prince is 'loosed from' the laws (*solutus* in the original Latin), that is above them, both derived ultimately from Ulpian. Jean Bodin (1529/30–96), the most important theorist of absolutism, constructed the first systematic account of sovereignty with the aid of the *Corpus* and the writings upon it of the medieval jurists (Bodin 1961).

The Reformation marked a watershed in political ideas, particularly with regard to the crucial matter of resistance to government. Many Catholics and Protestants accepted St Augustine's view of the essential purpose of Church and state, to keep fallen man in check but, in a period when Protestant rulers had Catholic subjects and Catholic rulers Protestant ones, it is not surprising that some of them, like Luther and Calvin, came to reject his related belief that resistance to established authority could not be justified ('Centre and periphery' in Part VI). But even Thomas Hobbes, the most original political thinker of the seventeenth century, whose political views departed in significant respects from those embodied in the classical and Christian traditions, still owed much to them.

## Instruments of persuasion

In the sixteenth and seventeenth centuries governments were alive to the psychological bases of power and authority, as their predecessors had been, so that there was nothing novel in Machiavelli's view that power was based upon reputation. Rulers deployed a wide variety of instruments to convey to their subjects the moral value and the utility of obedience and compliance: the sermons and writings of clerics; the works of the HUMANISTS; the insignia of power, such as crowns, orbs and sceptres; and ceremonial events, such as coronations, entries into cities and funerals (Muir 2005). From the second half of the fifteenth century literary forms of persuasion were given vastly greater possibilities of diffusion thanks to the invention of the printing press, although, as the German Reformation showed, this was a technical innovation that could also be exploited to great effect by opponents of the established order ('The long Reformation' in Part III).

If monarchs had simply been seen as lay persons, similar to their subjects save in respect of the power and authority they exercised, the reverence accorded them would have been less than it was. But the kings of France and England, for example, could claim a more exalted status, because they were anointed at their coronations in a manner reminiscent of bishops' consecrations, and also because they were held to have special healing powers as well. There was, however, more than one way of conceiving the relationship between monarchs and the political communities they governed. One persistent image, deriving from the ancient world, was that of the king as head of the body politic, who represented the kingdom as its delegate, whose authority derived from it. Another image depicted the king as personifying the kingdom; and this was the image Louis XI and Louis XIV used when they declared that they *were* France. There was a further conflict between a dynastic conception of the state as the ruler's property and the view of this relationship held by, for example, French lawyers, who considered the king to be a USUFRUCTUARY, enjoying the use of crown lands without owning them.

## Legislation and representation

One of the consequences of the revival of Roman law in Europe from the twelfth century onwards was that as much attention came to be paid to the legislative role of rulers as had previously been paid to their judicial one. Two of the four texts which comprised the *Corpus Iuris Civilis*, the *Code* and the *Novels*, were, after all, collections of imperial legislation. By the late sixteenth century legislation was taken, by Jean Bodin, to be the distinguishing mark of sovereignty (Box 3).

### Box 3

In his *Six Books of the Commonwealth* (1583) Bodin asserted that:

'the first mark of the sovereign prince is the power to give law to everyone in general, and to each person in particular; but this is not enough, for it is necessary to add, without the consent of anyone greater than he is, equal to himself, or lower than himself.'

(Bodin 1961, 221)

In England monarchs needed to get the consent of a parliament for new laws, in France they did not; and although in France the *Parlement de Paris* (a court of law rather than a 'parliament') could refuse to register royal legislation it considered harmful to the interests of the Crown, the king could override its opposition by having recourse to a *lit de justice*, a formal procedure involving a personal visit by the king to his court. From 1439 onwards in those parts of France known as the *pays d'élections* (because the *élus*, royal financial OFFICERS, resided there), the king could raise direct taxation without seeking the consent of a representative assembly, but in the rest of the country provincial estates had to be consulted. The Estates General was very rarely summoned in the sixteenth century; and its last meeting before the French Revolution took place in the years 1614 and 1615. In Europe as a whole the fortunes of representative assemblies differed markedly: in the Netherlands the States General played a decisive role in the rising against Spanish rule in 1576, subsequently becoming the central governing institution of the United Provinces; in Germany, by contrast, the imperial DIET and, in most cases, the estates of the various principalities played an ever diminishing role. Germany's example was not followed, however, by the Polish-Lithuanian kingdom, where the diet, essentially a noble parliament, increased its powers at the expense of the monarchy in this period, a tendency powerfully assisted by the replacement of hereditary by elective kingship.

## The administration of justice

In some sixteenth- and seventeenth-century European states the administration of justice was largely the responsibility of institutions and officials created before 1500, often long before. In England, for example, this was true of the central common law courts, such as King's Bench, and of the courts of equity, such as Chancery; and in the localities it was true of the justices of the peace, jurymen and assize judges. The most important Tudor addition to the local administration was the creation of the lords lieutenants and their deputies, with wide civil and military functions (Williams 1979). In France central law courts such as the *Parlement de Paris*, a sovereign body, had developed in the Middle Ages and so too, in the provinces, had the bailiffs or seneschals, bailiffs' lieutenants. In provincial administration the most significant change was the introduction in the seventeenth century of the INTENDANTS, commissioners sent out from the centre with wide powers (Bonney 1978).

Germany presented a more complex scene, for medieval emperors had never tried to impose a uniform administrative grid upon the *Reich*. There was both a territorial and an imperial system of justice. Princes and cities issued law codes inspired by Roman law. There were two imperial courts of appeal, the *Reichskammergericht* (established 1495) and the *Reichshofrat* (established 1498), but many German princes had the right to block such appeals, so that jurisdictional conflict was an abiding feature of German political life (Wilson 2011).

But such disputes were hardly confined to Germany. Elsewhere royal courts were often in conflict with ecclesiastical or seigneurial ones. An exception here was England, where little feudal or franchisal jurisdiction survived by 1500; in Ireland by contrast, subject to the king of England, great lords held sway beyond the areas known as 'the Pale'. In such jurisdictional battles the initiative was often in the hands of individual litigants, seeking the court best suited to their requirements (Guenée 1963, 133). But the choices of individuals could in their turn be limited by those of

---

**Box 4**

'[B]e it enacted, by authority of this present Parliament, that the king, our sovereign lord, his heirs and successors, kings of this realm, shall be taken, accepted, and reputed the only supreme head in earth of the Church of England.'

*(Act of Supremacy 1534; Web resources)*

---

individual rulers, such as the Tudor monarchs and Lutheran princes who broke with Rome and became heads of their respective churches (Box 4). In territories subject to Ottoman rule Christian, Jewish or local customary law was allowed to persist, but Islamic law had precedence.

## Public finance

The history of state finance in this period shows a similar mixture of innovation and continuity. In France, England and Italy direct and indirect taxation and recourse by rulers to credit from banks could be found throughout the late Middle Ages, as could, in areas like the Netherlands, life ANNUITIES (effectively a kind of pension granted in return for a large cash sum). In France the principal direct (*taille*) and indirect taxes (*gabelle, aides*) raised in the fifteenth century were still be to found in 1700. Tax regimes in Europe differed widely: in Spain and France, for example, the nobility was largely exempt from direct taxation; in England it was not. Some new taxes were introduced in this period, under the pressure of war: the EXCISE TAX in England, for example, and the MILLONES, an 'extraordinary' tax introduced in Castile in 1590 to supplement the main existing direct tax, the *servicio*. In France in 1522, Francis I created a further source of revenue by authorizing the sale of public office. The consequences of this dramatic measure of privatization were far-reaching, especially since officers who had bought their offices expected to be able to hand them on to their male heirs. It reduced the king's control over his own administration; it generated considerable administrative confusion, since new offices were created simply in order to sell them, not because they were needed, and existing offices were divided, with increasing frequency, into two or three parts; and, finally, it gave birth to a new form of nobility, the *noblesse de* ROBE, whose vested interests often conflicted with those of the Crown. One country that did experience a financial revolution, at the end of the seventeenth century, was England, with the establishment of the Bank of England and the National Debt (Dickson 1967). Few statesmen in France and England, however, had a good grasp of public finance: Cardinal Richelieu, for example, cheerfully admitted that he had none.

## Warfare and diplomacy

The conduct of diplomacy had been revolutionised in the fifteenth century by the introduction by the Italians of resident ambassadors, an innovation soon adopted by the major European powers. Their dispatches provided their governments with invaluable analyses of the domestic politics and foreign policy goals of the states to which they were sent.

It has also been claimed that there was a revolution in the conduct of warfare in this period that served to enhance considerably the power of the states that experienced it to withstand external enemies and repress domestic ones. But historians who accept the idea have differed markedly in their accounts of the chronology of this revolution, while others, by contrast, have laid stress upon the continuing salience of clientage, venality and inefficiency ('The impact of war' in Part VI).

## Social policy

In the sixteenth and early seventeenth centuries demographic growth and bullion imports from Spanish America caused a marked rise in prices and an associated increase in poverty, unemployment and vagrancy. Some governments used legislation to address these problems (in Germany the Imperial Police Ordinance of 1530), often with novel features: the English Poor Laws of 1572 and 1597/1601, for example, established a poor rate and recognised the category of the 'deserving' unemployed; but 'social policy' was hardly a novelty in Europe (medieval Italian COMMUNES had produced legislation of this sort, often justifying it in terms of its 'public utility', a key concept in Roman law). There was, however, a considerable growth in the number of such laws in Germany in this period. Passed within the wider framework of 'good police', a general state campaign to enhance public order and welfare, these were given a loose theoretical underpinning by a school of administrative theorists called the 'cameralists'. But those charged with implementing this legislation were far removed from Max Weber's classic definition of a rationalized and professional bureaucracy (Wilson 2004, 234–35); and their English equivalents, such as JPs, constables and overseers of the poor, were of an essentially 'amateur' stamp (Hindle 2000).

## Rulers and subjects

Several early modern states were 'composite monarchies', made up of diverse peoples and provinces with their own privileges and institutions that careful rulers needed to respect (Elliott 1992). The Habsburg and Ottoman Empires were perfect examples of this heterogeneity, the fruit of marriages, purchases or wars. It served to limit the power even of absolute rulers, but it also assisted it, for when rebellions occurred, they were often confined to a particular territory or city. One common cause of such upheavals was the failure by rulers to manage their noble subjects, whose wealth, social prestige, political alliances, clienteles and, sometimes, military resources made them the most important social group. They expected to receive PATRONAGE from the ruler, in the form of lands, titles or pensions, and to be consulted on matters of policy. Nobles and gentry played a crucial role in government, both at the centre and in the localities, and they constituted the officer class in European armies. This is why royal and princely courts were such crucial political institutions. At all costs kings had to avoid giving the impression that they were dominated by a faction or a favourite, a persuasion to which the exalted position of Cardinals Richelieu and Mazarin in seventeenth-century French government gave rise.

Below the nobility ranked the merchants, a vital source of tax revenue and loans, whose commercial and industrial enterprises were increasingly favoured by rulers pursuing what were later called a MERCANTILE SYSTEM, designed to boost the economies of their states at the expense of those of their rivals. The bulk of the population of Europe were, however, PEASANTS, providing Europeans with their food. They could be employed in some states in public works projects and their financial CONTRIBUTIONS, in the form of rents and seigneurial dues, tithes and taxes, were crucial to the maintenance of the established order. In some cases they were represented in the Estates but, even when they were not, their village communities and parishes possessed institutions and officers that enabled their interests to be defended. When these means of defence proved unavailing they sometimes had recourse to rebellion, but such uprisings, with a few exceptions such as the German Peasants' Revolt of 1524–26, rarely had radical aims. In France in the seventeenth century rebellious peasants often had the support of local nobles or even royal officers, anxious to prevent the burden of royal taxation depriving peasants of their ability to pay the rent ('Riot and rebellion' in Part VI).

Another 'estate' governments had to deal with was that of the clergy. In the late Middle Ages lay rulers had acquired considerable powers over churchmen, in matters of jurisdiction, taxation and appointments to BENEFICES. Clerics, for their part, were active in many areas of lay administration, in the case of Cardinal Wolsey in England, or of Cardinals Richelieu (Figure VI. 2) and Mazarin in France, at its summit. Before the Reformation Catholic teaching rarely encouraged the laity to challenge the accepted order, although medieval heretics, such as the Albigensians and Hussites, certainly did. After the Reformation, however, Catholics and Protestants developed theories of resistance, which played a key role in the civil wars of the period (Figure VI. 3; 'Dynastic politics, religious conflict and reason of state c.1500–1650' in Part VI; Greengrass 2014).

The political philosophies of Jean Bodin in France and Thomas Hobbes in England were powerfully shaped by their personal experience of the corrosive effects of radical religious disagreements, and both were led to argue that the only remedy was a formidable, absolutist state. Hobbes and John Locke both explored the key issue of political obligation by employing the intellectual contrivances of a state of nature

**Figure VI.2** The Cardinal de Richelieu, France's chief minister in the reign of Louis XIII, in a painting by Philippe de Champaigne (c. 1639) at the Château de Versailles. Cardinal Richelieu (1585–1642) c. 1639 (oil on canvas), Champaigne, Philippe de (1602–74) / Chateau de Versailles, France / Bridgeman Images.

**Figure VI.3** The Emperor Charles V (1500–58) is shown here in a portrait painted by his favourite Italian artist, Titian, after his triumph over the German Protestants at the battle of Mühlberg in 1547. 'The Emperor Charles V (1500–58) on horseback at Mühlberg', 1548 (oil on canvas). Titian (Tiziano Vecellio) (c. 1488–1576) / Prado, Madrid, Spain / Bridgeman Images.

preceding the creation of government and a social contract. They managed to arrive at conflicting conclusions: Hobbes argued that only under the most extreme circumstances was political rebellion justified; Locke, by contrast, took a far more permissive attitude to resistance. In England religious divisions helped to produce the first rudimentary political parties when, towards the end of Charles II's reign (1660–85), a sizeable portion of the political class tried to prevent the king's Catholic brother, James, from succeeding him. In the course of the so-called 'exclusion crisis' Whigs and Tories made their first appearance (Coward 1980, 285–86). Religious antagonism was also at the root of the 'Glorious Revolution' of 1688–89, when the crisis caused by James II's attempts to restore Catholicism to its former role in English life led his daughter Mary and her Dutch husband, William of Orange, to send an army to England, as a result of which James fled to France, leaving the way open for William and Mary to assume the throne.

## Eighteenth-century developments

In the eighteenth century monarchy continued to be the principal form of government, but republican government distinguished, for example, the Dutch Republic (Treasure 1985, 463–493); the city of Geneva, birthplace of Rousseau; and Venice, whose longevity and mixed constitution, a form favoured by Aristotle, continued to make it of absorbing interest to political thinkers.

In England one consequence of the removal of James II from the throne was a transformation in the role of parliament. In 1500 the king could rule without parliament, provided that he had no desire to introduce new laws or to levy the sort of taxation for which parliamentary consent was required. Charles I was still able to do this between 1629 and 1640, and Charles II between 1681 and 1685. After 1688 William III's determination to use English resources against the United Provinces' great enemy, Louis XIV, made the Crown heavily dependent on parliamentary taxation, and parliament used this dependence to obtain the right to assign revenue to specific purposes and audit royal finances. It was, therefore, the cost of Continental warfare, more than the Bill of Rights (1689) or the Triennial Act (1694), that made it impossible for the Crown to govern without parliament (which also became the ultimate guarantor of the repayment of royal debts). As so often in English history war had proved to be a most effective promoter of the growth of parliament. Although these developments represented a diminution in the power of the British monarchy, they also helped it to avoid the awful fate of its Bourbon rival, which might have survived with better management of its ever growing fiscal problems.

The monarchy lost other powers after 1688: queen Anne was the last English ruler to make use of the 'royal touch', the power of healing scrofula accepted for centuries in France and England as a distinguishing mark of sacral kingship; she was also the last ruler to use the royal veto. But the Crown remained, nonetheless, at the centre of the political world, with the theory of the Divine Right of Kings still commanding widespread support and considerably enhanced patronage resources (in the expanding army and civil administration) at the disposal of the king's chief ministers ('Epilogue'). Few members of the political class were wholehearted advocates of Lockean views of contract and consent, and fewer still of Hobbesian notions of absolutism.

Religion also continued to play a central role in the lives of the vast majority of Europeans, though the Enlightenment movement fostered more frequent attacks on the powers of the Catholic Church and the ANCIEN RÉGIME more generally ('Enlightenment' in Part V). Its political views, however, exhibited a considerable variety: Montesquieu, for example, a great fan of the British constitution, favoured a limited monarchy; Voltaire looked to enlightened despotism to spearhead reform; but for Rousseau the ideal was direct democracy, for he rejected representative government as inevitably associated with party and faction.

Enlightenment ideas mattered politically because they showed themselves capable of exciting the enthusiasm of rulers as diverse as those of Russia and Spain, Austria and Tuscany; even if in many cases the practical effects of such reforming initiatives were considerably less than had been hoped for. The most significant Russian monarch of the century, however, Peter the Great, could only to a very limited extent be described as 'enlightened', although certainly as 'westernising'. What he achieved was not to transform Russia's society and economy, but to make it a power of which, for the first time, all the leading players in European politics had to take serious account. He did this by constructing a fleet and dramatically improving the quality of the Russian army, which enabled him to defeat Sweden, and to establish Russia as a Baltic power, of which the enduring visual manifestation was his creation, St Petersburg (Anderson 1995). In France, at the heart of the Enlightenment movement, Louis XIV's successors were neither enlightened nor competent, and though they had some able ministers, the efforts of these men to reform the system were constantly blocked by privileged vested interests, whose resistance helped to make inevitable the fiscal crisis that engulfed the regime towards the end of the century ('Revolution' in Part VI).

## Assessment

A closer study of politics reinforces the view, found elsewhere in this volume, that there are few clear boundaries between the medieval and early modern periods. The Reformation did, however, mark a sharp break with the past, not merely in its consequences for religious belief and practice, but also because of the major impact that it had on political life and political theory. Between 1500 and 1648 civil and international conflicts in which religious discontents and divisions played a key role were far more salient than they had ever been before, a fact reflected, in different ways, in the works of Jean Bodin, Thomas Hobbes and John Locke. The duration and intensity of these wars, as well as of those in which religious differences did not play a part (such as the struggles between France and Spain), placed great strains upon the resources of states, leading to a growth in taxation, bureaucracy and the size of the armed forces, sometimes without corresponding improvements in efficiency (as for example in the extravagant proliferation of public offices in France). By contrast, in the eighteenth century, while religion remained of fundamental importance to Europeans, it was rarely the cause of violent domestic or international conflict, a development favoured and promoted by Enlightenment thinkers. In nearly all states throughout the period 1500–1800 the nobility and gentry occupied an exalted position in government and military affairs. Securing patronage, moreover, remained an essential element in social advancement, and dispensing it a key tool in political management.

## Discussion themes

1. What were the principal means employed by rulers to ensure that their subjects obeyed them?
2. Discuss the relationship between religion and political authority in this period.
3. To what extent did the powers of the state increase in this period?

## Bibliography

### (A) Sources

Bodin, Jean (1961), *Les Six Livres de la République* [1583], anastatic reprint, Darmstadt
*Corpus Iuris Civilis* (1988), I: *Institutiones et Digesta*, ed. P. Krueger and T. Mommsen, Hildesheim
Machiavelli, Niccolò (1998), *The Prince*, ed. and trans. S. J. Milner, London
St Augustine (1950), *The City of God*, books I-VII, in *Writings of Saint Augustine*, vol. 6, trans. D. B. Zema and G. R. Walsh, Washington

### (B) Literature

Anderson, Matthew S. (1995), *Peter the Great*, 2nd edn, London
Bonney, Richard (1978), *Political Change in France under Richelieu and Mazarin*, Oxford
*Bonney, Richard (1991), *The European Dynastic States 1494–1660*, Oxford
*Coward, Barry (1980), *The Stuart Age*, London and New York
Dickson, Peter (1967), *The Financial Revolution in England: A Study in the Development of Public Credit 1688–1756*, London
Elliott, John (1992), 'A Europe of composite monarchies', *Past and Present*, 137, 48–71
Greengrass, Mark (2014), *Christendom Destroyed: Europe 1517–1648*, London
Grossi, Paolo (2006), *L'ordine giuridico medievale*, Rome-Bari
Guenée, Bernard (1963), *Tribunaux et gens de justice dans le bailliage de Senlis à la fin du Moyen Age (vers 1380–vers 1550)*, Paris

Guenée, Bernard (1971), *L'Occident aux XIVe et XVe siècles. Les états*, Paris

Hindle, Steve (2000), *The State and Social Change in Early Modern England, c. 1550–1640*, Basingstoke

Muir, Edward (2005), *Ritual in Early Modern Europe*, 2nd edn, Cambridge

Rubinstein, Nicolai (1987), 'The history of the word *politicus* in early modern Europe', in: *The Languages of Political Theory in Early Modern Europe*, ed. A. Pagden, Cambridge, 41–56

Skinner, Quentin (1979), *The Foundations of Modern Political Thought*, 2 vols, Cambridge

Treasure, Geoffrey (1985), *The Making of Modern Europe 1648–1780*, London and New York

Williams, Penry (1979), *The Tudor Regime*, Oxford

Wilson, Peter (2011), *The Holy Roman Empire, 1495–1806*, New York

Wilson, Peter (2016), *The Holy Roman Empire: A Thousand Years of Europe's History*, London

## (C) Web resources

'The Act of Supremacy' (1534), on the 'Then Again . . .' website of David Koeller:  <http://www.thenagain.info/Classes/Sources/ActSupremacy.html>

'Periodical Historical Atlas of Europe, AD 1 to AD 2000', designed by Christos Nüssli (2003): <http://www.euratlas.net/history/europe/index.html>

# Dynastic politics, religious conflict and reason of state c. 1500–1650

*Humfrey Butters and Henry J. Cohn*

Starting our survey with the relations between two of the principal powers, it is noteworthy that both between 1494 and 1559 and between 1635 and 1659 France and Spain were at war, even though in the earlier period their conflicts were punctuated by peace treaties and truces. At stake were the strategic and economic interests of the two states and the territorial claims and prestige of their ruling dynasties; but the Reformation – and the confessional strife that it engendered – added a religious dimension to their struggles. In one significant respect, however, the earlier contest differed from the later one: in 1500 these two countries were the leading powers in Western Europe; by 1650 this was ceasing to be true of Spain, forced in 1648 to abandon its long and costly struggle to recover the northern provinces of the Netherlands.

In 1500 France and Spain had not enjoyed their pre-eminence for long, but the claims and rights which lay at the root of their conflicts were long-standing ones ('Europe in 1500' in Part I). Since the late thirteenth century the house of Anjou, whose titles passed to the crown of France in 1481, had been in dispute over the kingdom of Naples with the crown of Aragon, now joined with the kingdom of Castile by the union of the crowns effected by the marriage of Isabella of Castile  and Ferdinand of Aragon (Map 1, Appendix). The struggle had often taken a military form. The French crown had a claim to the Duchy of Milan, deriving from the marriage in 1387 of the duke's daughter and the Duke of Orleans. The Duchy of Burgundy, birthplace of Charles V, ruler of Spain from 1516, and of the Empire from 1519, was another bone of contention, since after the death in 1477 of the last duke, Charles the Bold, its northern provinces (the Netherlands) had been acquired by the Habsburgs, and its southern province, whose capital was Dijon, had been retained by the Valois of France; each dynasty, therefore, wished to acquire the part of the former Duchy that it did not possess. These were mostly crown territories and claims that rulers had no right to renounce ('The theory and practice of politics and government 1500–1800' in Part VI). The struggle between France and its Spanish and imperial opponents became further complicated by two other conflicts, in which religious convictions played a crucial role: that between the Habsburgs and the German Lutherans, and that between the Habsburgs and the Ottomans.

## The Italian wars

The series of wars initiated by the French invasion of Italy in 1494 caused extraordinary political instability (Mallet and Shaw 2012). Of the five major powers in Italy, Florence experienced four changes of regime between 1494 and 1530, and the Duchy of Milan and the kingdom of Naples underwent several; Rome was sacked in 1527; and in 1509, in the wake of defeat by the French at the battle of Agnadello, Venice lost most of its territorial state, though it contrived to recover the greater part of it by 1516 (Bonney 1992, 79–107). Frequently regimes were overthrown because of an alliance between their domestic opponents and their external enemies. It is not surprising that in the writings of Machiavelli, who lived through these upheavals, the relationship between interstate relations on the one hand and internal politics on the other is given greater prominence than in the works of any other major political theorist (Box 1).

Box 1

'The prince who earns this reputation for himself is held in high esteem, and as long as he is understood to be a great man and revered by his subjects, it is difficult to conspire against and attack such a person when they are esteemed. For a prince should have two fears: an internal one, in regard to his subjects, and an external one, in regard to foreign powers. he defends himself against the latter with good arms and good allies, and when he has good arms he will always have good allies. internal affairs will always remain stable whilst external matters are stable, unless they have already been disturbed by a conspiracy.'

(Machiavelli 1995, 99)

The French attempts to acquire the kingdom of Naples ended in failure. In 1495 Charles VIII's astonishingly rapid victory over the Aragonese regime and its papal and Florentine allies proved to be short-lived, thanks to inadequate supply routes and the formation of a powerful anti-French coalition; and when Charles's successor, Louis XII, tried to conquer the kingdom in concert with Ferdinand of Aragon, the latter outwitted him, expelling the French by force from Neapolitan territory in 1504. Louis, who had also inherited the Orleanist claim to the Duchy of Milan, managed to conquer it in 1499 and retain control of it, save for one brief interlude, until 1512. Pope Alexander VI and Venice were persuaded to support the initial conquest, the former by the promise of assistance in his project of asserting control over certain parts of the Papal States.

One prominent Italian statesman determined to free Italy from the foreign yoke was Pope Julius II. After his ephemeral alliance with the French and the other major powers against Venice, the League of Cambrai (1508), he was able to use the Spanish and the Swiss to expel the French from Lombardy in 1512. The net result, however, was to reinforce Spanish influence in the peninsula.

France did not succeed in winning Milan back until 1515, under Francis I. For a while the new ruler of Spain, Charles I of Habsburg, was too occupied elsewhere to do anything about this, but two years after his election as emperor in 1519 conflict between the French and the Spanish broke out on several fronts: in Luxembourg, in Spanish Navarre and in Lombardy. Once again France was expelled from the Duchy of Milan, and in 1525, after a promising start, Francis's attempt to win it back was ended by the battle of Pavia, the worst defeat suffered by French arms since Agincourt (1415), largely due to his strategic and tactical blunders. Pope Clement VII's fears about Habsburg domination of the peninsula led him to join other Italian powers and France in the League of Cognac (1526), but neither he nor Francis profited much from this alliance: in 1527 Rome was sacked by imperial troops and 1528 saw the failure of France's campaign to take Naples, which had initially prospered. In the following year, in the Peace of Cambrai, Francis gave up his Italian aspirations and towns and titles in the Netherlands, but kept the French province of Burgundy in return for a cash payment to Charles (Bonney 1992, 105).

Francis's renunciation of his Italian interests was, however, purely ornamental; in 1536 he invaded Savoy, in 1537 Piedmont, and these he still held when he died in 1547; but the kingdom of Naples and the Duchy of Milan remained in Habsburg hands. Charles, on the other hand, never managed to acquire the French province of Burgundy. In Germany, moreover, the emperor found it difficult to counter the spread of Lutheranism in the 1520s because of his military undertakings in Italy; and, subsequently, assistance provided by Francis and, more importantly, by his successor Henry II, played a significant part in enabling the Lutheran cause to resist Charles's attempts to subdue it ('The Long Reformation: Lutheran' in Part III). In 1552, five years after Charles's crushing victory over the Protestants at Mühlberg, Henry II – having contracted an alliance with the Lutheran princes – captured Metz, Toul and Verdun within a few months. Charles's expensive and ultimately unsuccessful siege of Metz, abandoned on 1 January 1553, was a major reason for his overall failure in Germany, of which the Peace of Augsburg (1555), which legalized Lutheranism, was the formal acknowledgement.

The French and the Lutherans were hardly the only opponents Charles had to face: after they had taken Constantinople in 1453 the Ottoman Turks spent several decades subduing most of the Balkans. Early in the sixteenth century, first under Selim I and then under Suleyman the Magnificent, they embarked upon a second, and generally successful, campaign of expansion. Having conquered Syria and Palestine in 1516 and Egypt in 1517, they captured Belgrade (1521), Rhodes (1522) and, after defeating a Hungarian army at Mohács (1526), occupied most of Hungary.

Charles V's brother Ferdinand ruled in what was known as 'royal Hungary'. The Turks failed, however, to take Vienna in 1529. Their influence extended into the western Mediterranean, where Hayreddin Barbarossa governed Algiers for them, becoming subsequently the admiral of their fleet. In 1536 the Ottomans signed a commercial treaty with Francis I, who had no scruples about allying with an Islamic power against his Catholic enemy. Through his relationship with the sultan, a Turkish fleet was able to spend eight months in Toulon in 1544. Charles was particularly concerned about the Ottoman threat to his Italian possessions and to Spain, whose substantial Moorish minority might support any Turkish incursions. His military operations in North Africa enjoyed mixed success: in 1535 he took Tunis, restoring a friendly Islamic dynasty, the Hafsids, as rulers, but failed to take Algiers (1541).

Charles's decision to abdicate in 1556 showed that he considered his career to have been a failure. He had certainly failed to inflict decisive defeats on the Ottomans or Lutherans, and the territories he had ruled were divided between his son, Philip, who took Spain, the Italian possessions, the Low Countries and the American colonies, and Ferdinand, who became emperor. Never again would the same man rule in Madrid and Vienna (Blockmans 2002).

Charles's French adversaries had little reason to rejoice: by the second treaty of Cateau-Cambrésis (1559), which ended the Habsburg–Valois conflict, they had to renounce their claims to Milan and Naples. Religious dissent, whose growth in Germany they had exploited, was now infecting their own lands: in May 1558 Henry II abandoned his Lutheran allies in order to deal with the spread of Calvinism in France. His early death, which triggered a royal bankruptcy and left his kingdom enduring the problems of a royal minority, helped precipitate the French Wars of Religion, which for nearly 40 years denied France the prominent role in European affairs that it had played since 1494 (Knecht 2000).

## The conflicts of the later sixteenth century

France's decline helped to assure Spain's predominance in Europe, but this – powerfully assisted by the arrival of increasing quantities of silver from the New World – was hardly uncontested. The Ottomans remained formidable for a while, although their failure to take Malta (1565) and their defeat by a joint Spanish and Venetian fleet at Lepanto (1571; Figure VI.4) boosted the morale of the Christian powers and discouraged the Turks from risking major naval encounters. In the decades after Suleyman's death in 1566 most of his successors were mediocre, a major defect in a state as dependent on central direction as the Ottoman one; this weakness, inflation and their involvement in war with Persia led the Turks to pose a lesser threat than before to the West.

The principal problem faced by Philip II was the Revolt of the Netherlands, caused mainly by his maladroit handling of leading members of the aristocracy such as Orange and Egmont, who had loyally served his father, and his insistence that the spread of

**Figure VI.4** The battle of Lepanto, fought between the fleets of the Holy League and the Ottomans on 7 October 1571 off the western coast of Greece, was the largest early modern naval confrontation, involving hundreds of ships on both sides. Greece / Turkey: The Battle of Lepanto, 7 October 1571, anonymous painting, late 16th century / Pictures from History / Bridgeman Images.

Calvinism and Anabaptism should be checked by the rigorous implementation of the heresy laws, despite urgings to the contrary by many Catholic nobles. The rebellion started with a series of ICONOCLASTIC riots in 1566 (Parker 2002; cf. 'The long Reformation: Reformed' in Part III). It had two contrasting effects on Spanish foreign policy: first, it forced Philip to commit financial and military resources to suppressing it that might have been used elsewhere; but second, foreign powers who assisted the rebels, or threatened to do so, faced war with Spain. The Spanish Armada (1588), whose defeat was due more to poor Spanish planning and bad weather than to the English fleet, was Philip's response to Elizabeth I's dispatch of an army to the Netherlands under the Earl of Leicester in 1585, after the assassination of William of Orange in the previous year had imperilled the rebel cause; and in the following years the Spanish commander in the Netherlands, the Duke of Parma, was sent to France to help prevent the accession to the throne of the Protestant Henry of Navarre, which Philip saw as a threat to his efforts to suppress the rebellion. Philip's interventions had the opposite effect to that intended: they were insufficient to defeat Henry militarily, and by helping to make his opponents, the Catholic League, appear to be the sedulous instruments of Spanish foreign policy, they contributed to Henry's victory (Lynch 1994).

To the east lay powers whose extensive territories were not matched by their military strength. Between 1462 and 1600 Muscovy grew from 168,000 square miles to over two million, making it vastly larger than the dual state of Poland-Lithuania (formed in 1569), the largest political formation in Europe; but Ivan the Terrible's attempts to establish Russia on the Baltic in the Livonian war against Sweden and Poland were unsuccessful: in 1582–83 he had to cede Livonia to Poland and Estonia to Sweden. In the Swedish Civil War, moreover, between Sigismund III of the house of Vasa and his uncle Charles (1598–99), it was the former who emerged defeated, despite the fact that he was ruler of Poland-Lithuania (Kirby 1990).

## The Thirty Years War

The most destructive conflict until the twentieth century, the Thirty Years War (1618–48), was the first European-wide war (plus maritime and colonial outliers) with large armies brutalizing civilian populations in a foretaste of later 'total wars'. Some major combatants joined the war only at a later stage, but all saw their interests as involved from the beginning (Asch 1997; Wilson 2008/2009/2010; Asbach and Schröder 2014). Long-standing disputes like those between Spain and the Dutch, France and Spain, or Denmark, Poland and Sweden over lands and influence in the Baltic became entangled with constitutional and confessional rivalries within the Holy Roman Empire, but never merged into a single, integrated war.

In Germany the Peace of Augsburg had outlived its earlier usefulness: the spread of Calvinism (not recognized in 1555), struggles over ecclesiastical property, and the succession of rulers strongly committed to the revival of Catholicism all proved too much for imperial institutions. Adjudication of disputes over church property by the main imperial supreme court collapsed. The failure of the imperial diet (1608) provoked the formation of Catholic and Protestant leagues, which were however weak and divided. Several times princely quarrels over territorial ownership threatened a German war, but none broke out until revolt erupted in Bohemia against an attempt by the newly elected Habsburg king Ferdinand to subordinate the nobles and reimpose Catholicism in a country with significant Protestant minorities. After radical noble leaders threw two royal regents out of a window of Prague castle, the Bohemian Estates deposed Ferdinand and elected Frederick V, Elector of the Rhine Palatinate (1619). Had this substitution prevailed, Protestant would have outnumbered Catholic votes in the imperial electoral college, which included the king of Bohemia, but immediately Ferdinand was elected emperor. Spanish forces and the Catholic League army, led by Duke Maximilian I of Bavaria, defeated the rebel cause at the battle of the White Mountain (1620). The leading rebels suffered death or exile and their confiscated lands went to Catholic loyalists like Ferdinand's commander Albrecht von Wallenstein. Ferdinand bestowed the palatine electoral title on Maximilian – after Frederick fled to the United Provinces – and imposed a more absolutist constitution on Bohemia (1627).

Spain's decision to intervene was motivated less by religion than the desire to prevent conflict in the Empire from threatening the Spanish Road, the route by which its armies moved from Italy to the Netherlands. Moreover, the preservation and extension of Spain's Netherlands and Italian territories and support for her Austrian ally would maintain the 'reputation' which every dynasty sought to uphold (Box 2).

The growth of Habsburg power spurred their opponents to act. English involvement in favour of James I's daughter Elizabeth and her exiled husband, the 'Winter King' of Bohemia, was limited, often comprising fruitless mediation between the parties. France preferred at first to wage a secret financial and diplomatic war, then engaged militarily with Spain in northern Italy (1628–31). Danish intervention in 1625, prompted by designs on the adjacent German bishoprics, led to defeat by the League's commander, Count Tilly (1626). Wallenstein conquered large tracts of northern Germany and took the Duchy of Mecklenburg for himself. He and Spain's first minister, the Count-Duke of Olivares, aimed to create a Baltic fleet to rival Sweden's. By 1629 the emperor was powerful enough to impose the Edict of Restitution, which ordered restoration of all bishoprics and monasteries seized by the German Protestants since 1552. Reaction within the empire to Habsburg power then led to Wallenstein's dismissal and the suspension of this Edict in 1630.

Protestant Sweden had temporarily resolved its conflicts with Denmark (1613) and Russia (1617), but during the 1620s engaged in a running war with Poland over the claims by the Catholic Polish Vasa King Sigismund III to both the Swedish throne and the rich provinces of Estonia and Livonia. Sweden briefly entered Germany to take Stralsund in 1628; after Denmark had withdrawn when defeated by the Habsburg forces, Sweden's second invasion in 1630 was principally a continuation of the war against Poland, especially as Poland had allied with the emperor.

The tide gradually turned against the Habsburgs. The Swedish warrior king, Gustavus Adolphus Vasa (1611–32), brought the German Protestant princes under his control through massive propaganda and pressure, received Russian and later French subsidies, and levied contributions in money and kind on friend and foe alike in Germany to support his large army consisting mostly of foreign mercenaries. His Breitenfeld victory (1631) led to the conquest of large swathes of Germany as far as the southern Rhineland and Bavaria. Although he died a year later at the battle of Lützen, Sweden consolidated its position under the leadership of its Chancellor and Regent, Axel Oxenstierna. Yet Swedish power, which had alarmed its Protestant allies, declined after a major defeat at Nördlingen (1634). Ferdinand II gained the loyalty of most Protestant and Catholic princes in the Peace of Prague (1635), which rescinded the Edict of Restitution and restored the territorial situation of 1627.

Both Swedish and Habsburg aggrandizement prompted French intervention in 1635. The French minister Cardinal Richelieu was always prepared to ally with Protestant as well as Catholic powers against Spain, arguing that the interests of his Catholic state required it. Thirteen more years of fluctuating military fortunes left the empire severely damaged, with an estimated loss of over five million people, one fifth of its population, albeit with wide regional variations. Spain was weakened from 1640 onwards after defeat by the Dutch fleet at The Downs and revolts in Catalonia and Portugal, and in 1643 by the French victory at Rocroi. Conflict continued for several years to secure territorial advantages even while peace negotiations were taking place in two Westphalian cities, Münster and Osnabrück.

Confessional considerations which played some part at the outset of war were usually subordinate to reason of state. More extreme protagonists wrongly believed in an international conspiracy by the other side, the one centred on Catholic Rome, the other on Calvinist Geneva. Bitter religious propaganda accompanied the war, although countered by a growing minority stream opposing it (Figure VI.5).

Strategic concerns and hopes of territorial gain increasingly prevailed, but the religious divide remained a factor until the Treaty of Westphalia (1648) removed key contentious issues. The Religious Peace was amended to allow 'exact equality' for the three main faiths in both worship and the functioning of imperial institutions, with the issue of Church property settled favourably for the Protestants. If a ruler later

**Figure VI.5** In this flysheet illustration of 1617, a poor shepherd begs God to be spared wars caused by the quarrels of the Pope, Luther and Calvin. 'Geistlicher Rauffhandel' [Clerical Brawl] (1617): Manfred Höfert, 'Freiburgs Geschichte in Zitaten': http://www.freiburgsgeschichte.de/ 1525-1618_Reformation.htm

converted, his subjects were not obliged to follow suit. Only the Austrian and Bohemian lands of Emperor Ferdinand III remained under his unfettered religious control. Although the central religious disputes were settled, the necessary reform of imperial institutions was referred to the imperial diet, which failed over decades to achieve any. The Swiss Confederation was granted formal 'exemption' from membership of the empire. The emperor had his traditional role confirmed while the territorial power of the German princes was strengthened, but short of complete sovereignty. Among the many territorial adjustments some fostered the rise of Brandenburg-Prussia; Denmark and Sweden gained territories in north Germany and seats in the imperial diet; and – thanks to the skillful diplomacy of its chief minister Cardinal Mazarin who master-minded the whole treaty – France acquired the Habsburg territories in Alsace which became a launch-pad for Louis XIV's invasions of Germany ('European politics from the Peace of Westphalia to the French Revolution c. 1650–1800', Part VI.3).

Spain had recognized the independence of the Netherlands, but successfully continued the war with France, taking advantage of the French *Frondes* (1648–53) against the unpopular Mazarin. England's Protector Cromwell later helped Spain to victory at the battle of the Dunes (1658). The Peace of the Pyrenees (1659) secured Artois and Roussillon for France and Dunkirk for England (Box 3), while Spain retained the rest of its Low Countries and northern Italy. Sweden resumed war in 1655 against a weakened Poland, but Poland received support from the powers dissatisfied with Swedish gains in 1648: Russia, the emperor, Brandenburg and Denmark. Although Denmark was defeated, the succession of a minor to the Swedish throne led to the ending of the war by the Treaties of Copenhagen and Oliva (1660). Overall, Spanish might was being slowly eclipsed, France became the dominant power

## Box 3

### British civil wars

The period of the English Civil War and Interregnum (1642–60) was one of internal conflict which distracted England from the Thirty Years War, but had similarities to it. The conflict was triggered by revolts in Scotland (1638) and Ireland (1641) and fought out between Charles I (1625–49) and his opponents, who accused him of being tyrannical towards both parliament and those Protestants who regarded his vision for the Church of England as a Catholic one. Religious radicalism and an unprecedented public debate on the right political order led to the execution of the king (1649), an act which startled contemporaries throughout Europe, and the establishment of a republican regime, based on England's first (and only) written constitution, the *Instrument of Government* of 1653. The increasingly unpopular regimes of the Protectors Oliver and Richard Cromwell prompted a reaction culminating in the restoration of Charles II (Hughes 1998; Woolrych 2004; see also 'Revolution' in Part VI).

in Europe, and Sweden emerged as the leading player in the Baltic, though only for the next half-century.

## Assessment

The Treaty of Westphalia, rejected by the Papacy, failed to secure the universal Christian Peace it had intended (Croxton 2013, 331–64, 383–87). It did not create the modern secularized state system, but took states further along that road on which they had already embarked. Religion continued to play a subordinate role in some later wars. The congress diplomacy of Westphalia established norms for settling future international conflicts and the content of peace treaties. With time a notionally united Christendom would become a comity of states governed by international law as outlined, for instance, in Hugo Grotius's *The Rights of War and Peace: Including the Law of Nature and of Nations* (1623). An era opened, that was to last beyond the French Revolution, of wars motivated principally by reason of state and considerations of balance of power.

## Discussion themes

1. Account for the dominant position of Spain in sixteenth-century European politics.
2. Assess the impact of dynastic succession on international relations.
3. Was the Thirty Years War 'the last of the religious wars'?

## Bibliography

### (A) Sources

Machiavelli, Niccolò (1995), 'The Prince' [1513], in: *The Prince and other Political Writings*, ed. S. Milner, London
Wilson, Peter ed. (2010), *The Thirty Years War. A Sourcebook*, Basingstoke

### (B) Literature

Asbach, Olaf and Schröder, eds (2014), *The Ashgate Research Companion to the Thirty Years' War*, Abingdon
* Asch, Ronald (1997), *The Thirty Years War*, Basingstoke
Blockmans, Wim (2002), *Emperor Charles V, 1500–58*, London
* Bonney, Richard (1992), *The European Dynastic States 1494–1660*, Oxford
Croxton, Derek (2013), *The Last Christian Peace: The Congress of Westphalia as a Baroque Event*, New York
Elliott, John (2000), *Europe Divided 1559–1598*, 2nd edn, Oxford
Hughes, Anne (1998), *The Causes of the Civil War*, 2nd edn, Basingstoke

Kirby, David (1990), *Northern Europe in the Early Modern Period: The Baltic World, 1492–1772*, London

Knecht, Robert (2000), *The French Civil Wars, 1562–1598*, 3rd edn, Harlow

Lynch, John (1994), *Spain 1516–1598: From Nation State to World Empire*, revised edn, Oxford

Mallett, Michael and Shaw, Christine (2012), *The Italian Wars, 1494–1559*, Harlow

Parker, Geoffrey (2002), *The Dutch Revolt*, revised edn, London

Wilson, Peter (2008), 'The Causes of the Thirty Years War', *English Historical Review*, 123, 554–86

* Wilson, Peter (2009), *Europe's Tragedy. A History of the Thirty Years War*, London

Upton, Anthony P. (2001), 'The First European War', in his *Europe 1600–1789*, London, 39–70

Woolrych, Austin (2004), *Britain in Revolution: 1625–1660*, Oxford

### (C) Web resources

'Geistlicher Rauffhandel' [Clerical Brawl] (1617), in Manfred Höfert, 'Freiburgs Geschichte in Zitaten': <http://diathek.kunstgesch.unihalle.de/dbview/fullview.php?id=21137>

'Treaty of Westphalia' (1648): <http://avalon.law.yale.edu/17th_century/westphal.asp>

# European politics from the Peace of Westphalia to the French Revolution c. 1650–1800

*Colin Jones and Mark Knights*

## Introduction

The eighteenth century could claim to be an age of reason ('Enlightenment' in Part V). It was also an age of war. Hopes that the Peace of Westphalia (1648) would mark a diminution in warfare proved very misguided. Hardly a year passed between 1650 and 1800 without fighting involving one or more European powers (see timeline). Casualties were often very severe. One and a quarter million individuals were killed in the War of the Spanish Succession – some 30,000 at the battle of Blenheim alone (1704). Deaths amounted to 350,000 in the War of the Austrian Succession, almost a million in the Seven Years War and around 2.5 million in the French Revolutionary and Napoleonic Wars.

Heavy war mortality was linked to significant growth in army size. Recruiting, maintaining and equipping huge armed forces constituted one of the most striking achievements of the powerful bureaucratic states which emerged over the eighteenth century ('The theory and practice of politics and government 1500–1800' in Part VI). Campaign army size in the Thirty Years War had numbered in the tens of thousands. By the time of the Seven Years War, the French and Russian armies were over a quarter of a million men strong, with Prussia not far behind. Peacetime armies were smaller – but they were now standing armies, maintained all year round and not solely for the campaigning season. Navies expanded too – the number of seamen in the British Royal Navy and the Spanish navy roughly tripled over the eighteenth century. These huge armies and navies, assembled largely through various forms of recruitment including brutal press-ganging, had to be paid for (Black 1990).

War – financing and supplying as well as strategizing – continued to preoccupy monarchs, governments and diplomats. Armed forces were the heaviest financial burden governments had to bear. But war also had a transformative effect on society and politics as a whole. International conflict provides a lens through which to view changing political structures and cultures. In this chapter, we will first examine international relations and the role of war within domestic politics. The second part will focus on the most important political event of the century, the French Revolution, which not only unleashed a massive wave of military violence but also reanimated ideological battles about the role of the people in political life.

## Towards a balance of power

Beneath the raw facts highlighted in the timeline we can detect a shake-up in the pattern of international politics, with certain great powers entering eclipse and others emerging. The Dutch were already in decline by 1700 (Israel 1995). Despite (or perhaps because of) the successful Dutch invasion of England in 1688 and William III's reorientation of English foreign policy against France, England (or Britain as it became with the Union with Scotland in 1707) emerged as a major international player at sea but also on land. With its allies, it temporarily subdued the dominant European power, France, in the Nine Years War and War of the Spanish Succession. Intense rivalry between Britain and France characterized much of the eighteenth century. After a lull in warfare following the death of Louis XIV in 1715, the War of the Austrian Succession witnessed the emergence of another new power, Prussia, bent on aggrandizement. Other Eastern European powers were on the rise, extending theatres of military operations. Russia became truly engaged in European affairs for the first time, acquiring territory at the expense of Sweden (whose empire collapsed) and Poland (which was carved up in a series of PARTITIONS by its hungry neighbours). Russia now also replaced the Holy Roman Empire as the chief enemy of the Ottoman Empire and made significant gains in the Crimea ('Peter the Great': Web resources). By 1700, the process by which the Habsburg Holy Roman Empire refocused into its Austrian core was well under way. With its extensive interests in the Balkans and in Italy as well as in Central Europe, Austria developed a pivotal position between Western and Eastern Europe. By around 1750, the network of great powers that would dominate nineteenth-century international relations – France, England, Austria, Prussia and Russia – was in place.

Also evident by 1750 was a new globalization of European conflict ('Expanding horizons' in Part IV). Until Westphalia, European conflicts had been largely fought within Europe; by 1750, they spread over many continents. By 1750, the English and French empires were extensive, while the Dutch and Portuguese overseas empires were far from moribund. Similarly, although Spain is said to have been in decline, by 1789 the Spanish Empire was larger than ever before, following the acquisition of Louisiana in 1763 and Florida in 1783. Conflicts between European powers now came to be accompanied by imperial war (Elliott 2006). Even in periods of peace in Europe, colonial wars flared and could (as in 1756) spark wider war. The key areas of tension between Britain and France were North America and the Caribbean, India and the Pacific (the latter a notable area of rival exploration). European wars had become global wars (Appendix Maps 3–4; Table VI.3.1; Figure VI.6).

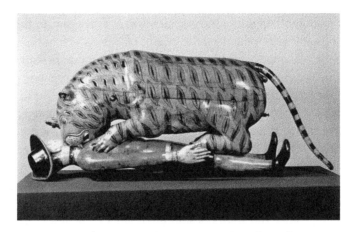

**Figure VI.6** Tipu's Tiger – a life-size model representing the sultan of Mysore mauling a European, probably a British soldier. The tiger symbolized resistance against European colonialization. 'Tipu's Tiger', c. 1790 (wood), Indian School (18th century) / Victoria and Albert Museum, London, UK / Bridgeman Images.

**Table VI.3.1** Imperial and colonial conflicts, with primary arenas of war

| 1664 | Anglo-Dutch War | North America |
|---|---|---|
| 1689–97 | King William's War (France, native Americans) | North America |
| 1702–13 | Queen Anne's War (France, Spain and native Americans) | North America |
| 1739 | Anglo-Spanish War | Caribbean |
| 1744 | Anglo-French War | Cape Breton Island |
| 1744–54 | Anglo-French War | India |
| 1756–63 | Seven Years War | North America, Caribbean, India, Mediterranean, Philippines, West Africa |
| 1770s | Spanish–Portuguese clashes | South America |
| 1775–83 | American War of Independence (Britain at war with France, Spain and United Provinces) | North America, Caribbean, Mediterranean |
| 1780–83 | Anglo-Dutch War | East Indies |
| 1788 | Anglo-Spanish War | Nootka Sound (now Vancouver Island) |
| 1792–1815 | French Wars | Caribbean, North Africa, East Indies, India, South America |

By the mid-eighteenth century, the globalization of European conflict was evident in colonial rivalries, which influenced the origins of wars as well as the ways in which they were fought. Colonies could be strategically important. Britain, for example, regarded the Cape of Good Hope as a crucial strategic point on important sea routes; viewed Gibraltar and Minorca as the key to maritime dominance in the Mediterranean; and valued Caribbean islands for providing essential raw materials and wealth. To maximize economic benefits, Britain, like its rivals, erected trade barriers against competitors, notably in the form of tariffs or in state support and protection for semi-private trading companies. Rivalry was especially acute in that it was assumed that in this MERCANTILE SYSTEM, the contest for wealth was a zero-sum game, and that victory for one power meant the decline of another. War was an economic enterprise in another way too, since the ability of states to conduct global warfare depended on their ability to finance them. As armies and navies grew larger and campaigns more extensive, so states were forced to raise more money, through a combination of taxation, loans and fiscal innovation. The great powers were becoming what historians have called 'FISCAL-MILITARY STATES' (Glete 2002).

Preoccupied with global commercial considerations, warfare lost the strongly religious character that had dominated Reformation Europe. To be sure, religious sensibilities could still infuse and inform conflict and alliances between states. Britain's long-standing feud with France and its colonies, for example, was sharpened by traditional Protestant antipathy to Catholicism, while its alliance with Prussia in the 1750s was hailed as Protestant. Yet wars were no longer confessional as they once had been, pitting Catholic against Protestant and Christian against Turk. The Grand Alliance fighting Catholic France included Catholic powers (and initially had the Pope's backing). Similarly, after the Austrian victory over the Ottomans in 1683, the (western) Christian crusade against the Ottomans waned.

Warfare was thus more secular and materialist than formerly (Pincus 2001). Yet ideology could still count. A related set of ideas – including opposition to tyranny, an emerging theory of international law (Grotius 1964), the right of resistance, and notions of natural liberty and equality – was having a growing effect on international relations. These concepts were honed in the revolts and revolutions of the period, notably in England in the 1640s and 1650s and then again in 1688–89 and in America in the 1770s and 1780s, but their influence was also palpable outside this context: the coalitions against Louis XIV's France, for example, were justified in terms of opposing French 'tyranny'. This set of ideas would be endorsed and strengthened in the French Revolutionary Wars (1792–1802), which raised the ideological aspect of warfare to an even higher level (Black 2002).

Prior to 1792, however, ideas played second fiddle in European politics to traditional dynastic considerations. Despite the apparent modernity of the increasingly global wars that wracked Europe between 1650 and 1789, dynastic issues still loomed large. Kings were there to reign, to fight, to win territory. Then again, dynastic crises brought on by the extinction or rupture of a reigning dynasty could lead to a collapse of traditional authority and European conflict over succession rights – as with England in 1688, Spain in 1701, Poland in 1733 and Austria in 1740.

Dynastic goals were increasingly pursued in a new context. First, the European international relations outlined so far were closely linked to domestic politics, both at national and local level. The 'great power' system, the mercantile rivalries, the global theatre of war and the development of fiscal-military states all had important transformative consequences for domestic politics. Events abroad stimulated a public appetite for news and provided matter for debate and discussion by a public that often had a vested stake in economic activity affected by state affairs, thereby stimulating the emergence and development of the 'public sphere' ('Enlightenment: England and France' in Part V). Paradoxically, while the fiscal-military state created more offices, jobs and bureaucracies (thereby imperilling traditional notions of custom and privilege), it also gave rise to a public that claimed powers to debate and discuss state policy, and to measure it against a notion of the public good. The public not only provided a pool of manpower to fight wars but was also imaginatively engaged in the wars being fought. Thus, for example, the wars between Britain and France helped manufacture and sustain ideas of a hated 'other', thereby promoting national identities, not just at the level of the elite; indeed, there was a real popular patriotism as well as popular radicalism (Figure VI.7). For their part, monarchs and governments had to accept that public opinion was a limiting factor on dynastic ambition – both in terms of external aggrandizement and as regards internal reforms. For all the attempts to create efficient and centralized states, most governments still relied heavily on voluntary office holders. In another paradox, then, the fiscal-military state often ran alongside a more traditional state in which authority was dispersed and negotiated at the local level.

Second, after the Peace of Westphalia the idea developed that European politics revolved around the notion of a 'BALANCE OF POWER', now involving all the great states of Eastern as well as Western Europe. In this 'great power system', or 'international system' (Scott 2006; Schroeder 1994), equilibrium between states was viewed as fragile. It could be preserved by diplomacy and if necessary by concerted action to reduce the power of any one over-mighty state. Thus in 1761, to give a single example, France and Spain signed a pact against Britain because of the latter's design 'of reigning despotically on all the seas, and . . . of aspiring to a position where no one shall have trade other than that which it pleases the British nation to allow to them' (Williams 1966, 90). Such an approach demonstrated that the dynastic interest of individual states could be inflected by wider considerations of European power equilibrium.

From the 1750s, this balance of power in Europe came under severe strain. Oscillations in the power struggle between England and France caused knock-on effects throughout the Continent. Britain's crushing of France in the Seven Years War meant that there was no western state capable of opposing the partitioning of much of Poland in 1772 between Austria, Prussia and Russia. The defeat of Britain

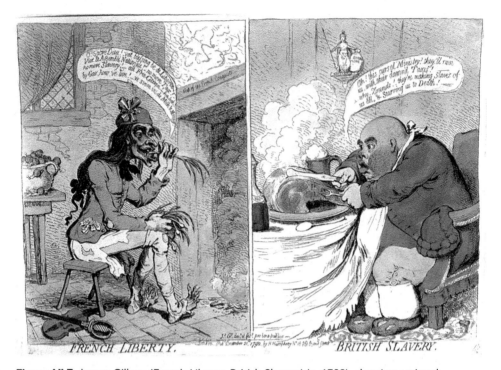

**Figure VI.7** James Gillray, 'French Liberty, British Slavery' (c. 1789), showing national stereotypes, including a well-fed John Bull © The British Library Board. All Rights Reserved / Bridgeman Images.

in the American War of Independence looked as though it would re-establish balance – but the financial burden of the war had been so heavy for France that it went into fiscal meltdown, triggering a political crisis which climaxed in the Revolution of 1789. The Austrians meanwhile had been dragged by Russian alliance into war against the Ottoman Empire, which helped Frederick William II of Prussia to take advantage of a political crisis in the Dutch Republic and establish Prussia's influence there at France's expense. When British Prime Minister William Pitt learnt of the outbreak of Revolution in France, he told his dinner companion that the event was 'highly favourable to us and indicates a long peace with France' (Blanning 2007, 616). France seemed in danger of disqualifying itself as a great power.

## The impact of the French Revolution

The French Revolution ('Epilogue'; Hunt and Censer: Web resources) revolutionized the conduct, reach and significance of European warfare. The changes were dramatic, from the moment that the French National Assembly declared war on Austria in April 1792. At that time, the French standing army numbered fewer than 200,000 men. By 1794 (when the monarchy had been abolished and a republic instituted), over one and a half million men were under arms or working in the military infrastructure. By the end of the decade, France had established something like hegemony in Continental Europe, in the process destroying the balance of power and transforming European politics. The effect was all the more startling, moreover, for being wholly unsuspected. Most statesmen had followed William Pitt in assuming the Revolution would muzzle rather than stimulate French external aggression. Even the French themselves seemed to agree: on 22 May 1790, the National Assembly had renounced wars of conquest.

It was ideological enthusiasm in defence of revolutionary values rather than bureaucratic efficiency which produced the new quantum leap in army size. With war almost at once going fairly disastrously, France was soon conducting a desperate war of national defence against the combined military forces of European states. On 23 August 1793, the National Assembly issued the famous LEVÉE EN MASSE ('mass levy') calling for all French males to be on military standby, summoning hundreds of thousands to the front, and ordering women, and the young and old to engage in helpful activity by gathering saltpetre for gunpowder, making clothes and tents for the army and so on. The decree was tantamount to the introduction of conscription, and offered the first foretaste of modern mass warfare (Box 1).

This mass military call-up formed part of a larger process of political mobilization. In order to get the popular classes – urban workers and the PEASANTRY – to fight, the National Assembly needed to offer something worth fighting for. The JACOBIN faction within the assembly introduced a package of measures – price freezes, land

## Box 1

1. 'From this moment until that in which the enemy shall have been driven from the soil of the Republic, all Frenchmen are in permanent requisition for the service of the armies. The young men shall go to battle; the married men shall forge arms and transport provisions; the women shall make tents and clothing and shall serve in the hospitals; the children shall turn old linen into lint; the aged shall betake themselves to the public places in order to arouse the courage of the warriors and preach the hatred of kings and the unity of the Republic.

2. The national buildings shall be converted into barracks, the public places into workshops for arms, the soil of the cellars shall be washed in order to extract therefrom the saltpetre. . . .

5. The Committee of Public Safety is charged to take all necessary measures to set up without delay an extraordinary manufacture of arms of every sort which corresponds with the ardor and energy of the French people. . . .

7. Nobody can get himself replaced in the service for which he shall have been requisitioned. The public functionaries shall remain at their posts.'

*(The Levée en masse: Decree of the National Assembly,*
*23 August 1793; Web resources)*

sales, welfare schemes, etc. – to boost popular morale. It stimulated soldiers of the Republic into a staunch commitment to the revolutionary values summed up in the famous triad, 'liberty, equality and fraternity', and a determination to root out all traces of the ANCIEN RÉGIME.

Ideology was back on the battlefield, producing a major transformation in the conduct of warfare. Ancien Régime standing armies had fought in a highly drilled and disciplined manner, going through their paces like clockwork soldiers (the metaphor was widely used at the time). The new massed hordes of revolutionary troops had time for neither training nor temporization. Using tactics discussed before 1789 but never tried, they fell on the enemy en masse and in broken order, fighting at close quarters and making speed and enthusiasm compensate for any professional deficiencies. 'Fire, steel [i.e. the bayonet] and patriotism', as the revolutionary general Lazare Hoche put it, was the revolutionary way (Jones 2002, 484).

This new form of mass warfare was designed for export. In November 1792, the Assembly issued a 'Decree of Fraternity', promising aid to all peoples 'wishing to recover their liberty'. The radical Jacobin Maximilien Robespierre counselled against ideologically driven expansion: no one, he stated, likes 'an armed missionary'. He was massively overruled, and French armies set out to spread the Revolutionary message throughout Europe, as a war of national defence transmuted into a war of territorial expansion.

The balance of power seemed like a forgotten dream, as French power and influence extended throughout Europe. In the east, Austria, Prussia and Russia took advantage of international mayhem in the west to complete the partition of Poland in 1793 and 1795. But by the late 1790s the rest of Europe was dominated by France. It had expanded its frontiers in the north to include most of the old Austrian Netherlands (now Belgium), on the east along the Rhine river and in the south-east into the areas of Piedmont and Nice. Land frontiers were ringed with French puppet regimes: the Batavian Republic (aka the Netherlands), the Helvetian Republic and, in northern Italy, the Cisalpine Republic. Sister republics were also established throughout the Italian peninsula as a result of the impressive military campaigns of the young Corsican general Napoleon Bonaparte.

These massive land gains went some way towards compensating for France's collapse as a global power. From 1793, the British Royal Navy bottled up the French Republic, severing its links with the colonies and excluding it from world trade. In the sugar-rich colony of Saint-Domingue (present-day Haiti), slave revolts had weakened French power even before the Royal Navy completed the task. Napoleon's adventurous effort to strike out against British power in the Near East also came to nothing: the Egyptian campaign of 1798 was little short of a fiasco.

The initial phases of French expansion had shown respect for a new principle in international law: self-determination. The former papal enclave at Avignon and the scattered feudal territories of German princes in eastern France were incorporated into France at the wish of their inhabitants and to the fury of their formal owners.

A concern for social justice was also evident in the wish expressed in the opening campaigns to wage 'war on castles, peace towards cottages'. Many of the liberal and egalitarian reforms of the Revolution such as the abolition of FEUDALISM, religious reforms and the introduction of a constitution were introduced into areas brought under French control. They assured the French of some measure of local support wherever they went. Yet as time went on the 'armed missionaries' started to produce local resentment and resistance. The Revolution's religious reforms did not always go down well in Catholic Europe. Furthermore, French occupation or influence tended to lead to plunder and extraction. Some parts of French Europe felt they were being treated like colonial possessions.

Napoleon Bonaparte sprang to the rescue – albeit only by overthrowing the constitutional regime of the Directory (1795–99) and instituting what was effectively personal rule. The period down to 1815 was to see a cynical return to Ancien Régime-style dynastic politics. Napoleon's brilliant adaptation of the military innovations of the Revolution allowed him to create a land empire across the face of Europe. But his grand strategy was ultimately ineffective. The great powers whose spirit of cooperation had been blown away by the speed and scale of French military revival in the early 1790s started to regroup. By 1812, they were on their way towards bringing Napoleon low and returning France to its 1792 frontiers. After 1815, Napoleon ended up in exile in the south Atlantic, but the balance of power had made a lasting return to the world of European politics.

## Discussion themes

1. Why were there so many wars between 1650 and 1815?
2. What was the domestic impact of war in this period?
3. How did European affairs change after the French Revolution?

## Bibliography

### (A) Sources

Grotius, Hugo (1964), *De iure belli ac pacis, libri tres* [1625; *The Law of War and Peace*], trans. Francis W. Kelsey, New York

### (B) Literature

Black, Jeremy (1990), *A Military Revolution? Military Change and European Society, 1500–1800*, London
* Black, Jeremy (2002), *European International Relations, 1648–1815*, London
* Black, Jeremy (2007), *The Pursuit of Glory: Europe, 1648–1815*, London
Blanning, T. C. W. (1996), *The French Revolutionary Wars, 1787–1802*, London

Elliott, John H. (2006), *Empires of the Atlantic World: Britain and Spain in America 1492–1830*, New Haven, Conn.

Glete, Jan (2002), *War and the State in Early Modern Europe: Spain, the Dutch Republic and Sweden as Fiscal-Military States*, London

Israel, Jonathan (1995), *The Dutch Republic: Its Rise, Greatness and Fall 1477–1806*, Oxford

Jones, Colin (2002), *The Great Nation: France from Louis XV to Napoleon, 1715–99*, London

Pincus, Steve (2001), 'From Holy Cause to Economic Interest: The Study of Population and the Invention of the State', in: *A Nation Transformed: England after the Restoration*, A. Houston and S. Pincus (eds), Cambridge, 277–98

Schroeder, Paul (1994), *The Transformation of European Politics 1763–1848*, Oxford

Scott, Hamish M. (2006), *The Birth of a Great Power System, 1740–1815*, London

Williams, Glyndwr (1966), *The Expansion of Europe in the Eighteenth Century: Overseas Rivalry, Discovery and Exploitation*, London

### (C) Web resources

Hunt, Lynn and Censer, Jack, 'Liberty, Equality, Fraternity: Exploring the French Revolution': <http://chnm.gmu.edu/revolution/>

'The *Levée en Masse*, August 23, 1793', IHSP: <http://www.fordham.edu/halsall/mod/1793levee.html>

Lynch, Jack, 'Eighteenth-Century Resources – History': <http://andromeda.rutgers.edu/~jlynch/18th/history.html>

'Peter the Great and the Rise of Russia (1685–1725)', IHSP: <http://www.fordham.edu/halsall/mod/petergreat.html>

# (B) Themes

## Locales

Historians pay increasing attention to the spatial dimensions of political life. Much recent research has focused on specific sites (e.g. princely courts and town halls) or ways in which rituals like coronations and processions turned churches and city streets into distinct political spaces.

In the course of state formation, territorial capitals and royal palaces absorbed growing shares of political exchange, involving both face-to-face encounters and, in ever greater measure, written correspondence with an army of officials. The prestige and attraction of such 'centres' was further enhanced through their expanding cultural, educational and scientific infrastructure. Even in the age of 'ABSOLUTISM', however, localities retained their own political sites and significance. Growing state interference in many walks of life required enforcement in parishes, towns and villages, where traditional forms of self-government were often adapted or instrumentalized rather than suppressed. Centre and periphery, furthermore, interacted through PATRONAGE relations, regional parliaments, provincial bodies and various other means of contact, turning early modern politics into an ongoing process of dialogue and negotiation.

The following two chapters examine the locales and channels of political exchange from princely courts down to village assemblies.

# Courts and centres

*Stéphane van Damme and Janet Dickinson*

## The courtier and the court

Written in a long tradition of advice literature for the aristocracy, Baldesar Castiglione's *Book of the Courtier* was one of the most influential texts of the Italian RENAISSANCE. Translated into virtually every major European language, it became the basic education manual for those who sought to make their way at court (Burke 1995, 61–65). Castiglione's advice, that the COURTIER be aware of and prepared for every opportunity to catch the eye of the ruler, provided a model of instruction not just for the sons of the aristocracy but for the mass of young men, educated in the universities and ACADEMIES of Europe, who aspired to rise up through the court hierarchy to serve their monarch. It also marked out the court as the pre-eminent site of political and cultural power in early modern Europe.

The court had begun to emerge as the location for the entourages of sovereigns in the Middle Ages. At this time the court was not yet a social focus, except on special occasions, and the king's most important subjects were not yet courtiers. Several centuries later, during the Renaissance, the institution of the court had become a central structure within royal power throughout Europe, the focus of attention from all levels of society and a vital point of contact between the government and the localities. Great nobles lived in and around the court, seeking and occupying its great offices. Local elites came to attend on their monarchs, to seek favour and to catch up with the latest fashions. PATRONAGE, a political system of allegiances founded upon pensions, rewards and prerogatives, extended the reach of the court to encompass all levels of government, connecting everyone involved in these complex networks of kinship and clientage back to the court and the monarch. In Rome, the constant flow of petitions to the papal court (the 'curia') forged a vital link between the Pope and those who swore allegiance to him. The weight of demand resulted in the reorganization and expansion of court administration in Rome as elsewhere in Europe.

The court was not just a collection of buildings or a governmental institution but a microcosm of political society, with its own distinctive culture. The sociologist Norbert Elias's work on the 'civilizing' of the nobility in early modern France, first published in 1939, heavily influenced subsequent accounts of the courts of Europe (Elias 2000). Historians have increasingly paid attention to the rituals that shaped life at court, to major events such as funerals, coronations and marriages, as well as to the daily ceremonies of attendance on the monarch's person. The role of women at all social levels has also received attention; the courts of consorts and other key members of the royal family have been revealed as playing important roles in the circulation of patronage and the conduct of politics. Alongside this have come studies of the practicalities of life at court – how the household was fed, clothed and housed, addressing questions of sanitation and simply of physical capacity. As the size of the court increased, so did the task of servicing its needs. Alongside the growth of court personnel came the physical expansion of the court itself, sometimes as an ad hoc set of additions to existing houses and palaces, sometimes as a result of grand building schemes. Around these developed gardens and spaces for the leisure activities of the court. Plays and costly entertainments were staged to amuse the court but also as a way of advising the monarch along the paths of virtue.

## The making of the court: an overview 1500–1800

It is difficult to generalize about the nature of European courts in the early modern period (Adamson 1999). Court culture reflected the personal tastes of monarchs and their subjects, and the economic and territorial limitations of the ruler's power determined the court's size and personnel. But although the structure, function and composition of Europe's royal courts evolved in various ways during the sixteenth and seventeenth centuries, they shared certain features. In most cases, the monarch, who had been itinerant in the past, settled in a principal residence. This residence attracted the nobility, who came to attend in increasingly assiduous fashion, before ultimately settling inside the palace itself or at the very least nearby. It brought together a diverse community composed of the royal family and princes of the blood, along with the great officers of the crown, some drawn from the ranks of the aristocracy, others from the rising order of university-educated bureaucrats and administrators. This courtly society and its mores set the tone for culture, manners and noble conduct, conforming to the vision that it held of itself.

In Spain, Philip II made an important contribution to the development of the court when he chose Madrid as his capital and primary residence in 1561. He remodelled the Alcázar by assigning particular importance to its official apartments, in marked contrast to the Spanish tradition of treating the palace as an annexe of a monastery, and extending his authority over a growing bureaucracy as well as the royal residences. During his reign, numerous courtiers settled in Madrid, which experienced urban expansion as a result. Architecture, decorative arts and cultural activities reached a great apogee thanks to the considerable sums invested in them, at a time when the Spanish Empire had entered its decline. Philip's grandson, Philip IV, built the Buen Retiro palace. By doing so, he provoked the emergence of an opposition: the court became in its eyes the symbol of ostentatious extravagance and the neglect of important realities rather than the site of glory and power. Upon Charles II's accession to the throne in 1665, the Spanish court regained its monastic atmosphere (characterized by an austere etiquette). This tradition was maintained by his successor, the Bourbon Philip V, Louis XIV's grandson, and likewise by the eighteenth-century monarch Ferdinand VI.

In England, the court declined in importance when parliament took control of government. The Glorious Revolution of 1688 marked a decisive shift of political power away from the court. The legislative concessions of William III and his successors reduced the court to a simple entourage which directly served the personal needs of the monarch. Notwithstanding the splendour of William III's rebuilt Hampton Court and the monarch's continued sway in parliament, the political significance of the Hanoverians of the eighteenth century did not approach that of the Continental European dynasties (Newton 2000).

## Spaces of the court

The establishment of the physical space of the royal court as a reflection of the power and 'magnificence' of the monarch was vitally important. In China the Yonge Emperor built the Forbidden City in 1406–20 on a scale that ensured that imperial power was focused there for the next 500 years. Other rulers sought to ensure their dynasty's longevity in similar terms. Safavid Shah Abbas I established 'a showcase of royalty and permanence' at Isfahan in Persia (Duindam 2016, 160). In England, the first Tudor monarch, Henry VII, consolidated his grasp on power by embarking on a series of building projects, spending the vast sum of over £600 a month on his new palace at Richmond. Completed in 1501, it cost well over £20,000; his subjects referred to it as 'Rich Mount'. Henry VIII was still more extravagant, drawing on funds raised from the dissolution of the monasteries to purchase and renovate a series of royal houses (Thurley 1993). By the time of his death in 1547, he owned fifty houses. The palace at Whitehall in London was one of the most significant, the seat of government until it was destroyed by fire in 1698. A sprawling complex of over 1,000 rooms, Whitehall was the only royal residence able to house the ever-expanding court, but it was not its permanent home. During the summer, the court was driven out by the sporadic outbreaks of plague that continued to hit London and by the demands of basic sanitation, the need for residences to be aired and cleaned before the vast entourage of retainers, servants and officials could return. Elizabeth I's progresses around the houses of her nobility were increasingly notorious for the demands she made on their hospitality. In 1601, learning of the queen's imminent arrival, the Earl of Lincoln fled his home in Chelsea and left the gates barred against the royal party (Cole 1999, 92–93).

While the Tudors largely resided in the vicinity of London, and Philip II of Spain built the Escurial alongside the Alcázar, the Valois court remained nomadic. The kings of France were accustomed to criss-crossing their kingdom, and this relationship with their subjects was essential for maintaining their authority. As the sixteenth century progressed, however, two practices alternated: Henry II and Henry III's courts were SEDENTARY whereas Charles IX, accompanied by his mother Catherine de Médicis, undertook between 1564 and 1566 a grand tour that logged 900 leagues (around 4,000 km) in 27 months, and involved over one hundred entries in the kingdom's cities. The itinerant nature of the court was a carefully orchestrated and prepared political act. It made it possible to establish a personal dialogue between sovereign and subjects, as well as to restore the pre-eminence of royal power during periods of trouble. In a well-regulated ritual, the king had to be seen within cities and towns as well as along the frontiers. The court was thus transformed into an immense caravan, transporting furniture, tapestries and china. The Renaissance court also travelled along the banks of the Loire, between royal residences – Amboise, Blois, Chambord, Chenonceau – as well as undertaking trips within Paris and its surroundings.

Eventually the king settled at Versailles. Beginning in 1673, his stays lengthened in time and – around the garden in which sumptuous festivals had been organized in 1664 – a veritable city began to emerge. The château was designed by the architect Jules Hardouin-Mansart in 1679–89: he assigned courtiers to the great and small stables and state servants to the wings. Some 3,000 people (out of the total of 10,000 who made up the court) were housed there. Most inhabited two-room apartments without kitchens, enduring crammed, dirty, uncomfortable conditions. Right up to the end of the ANCIEN RÉGIME, facilities (like the new opera house in 1770) continued to be added and helped to maintain international attention on Versailles (Newton 2000).

## Court ceremonial

The court was also a space where the iconography of monarchy was displayed and developed, where the monarchs could be presented to their subjects and to foreign visitors who faithfully documented every detail of the richly decorated chambers they processed through on their way to be received, establishing the monarch's magnificence and international reputation. At Whitehall in the 1630s, Charles I commissioned Peter Paul Rubens to paint a series of works glorifying his father's reign for the ceiling of the Banqueting House (Figure VI.8). Charles was later to pass under the image on the way to his execution in 1649.

Every aspect of life at court provided an occasion for the display of the monarch's magnificence. The seventeenth-century Spanish court was amongst many influenced by the example of the late medieval courts of the Dukes of Burgundy, in which every public action of the monarch was conducted according to an elaborate set of guide-lines, solemnly observed by members of the court. In France, the social rituals that shaped the life of the court, such as the *lever du roi*, contributed to the stratification of the royal entourage. Norbert Elias's work on the 'civilizing of courtly society' suggests that by the sixteenth century French monarchs used the court as an instrument to control the nobility, to pull it away from feudal tensions which had been so strong in France during the fifteenth century. Kings encouraged princes from the most

Figure VI.8 In an embodiment of the Stuarts' belief in the 'divine right' of kings, James I (holding a sceptre and with his foot on an imperial sphere) is lifted aloft by 'Justice'. Detail, from Peter Paul Rubens, 'The Whitehall Ceiling: The Apotheosis of James I' (c. 1630–35). © Banqueting House, Whitehall, London/Bridgeman Images.

'The Duchesse de Bourgogne's ladies, who are called ladies of the Palace, tried to arrogate the rank and take the place of [the ladies of the Duchess of Orleans] everywhere. Such a thing was never done [before]. They got the King's Guards to keep their places and push back the chairs belonging to my ladies. I complained first of all to the Duc de Noailles, who replied that it was the King's order. Then I went immediately to the King and said to him, "May I ask your Majesty if it is by your orders that my ladies have now no place or rank as they used to have? If it is your desire, I have nothing more to say, because I only wish to obey you, but your Majesty knows that formerly . . . the ladies of the Palace had no rank. . . ." The King became quite red, and replied, "I have given no such order, who said that I had?" . . . These women are becoming far too insolent now that they are in favour, and they imagined that I would not have the courage to report the matter to the King. But I shall not lose my rank nor prerogatives on account of the favour they enjoy. The King is too just for that.'

*(Duchess of Orléans 1704; Web resources)*

This extract from a letter by the Duchess of Orléans in 1704 highlights the enormous significance of rank and precedence at the court of Versailles.

powerful lineages to join their entourages, where they found many advantages in the form of offices, gifts and pensions which they in turn redistributed to their protégés. To be a courtier became a form of work which consisted in participation in monarchical rituals and benefiting from the privileges accorded by the king, distinguishing those who were authorized to enter the king's chamber or dine with him. Under Louis XV, this code was reinforced with the so-called 'Honours of the Court' of 1759 which restricted these privileges to candidates of proven nobility (Box 2).

Elias's interpretation of the domestication of the nobility does, however, remain a limited model of analysis. Only 5 per cent of nobles consented to live at Versailles, despite the fact that to ignore the court was a cause for suspicion under Louis XIV. Moreover, Elias's model of an oppressive monarchy and submissive aristocracy has been criticized and modified (Asch and Birke 1991, 3; Duindam 1995). Increasingly, the ritual life of the court has been read as a dialogue between the monarch and his or her subjects through which the latter could approach and advise their ruler at the same time as seeking favour and advancement. This has contributed to a deeper understanding of the relationship between the monarch and the nobility as being one characterized by shared interests and cooperation rather than conflict.

The exception to the increasingly formalized ceremonial seen at courts throughout Europe was that of Peter the Great at St Petersburg in Russia. In the 1720s, the French ambassador Jacques de Campredon 'noted the "informality" of the Russian court in comparison with others of his acquaintance'. Instead, Peter's taste for burlesque theatricality was reflected in bawdy parodies of court life, such as the parallel weddings of Peter's niece, Anna Ioannovna, to the Duke of Courland, and the royal dwarf Iakim Volkov's, where around seventy dwarfs were gathered to attend the service, 'accompanied by the stifled giggles of the congregation and the priest, and with the tsar himself holding the wedding crown over the head of the dwarf bride' (Lindsey Hughes in Adamson 1999, 312).

## Cultural patronage

Courts were also important and influential cultural centres. The Italian Renaissance was fostered by the artistic patronage of the rulers of a multiplicity of city-states and principalities. Castiglione's *Courtier* celebrated the cultural refinement of the court of Urbino, the birthplace of his friend, the artist Raphael, subsequently invited to work in Rome by Pope Julius II. Far into the early modern period, the papal court set the style for much of Europe with its artistic, musical and architectural patronage ('Arts and society' in Part V).

Artists, writers, scholars and craftsmen all looked to the court for patronage, turning it into a permanent workshop for artistic creation. Palaces throughout Europe attracted poets, musicians and men of letters as well as scientists. At the court of the Grand Duchy of Florence the naturalist Francesco Redi (1626–97) was the official physician of the Tuscan dukes Ferdinand II and Leopold. While he supervised the Grand Duke's pharmacy, Redi's most important laboratory was the court itself; his place at court gave him direct access to scientific specimens of inestimable rarity in the form of diplomatic gifts, hunting game and presents from renowned naturalists. By defining the court as an experimental space, Redi created a laboratory in perpetual movement, his position as a physician causing him to follow the court wherever it moved, his subjects of interest and research changing to reflect the court's wanderings. Stays in Pisa and Livorno provided him with the opportunity to observe marine life and even to dissect a shark (Findlen 1993). Courts accumulated paintings and objects of scientific curiosity (like instruments or specimens) and royal patronage led to the creation of academies, sometimes – as in London and Paris – preceded by informal meetings of learned circles. The Accademia dei Lincei flourished in Rome in the seventeenth century, as did the Accademia del Cimento, both of which pioneered experimental science ('The scientific revolution' in Part V).

Scientific patronage attracted growing princely interest and investment. By the eighteenth century, however, rulers tended to be figureheads rather than active scholars or academic arbitrators, as some of their predecessors had been (Box 3). New centres of power had emerged, in some cases initiated by royal patronage but becoming increasingly independent. New kinds of power were also developing along with the expansion of markets and global trade. Across Europe, stock exchanges were founded, following early examples in the Netherlands.

Monarchs and leading courtiers supported institutions of learning other than academies. The new Prussian Pietist University of Halle was founded in 1693 and the Hanoverian University of Göttingen in 1737. In Paris, where a university had existed since the twelfth century, royal patronage was at the origins of the Collège Royal (1530), while Cardinal Mazarin initiated the Collège des Quatre Nations (1660s). Further facilities like royal observatories (Paris 1668, Greenwich 1675, Berlin 1708) and botanical gardens (Paris 1635, Kew 1759) followed in the wake of the scientific revolution. In the eighteenth century, many learned societies – Bologna (1714), St Petersburg (1724), Stockholm (1739), Barcelona (1764) and Edinburgh (1783), to name just a few – obtained official state recognition (De Ridder-Symoens 1996).

## Assessment: the court in crisis

In seventeenth-century France, the court of Louis XIV competed with a burgeoning number of sites of aristocratic sociability in Paris as well as the entourages of princes of the blood. The development of private *hôtels particuliers*, princely residences like the Palais-Royal and fashionable venues like SALONS altered the court's role. The city competed with the court: Versailles's loss of influence reflected the capital's growing cultural prestige. As one contemporary observed: 'what else is Versailles . . . but a great servants' hall, with no topic of conversation but the master?' (Mercier 1999, 165).

In the eighteenth century, if the institution was not truly in decline, it was nonetheless increasingly questioned. Louis XV preferred less formality and enjoyed retreats to his châteaux in Choisy, Crécy and La Muette. While protocol was maintained, court etiquette increasingly bored its participants. Life at Versailles emerged as a subject of derision in numerous pamphlets published in the decades preceding the French Revolution. The negative image of royal mistresses like Madame Pompadour and queens like Marie-Antoinette fed a wave of critical and even pornographic literature.

Some royal courts, as in England and Spain, continued to exert political as well as cultural and social power and influence, monarchs adapting to new models of government and emerging notions of national identity. In late eighteenth-century Vienna, Emperor Joseph II abolished court etiquette, shut down the great palace of Schönbrunn (Figure VI.9), the 'Austrian Versailles', and moved into a small, unostentatious house in the Augarten, working there as a 'public servant' until his death in 1790 (Blanning 2002, 430–31; 'Enlightenment' in Part V). Over time, therefore, the court returned to something like its original function as the home of the monarch and his or her household.

**Figure VI.9** After the first plan for a magnificent new castle in Vienna, designed by the architect Johann Bernhard Fischer von Erlach in the 1690s, had been rejected on grounds of cost, a somewhat less ambitious – but still imposing – version was completed in 1713. This painting shows its courtyard as a hub for numerous activities. Schloss Schonbrunn, 1759–60 (oil on canvas), Bellotto, Bernardo (1720–80) / Kunsthistorisches Museum, Vienna, Austria / Bridgeman Images.

## Discussion themes

1. How important were courts as 'a point of contact' between rulers and ruled in the early modern period?
2. Did courts still hold power by 1800?
3. Was the culture of early modern courts more concerned with the pursuit of leisure or the exercise of power?

## Bibliography

### (A) Sources

Mercier, Louis-Sébastien (1999), *Panorama of Paris: Selections from* Le Tableau de Paris [1781–88], ed. Helen Simpson and Jeremy D. Popkin, University Park, Pa.

### (B) Literature

* Adamson, John ed. (1999), *The Princely Courts of Europe: Ritual, Politics and Culture Under the Ancien Régime 1500–1750*, London
Asch, Ronald and Birke, Adolf eds (1991), *Princes, Patronages and the Nobility: The Court at the Beginning of the Modern Age, c. 1450–1650*, Oxford

Blanning, T. C. W. (2002), *The Culture of Power and the Power of Culture: Old Regime Europe 1660–1789*, Oxford

Burke, Peter (1995), *The Fortunes of the Courtier: The European Reception of Castiglione's Cortegiano*, Oxford

Cole, Mary Hill (1999), *The Portable Queen: Elizabeth I and the Politics of Ceremony*, Amherst, Mass.

De Ridder-Symoens, H. ed. (1996), *Universities in Early Modern Europe (1500–1800)*, Cambridge

Duindam, Jeroen (1995), *Myths of Power: Norbert Elias and the Early Modern European Court*, Amsterdam

Duindam, Jeroen (2016), *Dynasties: A Global History of Power, 1300–1800*, Cambridge

Elias, Norbert (2000), *The Civilizing Process*, trans. Edmund Jephcott, ed. E. Dunning, G. Goudsblom and S. Mennell, Oxford

Findlen, Paula (1993), 'Controlling the Experiment: Rhetoric, Court Patronage, and the Experimental Method of Francesco Redi (1626–1697)', *History of Science*, 31, 35–64

Newton, William Ritchey (2000), *L'Espace du roi. La Cour de France au château de Versailles, 1682–1789*, Paris

Thurley, Simon (1993), *The Royal Palaces of Tudor England: Architecture and Court Life 1460–1547*, London

### (C) Web resources

Castiglione, Baldesar (1528), *The Book of the Courtier*, trans. Sir Thomas Hoby  (1561): 'Renascence Editions' <http://www.luminarium.org/renascence-editions/courtier/courtier1.html>

Duchess of Orléans, 'Letter' (1704), IHSP: <http://www.fordham.edu/halsall/mod/1704duchess.html>

# Centre and periphery

*Steve Hindle and Beat Kümin*

For a long time, the study of government focused on institutions such as princely courts and COUNCILS in central locations. During the latter half of the twentieth century, however, first social historians and subsequently practitioners of the 'new' political history began to examine power relations in much greater geographical range and social depth, revealing numerous, often overlapping, layers of government as well as chains of command and communication reaching from the privy chambers of imperial palaces to the vestries of rural communities (Te Brake 1998). Most surviving records concern the agency of men, but avenues of female influence can also be detected ('Gender and family' in Part II).

To be sure, European states at the beginning of our period were far from uniform in their degree of centralization or even of territorial integration. Some kingdoms, such as England, were relatively homogeneous, sharing an ancient legal system based on common law and a vernacular literature in which the English language was becoming increasingly standardized. Even here, however, the endemic political instability of the fifteenth century suggests that monarchy was neither strong nor stable. Other polities, such as the Holy Roman Empire or the kingdom of France, were highly regionalized, lacking the legal or linguistic integration which characterized England. The typical situation, however, was the kind of 'composite monarchy' pushed to extremes by Spain, which by the sixteenth century consisted of Castile, Aragon, the kingdom of Naples, the Spanish Netherlands, New World territories and (at least temporarily) Portugal (Elliott 1992). The highly fragmented political geography which Spanish rulers called 'these kingdoms of Spain' was, accordingly, writ large across most of the Continent.

From this uneven and generally low starting point, a process of TERRITORIAL-IZATION began to emerge from the mid-fifteenth century. This was spurred in part by the socio-economic pressures associated with population growth, social differentiation and rising levels of poverty; and in part by the confessional strife concomitant on the Reformation. Concern over social stability and political loyalty prompted more frequent central interventions into the localities. As a result, the two original purposes which characterized medieval polities – military defence and the rule of law – were increasingly complemented by a third priority – the advancement of the common weal through 'good police' ('The theory and practice of politics and government 1500–1800' in Part VI).

The concentration of power in one (princely) hand was ideologically justified by political thinkers like Jean Bodin in France and Thomas Hobbes in England. Hobbes in particular argued that in order to avoid a perennial and highly destructive clash of self-interests, subjects should transfer the power they hold under 'natural law' to a sovereign power (a 'mortal God') who could in turn guarantee security and peace. This conceptualization of the need to vest absolute power in a ruler was not, however, uncontested (Gingell *et al.* 1999). Spearheaded by Theodor Beza, Calvin's successor at Geneva, the so-called 'monarchomachs' developed a theory in which intermediate authorities enjoyed a right of resistance against those princes who behaved tyrannically, especially by pressurizing religious minorities to abandon their beliefs (Box 1). In the context of the English Revolution of the mid-seventeenth century, furthermore, the LEVELLER movement advocated not only popular sovereignty and a householder franchise, but also a fully-fledged programme of decentralization ('Introduction' in Part I; 'Revolution' in Part VI).

All political systems depend on the existence of chains of command through which centre and periphery can communicate. Early modern central institutions – once regarded as self-contained decision-making organs – now appear as 'points of contact' through which PATRONAGE, policy and power could be transacted. In the case of Tudor England, these included the king's court, the Privy Council and parliament (Elton 1974–76) as well as the Lord Lieutenancy (created in the mid-sixteenth century) and the itinerant judiciary (which played an increasingly important role in articulating royal policy in the localities by the reign of Elizabeth).

In charting the dynamic relationship between 'centres' – understood here as the main seats of government and learning – and 'periphery' in early modern Europe, this

## Box 1

'[If] the king should . . . send his lieutenants to compel us to become idolaters, and if he commands us to drive God and his service from amongst us; shall we not rather shut our gates against the king and his officers, than drive out of our town the Lord, which is King of Kings? Let the . . . magistrates and governors of the people of God dwelling in the towns, consider with themselves that they have contracted two covenants, and taken two oaths: The first and most ancient with God, to whom the people have sworn to be his people: The second and next following with the king, to whom the people hath promised obedience, as unto him which is the governor and conductor of the people of God.'

*(Du Plessis-Mornay 1579 in Web resources)*

In his *Vindiciae contra tyrannos* (French original 1579), the anonymous author – perhaps the Huguenot Philippe Du Plessis-Mornay – entrusts magistrates with a right of resistance against religious tyrants and, in other passages, against rulers endangering the commonwealth more generally.

chapter first describes the basic units of local government; proceeds to analyse the significance of regional and representative institutions; and then examines informal channels of political exchange which helped to hold polities together.

## Local government

For many if not most people on the periphery, of course, central institutions (as just defined) could appear remote and the village or town of residence formed the centre of their universe. Traditional institutions of local government varied remarkably in size and shape but certain parameters can be determined. Throughout Europe the nobility as a landowning class exercised political authority in their MANORS. A noble ESTATE might be under direct seigneurial control, or authority might be delegated to a steward, but either way there was almost invariably scope for some degree of popular participation, with leading tenants often enjoying the traditional right to sit on juries judging agricultural and other offences. Despite the waning of the military power of the aristocracy in many parts of Europe, the nobility continued to play a vital part in the power structure of most monarchies. Indeed, manorial and DEMESNE organization remained dominant in many regions, especially east of the river Elbe in territories like Brandenburg-Prussia or Muscovy (Hagen 2002). Poland-Lithuania, which lay between them, was a vast but unstable 'mixed' polity dominated by members of the SZLACHTA and effectively run as a noble republic, with rulers elected by an aristocratic elite, subject to binding agreements and faced with strong anti-monarchical identities in cities like Danzig (Friedrich 2000). Even in England's comparatively 'advanced' socio-political system, Georgian landowners regarded themselves as lords of the earth just as their forefathers had done. As long as both sides fulfilled their respective duties, the relationship between nobles and tenants was characterized by the mutual exchange of paternalism and deference ('Popular culture(s)' in Part V).

On the level of local communities, the extent of popular participation varied according to contextual factors like the strength of external authorities or the number and status of members. In the principal units of towns, villages and parishes ('Urban society' / 'Rural society' in Part II; 'Church and people at the close of the Middle Ages' in Part III; Kümin 2013), typical responsibilities included the supervision of economic affairs, public works (such as the building of churches or the maintenance of roads), poor relief and jurisdiction over petty offences. All of these required 'political' activities like regulation, the setting of priorities and the raising of funds. Local constitutions were based on a number of widely accepted principles: the equality of rights between all householders (usually married males); collective, if at all possible consensual, decision-making; the (often) annual election of accountable officials (councillors, churchwardens, etc.); high regard for custom and the priority of the 'common good' of the whole over the self-interests of individuals or particular groups (Figure VI.10). Ideally, these components (hallmarks of 'communalism' as conceptualized in Blickle 1998) gave rise to a participatory and highly sophisticated political

**Figure VI.10** Councillors dressed in official robes and accompanied by beadles leave the town hall, a representative building featuring the city crest (above the main door) as well as a shaming platform for offenders (centre right). As an Imperial Free City, Augsburg enjoyed a very high degree of local autonomy. 'December', painting after Jörg Breu d. Ä. (Augsburg, c. 1530): Deutsches Historisches Museum, Berlin, Germany / © DHM / Bridgeman Images.

culture in which written records gradually supplemented the traditional forms of face-to-face communication (Schlögl 2014). Arrangements of this kind were, however, vulnerable to inner frictions, oligarchization and the exclusion of growing sections of the local population. Many communities thus experienced periods of intense political conflict, sometimes even violent risings.

Many of the emerging early modern states gradually appropriated these local institutions to their own ends, either by dispensing patronage to those men who might exert influence on local politics or by incorporating local offices into the developing state structure. This process was relatively straightforward in the small-to-medium sovereign units of northern Italy, the south-west of the Holy Roman Empire and the Dutch Republic. In England, the Tudors effectively carried out a revolution in local government with minimal institutional reform: the existing network of ecclesiastical parishes was adapted for secular administrative purposes, and unpaid gentlemen magistrates were entrusted with supervisory duties at the county level (Hindle 2000). At the other extreme of the spectrum, Spanish kings established viceroys and regional councils to run the various parts of their empire, while leaving existing constitutional and institutional structures largely intact. Other polities attempted something in between these divergent strategies. French monarchs, for example, met their vast financial needs partly through the sale of heritable offices and supplemented existing regional structures with central officials (INTENDANTS) who were recruited from other parts of the country and directly dependent on the king.

In most of Europe, regardless of size and regime, there were clear trends towards the professionalization and bureaucratization of local government, especially through legally trained officials. This in turn reflects the broadening of university curricula (beyond arts and theology into law and 'good police') and the increasing rates of higher education among a governing elite influenced by Ciceronian civic HUMANISM, stipulating that a man was born not for himself or his kindred but for his country ('The Renaissance' in Part V; 'Courts and centres' in Part VI).

## Regional and representative institutions

At the regional level, there was very significant variation in institutional arrangements *within* individual territories. In the English case, distinct patterns of policy and personnel reflected differences between the south-eastern lowlands (where the royal writ ran directly), the midland and northern counties (with their strong legacy of semi-autonomous dukedoms and palatinates) and the periphery of the marches (where royal authority was weakest and local magnate power paramount). Most early modern states, moreover, had administrative divisions like provinces, districts or counties. These were defined by geographical, linguistic or political criteria and often featured their own law courts (like the French regional *parlements*) and administrative institutions.

A striking feature of the early modern political landscape is the large number of 'representative' assemblies ('Europe in 1500' in Part I). These parliaments, estates or

### Box 2

'Thus we have ordered and agreed to uphold that in future no secular or religious clergyman shall cite another priest or layman before an ecclesiastical court, nor to have them excommunicated, neither for matters of debt, defamation, nor any dispute. . . .'

'The form of our government is democratic: and the election and deposition of the magistrates, all kinds of officers, judges and commanders, both in our free and ruling lands and in those which are subject to us, belongs to our common man; he . has the power, according to his majorities, to create [and depose] them, to establish alliances with foreign princes and estates, to [decide] questions of war and peace, and to deliberate about all other matters pertaining to the high and lesser magistrates.'

*(Extracts from a 1524 ordinance and an early 17th century pamphlet in the Grisons; Blickle 1998, 91, 114–15)*

DIETS were advisory bodies composed of delegates from the principal social groups, typically the nobility, the clergy and the third estate (townsmen or PEASANTS), and were usually summoned by monarchs at times of financial or other crises (Graves 2001). The spectrum ranges from territorial and provincial diets, like the Brandenburg estates (*Landstände*), to assemblies representing entire kingdoms or empires, like the Swedish *Riksdag* (where, unusually, the peasants had their own chamber) and the English parliament (Stjernquist 1989; *Journals* 1547). Knowing that princes depended on their tax grants, assemblies exercised political leverage through GRAVAMINA formulated at the outset of a session, some of which then prompted central legislation and/or executive measures (Kümin and Würgler 1997). A particularly coherent and exceptionally powerful pyramid of such bodies existed in the republican territory of the Grisons, a federation of three Leagues in the Alps, where a largely peasant (male) population enjoyed representation on three levels: the local village council, regional league and federal assembly. In 1524 and 1526, the latter passed articles which effectively ended the secular rule of the local bishop and established a thoroughly communal form of government, in matters of both Church and state (Box 2; Head 1995).

Few assemblies could go as far as this. Indeed few acquired the right to sit regularly (even the English parliament only did so in 1694), but most managed to influence the political agenda and to moderate their princes' fiscal demands. By the end of our period, some – most famously the French *états généraux* in 1789 – actually managed to establish new political constitutions (Figure VI.11).

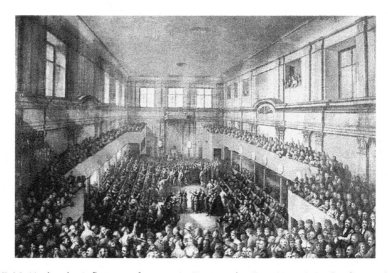

**Figure VI.11** Under the influence of events in France, the Four-Year Sejm (parliament) of 1788–92, seen here meeting at Warsaw's Royal Castle, adopted a new, reformist – if short-lived – constitution for the Commonwealth of Poland-Lithuania. Kazimierz Wojniakowski, 'The Vote upon the Constitution' (oil on canvas, 1806). © National Museum, Warsaw.

## Informal interaction

It would, however, be a mistake to emphasize the institutional arrangements in which political communication was embedded to the exclusion of the continuing and developing tradition of informal interaction. Early modern polities lacked the infra-structural reach of modern rational bureaucratic states, and their classes of salaried office holders were tiny by twenty-first-century standards. Most of those who held (usually unpaid) local office had obligations not only to their sovereign but also to their neighbours and kinsmen. In this sense, early modern states were only partially differentiated from the societies over which they exercised authority. Rulers therefore had to adopt a range of techniques through which they could encourage or enhance cooperation among their subjects. Consent could not usually be commanded, it had to be negotiated (Blockmans *et al.* 2009).

One of the most obvious strategies of negotiation was symbolic representation. Medieval kings and their courts had usually been PERIPATETIC; and although early modern monarchs often went on royal progress to show themselves to, and hear the grievances of, their people, they had to find other ways to mark their presence to a populace which might otherwise have been oblivious to their image, personality or policies. Charles V, for example, commissioned chronicles, portraits and coinage to disseminate his image to his subjects. The Tudors developed a wide-ranging strategy of propaganda, encouraging not only the purchase by the gentry of portraits of individual monarchs (especially of Elizabeth I) but also the painting of the royal arms on the whitewashed walls of post-Reformation parish churches.

Symbolic representation was, however, only the first stage in a process of 'presencing' royal authority in the localities. That was most easily (if sometimes expensively) achieved by spending the currency of patronage, especially the granting of office, gifts and favours to individuals on whose service and loyalty a ruler felt he could count. Patronage was most usefully dispensed to those brokers (officials, professionals, clergy, even publicans) who might effectively link more powerful individuals with their potential clients in localities, thereby creating a 'pyramid' stretching from the monarch's bedchamber to the peasant's kitchen. The widespread culture of gift-giving testifies to the strength, endurance and significance of reciprocal relations all across early modern society (Kettering 2002).

Such contacts were facilitated by improvements in communication infrastructure. From the RENAISSANCE onwards, scholars developed a 'republic of letters' based on an increasingly intricate correspondence network stretching well beyond the great centres. In the period 1723–77, for example, the Swiss doctor, poet and statesman Albrecht von Haller exchanged some 17,000 letters with no fewer than 1,200 correspondents all over Europe (Web resources). By this point, Europeans benefited from regular postal services (introduced for letters from the sixteenth century and for passengers from the late seventeenth century) which widened spatial horizons and made long-distance journeys more feasible, reliable and secure (Beyrer 2006). At the same time, numerous European states embarked on major road-building programmes, providing wider and more comfortable *chaussées* for traders, travellers – including early 'tourists' – and their own officials. The tyranny of distance was gradually being overcome.

Local developments also enhanced awareness of central (and political) affairs. There were few, if any, ACADEMIES, SALONS and COFFEE HOUSES in the provinces, but ever more uses for different forms of writing and by the end of the eighteenth century over half of adult males in North-western Europe could sign their names and still more could read a simple text ('Popular culture(s)' in Part V). Although the concept of an early modern 'educational revolution' is exaggerated, the Reformation-related emphasis on the ability to read the Scriptures, the rising demand for skilled administrators and the development of more sophisticated mechanisms for economic exchange certainly provided stimuli for learning (Stone 1965). In some, particularly Protestant, areas, the number of elementary schools increased substantially. Over a hundred educational ordinances had been issued in reformed territories of Germany by 1600 and, in the Duchy of Württemberg alone, the number of schools rose from 89 in 1520 to over four hundred by the end of the century (Strauss 1978). There was clearly a growing market for books and pamphlets: the 'popular' French *bibliothèque bleue* series, for example, reached circulation figures of over one million copies per year in the early eighteenth century (Andriès 1989; 'From pen to print' in Part V). Even in remote villages, the parsonage turned into something of a cultural centre, welcoming distinguished visitors, organizing concerts and building up sizeable libraries. By the end of the ANCIEN RÉGIME, furthermore, provincial (Western) Europe participated in the expanding associational culture of educational, charitable and leisure societies typically based in urban inns. To this extent, 'ingenious and learned men' were emphatically not confined to courts and centres ('Enlightenment: England and France' in Part V).

Humble people occasionally approached the highest authorities directly. Some secured personal audiences with eminent figures like Cardinal Wolsey at Whitehall or Louis XIV at Versailles. In a famous episode of 1779, a miller named Christian Arnold from Pommerzig repeatedly petitioned Frederick II ('the Great') of Brandenburg-Prussia to intervene in a lawsuit he had lost at successive levels of the jurisdictional hierarchy. Nobody believed his assertions that a gentleman had deprived him of his livelihood by diverting crucial water supplies. Fearing a miscarriage of justice in his name (and impressions of class-justice), the monarch quashed the highest verdict, imprisoned the judges and ordered compensation to be paid to Mr Arnold (Schulze 1996, 79). Petitioning became a ubiquitous strategy at all levels, be it to gain redress, seek a favour or alert officials to pressing problems. It could in turn shade into litigation, as subordinates sought to mobilize their rights at law, often contesting the arbitrary claims of the rich and powerful in the process. Underlying petitioning and litigation was the implied threat of direct action, culminating eventually in riot or even insurrection. Most rebels, after all, articulated their grievances first in 'loyal' petitions. In a very real sense, therefore, riot was a continuation of petitioning by other means ('Riot and rebellion' in Part VI).

## Assessment

Most Europeans enjoyed considerable political influence in their towns, villages and parishes. Although territorialization strengthened rulers from the fifteenth century, it would be too simplistic to describe this process as centralization. Indeed, state formation is perhaps best understood as increased interaction between centre and periphery, and in some respects it was stimulated by initiatives, petitions and protest 'from below'. Growing state authority could be a resource as well as a threat, allowing for a juridification of conflicts previously settled by violent means and an environment more conducive to supra-regional exchange. To be sure, these processes were neither uniform nor unproblematic. Both the Swiss cantons and the Dutch provinces successfully guarded their autonomy throughout the period, while the 'British problem', which paralysed three kingdoms in the mid-1600s, provides an example of extreme tensions between centre and periphery. By the eve of the French Revolution monarchs and central institutions were certainly more powerful than they had been at the close of the Middle Ages, but local political agency had by no means disappeared.

## Discussion themes

1. Which bonds linked monarchs to their subjects in early modern Europe?
2. Was the relationship between centre and periphery one of cooperation or of conflict?
3. Who governed the polities of early modern Europe?

## Bibliography

### (A) Sources

Gingell, John, Little, Adrian and Winch, Christopher eds (1999), *Modern Political Thought: A Reader*, London
*Journals of the House of Commons* (1547–), London


### (B) Literature

Andriès, Liese (1989), *La Bibliothèque bleue au dix-huitième siècle: Une tradition éditoriale*, Oxford
Beyrer, Klaus (2006), 'The Mail-Coach Revolution', *German History*, 24, 375–86
Blickle, Peter (1998), *From the Communal Reformation to the Revolution of the Common Man*, Leiden

Blockmans, Wim, Holenstein, André and Mathieu, Jon eds (2009), *Empowering Interactions: Political Cultures and the Emergence of the State in Europe 1300–1900*, Aldershot

Elliott, John H. (1992), 'A Europe of Composite Monarchies', *P&P*, 137, 48–71

Elton, G. R. (1974–76), 'Presidential Address: Tudor Government. The Points of Contact: I. Parliament / II. The Council / III. The Court', *Transactions of the Royal Historical Society*, 5th Series, 24, 183–200; 25, 195–212; 26, 211–28

Friedrich, Karin (2000), *The Other Prussia: Royal Prussia, Poland and Liberty 1569–1772*, Cambridge

* Graves, Michael (2001), *The Parliaments of Early Modern Europe*, London

Hagen, William (2002), *Ordinary Prussians: Brandenburg Junkers and Villagers 1500–1840*, Cambridge

Head, Randolph (1995), *Early Modern Democracy in the Grisons: Social Order and Political Language in a Swiss Mountain Canton, c. 1470–1620*, Cambridge

Hindle, Steve (2000), *The State and Social Change in Early Modern England*, Basingstoke

Kettering, Sharon (2002), *Patronage in Sixteenth- and Seventeenth-century France*, Aldershot

Kümin, Beat (2013), *The Communal Age in Western Europe c. 1100–1800: Towns, Villages and Parishes in Pre-modern Society*, Basingstoke

Kümin, Beat and Würgler, Andreas (1997), 'Petitions, *Gravamina* and the Early Modern State: Local Influence on Central Legislation in England and Germany (Hesse)', *Parliaments, Estates and Representation*, 17, 39–60

Schlögl, Rudolf (2014), *Anwesende und Abwesende. Grundriss für eine Gesellschafts-geschichte der Frühen Neuzeit*, Constance

Schulze, Hagen (1996), *States, Nations and Nationalism: From the Middle Ages to the Present*, trans. W. Yuill, Cambridge, Mass.

Stjernquist, Nils ed. (1989), *The Swedish Riksdag in an International Perspective*, Stockholm

Stone, Lawrence (1965), 'The Educational Revolution in England 1560–1640', *P&P*, 28, 41–80

Strauss, Gerald (1978), *Luther's House of Learning*, Baltimore, Md.

* Te Brake, Wayne (1998), *Shaping History: Ordinary People in European Politics 1500–1700*, Berkeley, Calif.

## (C) Web resources

Du Plessis-Mornay, Philippe [attrib.] (1579/1648), *Vindiciae contra Tyrannos: A Defence of Liberty against Tyrants*, extracts transcribed by J. P. Sommerville: <http://faculty. history.wisc.edu/sommerville/367/Vindiciae.htm>

Haller, Albrecht von (1708–77), 'List of Correspondents', compiled by the Haller-Projekt, Bern: <http://www.albrecht-von-haller.ch/medien/pdf/Korrespondenten. pdf>

# The impact of war

*Jonathan Davies*

## Introduction

War was a key characteristic of early modern Europe. The period from 1500 to 1800 saw frequent conflicts within European states, between European states and between European states and states across the globe. The preparations, conduct and costs of these conflicts shaped not only early modern Europe but also its relationships with the wider world (Sandberg 2016).

## Warfare and state formation: the military revolution debate

In 1955 Michael Roberts proposed the concept of an early modern military revolution which linked warfare and state formation. Focusing on the period from 1560 to 1660, Roberts argued that the introduction of the musket led to a revolution in tactics. He also highlighted the exponential growth in the size of armies across Europe, the development of strategies to mobilize larger armies and the impact of war on society as expenditure and bureaucracy increased. Roberts's thesis was developed and modified by Geoffrey Parker. Whilst he agreed about the major increase in army size, Parker stressed technology rather than tactics as the key driver of change. The use of heavy artillery resulted in larger and more elaborate fortifications which in turn stimulated the growth of armies. For Parker, the military revolution began around 1450 and spread slowly across Europe before ending around 1700. It also had a global significance since technological change and the rise of navies facilitated European overseas conquest. The arguments of Roberts and Parker have been challenged by many scholars (Rogers 1995; Parker 1996; Black 2002, 32–38). Instead there is an increasing preference to use a naval revolution to explain the relationship between warfare and state formation. F. C. Lane, an expert on Mediterranean maritime history, has argued that early modern states became producers of protection and that taxes can be seen as protection money. This theory has been developed by Jan Glete who views the integration of merchants, rulers and other interest groups in the rise of permanent navies as an important stage in the development of states. He also notes that royal power in the earliest FISCAL-MILITARY STATES (the Kalmar Union of Denmark, Sweden and Norway; Portugal; and England) was closely connected to naval power (Glete 2001, 54–55; Glete 2010, 312).

However, one should be cautious about seeing warfare as the main factor in the growth of states. In early seventeenth-century France, the 40,000 royal officials far outnumbered the 15,000 peacetime troops. Likewise, the 4,830 licensed preaching clergy of the Church of England in 1603 probably outnumbered all the judicial, fiscal, naval and military staff. One also needs to recognise the role of warfare in state fragmentation as well as in state formation. For example, the French Wars of Religion and the Dutch Revolt both produced serious political breakdowns (Gunn 2010, 70, 72).

## Support for war

The support of elites was essential in early modern warfare. The nobility provided leadership and troops and ship-owners made war at sea possible. As historians have moved away from absolutist readings of early modern politics, they have come to recognise how the waging of war rested on negotiation between the ruler and the elites (Gunn 2010, 64). But why did the elites support wars? Whilst there were financial reasons, there were also important cultural and social motivations. The traditional 'SWORD' nobility as defined by warfare and military service brought social esteem (Parrott 2010, 78–79; Sandberg 2010). The martial ethic of the nobility and royalty was expressed in chivalric orders, festivals, chronicles and pamphlets. It was also celebrated in art and architecture (Gunn 2010, 65, 69; cf, Figure VI.3). However, not everyone was in favour of war. During the sixteenth century it was opposed by humanists such as Erasmus and by radical Protestants such as the Anabaptists (Tallett and Trim 2010, 6).

## Militias, mercenaries and entrepreneurs

Early modern armies were composed of one or more of three elements: MILITIAS; mercenaries; and forces provided by military entrepreneurs. Militias had been used in antiquity and they were revived in the late middle ages (Tlusty 2011). From 1363 the English were required to practice archery regularly and they were called up repeatedly in the fifteenth century. Most early modern European states had militias trained in the use of the pike and firearms (Figure VI.12). The most famous militia is probably that raised in Florence by Machiavelli between 1503 and 1506 but other notable examples are the French légions of 1534, the English trained bands of 1573 and the militia raised by John VII of Nassau and Maurice of Hesse around 1600. Some militiamen such as the Swiss hired out their services as mercenaries. Their skill with weapons or tactics recommended them to rulers who could be reluctant to rely on their own citizens. As Machiavelli noted, '[The king of France] has disarmed all his subjects in order to rule them more easily'. Mercenaries often came from the borders of the states for whom they fought: Cleves for the Netherlands; the Grisons for Venice; the Tyrol or the Trentino for Spanish Lombardy; and Alsace or Lorraine for France

*Cum Priuile Reg.Jfrael exendir*

**Figure VI.12** A seventeenth-century illustration of military exercises for infantrymen. Jacques Callot 'Les exercices militaires', c. 1632. / Photo © Granger / Bridgeman Images.

(Machiavelli 2001, 28; Gunn 2010, 58–61). States could bear the ever-increasing costs of mercenaries so long as wars were relatively short. However, the Habsburg-Valois conflict which re-ignited in 1552 led to a financial crisis in 1557 with the French and Spanish crowns unable to pay their forces. During the late sixteenth and early seventeenth century prolonged wars in the Netherlands, France and Hungary saw growing reliance on military entrepreneurs who used their own money or credit to provide forces. Over 300 such entrepreneurs were active during the Thirty Years War and by 1634 Albrecht von Wallenstein had assembled a mercenary army of around 45,000 men (Parrott 2010, 74, 80–81; Parrott 2012). Until the late seventeenth century naval warfare was also characterized by entrepreneurship as sea captains and venture capitalists provided vessels, armaments and crew (Tallett and Trim 2010, 17).

Traditionally historians have been sceptical of the effectiveness of the early modern militia, preferring to see the origins of later armies in the large mercenary forces of the seventeenth century. However, there is now an argument that military entrepreneurship was a 'dead-end' and that militias were in fact the basis of state-raised, financed and administered standing armies (Parrott 2010, 76). Although standing forces (mainly of cavalry) had existed in Western Europe in the fifteenth century, they were relatively small; even the permanent forces of the king of France numbered no more than 6,000. The Spanish Army of Flanders in the 1580s and 1590s included veterans in permanent companies and *tercios* at the heart of its total force of 60,000 men. But the seventeenth century saw the greatest expansion of standing armies, especially in France. By the War of Devolution in 1667 the French army included 70,000 infantry and 35,000 cavalry. This increased to 140,000 on the eve of the Dutch War in 1672 and to 340,000 in the early 1690s. At a time of rural depression and demographic stagnation, this massive expansion was only achieved with the political and financial support of the elites (Gunn 2010, 54–55; Parrott 2012, 30, 274–75; Box 1).

Box 1

Between 1494 and 1559 a series of wars raged across the Italian states. Machiavelli's views on war, based on his personal experience as well as on his study of ancient histories and military treatises, shaped all his political writings but they are expressed most extensively in *The Art of War*, his only work to be published during his lifetime and the one which he himself may have valued most. A champion of militias, Machiavelli was scathing about the military and political damage caused by the use of mercenaries (Machiavelli 2001; cf. Mallett and Shaw 2012; Evans 1913 in Web resources):

> 'Mercenary and auxiliary arms are useless and dangerous; and if one keeps his state founded on mercenary arms, one will never be firm or secure; for they are disunited, ambitious, without discipline, unfaithful; bold among friends, among enemies cowardly; no fear of God, no faith with men; ruin is postponed only as long as attack is postponed; and in peace you are despoiled by them, in war by the enemy. The cause of this is that they have no love nor cause to keep them in the field other than a small stipend, which is not sufficient to make them want to die for you. They do indeed want to be your soldiers while you are not making war, but when war comes, they either flee or leave. It should be little trouble for me to persuade anyone of this point, because the present ruin of Italy is caused by nothing other than its having relied for a period of many years on mercenary arms.'
>
> *(Machiavelli 1998, 48–49)*

In assessing the development of military forces in early modern Europe, one also needs to recognise that the experience of the Ottoman Empire had a different trajectory to that of the West. Between 1420 and 1520 reliance on military enterprisers such as the march lords was replaced by state control. During the sixteenth century monetary stability and budgetary surplus permitted a virtual state monopoly over military provision. Although a decline in revenues put this system under strain between 1570 and 1720, the Ottomans managed to adjust to meet the challenges they faced (Murphey 2010, 136; 'European relations with the Ottoman world' in Part IV).

## Technology and logistics

The significance of gunpowder for warfare was recognised by contemporaries, as Robert Barret's dialogue between a country gentleman and a veteran of the Dutch Revolt demonstrates (Box 2).

However, one needs to add some caveats. Advances in metallurgy and weapon design and production were as important as the introduction of gunpowder for warfare on land and at sea. Technology did not determine the status of the European powers or the results of wars, not least because it was shared by states. Also, new technology

'*Gent.* . . .for in executing her Maiestie's commands, for trayning our men, providing of armour, I heare many say, what needs so much a do and great charge in Calliver, Musket, Pyke and Corselet? Our auncestors won many battels with bowes, blacke Billes and Iackes [the bill was a polearm weapon and the jack was a sleeveless tunic or jacket worn by foot-soldiers and others, usually of leather quilted, and in later times often plated with iron]. But what thinke you of that?

*Captaine.* Sir, then was then and now is now; the wars are much altered since the fierie weapons came up: the Cannon, the Musket . . . and Pistoll. Although some have attempted stifly to maintaine the sufficiencie of Bowes, yet daily experience doth and will shew us the contrarie . . .

*Gent.* Why do you not like of our old archerie of England?

*Capt.* I do not altogether disalow them; true it is, they may serve to some sorts of service, but to no such effect as any of the fierie weapons.

*Gent.* Will not a thousand bowes handled by good bowmen, do as good service, as a thousand . . . muskets, especially amongst horsemen?

*Capt.* No, were there such bowmen as there were in the old time, yet could there be no comparison.'

(*Barret 1598, 2–3*)

Robert Barret (d. 1607) spent most of his life fighting 'among forraine nations, as the French, the Dutch, the Italian, and Spaniard'. His dialogue *The Theorike and Practike of Modern Warres* is one of the most important military treatises of the period, introducing continental theory and practice to an English audience, including Shakespeare.

was mixed with the old. For example, although the Ottomans were the leading developers of firearms, they continued to deploy bows in their armies until the seventeenth century (Tallett and Trim 2010, 3, 23–24).

The ability to use technology was as significant as its possession. Ottoman military success depended on its capacity to mobilize very large armies for long campaigns rather than on its access to advanced technology (Tallett and Trim 2010, 23). Between 1365 and 1720 the Ottomans outperformed the other European powers not only in the mobilisation of troops but also in finance, food supply and transport, enabling them to provision war zones before campaigns began. However, a reversal began in the early eighteenth century. The Ottomans' opponents came to eclipse them in the scale and management of resources as well as in the standards and discipline of their armies. The Ottoman army became increasingly privatized as the forces of the other European powers became more state-regulated and centralized (Murphey 2010).

# The experience of war

Assessing the experience of warfare in early modern Europe is not easy. We lack key information such as mortality levels, numbers of troops and economic data. We also need to appreciate that prolonged campaigns, civil wars, religious wars and raids produced different experiences of warfare. There was also significant geographical variation with some regions suffering significantly whilst others were not affected directly. The prosperity of areas such as the Rhineland, Westphalia and northern Italy attracted armies which needed to live off the land. Regions which were contested politically were also the focus of military conflict: the Italian states, the Low Countries, northern France and the Habsburg-Ottoman border. As troops moved across Europe from recruitment areas to war zones, military corridors such as the 'Spanish Road' from northern Italy to the Low Countries were hit hard. The direct impact of war on different regions could vary widely even during the same conflict. For example, Kent escaped the armies of the English Civil War and during the Thirty Years War Pomerania, Mecklenburg and Württemberg were damaged far more than other German states. Whilst some villages in Württemberg lost 60 per cent of their inhabitants, the population of Lower Saxony declined by only 10 per cent (Tallett 1992, 148–51, Helfferich 2009; Wilson 2009).

As with geographical differences, so there was variation in the impact of war on different social classes with the richer usually suffering less than the poor. Although Nördlingen was a frequent target in the Thirty Years War, the most prosperous 2 per cent of its citizens actually increased their share of the city's wealth from 21 per cent to 40 per cent between 1579 and 1646 with the greatest growth occurring during the 1630s and 1640s. As soldiers sought supplies, the richer – who could exploit economic opportunities – adapted better than the poor to the consequent inflation, which could

---

**Box 3**

Peter Hagendorf served as a professional soldier for 25 years and kept a diary. Since most German troopers were illiterate, this is a rare source. He was married to his first wife, Anna, for six years and throughout the marriage she and later their children accompanied him on campaign. Hagendorf was injured at the sack of Magdeburg in 1630.

'When I was bandaged my wife went into the city, even though it was on fire everywhere, as she wanted to fetch a pillow for me to lie on and cloths for dressings, so I had the sick child lying by me too. Then the cry reached the camp that the houses were all collapsing on top of each other, so that many soldiers and women who were wanting to do a bit of looting were trapped inside them. As a result I was more worried about my wife, because of the sick child, than about my wounds.'

(Mortimer 2002, 35)

**Box 4**

Pierre Vuarin described the impact of soldiers on the Duchy of Lorraine in his journal of 1622.

'In transit they killed everyone they encountered as if it were open warfare. They burnt villages, raped girls and women, pillaged and damaged churches and altars, carried away everything of value and did unheard of damage even though His Highness [Duke Henry II] provisioned them. Further they cut growing corn as feed for their horses which they stabled in churches. Everywhere they did infinite damage, stealing furniture and livestock, which they managed to discover even when hidden in the remoteness of woods. For five whole days they [the Prince of Phalsbourg and his men who were supposed to be repelling the invaders] lived off the country, pillaging and extorting money like the enemy forces . . . The poor villagers returning to their villages after the passing of the soldiery picked up infections from human and animal carcasses left behind by the marauders. A third died from dissentry and other infectious diseases in the villages through which the soldiers had passed.'

*(Daniel 1974, xix)*

be significant. For example, the price of corn in Lorraine rose from 6 francs in 1632 to 37 francs in 1638 (Tallett 1992, 158–61).

Attempts to analyze the experience of early modern warfare must also address problems with contemporary accounts. Few diarists keep up-to-date records. Whilst some events may have been noted at the time, others may have been recorded weeks, months or years later and there is the danger that they were moulded by hindsight (Mortimer 2002, 17–21). Nevertheless, they can give valuable insights into military and civilian experiences (Box 3).

The duchy of Lorraine was a crossroads for armies and so suffered particularly badly from warfare (Box 4). The sufferings of Lorraine at the hands of soldiers and the violent revenge taken by peasants were represented by Jacques Callot in his series of engravings entitled *The Miseries of War*. As with the written records, one needs to beware hyperbole and elaboration in these visual sources. However, they are testimony to the undoubted desolation among many (Callot 1633 in Web resources; Daniel 1974).

## Assessment

For 60 years discussions of early modern warfare have been dominated by the military revolution debate. This has provided a wealth of information about institutional development and the relationship between war and society (Hale 1998). However, other key issues have been relatively neglected. In particular, we need to focus on the reasons for and conduct of wars (especially the nature of large-scale violence), on explaining success and failure, on examining the consequences of conflict, and on how warfare shaped relations between Europe and the rest of the world (James 2013; Sandberg 2016).

## Discussion themes

1. Was the 'military revolution' cause or consequence of a more sophisticated state apparatus?
2. How deeply did warfare disrupt the lives of early modern Europeans?
3. How did warfare shape relations between Europe and the rest of the world?

## Bibliography

### (A) Sources

Barret, Robert (1598), *The Theorike and Practike of Modern Warres*, London
Daniel, Howard ed. (1974), *Callot's Etchings*, New York
Helfferich, Tryntje ed. (2009), *The Thirty Years War: A Documentary History*, Indianapolis
Machiavelli, Niccolò (1998), *The Prince* [1513], trans. Harvey C. Mansfield, Chicago
*Machiavelli, Niccolò (2001), *The Art of War* [1521], trans. Ellis Farneworth and Neal Wood, Cambridge, Mass.
Mortimer, Geoff (2002), *Eyewitness Accounts of the Thirty Years War 1618–48*, Basingstoke

### (B) Literature

Black, Jeremy (2002), *European Warfare 1494–1660*, London
Glete, Jan (2001), *War and the State in Early Modern Europe: Spain, the Dutch Republic and Sweden as Fiscal-Military States*, London
Glete, Jan (2010), 'Warfare, Entrepreneurship and the Fiscal-Military State', in: *European Warfare 1350–1750*, ed. Frank Tallett and D. J. B. Trim, Cambridge, 300–21
Gunn, Steven (2010), 'War and the State in Western Europe, 1350–1600', in: *European Warfare 1350–1750*, ed. Frank Tallett and D. J. B. Trim, Cambridge, 50–73
Hale, John R. (1998), *War and Society in Renaissance Europe 1450–1620*, Stroud
James, Alan (2013), 'Rethinking the Peace of Westphalia: Toward a Theory of Early Modern Warfare', in: *Aspects of Violence in Renaissance Europe*, ed. Jonathan Davies, Farnham, 107–26.
Mallett, Michael and Shaw, Christine (2012), *The Italian Wars, 1494–1559: War, State and Society in Early Modern Europe*, Harlow

Murphey, Rhoads (2010), 'Ottoman Military Organisation in South-Eastern Europe, *c.* 1420–1720', in: *European Warfare 1350–1750*, ed. Frank Tallett and D. J. B. Trim, Cambridge, 135–58

Parker, Geoffrey (1996), *The Military Revolution: Military Innovation and the Rise of the West, 1500–1800*, Cambridge

Parrott, David (2010), 'War, State and Society in Western Europe, 1600–1700', in: *European Warfare 1350–1750*, ed. Frank Tallett and D. J. B. Trim, Cambridge, 74–95

* Parrott, David (2012), *The Business of War: Military Enterprise and Military Revolution in Early Modern Europe*, Cambridge

*Rogers, Clifford J. ed. (1995), *The Military Revolution Debate: Readings on the Military Transformation of Early Modern Europe*, Boulder, Co.

Sandberg, Brian (2010), *Warrior Pursuits: Noble Culture and Civil Conflict in Early Modern France*, Baltimore

* Sandberg, Brian (2016), *War and Conflict in the Early Modern World: 1500–1700*, Oxford

Tallett, Frank (1992), *War and Society in Early Modern Europe, 1495–1715*, London

Tallett, Frank and D. J. B. Trim (2010), 'An Overview of Change and Continuity', in: *European Warfare 1350–1750*, ed. Frank Tallett and D. J. B. Trim, Cambridge, 1–26

Tlusty, B. Ann (2011), *The Martial Ethic in Early Modern Germany: Civic Duty and the Right of Arms*, Basingstoke

Wilson, Peter H. (2009), *Europe's Tragedy: A New History of the Thirty Years War*, London

## (C) Web resources

Callot, Jacques (1633), 'The Miseries of War', in: Chris Mullen, 'The Visual Telling of Stories': <http://www.fulltable.com/vts/c/callot/callot.htm>

Evans, A. W. ed. (1913), *Blaise de Monluc* (Being extracts from Charles Cotton's translation of the 'Commentaires'), Chicago: <http://archive.org/details/blaise demonluc00montiala>

Pepys, Samuel (1906), *Memoires of the Royal Navy, 1679–1688*, Oxford: <http://archive.org/details/pepysmemoiresro00pepygoog>

# Riot and rebellion

*Bernard Capp*

## Introduction and context

In 1500 most early modern rulers enjoyed only limited control over their dominions. Many great nobles could still deploy military forces of their own, and secure support from their tenants and dependants. Governments, perennially short of money, were also hampered by poor communications and their rudimentary bureaucratic machines. All this left rulers vulnerable whenever they attempted to impose new burdens or drive through unpopular policies. While small-scale disorders usually lasted only a few hours and had only local significance ('Popular culture(s)' in Part V), rebellion, both aristocratic and popular, posed a major recurring challenge throughout Europe. This chapter surveys the nature and significance of rebellions: their triggers, objectives, course and consequences. And it looks at the revolutionary voices and movements that also appeared, more briefly, in some areas (see 'Revolution' in Part VI).

Aristocratic rebellions, often led by disgruntled members of the royal family, were sometimes aiming at the throne itself, and the stakes were high. Henry Tudor's victory at Bosworth in 1485 established the Tudor dynasty in England; by contrast, the young Duke of Monmouth's attempt in 1685 to wrest the crown from his uncle, James II, ended with his execution on the scaffold. Other aristocratic rebels, such as the prince de Condé in France in 1651, were seeking political domination rather than the throne itself. The abortive rising by Elizabeth's former favourite, the Earl of Essex, in 1601 had been intended to display his strength and recapture his influence at court (Zagorin 1982, vol. ii; Dewald 1996, 134–39). This chapter focuses primarily on popular rebellions, usually triggered by economic grievances, and on provincial rebellions, a third, overlapping, category. Often provoked by new fiscal demands from central government, these could sometimes unite PEASANTS, townsfolk and aristocrats in defence of traditional liberties and customs.

To make sense of these upheavals we need to look briefly at the wider context. The early modern period witnessed rising populations, soaring prices and rents, falling real wages and the upheavals of the Reformation. It also saw a significant increase in the power and ambitions of the state, reflected in spiralling taxation, mainly to pay for larger, more professional royal armies, and in attempts to exert control over the more distant, often semi-autonomous provinces. Moreover, several monarchs, especially the Habsburgs, ruled over multiple kingdoms, and this inevitably brought with it many problems (Evans 1979). Some were fiscal. The British Isles provide a striking example. Though Wales was united with England in 1536, Ireland and (from 1603) Scotland proved far more challenging, not least because of profound religious differences. Catholic Ireland posed a major threat to Elizabeth. Plans for large-scale English settlement achieved only limited success, and rebellion in the 1590s helped cripple the English treasury. Charles I's attempts in the later 1630s to tighten his control over Scotland and Ireland provoked rebellions in both, and English authority was only regained by invasions led by Oliver Cromwell in 1649–50. It is estimated that one-third of the Irish population perished in the troubles of the 1640s and 1650s. Similar problems followed a generation later, after the Glorious Revolution of 1688. Catholic Ireland refused to recognize the new king, William III, prompting another invasion, while Scottish dissent spawned an enduring Jacobite movement.

Such factors underlay many of the tensions that triggered popular protest. But equally important is that most people, at all social levels, accepted the fundamental principles of order and hierarchy instilled over generations by custom, religion and law (Wood 2002). The Church, whether Catholic, Protestant or Orthodox, upheld the God-given authority of kings, magistrates and all in God-given power. To abuse them was sedition, to defy them treason. Very few possessed the ideological weapons required to challenge the existing order and imagine a state or society organized along radically different lines. Most rebellions were therefore essentially limited in aim, setting out to prevent or reverse unwelcome change, usually fiscal or religious. Most early modern rebels, however embittered, stressed their fundamental loyalty, and generally convinced themselves that evil ministers were to blame for their sufferings. A fierce uprising in Moscow in June 1648 saw angry crowds clamouring for Tsar Alexis to relieve them from heavy taxes from which the clerical and lay elites were largely exempted. Alexis was forced to have several of his leading officials executed to assuage popular fury, and the exemptions were abolished, a useful reminder that popular protests did not always fail (Dukes 1990, 32–38). The leaders of the greatest upheaval in Tudor England, the Pilgrimage of Grace (1536), similarly stressed their loyalty to the sovereign, Henry VIII. Blaming the break with Rome on his evil ministers, they called for Thomas Cromwell to be executed and heretical bishops burned at the stake.

## Taxation and state power

Many rebellions, perhaps most, were triggered by demands for higher taxes. One of the earliest and most dangerous was the revolt of the *Comuneros* in Spain in 1520–21, which began as a protest by the cities of Castile against royal power encroaching on their traditional privileges, exacerbated by suspicion of the influence of foreign ministers. Royal demands triggered particular hatred when imposed on provinces previously sheltered by custom and privilege, especially when monarchs were ruling over multiple kingdoms. Spain, struggling in the seventeenth century to maintain its earlier pre-eminence, offers a striking example of what might follow. Olivares, chief minister to Philip IV, tried to spread the military and fiscal burden between all his dominions by the Union of Arms (1626), a policy that ended disastrously when Spain became embroiled in all-out war with France from 1635. An army of 9,000 stationed in Catalonia, a frontier province, triggered a major revolt in 1640. Angry peasants and townsfolk attacked royal officials in protests that culminated in the murder of the viceroy in Barcelona, and the collapse of provincial government. With the local authorities now assuming control to prevent total anarchy, the rebellion drew support from across the whole of society. In 1641 its leaders declared Philip deposed, but knowing they were too weak to survive alone they accepted the sovereignty of Louis XIII of France. In the short term, French military aid saved the rebellion, but French rule proved as oppressive as that of Madrid, and Catalonia eventually returned to the Spanish crown, where it has remained (uneasily) to the present day (Elliott 1963). By contrast Portugal, which also rebelled in 1640, managed to throw off the Spanish yoke, and regained its independence. A few years later, in July 1647, rebellion broke out in Naples, also part of the Spanish dominions, and one of Europe's largest and poorest cities. This too was triggered by Spain's fiscal demands, compounded by the corruption of local officials. Initially this was a plebeian outburst, led by a young

**Figure VI.13** A spontaneous riot against a new tax in Spanish-ruled Naples turned into a major uprising. Though Masaniello was quickly murdered, the rebellion spread and lasted for months. Piazza del Mercato in Naples, detail from the Revolt of Masaniello, by Domenico Gargiulo known as Micco Spadaro (1609 or 1610, c. 1675). De Agostini Picture Library / Bridgeman Images.

fish-vendor nicknamed Masaniello, and angry crowds gave vent to bloody vengeance on their oppressors. But when Masaniello was murdered after a chaotic rule lasting only ten days, the rebels fragmented into rival factions, some looking for the restoration of local privileges within the Spanish monarchy, others inviting the French Duke of Guise to lead a Neapolitan republic. It was not to be; alarmed by the violence and volatility of the mob, the Naples elite held aloof, and by 1648 Spain had regained control (Figure VI.13; Zagorin 1982, i. 247–49).

The kings of France faced rather different but related problems. French nobles rebelled in pursuit of personal, political and religious objectives, while local and regional popular risings were generally triggered by grievances over taxation. With France repeatedly at war, the need to fund huge armies drove royal policy throughout the period. The nobility and many office holders were exempt from most taxes, so the fiscal burden fell primarily on the peasantry and towns (Le Roy Ladurie 1987). Most protests were local. Primarily concerned to defend their own customs and privileges, magistrates and citizens alike tended to see other towns as rivals, rather than make common cause. Their genuine loyalty to the crown was tempered by a sense of reciprocal obligations: rulers, they felt, should respect traditional customs and laws, provide security, and protect the town's interests. Urban protest often reflected a deep sense of injustice as well as economic hardship, though the anger was generally directed at tax officials rather than the monarch.

Popular protest, both urban and rural, peaked in the period 1630–70, following France's entry into the Thirty Years War. Large-scale rural protests, such as the *Nouveaux Croquants* in 1637 and the *Nu-Pieds* in Normandy in 1639, galvanized rage against tax officials, sometimes supported by local landowners and village priests. In urban centres, rumours of a new levy would trigger angry talk in the market-place and could quickly lead to violence if local magistrates failed to defuse the situation. Angry crowds turned on the tax officials, sometimes killing them and mutilating their bodies, and might turn against local magistrates too if they were suspected of complicity. The absurd but telling cry, 'Long live the king, death to the tax collectors!', captured the mindset of the protesters. The magistrates, nervous and sharing much of the traditionalist outlook of the protesters, often responded very cautiously. In theory the state could have deployed the army to crush disturbances, but ministers knew they were facing a bush-fire where trouble might flare up elsewhere at any moment. It often seemed wiser to compromise, reducing or dropping a novel levy and withdrawing hated officials. Ministers, realistic and pragmatic, experimented endlessly with new devices to raise money, and if some provoked massive opposition it made more sense to back down than devote time and resources to a major confrontation. William Beik identifies 30 to 40 major urban revolts in this period, and thousands of minor episodes. There might be a few casualties on each side, officials and rioters killed in street clashes, and sometimes a few token executions afterwards, but large-scale repression was the exception rather than the rule (Box 1).

Box 1

'some inhabitants of the quarter started crying out that they were posting the gabelle [salt tax]. They roused the neighbours and in a moment there were almost eighty or a hundred persons, men and women, armed with swords, halberds, clubs, iron skewers, and a few firearms, lighting up the streets with torches of straw . . . and shouting that they wanted to kill the gabeleurs.'

*(Beik 1997, 62)*

A rising in Agen (south-western France) in 1672. Note the participation of women, often involved in local protests ('Popular culture(s)' in Part V).

A protest in 1645 in Montpellier, in south-western France, illustrates many of these features. When an official arrived to impose a new levy in return for confirming the city's privileges, wild rumours quickly spread and women took to the streets protesting at reports that they would be taxed on each child. Roving bands were soon hunting down the hated official, and his documents were seized and shredded. The authorities responded by seizing two looters, sentenced to death but quickly freed by angry crowds who broke open the prison. Passions boiled over in a wave of attacks and looting, with several officials murdered, their bodies mutilated and dragged through the streets. When Marshal Schomberg arrived to restore order he found himself massively outnumbered and judged it best to back down. The new levy was withdrawn, and tensions gradually eased. The protesters had won, for there were no reprisals. The whole province remained on edge throughout the summer, and the authorities dared not provoke further trouble (Beik 1997, 117–26). Over the century as a whole the French crown grew immeasurably stronger, but that success was qualified by a host of local compromises and occasional defeats.

## Religion, social protest and rebellion

It was Germany that witnessed the greatest popular upheavals of the period. The Peasants' War of 1524–25 was not a provincial revolt against central authority but a huge wave of local and regional uprisings, essentially over social and economic grievances. Peasant unrest had a long tradition in Germany; SERFDOM still survived or had been reintroduced, and the free peasants too had numerous grievances against their landlords, both lay and ecclesiastical, over issues such as rent, labour dues, and access to the commons for hunting, fishing and wood-gathering. With political power divided between a plethora of princes and local rulers, anger was often directed at both landlords and rulers, categories that to some degree overlapped, and many also resented the wealth and privileges of the Church. The Peasants' War was not a movement of the destitute and desperate, however; the rebels were defending

## Box 2

'It has hitherto been the custom for the lords to treat us as their serfs, which is pitiable since Christ has redeemed and bought us all by the shedding of his precious blood. . . .

It has hitherto been the custom that no poor man has been empowered to catch game, wildfowl or fish in flowing water, which we consider quite improper and unbrotherly, indeed selfish and contrary to the Word of God. . . .

The sixth [article] concerns our grievous burden of labour services, which are increased from day to day in amount and variety. . . .'

*(From the Twelve Articles of the Swabian peasants;
Scott and Scribner 1991, 253–57)*

traditional rights and determined to strengthen their local communities against both landlords and local rulers. They were also clearly stimulated by the Lutheran Reformation, and its example of successful defiance of both Church and state ('The long Reformation: Lutheran' in Part III). The leaders were often artisans, minor officials and townsmen, with some Protestant ministers and a few lesser nobles, and they won the support of substantial peasants, including village leaders. While each local rising had its own grievances and objectives, the Twelve Articles drawn up by the rebels in Swabia, frequently reprinted, summed up objectives that were widely shared (Box 2).

They demanded the restoration of common lands and rights, the reduction of rents, dues and labour services, and the restriction of lords' criminal jurisdiction. They also called for the election of parish clergy and a reduction in tithes. Equally striking is their appeal to Christ's sacrifice: these were demands inspired by religious idealism as well as custom. Some movements demanded the removal of local rulers, and direct rule by the emperor, and some urban protests demanded the abolition of clerical privilege and rule. While the rebels did not demand the overthrow of princes or landlords, they envisaged a new order with greatly strengthened peasant and urban communities. Most bands operated within their own principality, but in the more fragmented south-west a super-regional association emerged, formally constituted by the Federal Ordinance on 7 March 1525 (Scott and Scribner 1991, 130–32). But ultimately the peasant bands stood little chance against professional troops, and were crushed, with thousands slaughtered. Never again did early modern Europe witness a popular movement of comparable scale or significance (Blickle 1981).

Mid-Tudor England was similarly beset by chronic problems, political, religious and economic, all of which triggered popular upheavals. The Pilgrimage of Grace, which saw much of the north of England up in arms in 1536, repudiated the break with Rome and the spread of Protestant HERESY. But in the Pontefract Articles the

Box 3

**Extracts from the Pontefract Articles (1536)**

'Item to have the heretiqes, bisshoppis and temporall, and ther secte to have condign punyshment by fyer or such oder, or else to trye ther quareles with us and our parte takers in batell. . . .

Item to have the lord Crumwell [and others] to have condigne ponyshment, as the subverters of the good laws of this realme and maynteners of the false sect of those heretiqes and the first inventors and bryngars in of them.'

*(Fletcher and MacCulloch 2005, 135–37)*

Thomas Cromwell, Henry VIII's chief minister at this time, was blamed for the break with Rome. Note that English spelling was not standardized until the eighteenth century.

protesters also complained about taxes, oppressive landlords and the evil of ENCLOSURE, and their demand for a parliament to be held in York or Nottingham reflects the frequent sense that regional concerns were ignored by distant central governments (Box 3).

Kett's rebellion in 1549 in Norfolk was largely driven by economic grievances, especially rent increases, enclosures, and lords who overstocked the commons and undermined the common rights of ordinary villagers (Web resources). It was only one of a spate of protests and riots across England that year. While most were contained, the Western Rebellion (in Devon and Cornwall) posed a significant threat before being crushed on the battlefield. These rebels too had economic grievances but their major complaint was against the new Protestant Church settlement, and the new Prayer Book which accompanied it. Kett's rebellion, by contrast, showed some sympathy for Protestant reform, and its articles carried echoes of the German peasants' religious idealism. Such diversity, within a single country in the same year, underlines the challenges facing early modern governments.

Rebellions often reflected a remarkably wide range of discontents, for once up in arms, it was natural to air every grievance, however narrowly sectional. Kett's articles included one relating to whaling, a pressing concern for Yarmouth fishermen but for few others. Secular and religious issues also frequently became entangled, as in the German Peasants' War or the Pilgrimage of Grace, and sometimes in provincial resistance to central authority. A striking example is the rebellion of the MORISCOS in Granada in 1568–70. Many of the Moriscos had remained attached to their old language and cultural traditions, and when Philip II ordered the total suppression of Moorish culture he provoked a bloody and stubborn rebellion ('Jews and Muslims' in Part III).

In Western Europe, popular rebellion was primarily a phenomenon of the sixteenth and the first half of the seventeenth centuries. As the power of the state steadily increased, popular rebellion became increasingly unrealistic. The eighteenth-century Jacobite risings in the Scottish Highlands and attempts by Corsica to secure its independence were both on the margins of Europe. It was very different in Central and Eastern Europe, where state power was less developed. Russia, which had experienced a catastrophic 'Time of troubles' between the death of Ivan the Terrible in 1584 and the election of Michael Romanov in 1613, was also to witness a succession of massive peasant rebellions, led by Stenka Razin (1670–71), Bulavin (1707–8) and Pugachev (1773–74) (Dukes 1990). In Hungary, Bohemia and Silesia too, peasant uprisings posed a major challenge to royal authority in the 1670s and 1680s. In the west, by contrast, the major threat to the ANCIEN RÉGIME was to come from revolutionary movements, not popular rebellions.

## Revolutionary movements

Where were the early modern revolutionaries, men aiming to overturn the entire political or social order, rather than simply reform a perceived abuse or remove a hated minister or ruler? They were few, limited in influence, and for the most part inspired by a religious, often MILLENARIAN fervour. Medieval Continental Europe had a long tradition of millenarian movements, and echoes resound among some of the leaders of the German Peasants' War. Thomas Müntzer, a radical preacher, announced the imminent overthrow of kings and princes; with God's help, the peasants would establish a kingdom of heaven on earth and put the ungodly to the sword. In the Tyrol Michael Gaismair called for the destruction of privilege, cities and castles, and a simple new world of rural equality and social justice.

Though Müntzer's influence was limited and short-lived, a similar vision was implemented at Münster (in north Germany) a decade later. After the authority of the prince-bishop had been swept aside, thousands of ANABAPTISTS poured in from the Netherlands and Germany. In 1534 the revolutionaries seized control and set out to turn Münster into the New Jerusalem. Under the theocratic rule of two self-appointed leaders, who were Dutch immigrants, private property and money were abolished, and polygamy was made compulsory, part of a new legal code modelled on the Old Testament which established the kind of draconian rigour familiar in modern times under the Taliban. John of Leyden enjoyed a brief reign as messianic king until neighbouring Catholic and Lutheran rulers joined forces to besiege and capture the city. The Anabaptist experiment ended in slaughter.

The story of Münster was still remembered and often cited in England over a century later, to warn against the radical groups which emerged after the English Civil War. The war itself ushered in a limited political and religious revolution, with monarchy swept away in 1649 and the established Church remodelled under Puritan leadership (Woolrych 2002; Hill 1991; cf. 'Revolution' in Part VI).

We can find other revolutionary voices in early modern Europe, but most remained voices in the wilderness. By the eighteenth century the state had become, in most cases, far stronger and the age of popular rebellions was passing away. The 'Glorious Revolution' of 1688 in England was orchestrated by the elites, and was dubbed 'Glorious' not least because popular passions remained firmly contained. It was the American Revolution, proclaimed by the Declaration of Independence in 1776, that offered the first hint of the far more sweeping revolutions that were soon to erupt in Europe.

## Discussion themes

1. Why were rebellions generally limited in their aims? Were they bound to fail?
2. Do rebellions suggest the weakness or the underlying resilience of early modern states and societies?
3. What part, if any, did ideology play in the rebellions and revolutionary movements of this period?

## Bibliography

### (A) Sources

Scott, Tom and Scribner, R. W. eds (1991), *The German Peasants' War*, Atlantic Highlands, NJ
Wolfe, Don ed. (1944), *Leveller Manifestoes of the Puritan Revolution*, New York

### (B) Literature

Beik, William (1997), *Urban Protest in Seventeenth-century France*, Cambridge
* Bercé, Yves-M. (1988), *Revolt and Revolution in Early Modern Europe*, Manchester
Blickle, Peter (1981), *The Revolution of 1525: The German Peasants' War from a New Perspective*, Baltimore, Md.
Dewald, Jonathan (1996), *The European Nobility 1400–1800*, Cambridge
Dukes, Paul (1990), *The Making of Russian Absolutism, 1613–1801*, 2nd edn, Harlow
Elliott, John H. (1963), *The Revolt of the Catalans*, Cambridge
Evans, R. J. W. (1979), *The Making of the Habsburg Monarchy 1550–1700*, Oxford
* Fletcher, Anthony and MacCulloch, Diarmaid (2005), *Tudor Rebellions*, 5th edn, London
Hill, Christopher (1991), *The World Turned Upside Down*, Harmondsworth
Le Roy Ladurie, Emmanuel (1987), *The French Peasantry 1450–1660*, Aldershot
Magagna, Victor (1991), *Communities of Grain: Rural Rebellion in Comparative Perspective*, Ithaca, NY
* Parrott, David ed. (1998), *Resistance, Representation and Community*, Oxford
Te Brake, Wayne (1998), *Shaping History: Ordinary People in European Politics 1500–1700*, Berkeley, Calif.

Wood, Andy (2002), *Riot, Rebellion and Popular Politics in Early Modern England*, Basingstoke

Woolrych, Austin (2002), *Britain in Revolution, 1625–1660*, Oxford

Zagorin, Perez (1982), *Rebels and Rulers 1500–1660*, 2 vols, Cambridge

## (C) Web resources

'The Revolt of 1525': <http://germanhistorydocs.ghi-dc.org>

'Slave Revolt in Jamaica 1760–1761': <http://revolt.axismaps.com/>

Wood, Andy, 'Kett's Rebellion of 1549', in *Virtual Norfolk*: <http://www.webarchive.org.uk/pan/12032/20051206/virtualnorfolk.uea.ac.uk/kett/index.html>

# Revolution: England and France

*Bernard Capp and Colin Jones*

Revolutions are messy affairs for those involved. Contemporaries who lived through the revolution that followed the English civil wars (1642–46, 1648) found it hard to make sense of what they had experienced. Modern historians have found it impossible even to agree on a label: it has been described as a 'puritan revolution', 'great rebellion', the last of Europe's wars of religion, or the first modern revolution. The French Revolution that started in 1789 was equally confusing for participants. But no one was in any doubt that it was a 'revolution'. Although the scale and significance of the 'revolutionary' events down to 1799 have been debated, there has never been any quarrel with the term 'French Revolution'. Prior to 1789, the French had used the term in the plural when referring to major political turbulence and changes of regime. Thus England had had its 'revolutions' in the 1640s, just as America did in the 1770s and 1780s. When it came, 1789 was emphatically singular not plural. Indeed, it was not just 'a' revolution, it was 'the' Revolution, an epochal event that was held to redefine the shape of human history (Auslander 2009).

In the cases of both countries, there was a strong element of surprise. The Scots who rose against Charles I's attempt to impose a new prayer book in 1637, and the MPs who assembled at Westminster three years later neither wanted a revolution nor imagined one was coming. The situation was similar in France. Prior to 1789, some contemporaries had spoken of the Enlightenment ushering in a cultural transformation, while the financial problems of the monarchy from the mid-1780s gave warning of significant reforms in view. Yet the revolution of the summer of 1789 was like a bolt from the blue.

If both revolutions came as a surprise, once they were under way they generated a similar array of issues, including financial crisis, religious turbulence, regicide, political extremism and warfare. And both ended in a restoration of sorts.

## England

### Origins

Lawrence Stone, following the seventeenth-century political philosopher James Harrington, traced the origins of civil war to the massive shift in economic power that followed Henry VIII's seizure of monastic lands and their subsequent sale, along with most crown lands. Long-term social-economic explanations now find little support. More recently, 'revisionist' historians saw the English polity as basically stable until Charles I's unnecessary meddling in Scottish affairs. This interpretation has also failed to win general backing. Two points seem beyond dispute, however. First, England in the 1630s was remarkably peaceful. But second, the Scottish rebellion, and the king's need to raise an army to suppress it, revealed that he had forfeited much of his political capital. The Short Parliament (April–May 1640) and Long Parliament (from November 1640) demanded major concessions before approving new taxes, London preachers hailed the Scots as liberators, and newly conscripted soldiers deserted en masse. The grievances were partly financial, over the king's resort to prerogative powers to raise money in the 1630s, rather than face a parliament. They were also religious: the king's insistence on ritual and uniformity, his foreign Catholic queen, and his authoritarian, high-church archbishop of Canterbury, William Laud, led many to fear a dangerous slide back towards popery (general surveys in Woolrych 2002, Braddick 2008).

In 1640, many saw the Scottish crisis as a golden opportunity for a radical change of direction. They were happy to blame Charles's 'mistakes' on evil advisers, and forced the king to abandon his previous policies and ministers, including Laud and the hard-line Earl of Strafford. The slide into civil war in 1642 was triggered by distrust rather than fundamental constitutional or religious differences. Doubtful that Charles would stand by his concessions, his critics insisted that the current parliament could not be dissolved without its own consent, that henceforth parliaments must assemble at least every three years, and that they should have the power to vet royal councillors. The Irish rebellion in November 1641 brought the issue into still sharper focus, for the parliamentary leaders refused to entrust an army to any general nominated by the king. Moderates, disgusted, felt that would reduce the king to little more than a figurehead. They were also deeply alarmed by the huge crowds repeatedly demonstrating and petitioning in London, and by the breakdown of order in the provinces. For many, fears over law and order came to outweigh any concerns over tyranny or popery. The king's botched attempt to seize five leading radical MPs in January 1642, triggering his flight from London, marked the final breakdown of trust, and an inexorable slide into violence.

## War

Both sides declared they were waging a defensive struggle to preserve the true faith and protect the legitimate rights of king and parliament alike. Parliament insisted it was fighting to liberate the king from his evil counsellors. While not wholly disingenuous, that was far from the whole truth. Many parliamentarians were inspired by the religious vision of a purified Church and a nation reformed or coerced into becoming a Second Israel. Others, while still committed to monarchy, had absorbed the HUMANIST values of classical republicanism at grammar school and university, and focused on the goal of liberty. The concept of active citizenship was strongly entrenched not only among the elites but within corporate (self-governing) towns and cities throughout the land. Liberty and reformation gave the parliamentarians two positive ideals, and they could ignore for the moment the potential conflict between them.

The war ended in 1646. Parliament owed its victory to vastly superior financial resources (especially through its control of London), its military alliance with the Scots in 1643, and the effective reorganization of its forces in 1645. The New Model Army, led by Fairfax and Cromwell, imposed tight discipline and gave priority to commitment and ability rather than birth in the selection of officers. Victory did not necessarily mean revolution, however. The parliamentary leaders wanted a negotiated settlement, and expected that Charles would now prove ready to make concessions. Charles had other ideas, and the political situation grew increasingly unstable. The breakdown of ecclesiastical authority had allowed the rise of separatists (Congregationalists, Baptists, and others) who demanded religious freedom in any settlement. Though relatively few in numbers, their cause was taken up by the new LEVELLER movement, which demanded that any settlement must deliver sweeping reforms to benefit ordinary people. The Levellers proclaimed the sovereignty of the people, and called for the removal of the king and House of Lords. They wanted a written constitution providing for annual parliaments, an extended franchise, and devolution, along with a raft of social and economic reforms. Some rejected the existing order as a Norman Yoke, invoking a mythical age of Anglo-Saxon liberty crushed by the Norman invaders in 1066 and their Stuart successors. Others spoke of innate human rights under the 'Law of Nature', the right to self-preservation which, their opponents warned, could easily be interpreted to justify seizing the lands and wealth of the rich. Significantly, the army began to take a direct interest in political events. Many of the officers, including Cromwell, defended religious freedom for the separatists, while the Levellers made significant headway among the junior officers and cavalry regiments. An army revolt in spring 1647, triggered by material grievances and the threat of disbandment, led to the celebrated Putney Debates in October–November, with leading officers debating constitutional issues with elected representatives of the common soldiers (Box 1).

All these developments were soon overshadowed by the king's attempt to reverse the outcome of the civil war. Charles won the support of the Scots and of many Englishmen alarmed by recent developments, and a second civil war erupted in 1648. The royalists were soon defeated, and this time the sequel was very different. While most MPs still hoped for a negotiated settlement, the army leaders had lost patience and now saw Charles as a war criminal, a 'Man of Blood'. He had deliberately plunged the country back into civil war, and must now be called to account. God, they believed, demanded punishment for such a heinous crime, a duty which overrode the king's claim to authority and protection by divine right. In December 1648 a military coup,

Pride's Purge, removed moderates from the House of Commons, clearing the way for the radicals to establish a new high court to try the king (Figure V.14). Though Charles predictably refused to recognize its authority, his condemnation was a foregone conclusion. He was executed on 30 January 1649, before a huge and stunned crowd. Cromwell was among the regicides, a late but resolute convert to the belief that there was no alternative (Peacey 2008).

## Commonwealth and protectorate

Many kings had been deposed or assassinated, but never before had one been put on trial by his own subjects. It was a revolutionary step, quickly followed by the abolition of monarchy and the House of Lords, and a declaration proclaiming that England was now a commonwealth. We should recognize, though, that this was not a revolution driven by ideology, like the Bolshevik Revolution of 1917. Cromwell was never a committed republican, and neither were most of his colleagues. Their dissatisfaction was with King Charles, not with monarchy itself. The 'Rump' of the House of Commons, and its Council, took over the running of government, but they failed to agree on any long-term constitutional proposals.

This, then, was a limited revolution. It did not usher in the sweeping social upheavals of the French Revolution or the twentieth-century revolutions in Russia and China. It was not immediately clear, however, that this would be the case. England in 1649 was a dangerously volatile place, hit by successive harvest failures and soaring prices. Radicals, convinced by recent upheavals that a new order was possible or even inevitable, were now demanding sweeping reforms (Bradstock 2011). In 1649 the

**Figure VI.14** The trial of Charles I in
Westminster Hall, 27 January 1649:
revolutionary, and deliberately public: Private
Collection / Bridgeman Images.

DIGGERS, a newly formed communist movement, established settlements in Surrey
and elsewhere, and while rejecting violence they called on labourers to refuse any
longer to work for wages. Such a withdrawal of labour would have crippled the
traditional social and economic order (Hill 1973). Another group, the Fifth
Monarchists, saw the execution of the king as preparing the way for England to become
a new Israel, ruled over by the godly as the instruments of King Jesus. Much of the
new regime's energy was spent heading off radical threats, asserting its authority over
Ireland and Scotland (both invaded by Cromwell, in 1649 and 1650), and defending
itself from a universally hostile Europe. On all these fronts, it succeeded. It did not
'fail' to push through major social reforms, as radicals complained; on the contrary,
it was proud to have blocked such pressures and delivered a welcome measure of
stability. Its own reforming energies were directed towards religious and moral
reformation: new laws to uphold the Sabbath and suppress swearing and sexual
immorality. In 1650 adultery was made a felony, carrying the death penalty, though
the measure proved very hard to enforce. After a brief experiment with an unelected
'Parliament of Saints', Cromwell himself ruled as Lord Protector from December 1653,
with a new written constitution spelling out his own powers and those of the Council
and of regular parliaments. He declared that his priority now was to maintain public
order, likening himself to a parish constable keeping the peace among quarrelsome
parishioners, though he still retained his commitment to moral and godly reformation.

Cromwell was dismayed to find harmony still impossible to achieve; when supporters in parliament offered him the crown in 1657, he was strongly tempted, half-convinced that a return to England's traditional system could deliver a lasting settlement. But many army officers remained deeply hostile, and Cromwell himself doubted that God could favour a return to monarchy when it had been swept away by divine PROVIDENCE only a few years earlier. After weeks of hesitation, he declined the offer (Morrill 1990).

## Aftermath

Cromwell died in September 1658. His son Richard, succeeding him, had none of his father's personal authority or military fame and was soon pushed aside by the generals, who saw no reason to defer to him. In January 1660 General Monck, commanding the only army still paid and disciplined, marched down from Scotland, with no fixed plans. He was soon persuaded by the reassembled Long Parliament to invite back the king's son from exile.

The Cromwellian regime had successfully asserted its authority both at home and abroad, with Continental powers awed by his huge navy. There was never any prospect of his regime being swept away by foreign armies, as happened to Napoleon. But Cromwell never attracted large-scale elite or popular support. When the army turned against his family, the regime collapsed, and when it failed to devise any acceptable alternative, the way was opened for the king to return.

## France

## Origins

As was the case for England, the outbreak of revolution in France has traditionally been linked to social and economic roots. But historians have differed over what these were. Many have seen the 1789 revolution as a 'revolution of poverty', caused by the economic backwardness and France's seigneurial and FEUDAL system. The French PEASANTRY, who composed three-quarters of the population, lived in fear of dearth. Bread prices rose over the century, and living conditions got despairingly worse. Yet in contrast other historians have judged that ultimately 1789 was a 'revolution of prosperity': the expansion of CAPITALISM was creating a strong bourgeois class eager to contest the power of the aristocracy (a survey in Jones 2002).

In recent years, there have been moves to downplay long-term socio-economic causation and to highlight the importance of politics. The emergence from around 1750 of a 'bourgeois public sphere', stimulated by improvement in trade and communications, produced a greater engagement with political affairs. 'Public opinion' became a factor in ways that had never been the case hitherto. On top of this was the financial crisis of a monarchy that had become fatally overstretched by fighting expensive wars over the previous century. French involvement in the American War of Independence, a brilliant diplomatic and military success (see 'European Politics' in Part V), was a financial catastrophe. By 1786, state bankruptcy loomed and was a severe test of political management. This was especially so because higher taxes and state borrowing depended on the goodwill of wealthy individuals across society who set the tone for public opinion and who resented being excluded from the aristocratic decision-makers around Louis XVI. The king overflowed with goodwill, but in the looming political crisis he proved dim, depressed and indecisive. In late 1788, he was forced into calling the Estates General, a national representative body that had last met in 1614.

In the context of a lively public sphere, the archaic rituals of electing representatives for the Estates General in the spring of 1789 approximated to a modern electoral consultation (Jones 2002). This raised widespread expectations for reform throughout France, just as, ominously, an appalling subsistence crisis was hitting the countryside. As soon as the Estates General met, moreover, it was clear that the king could not live up to people's hopes. While he dithered, the commoner deputies in the Estates General assumed the title and powers of a National Assembly (constitutionally, this

**Figure VI.15** The Taking of the Bastille, 14 July 1789 (oil on canvas), French School, (18th century) / Chateau de Versailles, France / Bridgeman Images.

was *the* revolutionary act). In Paris, the storming of the old fortress-prison, the Bastille, on 14 July 1789 signalled that the French capital was in no mood for political compromise (Figure V.15). The stakes were raised even higher when rural France, suspecting an aristocratic backlash against reform, rose violently against their seigneurial overlords. The scale of peasant revolt was such that the National Assembly accepted the overthrow of the feudal system as a *fait accompli*. What had started as financial crisis was ending up as social revolution.

## From *Rights of Man* to a state of war

Hopes for human betterment that had long been nurtured (see 'Enlightenment: England and France' in Part V) came to the fore and offered the new National Assembly a template for social progress grounded in fundamental individual rights. The Declaration of the Rights of Man promulgated on 26 August 1789 offered a panoply of liberties (expression, press, belief, trade, etc.) and equalities (before the law, in tax liability, etc.) that seemed truly, well, . . . revolutionary (Hunt 2007; Box 2). In a heady mood of hope and optimism, the deputies set about reorganizing France as a genuinely modern society. In terms of throwing off the shackles of the past and reorganizing a society on abstract principles, nothing on this scale had ever happened before.

Hopes for continued unity and harmony proved difficult to sustain, and even those favourably disposed to the revolution disagreed on important issues. Most deputies supported a property franchise, for example, while radical groups – including clubs and societies outside the Assembly such as the JACOBIN network – argued for universal manhood suffrage (in this as in so much in the Revolution, women did not get much of a look in). Disagreement was even more fundamental in the case of groups which had lost most. Many churchmen initially welcomed religious reform. Yet the Civil Constitution of the Clergy of 1790–91, which effectively made the Church a department of state, disenchanted many members of the cloth, also because freedom of religion seemed to put Protestantism on the same level as Catholicism. The 'non-juring' clergy, who refused the constitutional oath of allegiance, would join the nobles as a second thorn in the Revolution's side. The third was the monarchy. The king had perhaps lost most of all, not least his Divine Right status and his capacity to legislate (a role which now fell to the National Assembly) – and he bitterly resented his circumstances.

These three oppositional forces stimulated disharmony in the legislative arena and beyond. From 1790 onwards economic disruption triggered severe problems of law and order. Many nobles and clergymen emigrated, seeking military aid from France's enemies to overthrow the new regime. The king failed to deter them. An attempt by Louis and his family to flee the country – the 'Flight to Varennes', 21 June 1791 – turned into a fiasco. From the autumn of 1791 onwards, the GIRONDIN grouping of deputies in the Assembly pushed for an aggressive foreign policy to rally patriotic

## Box 2

'The National Assembly recognizes and declares, in the presence and under the auspices of the Supreme Being, the following rights of man and the citizen.

1. Men are born and remain free and equal in rights. Social distinctions can be based only on public utility.
2. The aim of every political association is the preservation of the natural and imprescriptible rights of man. These rights are freedom, property, security and resistance to oppression.
3. The source of all sovereignty resides essentially in the nation . . .
4. Liberty consists in the power to do anything that does not injure others . . .
6. Law is the expression of the general will. All citizens have the right to take part personally or by their representatives in its formation . . .
10. No one should be disturbed on account of his opinions, even religious, provided their manifestation does not upset the public order established by law . . .
11. The free communication of ideas and opinions is one of the most precious of the rights of man. Every citizen can then freely speak, write and publish . . .
13. A general tax is indispensable for the maintenance of the public force and for the expenses of administration, common; it ought to be equally apportioned among all citizens according to their means.'

Extracts from 'The Declaration of the Rights of Man' of 26 August 1789.

*(Mason and Rizzo 1999, 103–4)*

## Box 3

'A sans-culotte, sirs, you Rogues? It is a being who always goes about on foot, who has no millions as you would like to have, no chateaux, no valets to serve him, and who is housed simply with his wife and children, if he has them, on the fourth or fifth floor. He is useful, because he knows how to work a field, how to forge, saw, file, roof, make shoes, and spill his blood to the very last drop for the good of the Republic. In the evening he goes to his section, not powdered, perfumed, and outfitted in the hope of attracting the attention of all the citizennesses in the stands, but rather to support the good motions with all his energy, and to crush those that come from the abominable faction of the statesmen.

'For the rest, a sans-culotte always has his sabre with the razor's edge, to cut off the ears of all the malefactors. Sometimes he walks with his pike; but at the first sound of the drum he can be seen leaving for the Vendée, for the army of the Alps or for the army of the North.'

Extract from *What is a Sans-Culotte?* of 1793.

*(Mason and Rizzo 1999, 197–98)*

forces against foreign powers, *émigrés* and internal enemies. War was declared against much of Europe on 20 April 1792. When things went badly, many supporters of the Revolution blamed the king, nobility and non-juring clergy. With foreign troops threatening a breakthrough on the north-eastern front leaving Paris open to invasion, the radical popular movement in Paris – the so-called *sans-culottes* – launched an insurrection which on 10 August 1792 overthrew the king (Box 3).

## Republic and terror

In 1789, only a handful of intellectuals had imagined France without a king. Now, given Louis XVI's behaviour and the unpredictable turn of events, no other option was thinkable. A new national assembly, the Convention, voted in by manhood suffrage, duly declared a republic on 21 September 1792. Victory at the battle of Valmy on the same day allowed the assembly breathing-space by removing the immediate threat of allied invasion. That autumn also, however, saw the 'September Massacres', whereby Parisian *sans-culottes*, fearing an internal plot, massacred prisoners in the Parisian gaols. These events convinced monarchists of the nefariousness of the Revolutionary cause, but they divided republicans too. The Girondins recoiled in horror, blaming the Parisian popular movement and its defenders in the Convention, the so-called MONTAGNARDS, prominent among whom was Maximilien Robespierre.

By spring 1793, war was going badly again. In the west, the department of the Vendée rose in open revolt against the Convention. Here, as in many other rural areas, the Revolution had failed to deliver all the benefits it had promised, and there was resentment against higher taxes, demands for military service and religious reforms viewed as anti-Catholic. Stoked up by nobles and non-juring clergy, peasant revolt in the west rumbled on throughout the 1790s. In the short-term, over 1793 and into 1794, however, it was contained, and allied incursions kept at bay – but only by the Convention adopting policies of Terror.

Terror had three main facets (Edelstein 2009). First of these was the centralization of power. Legislative and executive power was vested in a committee of the Convention, the Committee of Public Safety (CPS), whose most prominent member from July 1793 was Robespierre. The CPS was a war cabinet, a ministry of information for ideological rectitude and a ministry of the interior, enforcing emergency policies. Second, Terror involved the deliberate inculcation of fear as a weapon of government. The Revolutionary Tribunal savagely judged any crimes adjudged to be counter-revolutionary, and the newly invented guillotine was a potent symbol of Terror. Third, the government sought to mobilize popular support for revolutionary government by introducing egalitarian social policies. The LEVÉE EN MASSE introduced on 23 August 1793 was the first conscription law of modern times. The CPS gave the mobilized masses something worth fighting for: the vote, the sale of Church lands, price controls on basic commodities, a range of welfare programmes, and so on.

The enthusiasm of the popular classes in fighting for the revolutionary cause proved ultimately more than a match for the allied forces. By summer 1793, Revolutionary armies were invading France's neighbours. What had started as a war of national defence was becoming a war of expansion. The feeling in the Convention that the time had come for a slackening of the grip of Terror was not, however, shared by Robespierre and the most ideologically driven members of the CPS, who looked for an intensification of Terror so as to create a 'republic of virtue'. On several occasions since the summer of 1793, the Montagnards had purged the Convention of their more lukewarm opponents (starting with the Girondins in June of that year). Robespierre's threat to institute a new purge led deputies of all political persuasions to combine to overthrow him on 27 July 1794, or 9 Thermidor Year II in the new revolutionary calendar (see Figure VII.1, page 409).

## The aftermath of terror

Many histories of the Revolution end at 9 Thermidor, viewing the rest of the decade as a warm-up act for Napoleon Bonaparte who was to seize power by the *coup d'état* of 18 Brumaire Year VIII (9 November 1799). True, most of the heroic as well as the blackest days had by then passed. Yet post-Thermidorian statesmen still had an enormously difficult political challenge to tackle, and the outcome was far from inevitable. Finally, in 1795, a new constitution was introduced which aimed to create a liberal regime, the Directory, which placed liberty over equality, and in which political power was restrained through a complex system of checks and balances.

It was difficult to run such a fragile political system in a post-Terror atmosphere and with the state still at war. In the event, a regime which stressed the primordial importance of the rule of law found itself endlessly flouting the rule of law for reasons of political pragmatism. Once war started to go badly in 1798–99, it seemed unlikely that the Directory could cope. Faced with the choice between a popular regime of Terror on the lines of 1793–94 and an authoritarian regime headed by a charismatic military figure, politicians chose the latter. Napoleon had won enormous popularity by his victories in the Italian campaigns of 1796–97 and would be in power until 1815. Besides redrawing the map of Europe, he imposed order within France. Although the Napoleonic regime endorsed many Revolutionary gains, it also established a political culture in many respects closer to ANCIEN RÉGIME absolutism than to the polemical world of 1790s politics.

## Assessment

The English revolution lacked the ideological and social underpinnings to secure its long-term survival. Republicanism grew, without ever attracting more than a small minority. Puritanism, a powerful force, splintered into an array of rival denominations, and harsh puritan discipline in the localities alienated many. In 1660 a nation terrified of anarchy placed few restrictions on Charles II, welcomed home as a symbol of order and tradition. But the clock could not be turned back altogether. The restored Church of England failed to secure the monopoly it demanded; moreover, no one could forget that a king had been put to death by his own subjects, and that his son now wore the crown by parliament's invitation. Whatever the RHETORIC, 'divine-right' monarchy was never the same again and when James II failed to recognize these new political realities, he was swiftly driven from his throne in 1688.

The French Revolution lasted only a decade, and Napoleon did his best to water down much of its democratic implications, a task that the restored Bourbons after 1815 continued with gusto. Yet the long-term influence of the Revolution has been immense. Most significantly perhaps, it has offered a script for political modernity based on individual liberties. Not all have followed that script – and the English in particular have a rather different narrative dating back to Magna Carta (as British Prime Minister Margaret Thatcher was impolite enough to remind French President François Mitterrand at the time of the bicentennial celebrations in Paris in 1989). But much of the French Revolutionary message was spread across Europe on the bayonets of Revolutionary and Napoleonic armies down to 1815, before being globalized through the French Empire from the early nineteenth century onwards. France has been a model for other political revolutions, 1917 in Russia not least, and ultimately has influenced states that have never thought themselves revolutionary in the slightest. The United Nations' Universal Declaration of Human Rights of 1948 was manifestly modelled on the 1789 Declaration of the Rights of Man. In this way, the French Revolution has powerfully shaped the way we think about democracy in the twenty-first century.

The English and French revolutions followed broadly similar trajectories. Initially moderate, both developed a radical character culminating in regicide, and then consolidation under the rule of a military hero. In both cases, the monarchies restored in 1660 and 1815 proved fragile. The contrasts, however, are equally striking. England did not experience a Terror; while in France civil war was a less potent force. Religion played a far greater role in England, democratic ideology in France. The Declaration of the Rights of Man makes the French Revolution look recognizably modern; the nearest English equivalents were manifestoes by the Levellers, a group that never came close to wielding power. And while French people today are generally proud of their revolution, the English remain deeply divided over theirs.

## Discussion themes

1. What is a 'revolution'?
2. Compare and contrast revolution in seventeenth-century England and eighteenth-century France.

## Bibliography

### (A) Sources

Firth, C. H. ed. (1992 [originally 1891]), *The Clarke Papers*, Woodbridge
Hill, Christopher ed. (1973), *Winstanley: The Law of Freedom and other Writings*, Harmondsworth
Mason, Laura and Rizzo, Tracey (1999), *The French Revolution*, Boston and New York
Nalson, John (1684), *A True Copy of the Journal of the High Court of Justice for the Tryal of K. Charles I*, London

### (B) Literature

Auslander, Leora (2009), *Cultural Revolution: Everyday Life and Politics in Britain, North America and France*, Berkeley
Braddick, Michael (2008), *God's Fury, England's Fire: A New History of the English Civil Wars*, London
Bradstock, Andrew (2011), *Radical Religion in Cromwell's England*, London
Edelstein, Dan (2009), *The Terror of Natural Right: Republicanism, the Cult of Nature and the French Revolution*, Stanford
Hunt, Lynn (2007), *Inventing Human Rights: A History*, New York
Jones, Colin (2002), *The Great Nation: France from Louis XIV to Napoleon 1715–99*, London
Morrill, John ed. (1990), *Oliver Cromwell and the English Revolution*, London
Peacey, Jason (2008), *The Regicides and the Execution of Charles I*, Basingstoke
Woolrych, Austin (2002), *Britain in Revolution, 1625–1660*, Oxford

### (C) Web resources

'Women's Lives in the British Civil Wars': <http://earlymodernweb.org/warlives/wlintro.htm>
'Levellers Day': <http://levellersday.wordpress.com/>
'Liberty, Equality, Fraternity: Exploring the French Revolution', edited by Jack Censer and Lynn Hunt: <http://chnm.gmu.edu/revolution/>
'*Tableaux de la Révolution* database', Waddesdon Manor, Rothschild Collection: <https://waddesdon.org.uk/the-collection/tableaux-de-la-revolution/>

# PART VII
# EPILOGUE

# Europe in 1800

*Humfrey Butters*

If, by an astonishing feat of technological precocity, it had been possible to lodge our Venetian ambassador ('Europe in 1500' in Part I) in a deep freeze in 1500 and then to defrost him around 1800, what changes would this long-suffering observer have noticed in the European world? He would certainly have been greatly shocked to learn that not merely Europeans but all inhabitants of the planet now lived in a different universe, a heliocentric rather than a geocentric one, in which the same laws of physics obtained everywhere, in defiance of Aristotle's view that there were radical differences between the earth and the other planets ('The scientific revolution' in Part V).

## Economic developments

He would have been, as a loyal son of his native city, particularly disturbed by the dramatically altered position of Venice, at the centre of the European economy in 1500, on its margins in 1800. This was one striking example of a much wider phenomenon, the development of a global economy, a long-term consequence of the voyages of Columbus and Vasco da Gama, whose principal beneficiaries in Europe were the northern rather than the southern powers ('Expanding horizons' in Part IV). Europe had changed in another significant respect: its population was far larger. In the eighteenth century alone it grew from about 120 to c. 190 million (Blanning 2002, 123) and an increasing proportion of that population lived in towns: in England, for example, the percentage was 5.5 in 1520, 27.5 in 1801 (Brewer 1989, 181).

The two most vigorous economies were those of France and Great Britain, and although it is easy to assume, and *was* previously assumed, that the latter's INDUSTRIAL REVOLUTION must have given it an easy superiority in the eighteenth century, this is not the case: one economic historian, indeed, has argued that in France manufacturing output grew more rapidly between the decade 1700–1710 and the decade 1790–1800 than in Britain, even though judged qualitatively British manufacturing was superior to that of its French rival. Historians in general are now more sceptical than they were before about the value of the term, for although the industrial sector undoubtedly grew substantially in the course of the eighteenth and nineteenth century, the dramatic and rapid transition from an economy based on agriculture and handicraft to one based on mass, mechanized production to which the phrase Industrial Revolution refers simply did not take place: in 1841 only 25 of the firms in Lancashire involved in spinning and weaving had a workforce of over a thousand, nine hundred and fifty did not (Hilton 2006, 11); and in those sectors of British industry not devoted to producing textiles, the bulk of production was based on traditional methods. Nor is it true that Britain owed its prosperity in the nineteenth century primarily to manufacturing: import and export figures for 1846, for example, indicate clearly that foreign commerce played a far more important role, a fact that would have reassured our ambassador, coming as he did from a city whose wealth had been based largely on foreign commerce.

## Social structure

In the eighteenth century the numbers, wealth, political importance and social standing of those engaged in European commerce, banking and industry were undoubtedly greater than they had been in 1500. At the same time from Denmark to Naples the whole system of FEUDAL or seigneurial privileges was subjected to unprecedented attack by Enlightenment thinkers and reforming ministers ('Enlightenment' in Part V). But it would be quite mistaken to deduce that henceforth European political and social life were dominated by businessmen and industrialists from the middle ranks of society. First of all because the nobility and gentry continued to play a central role in political life. Two British examples illustrate this point rather well. At the beginning of George III's reign (1760) Cornwall had more merchant MPs than any other county, and yet there were only six of them out of a total of 48 (Namier 1968, 355); and in Lord Salisbury's Cabinet of 1895, not for the first time, nobles outnumbered commoners (Powis 1984, 69). Secondly, the majority of those from the middle ranks who came to play a significant part in politics were not in the main businessmen. In France in 1792 the latter constituted only ten per cent of the membership of the National Convention (Jones 2002, 462), though this revolutionary assembly was dominated by members of the third estate. Thirdly the nobility and gentry were involved in a variety of ways in business and manufacturing, despite longstanding prejudices against 'trade'.

PEASANTS still formed the majority of the population in most European states. Their conditions varied considerably: serfdom still survived in parts of Germany, Eastern Europe and Russia, though it disappeared in Prussia between 1807 and 1848; in Western Europe it had already largely vanished by 1500, but seigneurial dues and services often survived, to be swept away in France by the Revolution; in England, however, these were largely unknown. In France, even before the abolition of the feudal system, conditions for the peasantry were improving in some respects, so that the population as a whole was able to grow by 25 per cent between 1715 and 1789.

Women were coming to play a more public role in some respects than they had played before, though even French revolutionaries of the male sex were rarely keen on giving them the vote. Women authors were now more prominent than they had

**Box 1**

There were some vigorous campaigners for women's education in the eighteenth century. Daniel Defoe was one of them:

'I have often thought of it as one of the most barbarous customs in the world, considering us as a civilized and a Christian country, that we deny the advantages of learning to women. We reproach the sex every day with folly and impertinence; while I am confident, had they the advantages of education equal to us, they would be guilty of less than ourselves.'

*(Defoe 1719; Web resources)*

been in 1500 and the percentage of literate females had nearly doubled between the reign of Louis XIV and the 1780s (Box 1; Jones 2002, 185).

Social hierarchy worked as before to the advantage of some women, so that, for example, a male from the middle or lower ranks of society would normally have been singularly ill advised to insult or displease a female noble. And, as before, the 'double standard' in sexual matters was a sign of inequality, for it showed that a higher value was put on womens' virginity than on that of men. At law, however, men's standing was generally superior to that of women. Economic changes sometimes benefited women: the expansion of the textile industry in England brought employment to many, in part because they were generally paid less than men (Hilton 2006, 362).

## The role of religion

One feature of Europe in 1800 that would certainly have upset our Venetian ambassador was the existence and importance of Protestantism. But Christianity itself had not become a marginal feature in the more tolerant world of the eighteenth century ('Religious culture' in Part III). In England the Church of England was still the established church and, in theory, Nonconformists and Catholics were both barred from formal participation in politics. Anglicanism's official position did not prevent it, moreover, from generating reforming movements of considerable importance, as the example of John Wesley and of the evangelical revival in general shows. Intensely committed to the moral improvement of society, evangelicalism's greatest monument was the abolition of the slave trade.

In France the continuing authority of the Catholic Church, and the machinery of government censorship had made it difficult, sometimes dangerous, for much of the eighteenth century to try to publish heterodox ideas; but the French Revolution changed all that. By establishing freedom of thought in religion, abolishing the ecclesiastical tithe, nationalizing church property and establishing the civil constitution of the clergy, the revolutionaries were implementing Enlightenment ideas, but the

> **Box 2**
>
> Despite the fact that Jean Jacques Rousseau was an outspoken political and social radical, he considered religious belief indispensable to the ideal society he described in *The Social Contract* and devised a 'civic faith' for it. Its fundamental tenets included belief in God and in an afterlife. He also made it clear that this was no optional extra:
>
> > 'If anybody, after having publicly accepted these same dogmas, conducts himself as if he did not believe them, he shall be punished by death; he has committed the greatest of all crimes.'
> >
> > *(Rousseau 1915, ii, 132)*

dechristianization campaign that took place during the most radical phase of the Revolution went far beyond what most PHILOSOPHES had contemplated (Box 2).

These various attacks on the Catholic Church created a profound fissure in French social and political life that lasted till the end of the twentieth century.

## Enlightenment and public sphere

One topic much discussed by historians in recent decades has been the formation in this period, thanks to such developments as the expansion of the urban sector, the growth of literacy, improvements in communications, the rise of newspapers, and the appearance of COFFEE-HOUSES, of a 'bourgeois public sphere' in which 'public opinion' could express itself (Blanning 2002). The expression 'bourgeois public sphere' was coined by the German sociologist Jürgen Habermas, a member of the Frankfurt school of MARXISTS, which sought to give far greater weight to 'cultural' factors and less to economic ones than Marx had done (Habermas 1989). The view has several defects. Firstly, eighteenth-century nobles and clergy played just as significant a role in the 'public sphere' as the bourgeoisie did. Secondly, Habermas maintains that in the Middle Ages there was no clear distinction between public and private, an opinion to be found long ago in the writings of distinguished medievalists such as Gierke and Maitland, but now largely discredited by the work of later scholars (Post 1964). Thirdly, he considered that medieval political representation was of a completely different type from the parliamentary sort, since the powerful 'represented' their power directly, that is 'made it present' through symbols and rituals to a passive populace. This notion of representation captured one important aspect of medieval and early modern political culture, but only one. The view, common in the fifteenth century, that power was based on opinion or reputation implied that the 'people' were far from passive. In the *Prince* Machiavelli had urged European rulers to please the 'people', if they wished to retain power, a timely message given the high casualty rate suffered by Italian regimes in his lifetime. Fourthly, the reason, moreover, why medieval rulers often insisted that those who sent representatives to parliaments and estates should give them full powers, was that without the granting of this authority, the former would not be bound by the consent of the latter. Finally, the contention that 'rational argument' in a 'public sphere' was unknown before the eighteenth century can only be defended by defining 'rational' and 'public' so eccentrically that it becomes true by definition. The great upheavals of the sixteenth and seventeenth centuries, for example, such as the Reformation or the English Civil War, were marked by countless public discussions involving the popular classes as well as their social superiors. Nor was such 'popular participation' confined to periods of crisis and social turmoil (Te Brake 1998).

It cannot be denied, however, that in the eighteenth century there was an *expansion* of the public sphere. The Enlightenment benefited from that development. This movement was influenced by, but also helped to promote, a gradual lowering of the temperature of religious debate. One sign was the emergence of DEISM, whose advocates believed in a God who, having created the universe as a perfect machine, had no need to intervene in its workings by revealing himself to man. Deism was the creed of a small minority and agnosticism (or atheism) of an even smaller one, but their emergence, in however guarded a form, is undoubtedly significant. More widely diffused among the educated, and especially anyone sympathetic to the Enlightenment, was the conviction that Isaac Newton's largely mechanistic account of the universe was correct. The immense prestige attaching to the discoveries of Newton and of other theorists of the natural world encouraged Enlightenment thinkers to hope that similarly profound breakthroughs could be made by students of society, of economics and of political structures: if they adopted the same methods, they should be able to reveal the operation of general causal laws like those governing the physical universe. This aspiration lay behind such classics of Enlightenment thought as Montesquieu's *Spirit of the Laws* and Adam Smith's *The Wealth of Nations*. One impressive feature of mechanistic theories of the universe, whether those of Newton, or of his predecessors Descartes and Galileo, was the central role played in them by mathematics; to reproduce that element in moral philosophy or in economics an appropriate unit of measurement had to be discovered to allow quantification to proceed. For Utilitarianism this was happiness, for economics the labour theory of value, judgements which had an immense impact on society and government in nineteenth-century Europe.

Many of these new ideas our ambassador would have found puzzling, or even unfathomable, but he would undoubtedly have been reassured to learn that in 1800 a classical education was still normally seen as necessary for a gentleman, and that most thinkers of the Enlightenment were steeped in classical culture. In the course of the eighteenth century French replaced Latin as the most popular language for scholarly works; but the Latin and Greek classics continued to be the common currency of the educated upper classes. RHETORIC was still an important subject, as it had been for Renaissance HUMANISTS: Adam Smith lectured on it, and Gibbon considered it an essential element in literary criticism. Even the Enlightenment's signal contributions to the early development of the 'social sciences', discussed above, were strongly influenced by the humanists' extensive deployment of the comparative method, and by the interest shown in humanist scholarly commentaries on classical texts in subjects such as religion, law, morality and customs (Butters 2008, 484–85).

## Political life

It was not only the French revolutionaries' attacks on Catholicism that would have shocked the ambassador: he would have been profoundly disturbed by the overthrow of the monarchy, the execution of Louis XVI, and the destruction of seigneurial rights and privileges. The brave new world that emerged he would have struggled to comprehend, though as a good Venetian he might have had a sneaking initial sympathy for its republicanism. But even this would have been short-lived, firstly, because in 1797 the French did what no foreign power had been able to do before, they conquered Venice; and in the second place, because the rise of Napoleon brought an end to French republican government.

The overthrow of the old order in France and the conquest of his native city were not the only momentous changes that would have persuaded our ambassador that his world had passed away: in 1806 the Holy Roman Empire, a persistent, if not absolutely continuous, feature of European political life since Charlemagne's coronation on Christmas Day 800, came to an end, destroyed by the military challenges of the French revolutionary, and then the Napoleonic, armies. No eighteenth-century observer would have been surprised that the two leading states which survived the disappearance of the empire were Austria and Prussia, but our ambassador would have been, since although Prussia existed in 1500, it was hardly a great power (Wilson 2004).

The British monarchy did not suffer the same fate as its Bourbon rival, and indeed it profited from the horror and disgust many Britons felt as they observed the excesses of the Revolutionary Terror, while experiencing a certain grim satisfaction, however, that some of the leading promoters of the Terror themselves fell victim to it (Figure VII.1; Box 3).

The Crown was, however, a very different institution from its predecessor in 1500, and not just because it was British rather than English. The balance of power between the monarchy and parliament had shifted decisively in favour of the latter, and it was no longer possible for the king to rule for any sustained length of time without summoning the Commons and the Lords (Clark 1987, 'The theory and practice of politics and government 1500–1800' in Part VI). On the other hand, the civil and military establishments over which the Crown presided were also vastly more extensive, thanks in large part to Britain's prolonged involvement, for the first time since the end of the Hundred Years War in 1453, in a series of Continental conflicts that began with the replacement of James II by Mary and her Dutch husband William, who was keen to use England's resources against Louis XIV. In the Nine Years War

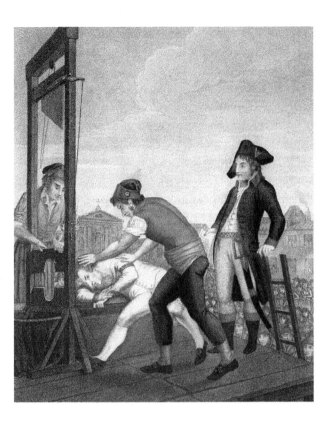

**Figure VII.1** Many contemporary observers interpreted the execution of Maximilien Robespierre, the figurehead of an increasingly ruthless and unpopular regime (which persecuted all political opponents in 'The Reign of Terror'), as a symbol of the degeneration and failure of the French Revolution. 'The Death of Robespierre, 28 July 1794' engraved by James Idnarpila (1799), after J. Beys / Musée de la Ville de Paris, Musée Carnavalet, Paris, France / Bridgeman Images.

## Box 3

Sir Samuel Romilly (1757–1818), a prominent legal reformer, considered that the French Revolution had tended to discredit reforming projects in general in England:

'If any person be desirous of having an adequate idea of the mischievous effects which have been produced in this country by the French Revolution and all its attendant horrors, he should attempt some reforms on humane and liberal principles. He will then find not only what a stupid spirit of conservation, but what a savage spirit, it has suffused into the minds of his countrymen.'

*(Bagehot 1881, 291–92)*

(1689–97), known as 'William's war', the army employed an average of around 76,000 men, the navy around 40,000 (Brewer 1989, 30); in 1803, facing the threat of a French invasion, the British government had over 800,000 men in its armed forces (Hilton 2006, 102). The civil bureaucracy grew mightily as well: an incomplete record of central administration lists 2,524 full-time civil servants in the fiscal sector in 1690; in 1782 / 3 the corresponding figure was 8,292 (Brewer 1989, 66–67).

The conflicts between France and Britain that ended in 1815 were global. It says much for Britain's resources and resourcefulness that she was able to survive the loss of her American colonies and still play an important part in the downfall of Napoleon; but this was a triumph for which several powers could claim a share of the credit, not least of all the Russians, whose defeat of his ill-judged invasion of 1812 was decisive. The rise of Russia to great power status was another striking feature of the eighteenth century that would have amazed our Venetian ambassador, but he would have been even more surprised to learn that by 1850 about 25 per cent of the world's population was subject to British rule. Poland, by contrast, which when joined with Lithuania had constituted the largest state in sixteenth-century Europe, had suffered the immense humiliation of being partitioned by its European rivals in the eighteenth century ('European politics from the Peace of Westphalia to the French Revolution *c.* 1650–1800' in Part VI).

There was much, therefore, for our Venetian friend to digest when he surveyed the world in 1800. As a classicist he might have been led to reflect on the contrast between it and the smaller, more reassuring one evoked in Socrates's famous remark that those who dwelt around the Mediterranean in his day were like frogs squatting around a pond.

## Discussion themes

1. What were the principal economic changes experienced by Europeans between 1500 and 1800?
2. To what extent had the position of the nobility in European society altered between 1500 and 1800?
3. How far had European thought been 'secularized' by 1800?

## Bibliography

### (A) Sources

Rousseau, Jean Jacques (1915), *The Political Writings of Jean-Jacques Rousseau*, ed. C. E. Vaughan, 2 vols, Cambridge

### (B) Literature

Bagehot, Walter (1881), *Biographical Studies*, ed. R. H. Hutton, London
*Blanning, Timothy (2002), *The Culture of Power and the Power of Culture: Old Regime Europe 1660–1789*, Oxford
Brewer, John (1989), *The Sinews of Power. War and the English State 1688–1783*, London

Butters, Humfrey (2008), 'Machiavelli and the Enlightenment: Humanism, Political Theory and the Origins of the "Social Sciences"', in: *Florence and Beyond. Culture, Society and Politics in Renaissance Italy*, ed. D. Peterson and D. Bornstein, Toronto, 481–97

Clark, Jonathan (1987), *English Society 1688–1832. Ideology, Social Structure and Political Practice during the Ancien Régime*, Cambridge

Habermas, Jürgen (1989), *The Structural Transformation of the Public Sphere*, Cambridge

*Hilton, Boyd (2006), *A Mad, Bad, and Dangerous People. England 1783–1846*, Oxford

Jones, Colin (2002), *The Great Nation: France from Louis XV to Napoleon*, London

Namier, Lewis (1968), *The Structure of Politics at the Accession of George III*, 2nd edn, London

Post, Gaines (1964), *Studies in Medieval Legal Thought: Public Law and the State 1100–1322*, Princeton, NJ

Powis, Jonathan (1984), *Aristocracy*, Oxford

Te Brake, Wayne (1998), *Shaping History: Ordinary People in European Politics 1500–1700*, Berkeley, CA

Wilson, Peter (2004), *From Reich to Revolution: German History, 1558–1806*, Basingstoke

## (C) Web resources

Daniel Defoe, 'On the Education of Women' (1719), IHSP: <http://www.fordham.  edu/halsall/mod/1719defoe-women.html>

# APPENDICES

**Map 1** Europe c. 1500.

**414**  Maps

**Map 2** Europe c. 1800.

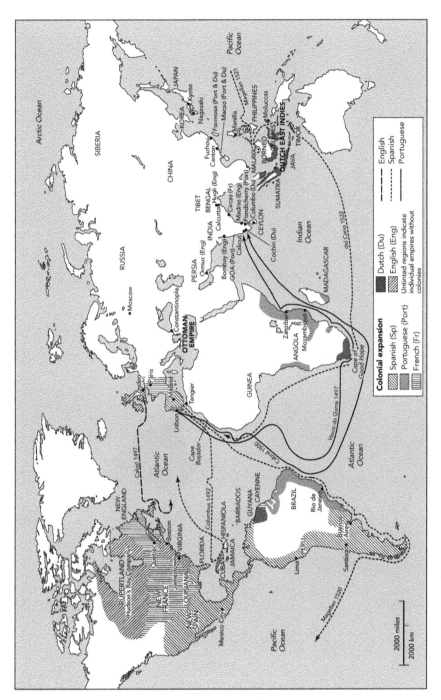

**Map 3** European explorations and empires 1400–1700.

This map features principal voyages, main areas of colonial expansion and a selection of place names mentioned in the preceding chapters. It cannot reflect the complexity of the situation in all regions of the globe.

Within the map:

Arctic Ocean

SIBERIA

RUSSIA

•Moscow

CHINA

TIBET

PERSIA

INDIA

BENGAL

Ormuz (Eng)
Calcutta
Hugli (Eng)
Bombay (Eng)
GOA (Port)
Calicut
Cochin (Du)
CEYLON

Circas (Fr)
Madras (Eng)
Pondicherry (Fr)
Columbo (Port)

Indian Ocean

MADAGASCAR

Zanzibar
Mozambique

ANGOLA

GUINEA

Cape of Good Hope

KOREA
JAPAN
Kyoto
Nagasaki

Fuzhou
Canton
Formosa (Port & Du)
Macao (Port & Du)

PHILIPPINES
Manila
Moluccas

MALAYA
BORNEO
DUTCH EAST INDIES
SUMATRA
JAVA
TIMOR

del Cano 1522

Magellan 1521

Vasco da Gama 1497

Cabral 1500

OTTOMAN EMPIRE

Constantinople

Paris
London
Madrid
Lisbon
Tangier

Cape Bojador

Atlantic Ocean

Cabot 1497

NEW ENGLAND
Boston
Quebec
NEW FRANCE
Hudson's Bay Company
RUPERTLAND
NEW SPAIN
LOUISIANA
VIRGINIA
FLORIDA
Mexico City
CUBA
HISPANIOLA
JAMAICA
BARBADOS
GUYANA
CAYENNE

Columbus 1492

BRAZIL
Rio de Janeiro

PERU
Lima
Santiago
Buenos Aires

Magellan 1520

Atlantic Ocean

Pacific Ocean

Pacific Ocean

2000 miles
2000 km

**Colonial expansion**

Spanish (Sp)
Portuguese (Port)
French (Fr)
Dutch (Du)
English (Eng)
Untinted regions indicate individual empires without colonies

– – – English
– · – · Spanish
——— Portuguese

COMPANION WEBSITE

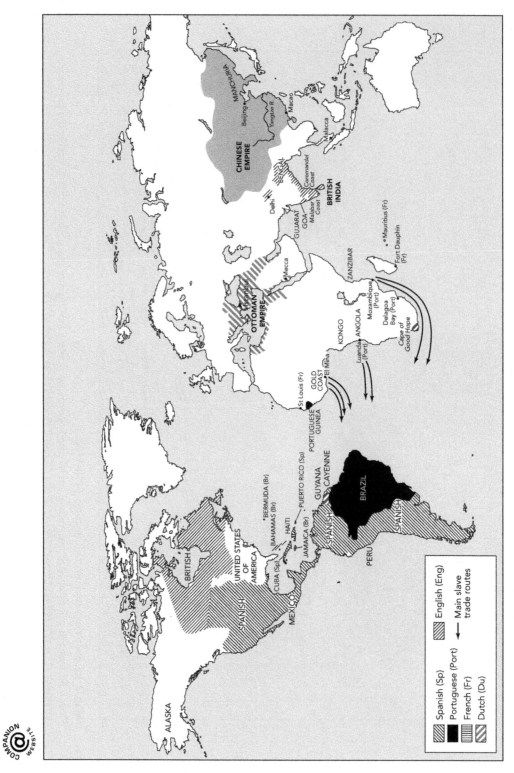

**Map 4** The world c. 1800.

# Glossary

**A PRIORI** Style of thinking based on derivation from fixed principles; the Enlightenment rejected this approach in favour of more 'inductive' (rather than 'deductive') or empirical reasoning derived from individual experience.

**ABSOLUTISM** The view that the ruler was a source of law and so not legally subject to it.

**ACADEMIES** Centres of learning often founded by princes in the context of the scientific revolution.

**ACCULTURATION** The repression of traditional, 'superstitious' customs and beliefs by the dominant, elite culture.

**AGRICULTURAL REVOLUTION** The period after *c.* 1750 when changes in agricultural output and the technology and organization of production (such as ENCLOSURE, crop rotation, improved drainage and fertilization) are believed to have led to fundamental transformations.

**ANABAPTISM** Radical movement of Christians rejecting both Catholicism and mainstream Protestantism; characterized by principles of separation from the world and baptism of adult believers.

**ANCIEN RÉGIME** The way in which French revolutionaries after 1789 referred to the former (*ancien*) social and political system.

**ANNUITY** A financial investment yielding a regular/yearly payment.

**ANTICHRIST** The devilish opponent of Christ, His exact opposite, used by Protestants to mean the Pope.

**ANTICLERICALISM** Although coined for a later period, the term is now generally used for resentment of members of the clergy and their wealth/privileges, which varied greatly between periods and regions.

**ANTIQUITY** The age of ancient Greece and Rome, singled out as a separate period by the RENAISSANCE HUMANISTS.

**BALANCE OF POWER** The notion that no state, or group of states, should monopolize power, but exist in an equilibrium with others.

**BANDEIRANTES** Frontiersmen of the Brazilian interior, usually from São Paulo, pursuing precious metals and Indian slaves.

**BANYAN** A man's informal robe made of Asian cotton or silk and worn in Europe in the late seventeenth and eighteenth centuries.

**BAROQUE** An architectural and artistic style marked by elaboration and opulence flourishing in *c.* 1600–1750. It became closely associated with the Catholic Reformation and the term is sometimes used for the period as a whole.

**BENEFICE** An ecclesiastical living.

**BENZOIN** A resin that was (and is) used as a common ingredient in incense-making and perfumery because of its sweet vanilla-like aroma.

**BLACK DEATH** The most serious outbreak of PLAGUE across Europe 1347–49.

**BOCAGE** The Norman French word for a terrain of mixed woodland and pasture.

**BRIDEWELLS** The collective term for houses of correction or prisons named after the penal institution established in London in the 1550s.

**BUCCANEERS** from French *boucanier*, or one who uses a *boucan* for grilling and smoking meat; a frontier settler in the Caribbean, living informally on island coasts and engaged in piracy.

**BUDDHISM** The religious system founded by Buddha in India in the fifth century BCE, from where it spread to East Asia.

**CALICOES** General term used by Europeans to refer to cotton textiles imported from India.

**CALIPH** A title indicating the preeminent Muslim ruler in the world. The Ottoman Sultans claimed to be caliphs after their conquest of Egypt, Syria and the Hijaz in 1517.

**CAMEOS** Small-scale shallow relief decoration executed in gemstones.

**CAPITALISM** An economic system based on the principles of private property, profit orientation and intensive market exchange.

**CAPITULATIONS** Unilateral grants of privilege made by the Ottoman Sultan to the merchants of particular European nations, detailing conditions of trade including duties and tax rates.

**CARTESIANISM** A way of doing philosophy owing its central tenets to René Descartes.

**CATECHISM** A book of religious instruction set out in a simple question-and-answer format; also refers to the teaching of basic religious knowledge.

**CHANTRY** An ecclesiastical BENEFICE endowed for a priest to celebrate daily masses for the souls of founders and other beneficiaries (for a number of years or in perpetuity).

**CHARIVARI** Rowdy processions mocking those seen as flouting the values of the community, especially wives who beat and cheat on their husbands, and marriages (especially second marriages) with a great disparity in age between bride and groom (see also SKIMMINGTON).

**CHINTZ** Painted or printed cotton originally produced in India and later imitated by European manufacturers.

**CHOSROES** The name of two emperors of the Sassanian dynasty in pre-Islamic Persia. The name was later used in many Asian societies as a synonym for 'emperor' in the same way that 'Caesar' was used in Europe.

CITY-STATES Originating as the principal socio-political unit in the ancient world and revived in the Middle Ages. Distinguished from normal cities and towns by the extent of their political independence and by being composed of a city and a territory beyond its walls.

COFFEE HOUSES Originating in the mid-seventeenth century, urban cafés became key places in which Enlightenment sociability (discussion and debate, newspaper-reading, networking) was conducted.

COMMUNES Italian CITY-STATE republics.

COMPLEXION The balance of the qualities of hot, cold, moist and dry resulting from the mixture of the ELEMENTS in the human body. Each person was born with an idiosyncratic complexion which had to be kept in its innate balance. Any imbalance of people's complexion could result in disease.

CONFESSIONALIZATION A scholarly concept, developed by Wolfgang Reinhard and Heinz Schilling, which sees early modern Europe shaped (and modernized) by the disciplining campaigns of the major confessions and the close collaboration between Church and state.

CONSISTORY The local governing body of Reformed churches including ministers and lay elders.

CONTRIBUTIONS Tributes in money and kind levied by occupying armies.

CONVERSO A converted Jew or New Christian.

COUNCIL The elected governing body in many European towns.

COURTIERS Those who lived at and visited the court to attend on the monarch. In the early modern period their manners and behaviour were increasingly codified.

CRIOLLOS From spanish *criar*, 'to raise'; people of Spanish descent born in the Americas.

DAOISM One of the main religions of China, based on the search for the Dao ('the Way') through meditation, public worship and alchemy.

DEISM A worldview in which the universe functions according to rules established at its creation without further intervention by God.

DEMESNE Land under the direct ownership (and sometimes cultivation) of a lord.

DEMONOLOGY The study of the operation of the devil in the world.

DEVSHIRME The Ottoman practice of levying boys from the empire's Christian population, who became slaves, converted to Islam, and were trained at the palace before entering imperial service as administrators and soldiers.

DIET A representative assembly (e.g. the German Imperial Diet).

DIGGERS A short-lived communist movement in England, 1649–50, led by Gerrard Winstanley.

DIVERGENCE The term used by historians to refer to the point in time when North-west Europe began to develop economically at a far greater rate than the rest of the world.

**DIVINE (OR DOUBLE) PREDESTINATION** The belief that God has chosen some for eternal life in heaven and others for eternal damnation in hell.

**DOWRY** Payment in land and/or money by the bride's parents to the bridegroom's family.

**EAST INDIA COMPANY** A joint-stock company established in 1600 and granted the trade MONOPOLY in the East Indies by royal charter.

**ELECT** Those who have been 'elected' by God for eternal life in heaven.

**ELEMENTS AND QUALITIES** According to Ancient Greek theory of nature, the four elements earth, water, air, fire (plus a fifth element called aether which filled the superlunary sphere) explained the nature and complexity of all matter in the sublunar sphere. Each element expressed the effects of a combination of four basic haptic (tangible) qualities (hot, cold, moist, dry) which are themselves paired in polar opposites (hot/cold, moist/dry).

**ENCLOSURE** The process by which common ownership rights were extinguished, usually accompanied by the hedging or fencing of property, and often by the conversion of arable to pastoral farming. In another sense: the state of being enclosed, especially in a religious community separated from the outside world.

**ENCOMIENDA** From spanish *encomendar*, 'to entrust'; royal grant of tribute paid by groups of Indians (in goods, labour or money), in return for commitment by the holder (or *encomendero*) to Christianise Indians.

**ENCYCLOPÉDIE** 'The Bible of Enlightenment', edited by Denis Diderot, assisted by Jean-le-Rond d'Alembert. Published between 1752 and 1777 in 32 volumes (of which 11 were illustrations), it arranged knowledge alphabetically and sought to cover all aspects of the human and natural world.

**ENGENHO** Sugar mill / plantation.

**ENLIGHTENED ABSOLUTISM/DESPOTISM/MONARCHS** Name which modern historians have given to those eighteenth-century rulers/regimes influenced by Enlightenment ideas like equity and rationality (while invariably pursuing rather traditional state policies).

**ENTREPÔT** Originally a term for a storehouse, in the early modern period also used for a city, often a port (like Amsterdam), to which goods from a variety of places are brought for storage, and further distribution. Entrepôts existed throughout Asia.

**ESCHATOLOGY** Beliefs connected with the end of the world.

**ESTADO DA INDIA** 'State of India'; Portuguese India, but a term loosely applied to all Portuguese settlements and FEITORIAS between the Cape of Good Hope and Japan.

**ESTATES** A term used for landed possessions, corporate social groups (nobility, clergy, commoners) and certain types of representative assemblies.

**EUCHARIST** CEREMONY/SACRAMENT in which bread and wine is blessed and consumed as a re-creation of the Last Supper.

EXCISE TAX English tax on goods produced and consumed within the realm.

EXPERIMENTAL PHILOSOPHY The name given to a NATURAL PHILOSOPHY relying on the gathering of facts through experiments, as promoted by late seventeenth-century English thinkers, particularly the leading members of the Royal Society.

EXTENDED / MULTIPLE HOUSEHOLD Family units containing adult siblings of the husband or occasionally wife, and/or three generations rather than two.

FEITORIAS Small, sometimes fortified, trading agencies, or 'factories' (Old English) planted at strategic points along trade routes.

FEUDALISM A pyramid of personal relationships between people of unequal standing developed in the Middle Ages, in which lords grant their tenants lands and resources in return for advice, dues, labour services and general support.

FISCAL-MILITARY STATE A state capable financially and economically of sustaining large-scale warfare.

FRATERNITY An association of members for the support of religious and charitable activities, often with particular emphasis on the provision of elaborate funerals and sometimes with their own altar and priest(s).

FRENCH POX A new and previously unknown disease in Europe, which, according to common opinion at the time, first appeared among the soldiers of French king Charles VIII (reigned 1483–1498) during his invasion of the Italian peninsula in 1494. Of disputed origin, it became known as syphilis from the sixteenth century.

FRESCO TECHNIQUE The technique of painting with water colours on wet plaster, used for large paintings on walls.

GEOCENTRIC Used in astronomy to indicate an understanding of the cosmos that is centred on the earth.

GHETTO Named after the foundry located in the first ghetto in Venice, the area of a city in which the (usually) Jewish minority was made to live and to which it was confined at night.

GIRONDINS Loosely organized political grouping in the French National Assembly from 1791 to 1793. Included deputies from the department of the Gironde around Bordeaux, whence the name. Most were purged from the Convention in June 1793.

GRACE The supernatural assistance of God to make Christians more holy (sanctified), understood by Catholics to be principally delivered by reception of the SACRAMENTS. Much theological debate has focused on whether the free gift of God's grace is a necessary precondition for all good works, and the role that human free will plays in cooperating with grace.

GRAVAMINA Lists of complaints and concerns compiled in the context of representative assemblies and submitted to the ruling prince.

GUILDS Associations for the regulation of the affairs of a particular trade or profession. They were formally instituted with exclusive groups of master craftsmen who decided on rules of manufacture and provided mutual support for members.

HANSEATIC LEAGUE A medieval alliance of trading GUILDS and cities in northern Germany and the Baltic.

HELIOCENTRIC Used in astronomy to indicate an understanding of the cosmos that is centred on the sun.

HERESY Religious doctrines and practices considered unacceptable by ecclesiastical authorities. Offenders faced court proceedings, humiliating penalties and – in the most serious cases – death at the stake.

HERMAPHRODITES People with both male and female genitals.

HOLY LEAGUES Ad hoc alliances of Christian nations formed to fight wars against the Ottomans, authorized by the Pope.

HUGUENOTS Name given to followers of the Reformed religion in sixteenth-century France.

HUMANISM An intellectual movement engaging (in more or less explicit distancing from SCHOLASTICISM) in philological critique of key texts, education and the advancement of Christian values and morals in this world. It flourished around 1500 and featured protagonists like Erasmus of Rotterdam and Thomas More. Its members aimed for a return to the ideals of classical ANTIQUITY through close study of original Greek and Roman writings.

HUMOURS The four humours, fused in the blood of the veins and produced from foodstuff in the stomach and liver, were black bile, red or yellow bile, phlegm (or melancholy) and blood. Most diseases and disabilities supposedly resulted from an excess or deficit of one of these four humours.

ICONOCLASM The act of breaking or destroying images and objects of veneration, especially in churches. Protestant groups were often particularly keen to implement the ban against images contained in the Ten Commandments.

IMPERIALISM The expansion of territory through conquest and the establishment of economic and political control that subordinates the residents of those territories.

INDEX LIBRORUM PROHIBITORUM A list of books banned by the Catholic Church, periodically updated from the sixteenth to the twentieth century.

INDULGENCE Grant of a reduction of time to be spent in PURGATORY (i.e. a full or partial remission of sins already forgiven), issued by ecclesiastical authorities (out of the 'treasury of merit' accumulated by saints) in return for pious activities such as pilgrimages or attendance at specific MASSES. Reformers criticized abuses like the sale of such documents.

INDUSTRIAL REVOLUTION In conjunction with the AGRICULTURAL REVOLUTION, the transformation of society prompted by a combination of technological advances (steam engines, spinning frames, general mechanization), new forms of economic organization (factory production) and developments in transport infrastructure (railways, canals); conventionally understood to have occurred first in eighteenth- and nineteenth-century England.

INQUISITION A Catholic ecclesiastical body concerned with the preservation of doctrinal orthodoxy and the detection and punishment of HERESY.

INTENDANTS Royal administrators in French provinces, much used by Richelieu and Mazarin, who owed their powers to a commission, revocable by the government, rather than to the purchase of an office. They became symbols of centralization.

JACOBIN Member of the network of politically radical clubs (or Friends of the Constitution), set up from late 1789 onwards. The most famous and influential was the Paris Jacobin Club which contained many left-wing members of the National Assembly.

JANSENISM Reform movement within (particularly French) Catholicism, stressing human sinfulness and the unmerited gift of God's GRACE.

JESUITS Also known as the 'Society of Jesus', a religious order founded by the Spaniard Ignatius Loyola (1491–1556) in 1534 and sanctioned by Pope Paul III in 1540. Loyola and his followers played a key role in the global Catholic Reformation, especially in the education and spiritual guidance of social elites, and attracted much hostility from Protestant contemporaries.

JOINTURE Provision made in the marriage settlement for the bride's maintenance, should she outlive her husband.

JOURNEYMEN Craftsmen employed by MASTERS who could manufacture but not sell goods.

JUSTIFICATION The act whereby God makes a person just, and also the change in a person's condition when passing from the state of sin to that of righteousness.

LACQUER A series of techniques used to decorate metal or wood objects (e.g. pieces of furniture, boxes, bowls) by using the resin produced by lac insects.

LENT The period of 40 days preceding Easter marked by abstinence and fasting, commemorating Christ's fasting in the wilderness; also used as a metaphor for sobriety and moral restraint.

LEVÉE EN MASSE The law of 23 August 1793 mobilizing the French nation for the war effort, most notably through military service. This was the first modern call for national conscription.

LEVELLERS A radical movement, centred in London in the late 1640s, calling for the end of privilege, social reforms and a written constitution.

LIBERTY OF A CHRISTIAN Protestant view that the Christian needs no intermediary to God.

LORD'S SUPPER Protestant term for the EUCHARIST.

**MACE** A spice made from the red covering (also known as aril) of the nutmeg seed. Mace was in demand in Europe as a flavouring for both sweet and savoury dishes.

**MALEFICIA** The harmful acts committed as a result of witchcraft.

**MALTHUSIAN TRAP** Named after the political economist Thomas Malthus, the check to population growth (subsistence crisis) resulting from the inability of agricultural supply to keep pace with rising demand.

**MANCHU** The nomadic people inhabiting the vast steppe lands in China's northeastern region (north of Beijing and Korea) who conquered the Ming dynasty and founded the Qing in 1644.

**MANOR** An agricultural estate under the economic control and jurisdiction of a FEUDAL lord (noble or ecclesiastical institution).

**MARRANO** A Spanish CONVERSO.

**MARXISM** A theoretical framework, developed by the nineteenth-century philosopher Karl Marx, which relates the development of social organization to the prevailing material and economic conditions.

**MASS** Also known as the EUCHARIST – one of the principal SACRAMENTS of the Catholic Church centring on a ritual re-enactment of Christ's sacrifice on the cross. Due to their meritorious attributes, individuals and groups endowed ever more (specialized) masses in the course of the late Middle Ages. While required to attend the parochial high mass regularly, most Christians received communion only once a year during the Easter season, after the confession and absolution of their sins.

**MASTERS** Craftsmen who could employ others and manufacture and sell goods.

**MAYOR** The elected leader of the governing body or COUNCIL in many European towns.

**MERCANTILE SYSTEM** Also known as mercantilism, characterized by protectionist trade tariffs, the use of MONOPOLIES and an ideal of excess of exports over imports. Adam Smith's *Wealth of Nations* (1776) rejected its economic model in favour of free trade, but in doing so popularized the term, which was coined by the Marquis de Mirabeau in 1763.

**MESTIZO** A person of mixed parentage, in Spanish America a person of mixed European-Indian descent.

**METHODISM** Protestant Church, originating as a reform movement within the eighteenth-century Church of England and emphasizing heartfelt conversion.

**MÉTIS** French-Canadian term for a person of mixed European-Indian descent.

**MICROHISTORY** A methodical approach seeking to illuminate general issues and macro-historical trends through close studies of individuals and local communities.

**MILITIA** A military force raised from the civilian population of a country or region, as distinguished from mercenaries or professional soldiers.

MILLENARIAN Belief in an imminent, thousand-year reign of Christ on earth, either in person or through his self-appointed 'saints'.

MILLINERY Making/selling hats, bonnets, ribbons, gloves.

MILLONES An 'extraordinary' tax in Castile voted by representatives of the realm in the *Cortes*.

MISCEGENATION Procreation by people of different races (e.g. Africans, Europeans, and Amerindians in the Americas).

MONOPOLY The exclusive right granted by a state (usually a European power) to control the trade in a certain commodity.

MONTAGNARD Name given to left-wing deputies headed by Danton and Robespierre who occupied benches at the very top and on the left of the steep-banked hall in which the French National Convention met. Most were members of the Paris JACOBIN Club.

MORISCO A converted Moor in Spain, a New Christian.

MOVABLE TYPE Metal typeface that could be arranged, rearranged and re-used on the printer's block.

MULATTO A person of mixed European-African descent.

MUSK An aromatic substance commonly used for making perfume. It is often made from the glandular secretions from animals such as the musk deer, or from certain plants emitting similar fragrances.

MUSLIN Very fine, semi-transparent plain white cotton cloth, produced in a variety of qualities in, for example, Bengal. It was the most expensive and most widely appreciated of the cotton textiles.

MYSTICISM A spiritual movement striving for a more direct / personal relationship to God, usually through frequent prayer, introspection and close engagement with religious literature.

NATURAL PHILOSOPHY A category referring to systematic knowledge of all aspects of the physical world, including living things, which the sixteenth and seventeenth centuries routinely understood to be God's creation. It therefore has strong theological connotations.

NICODEMISM Outward conformity which does not reflect inner conviction (after Nicodemus in the Bible who would only visit Jesus at night).

NON-NATURALS Six influences the human body was incessantly exposed to: air, evacuation and retention, food and drink, motion and rest, sleeping and waking, and passions / emotions.

NUCLEAR HOUSEHOLD A family unit comprising one married couple and their children.

OFFICERS The term characterizing those members of the French royal administration, who had normally acquired their post by purchase.

ORIENTALIST Having a distorted and prejudiced view of the non-European inhabitants of Asia.

PARTITION The division of a state into parts acquired by other states.

PATRIARCH A bishop in the Orthodox Church with jurisdiction over other bishops.

PATRIARCHY A society in which male authority and privilege within the family, institutions and society at large are underpinned by laws, regulations and custom.

PATRONAGE (A) A political system whereby favour, office and reward was distributed by men and women in powerful positions to those further down the social system, reinforcing and creating a set of bonds and allegiances; (B) The protection of (and commissioning of artworks from) artists by a wealthy and powerful person.

PAULISTAS Inhabitants of the Brazilian town of São Paulo.

PEASANTS Agricultural producers with limited market involvement, using mainly family labour and operating under seigneurial constraints.

PENANCE The SACRAMENT by which Christians express sorrow for sin and receive God's forgiveness. In Catholic practice this is done through confession to a priest (auricular confession) who confers absolution. Penance is also used to mean the action required to demonstrate true repentance: 'doing penance' by saying prayers, fasting etc.

PERIPATETIC RULER A king/prince whose court moves around the territory. (See also SEDENTARY RULER).

PHILOSOPHES 'Philosophers' or 'natural philosophers': the writers and thinkers of the French Enlightenment.

PIETISM Reform movement within Lutheranism, stressing Bible-reading and practical piety in place of doctrinal speculation.

PLAGUE A highly infectious disease, called the BLACK DEATH or simply pestilence by early modern contemporaries, which appeared in Europe in the middle of the fourteenth century. It frequently reappeared until it vanished from the Western European continent at the beginning of the 1720s.

PORTOLAN CHARTS Charts with written sailing directions, based on sailors' direct observations of coasts and harbours, their measurements of distance and indications of position, taken by compass bearings. In use for maritime routes in Europe until the 1700s.

PRESBYTERIAN A church governed by elders including ministers and laypeople.

PRIESTHOOD OF ALL BELIEVERS The idea that Christians are their own priests and have the duty to bring the message of the Gospel to others.

PROTO-INDUSTRIALIZATION Systematic, wide-scale and decentralized manufacture prior to the INDUSTRIAL REVOLUTION and the establishment of factories.

PROVIDENCE The belief that God intervenes in the world and leaves clues there as to His Will.

PURGATORY An intermediary place between earth and heaven where flames of fire cleansed people's souls of any remaining blemishes of sin before they could enter Heaven. The duration of this stay could be reduced by good works and pious activities.

'PUTTING-OUT' SYSTEM Work, usually in textiles, given by merchants to rural households as a way of cutting manufacturing costs.

REAL PRESENCE The belief that Christ is present in the bread and the wine of the EUCHARIST.

RENAISSANCE Renewed engagement with Classical culture by scholars and artists, a movement starting in late medieval Italy and spreading north of the Alps by the sixteenth century.

RHETORIC The art of fine speaking and writing, first developed in the Graeco-Roman world.

ROBE Along with SWORD, one of the two major designations used from the sixteenth century onward to classify the nobility in France. Nobles of the robe (*noblesse de robe*) were individuals and families who traced their ennoblement from the acquisition of a royal office.

ROMAN LAW A civil code, compiled in the sixth century by the Roman Emperor Justinian, which was used in many parts of early modern Europe.

SABBAT A gathering of witches.

SACRAMENTS A set of rituals performed by members of the clergy to channel God's GRACE to Christians; in the late medieval Church, the seven sacraments included baptism, confirmation, MASS, PENANCE, marriage, ordination (of priests) and extreme unction.

SACRAMENTALS Religious practices (like the blessing of candles and holy water) which are not SACRAMENTS, but aids to devotion; popularly believed to have quasi-magical properties.

SACRAMENTARIAN Rejecter of the REAL PRESENCE at the EUCHARIST.

SALONS Comfortable private homes in which individuals (usually women) from the upper orders hosted informal intellectual sessions involving debates and discussions, play-readings, musical recitals and other forms of Enlightenment sociability.

SCHMALKALDIC LEAGUE Alliance for self-defence of Protestant princes and cities, 1531–46.

SCHOLASTICISM A general term for a number of theological schools striving for a coherent and logical analysis of all aspects of the Christian faith; often criticized by HUMANISTS for a tendency of over-elaboration and preoccupation with detail.

SEDENTARY RULER A king/prince settled in a principal residence (see also PERIPATETIC RULER).

**SERFDOM** The condition of unfree PEASANTS, characterized by (more or less severe) restrictions on personal mobility, property-holding and choice of spouses as well as the obligation to provide particular dues and services.

**SHARE-CROPPING** A form of tenancy in which the tenant did not pay a money rent, but handed over to the landlord half of the harvest each year.

**SHI'ISM** The denomination of the different groups of Shi'a Muslims who believe that the members of Mohammed's family and his descendants were the rightful leaders of the Muslim faith (see also SUNNISM).

**SIGNORI** The 'despots' who overthrew the republican regimes of most Italian CITY-STATES and were the protagonists in Burckhardt's account of the RENAISSANCE.

**SKIMMINGTON** A form of CHARIVARI especially popular in South-west England, in which a figure representing the 'mannish' woman beats her feeble husband with a ladle; the name may come from the skimming ladle used by dairywomen.

**SOLA SCRIPTURA** Latin phrase meaning that the Bible should be the sole source of authority for Christians.

**SUNNISM** The largest denomination of Islam, which since his death in 632 has been under the authority of the CALIPHS, the political successors of Mohammed (see also SHI'ISM).

**SWORD** Along with ROBE, one of the two major designations used from the sixteenth century onward to classify the nobility in France. Nobles of the sword (*noblesse d'épée*) were families who traced their ennoblement to France's medieval nobility whose responsibility and privilege it was to bear arms.

**SYNCRETIC/SYNCRETISM** The fusing together of Christian and non-Christian beliefs and practices. An attempt at bringing diverse religions or religious sects together under a single heading (Confucianism, DAOISM and BUDDHISM in the Chinese case).

**SZLACHTA** Nobility in the Commonwealth of Poland-Lithuania.

**TEMPERA TECHNIQUE** Painting technique in which dry pigments are mixed with egg yolk and water, used especially for altarpieces.

**TENURES** The contractual basis on which land is held by a tenant from a landlord.

**TERRITORIALIZATION** A process in which rulers of polities began to exert ever-greater influence across the full geographical range of their dominions.

**TRANSUBSTANTIATION** Catholic doctrine according to which – in the SACRAMENT of the MASS – the material features ('accidents') of bread and wine remain, but their essence ('substance') becomes the body and blood of Christ.

**TRIDENTINE** Adjective derived from Trent (*Latin*: Tridentum), and used to designate the style of Catholicism which the Council of Trent aimed to promote.

**USUFRUCTUARY** One who enjoys the fruits or revenues of property without owning it; a term applied by lawyers to monarchs.

VASSAL A FEUDAL term denoting one who owes service to an overlord in return for land or money.

VEREENIGDE OOSTINDISCHE COMPAGNIE A joint-stock company, established in 1602 and granted a MONOPOLY of Asian trade by the parliament of the Dutch Republic. In 1621 the Dutch also established a West India company.

VULGATE The Latin translation of the Bible made by St Jerome in the early fifth century; confirmed by the Council of Trent as the official Roman Catholic version.

YIELD–SEED RATIOS The conventional measure of agricultural productivity, expressed as output per unit of seed sown.

# Index

Entries in SMALL CAPS denote that the term appears in the glossary. Page numbers followed by a 'b' indicate material that appears in the chapter boxes. Page numbers followed by an 'f' indicate material that appears in a figure. Page numbers followed by a 't' indicate material that appears in a table. Monarchs are listed under their national entries.